V. O. KLIUCHEVSKII,
HISTORIAN OF RUSSIA

Drawing of V. O. Kliuchevskii. Artist unknown. March 27, 1907. Source: *Sbornik statei posviashchennykh Vasiliiu Osipovichu Kliuchevskomu* (Moscow, 1909).

V. O. KLIUCHEVSKII, HISTORIAN OF RUSSIA

Robert F. Byrnes

INDIANA UNIVERSITY PRESS

Bloomington and Indianapolis

© 1995 by Robert F. Byrnes

The paper used in this publication
meets the minimum requirements
of American National Standard
for Information Sciences—Permanence of Paper
for Printed Library Materials,
ANSI Z39.48-1984.

Manufactured in the
United States of America

Library of Congress Cataloging-in-Publication Data

Byrnes, Robert Francis.
V. O. Kliuchevskii, historian of Russia / Robert F. Byrnes.
p.   cm.
Includes bibliographical references and index.
ISBN 0-253-32940-X (cl : alk. paper)
1. Kliuchevskiĭ, V. O. (Vasiliĭ Osipovich), 1841–1911.
2. Historians—Russia—Biography.   3. Russia—History.   I. Title.
DK38.7.K53B97   1995
947é.007202—dc20
[B]   95-18202

1   2   3   4   5   00   99   98   97   96   95

FOR ELEANOR,
ONE OF THE WONDERS
OF THE WORLD

A teacher affects eternity: he can never tell when his influence stops.

—Henry Adams

Moving by touch in the darkness, we see in the path ahead the glow from a candle behind us. This comes from our conductor, history. Its lamp and experiences selected from the past light the way for us.

—Vasilii O. Kliuchevskii

CONTENTS

Contents

ACKNOWLEDGMENTS

Many men and women over a long period have contributed to this volume on the great nineteenth-century Russian historian Vasilii O. Kliuchevskii. My interest began many years ago in an undergraduate course on the seventeenth century in which Professor Laurence B. Packard assigned pages from Kliuchevskii's *Course of Russian History*. In my first year of graduate study, Professor Michael Karpovich, who I learned later had studied with Kliuchevskii, assigned several sections of his mentor's master work in a survey of Russian history. Even in a clumsy translation into English, Kliuchevskii's erudition, common sense, brilliant insights, and skill in expression excited my interest. Later, when I planned to devote my first book in Russian history to Kliuchevskii, Geroid T. Robinson suggested that such an analysis required deep knowledge of Russian history and of Kliuchevskii's time and access to archives not then open.

Influenced directly by the scholarly values of these men and of Kliuchevskii, I have sought to provide an accurate and clear account of the life and work of a historian who all observers agree was exceptionally gifted, perceptive, and significant. I have not praised or criticized his methods or views, except in clearly defined instances that note his neglect of information easily available then or presuppositions that affected his judgment. On occasion, in order to provide additional enlightenment concerning his insights, I have described the views of other scholars concerning his procedures and conclusions, but without praising or condemning them or him.

This volume rests upon research in the rich primary source materials on Kliuchevskii's life and work as well as all data that I could locate concerning the men and women who studied with and taught him or who were friends or associates. I have also scrutinized carefully the archival and published materials of the institutions at which he taught and of institutions such as the Ministry of Education and the Moscow Police Department for materials in their archives. The vast secondary literature on Russia in the second half of the nineteenth century published by scholars in several countries has been valuable, as have the numerous journals I have reviewed.

I am grateful both to the men and women who collected, organized, and preserved those sources and to the archivists and librarians who have been solicitous and generous in making them available. The Manuscript Division of the Russian State Library and the archives of the Institute of Russian History of the Russian Academy of Sciences in Moscow were especially rich and their staffs helpful, as were those of the Russian State Historical Museum, the Russian State Historical Archive, the Russian State Archive of Literature and Art, and the State Archive of the Russian Federation. Similarly, staff members of the Russian State Library, libraries of the Moscow and St. Petersburg State Universities, the State Public Historical Library in Moscow, the Russian National Library in St. Petersburg, the Academy of Sciences Libraries in Moscow and St. Petersburg, and the Fundamental Social Sciences Library in Moscow were diligent in making materials available. Librarians in many American and European libraries were equally skillful and generous in providing assistance.

Research is expensive, especially when it demands prolonged periods of residence in distant parts of the United States and in foreign countries. For financial support for travel and other research assistance, I am deeply grateful to the Indiana University Office of Research, the American Council of Learned Societies, the Rockefeller Foundation, the Fulbright Commission, the Netherlands Institute for Advanced Study, the International Research and Exchanges Board, the Kennan Center for Advanced Russian Studies, the Woodrow Wilson Center, the Hoover Institution, the Earhart Foundation, and the John M. Olin Foundation.

Gustave Alef, Ben Eklof, and Robert H. Ferrell commented generously and carefully on the bulk of this manuscript, identifying issues and questions I had ignored and errors of fact and interpretation. They saved me from a number of embarrassing errors, omissions, redundancies, and infelicities of style. George Enteen, Hans Torke, and Susan Byrnes Wallace each helped improve individual chapters. I profited also from discussions with Vladimir A. Dunaevskii, Raisa V. Kireeva, and the late Academician Militsa V. Nechkina, who have devoted much of their lives to study of Kliuchevskii and whose published works were full of insights. However, I bear full responsibility for this text.

Over the years, a number of graduate students, beginning with Dr. Etta Perkins and ending with Dr. Eli Weinerman, have contributed unstinting research assistance. Betty Bradbury, Debbie Chase, Lori Citti, and Marina Eskina have somehow mastered my handwriting and uncomplainingly typed numerous drafts of this volume. I appreciate their loyal and important contributions.

I am grateful to the editors of the following journals for granting permission to reprint materials originally published in their journals in different form: *Canadian-American Slavic Studies, The History Teacher,* the *Journal of Modern History, Modern Greek Studies, Russian History/Histoire Russe,* the *Review of Politics,* the *Russian Review,* the *Slavic Review,* the *Slavonic and East European Review,* and *Survey.*

The translation of Russian terms and the spelling of Russian names constitute perpetual problems for American scholars. In the text of this book, I have used the customary American spelling of the names of Russian rulers and a few well-known writers and composers (e.g., Dostoevsky, Tolstoy, Tchaikovsky). For all others I have followed the Library of Congress system. All dates in this volume are old style, or according to the Julian calendar, which in the nineteenth century was twelve days behind the Western, or Gregorian, calendar.

Acknowledgments

Nothing I have ever undertaken could have been completed without the happy, constant support of my wife. Not only has she contributed hours of labor searching through bibliographies, guides, and catalogues and completing accurately the many essential but dull chores scholarship requires, but she was a thoughtful and discerning reader of drafts. One of the wonders of the world, she has made my life one of perpetual joy.

INTRODUCTION

This volume describes the career and scholarship of V. O. Kliuchevskii (1841–1911), whom many specialists consider Russia's most distinguished historian and whose teaching, writing, and training of young scholars have markedly affected the way Russians and others view Russia's past. Much of his renown rests upon his five-volume *Course of Russian History,* the printed version of the survey course he taught for more than forty years, which is almost certainly the most widely read and influential study of Russian history ever published. He was a brilliant teacher: his dedication, erudition, and superior skills as an instructor excited thousands into an interest in their national past. From 1868 until 1910, he taught 110 academic years—35 at the Moscow Ecclesiastical Academy, one of the Russian Orthodox Church's four senior seminaries, located in Trinity Monastery, Russia's most sacred patriotic shrine; and 31 at Moscow University, Russia's most respected educational institution and a center for Western thought. In addition to these two national and nationalistic institutions, one looking inward and the other westward, he also lectured at institutions for military cadets and women and at the School of Painting, Sculpture, and Architecture.

The son of a poor parish priest in Penza, Kliuchevskii made his own way from the province to and through the university to a senior position in Russian history. He became a self-trained scholar whose integrity, emphasis upon primary sources, independent thinking, incessant questioning ("Why this way and not that way?"), and dispassion led him away from the historical school that had concentrated on the state. His emphasis on the economic, social, and institutional "structural materials" of society placed a profound stamp upon much study of Russian history and prepared some Russians to adopt a Marxist approach. Similarly, his conclusion that history flowed as a slow river, unaffected by ideas or powerful individuals, may have contributed to acceptance of Marxist determinism.

The men whom Kliuchevskii attracted into professional study of history and helped train adopted his principles and techniques. Most remained in Russia after 1921 under difficult circumstances, continued their research, preserved Kliuchevskii's principles, and helped to train the first and second generations of Soviet historians, even playing important roles in producing Soviet history textbooks after 1935. One edited the first Soviet editions of the *Course of Russian History,* published between 1918 and 1923, and three others the editions published in 1937 and 1938, ensuring their accuracy. The large editions published in the late 1950s and between 1987 and 1993 (325,000 copies in those latter years alone) demonstrate that Kliuchevskii remains an attractive alternative to official Soviet histories. Moreover, translated into eleven languages, the *Course of Russian History* helped shape the way scholars outside Russia, especially in the United Kingdom and the United States, viewed Russia's past when they began study of Kliuchevskii's homeland.

Kliuchevskii was a reserved, shy "countryman" who loved old Russia, lived in old Russian style on the then-outskirts of Moscow, and enjoyed gardening and fishing. These qualities, the poverty he had experienced, and the difficult early years in Moscow deeply affected his view of Russia's past. For him, his country was always "on the brink," surviving with difficulty because of the "harsh circumstances" of its first centuries, vast expanse, internal divisions, and the perpetual threat of powerful external enemies. He assigned to those elements responsibility for the absolutist and later autocratic form of government that he considered "natural and necessary" for Russia.

Kliuchevskii spent his entire adult life in the city of Moscow and the Moscow region, concentrating upon his work except for a small circle of academic friends. He traveled to St. Petersburg only as a graduate student who needed access to research materials and as a senior scholar to whom the government turned for advice in 1905. He visited Kiev only once, in 1874, and never visited Warsaw, Odessa, or other major cities. He never traveled east of the Urals and was totally ignorant of the non-Russian and non-Orthodox populations. He had no friends in society or in the court. Similarly, he was uninformed of the way in which peasants and workers lived. He did not notice the changes industrialization was producing before his eyes. He never traveled abroad.

At the same time, Kliuchevskii's early years in Moscow were those of Alexander II's reform period, when prospects for continued relaxation of state controls seemed bright. Moreover, the able scholars with whom he and other members of his talented generation worked had traveled and studied in Europe. They not only passed along their awareness that Europe was freer, more prosperous, and more powerful than Russia, but introduced him to the work of Guizot, Taine, de Tocqueville, and Buckle, whose ideas permanently affected him. In sum, his history of Russia was a brilliant intellectual creation deeply marked by limited exposure to Russian life, awareness of the work of exciting British and French scholars, membership in an academic community of very high quality, and years of study in Russian archives and libraries.

Kliuchevskii concluded as a young man that European peoples were building nation-states, a process in which Russia lagged. In his judgment, historians were just as important as Bismarcks and Cavours in forming nations: knowledge of the past could bind people together as much as successful military actions. Convinced that Russia was a state but not a nation, he devoted his life as a teacher to making Russians aware of their past and helping them acquire national consciousness through knowledge of their history.

Kliuchevskii considered himself and those he instructed members of a missionary order that Timofei Granovskii, an inspiring and beloved teacher of Western and Russian history at the university from 1839 until his early death in 1855, had established to carry knowledge from the university to the nation. His principal instruments in this dedicated work were a coherent, synthetic view of the full sweep of Russian history, designed to encourage students and readers to understand the follies and disasters as well as the glories and achievements of their country's long history. All his books and articles kept what *Annales* historians term *la longue durée* in perspective. Some judgments now appear elementary and antiquated because succeeding generations have transformed them into conventional wisdom, and later scholars have had access to information not available to him. But scholars of every persuasion in every country continue to study the questions he raised, follow his approaches, and agree that his research was profound and that his judgments were both imaginative and sound.

Kliuchevskii's history was profoundly nationalistic, but cultural and territorial rather than ethnic, and mild, not aggressive. One of his most significant theses was that the Russians and the first Russian state had their origins in Kiev in the tenth century. This judgment, which was not original or even unusual then, meant that there were no Ukrainians or Belorussians; they were Russian. This collided with the views of Ukrainian and Belorussian scholars, and later of scholars in other countries as well, who concluded that the Kievan state was the mother of Ukraine and fourteenth-century Moscow the founding site of Russia. These disagreements, and those between rival nationalist groups, became bitter in the twentieth century, helping to bring down the Russian empire in 1917 and leading to the establishment of independent Ukraine and Belorus in 1991.

Relations with the West throughout Russian history constituted a central issue for Kliuchevskii, who considered Russia a part of Europe but on its fringes. In early centuries, Russian culture had quietly absorbed Western ideas and products without visible effect. However, the attempts by some Russian Orthodox Church leaders in the second half of the seventeenth century to use Western scholarship to eliminate minor errors in the liturgy shattered Church and national unity. It also revealed the arrogance and intellectual poverty of the Church, which had earlier contributed to religious and national unity, "civilizing" the Russian people, and keeping alive the "bare bones" of education. Although Kliuchevskii was devoutly Orthodox, he assigned the Church a very modest role in Russian history and described its weakness as a principal reason why Western influence poured into Russia after the schism.

Kliuchevskii was perceptive in describing the dilemma that Russian rulers faced after the seventeenth century, a quandary that Soviet rulers failed to resolve and that many countries throughout the world confront today. Briefly, Peter the Great, Catherine the Great, and their successors recognized that European states' growing power after the sixteenth century had widened the economic and military gap that separated Russia from the West. They concluded that Russia could preserve its independence *only* if it borrowed, utilized, and absorbed the instruments and techniques that had given the West superiority. However, borrowed instruments brought along with them the values and beliefs responsible for Europe's advance, which dissolved the culture and institutions that had made Russia distinct. Consequently, Russia's most Westernizing rulers tightened controls, enlarging the authority of the centralized state that was the primary cause of backwardness. In sum, efforts to "catch up" by borrowing strengthened the autocracy, as circumstances and external pressures had earlier.

Kliuchevskii's view of the Church's weaknesses, analysis of the riddle that bedeviled Russia's leaders, and growing awareness of the government's inability to resolve other national problems made him increasingly fearful. His gloom and pessimism resembled Chekhov's. Change, he concluded, came slowly in Russia. Russia's history was a perpetual flow, in which every element was related to every other and all changed constantly. The past was a seamless web with no sharp breaks caused by revolutions or individual leaders. This persuaded him that no tsar or radicals of the left or right could affect the tide and that passivity was the proper response: the autocracy would one day wither away, but so would its successor system of rule.

For some, Kliuchevskii was attractive because of his candor, his faith in his country and countrymen, and his conviction that the West's blessings would inevitably come to Russia. He impressed others with his affection for old ways, disinterest in politics, passivity, and criticism of those who thought they could direct Russia's future.

Whatever observers concluded about Kliuchevskii's views of the past, all recognized his scholarly qualities, dispassion, and keen insights, and the genius with which he taught and wrote.

The central fact of Kliuchevskii's career and scholarship is his dedication to teaching, by both lecturing and writing, in order to create national consciousness and a nation. His extraordinary capabilities as a teacher developed from the infinite attention he devoted to his craft, beginning with reflection on the purposes and organization of each lecture, immense knowledge, and constant probing for explanations. His vocabulary was rich. He skillfully portrayed situations so that his students felt that he, and they, were participants. His portraits of individuals were unforgettable, and aphorisms helped every student or reader understand and remember. He was also a distinguished actor and used his husky tenor and clarity of pronunciation with exquisite care. His skill in providing the full sweep of Russian history and at the same time introducing details and portraits of individuals helped raise the study of history to an art. In the classroom, this mild and modest man was transformed into a superb lecturer.

Kliuchevskii's writing was just as compelling: he "polished the marble" of every word, rewrote and rewrote and rewrote to make certain that he was correct and clear. With him, historical writing became a form of literature, as it was in the United States then.

Above all, he loved his subject and his students. The hundreds of teachers scattered throughout European Russia at his death and the scholar-teachers who continued teaching after the revolution represent one tribute, as does the *Course of Russian History* another. The outstanding scholar can in truth have almost eternal influence. His work in the classroom, his public lectures, and his scholarship made him one of the most distinguished representatives of a remarkable flowering of Russian culture that included giants such as Tolstoy, Chaliapin, Repin, Dostoevsky, Chekhov, and Tchaikovsky. They also place him at Edward Gibbon's level as a supreme scholar and writer.

PART ONE

The Beginnings

ONE

"Under the Bells" of Penza

Vasilii O. Kliuchevskii was born January 16, 1841, in Voskresenskoe, a village of less than a thousand inhabitants 8 miles from the provincial capital, Penza, 450 miles by road southeast of Moscow. He lived in hamlets east of that city until his father, a poor Orthodox priest, died in 1850, when his mother joined her mother and other relatives in Penza. His paternal ancestors for four generations were Russian Orthodox priests, as were his maternal grandfather and uncles. Until he made his way into the History-Philology Faculty of Moscow University when he was twenty years of age, he studied at home with his father and then in the Penza parish and district Church schools and seminary. After he left Penza, he spent his next fifty years within two miles of the Kremlin and Moscow University, from which he received his degrees.

He taught thirty-five years at the Moscow Ecclesiastical Academy, one of the Russian Orthodox Church's four elite institutions, and thirty-one years at the university, then the nation's leading educational institution, and a total of more than forty years at Moscow institutions for women, artists, and army cadets. The Moscow area, center of Orthodox and patriotic Russia, remained his home except for rare visits to St. Petersburg and monasteries in European Russia that possessed important archives and libraries. He never visited Helsinki or Warsaw or traveled abroad. He was in Kiev only once, to attend a conference in 1874. Provincial, even frontier, Penza and the Russian Orthodox Church established his intellectual foundations, and he lived his entire adult life in Moscow. From this central vantage point, he described in brilliant fashion the history of Russia and the Russians.

Kliuchevskii's great-great grandfather, Ivan Afanas'ev, who died in 1764, was a priest in a small village fifty miles west of Penza. One son, Stepan Ivanov, in 1780 became a deacon in the neighboring village, Kliuch, three or four miles north of Chembar, where another son, Iosif, had become sexton and later priest. Indeed, the family name derives from this village: the Penza seminary rector gave the name to Kliuchevskii's father. When Stepan Ivanov died in 1802, one of his sons, Vasilii, succeeded him. The latter died in 1816, leaving five children, the youngest of whom, Iosif, only six months old, became the historian's father.

Iosif attended a parish school and the district church school in Nizhnelemov, thirty miles north of Kliuch, until 1832, when he entered the seminary in Penza. He graduated in 1838 and that November obtained permission to marry seventeen-year-old Anna F. Moshkova, daughter of a Penza archpriest. They married May 6, 1839, the day Iosif became deacon in the St. Nicholas Church in Penza and teacher in the parish school. In June 1840, Iosif Kliuchevskii became priest in Voskresenskoe. There the historian was born and lived until 1845, when Iosif became a priest in the large Church of the Trinity in Gorodishche, a town ten miles farther east that had a population of 4,800 in the 1890s, presumably after considerable growth. The following year, the Kliuchevskiis moved to another tiny village, Mozharovka, deep in the pine forests. There Kliuchevskii's father drowned in 1850, when he was only thirty-four. He left his widow with three children: Vasilii, nine; Elizaveta, five; and Nadezhda, five months.

Under the best of circumstances, the life of a priest and his family in rural Russia in the nineteenth century was harsh, marked by the grinding, inescapable poverty that most peasants endured. As a parish schoolteacher in 1838, Kliuchevskii's father had an income of 100 rubles a year. (The Russian silver ruble throughout Kliuchevskii's life had approximately the same value as fifty American cents then.) In 1840 he received 300 rubles in Voskresenskoe, but he dreamed of a parish that would provide 500. The life of the Kliuchevskiis was no doubt similar to that described in Russian novels and in recollections of Father Aleksandr A. Golubtsov, a student and later colleague and friend of the historian, whose mother was illiterate and whose father had been a rural priest in Kostroma: searing poverty, an income of 150 rubles, meat rarely, and tea only on holidays.

Conditions worsened after the death of the future historian's father. His mother somehow acquired a small wooden house, which still survives, at No. 66 Popovka Street in Penza (named Kliuchevskii Street in 1991) in the parish of Father Ivan V. Evropeitsev, who had married one of her sisters. (Her other sister also married a priest, who lived in Saransk.) She survived in part by renting half of the tiny dwelling to lodgers for three rubles a month. Vasilii assisted with his stipend as a student and by tutoring youngsters for three rubles a month. The family suffered in the winter and sometimes lacked candles, a handicap for a boy who loved to read. The youth did not wear shoes until he began attending the parish school in 1851. Most of his classmates were as poor, or almost so. His sister, Elizaveta, who married a priest in 1861 and lived in a Penza village throughout her life, later remarked, "No one was poorer than we."[1]

Kliuchevskii's mother was an unpleasant, harsh woman never close to her son. She gave birth to two illegitimate daughters, Mariia and Anastasiia. These were humiliating years, and Kliuchevskii acquired a stutter. He was so skillful at hiding this by creating pauses during lectures that few students were aware of the handicap.

Penza was in a plateau area noted for a moderate, dry climate and for rivers, lakes, pine forests, and little good soil. Founded in the 1660s as a fortress against the Mordovians and Meshcheriaki on the high slopes of the river Mura, it became a regional administrative and trading center, with lumber rafts traveling along the Mura to the Volga. The Holy Synod established a seminary there in 1800, and Penza became a provincial capital in 1801. The city established a four-class *gimnaziia* or high school in the governor's palace in 1804 and a parish school fourteen years later. It became a bishopric in 1828 and enjoyed a repertory theater on occasion after 1853. It contained 20,000 inhabitants in 1840 and 27,000 in 1865, almost entirely Russian and Orthodox. In 1865, the city had two monasteries, twenty-nine Orthodox churches, five chapels, a seminary, two parish schools, and one Lutheran church. The 1897 census revealed 51,662 members of the Russian Orthodox Church, 85 Old Believers, 839 Roman Catholics, 496 Jews, 422 Muslims, 86 Protestants, and 95 "others."[2]

The province contained a number of villages inhabited by non-Russians, Mordovians, Meshcheriaki, and Tatars. These concentrated around Chembar, fifty miles west of Penza, and in the areas east of the towns in which he spent his first ten years. No evidence has survived that Kliuchevskii had any relations with or interest in these groups, or that he realized that some inhabitants of Russia were neither Russian nor Orthodox.[3]

Penza in the 1850s was a peaceful, isolated provincial center. Wolves and bears prowled the forests in the surrounding territory, and winter snows often isolated the villages. When young Kliuchevskii traveled to Moscow in 1861, his first trip of more than twenty or thirty miles, the journey by cart to Vladimir consumed a week. A railroad broke the city's isolation in 1874, when the population was 30,000, but the community that he knew was as remote from the rest of the world as that described in the novels of M. N. Zagoskin, who lived there until 1802.

Penza nevertheless produced a number of men important in history, and other eminent figures lived there at least briefly. Radishchev, Marshal A. V. Suvorov, V. E. Meierkhol'd, Marshal M. N. Tukhachevskii, and Ogarev were born in or near Penza and spent early years there. Speranskii, Belinskii, and Chernyshevskii lived there for several years. Aleksandr Kerenskii's father, Fedor, a distant relative and acquaintance of Kliuchevskii, graduated from the seminary in 1859, and Il'ia N. Ulianov, Lenin's father, taught in that first high school from 1855 until 1863.

When one considers Penza's primitive character, the documents for Kliuchevskii's early life are remarkably rich. For example, the seminary's investigation of an incident in which two seminarians threw rocks through the inspector of students' window provides fifty pages of information concerning that piquant event and relations between faculty, staff, and seminarians.

In the 1850s, Russia had about 75 high schools with 18,000 students in a total population of 60 million. Parish primary schools and district church schools were much more numerous, perhaps 4,000 with an enrollment of 160,000. But acquiring even an elementary education was a difficult achievement for children of parents not large landowners and serf-owners or in the upper levels of the bureaucracy. In the 1850s, only 5 or 6 percent of the population was literate, and less than 1 percent attended any sort of school. According to the 1897 census, 23.7 percent of the males and 6.3 percent of females in Penza province were literate.[4]

The state's policy toward education was ambivalent. Nicholas I and his ministers appreciated the growing need for literate men to staff the bureaucracy and strengthen Russia at a time of increasing involvement in European affairs. But they were frightened by the consequences of expanding education in a conservative, repressive state. In Count S. S. Uvarov's striking phrase, the tsar "wanted a fire that would not burn."

Kliuchevskii's uncles and other relations had graduated from a seminary, and his father and some other relatives taught briefly in parish schools. His father, close to his eldest child and only son, taught him to read and write, using lives of saints and Church writings. He was apparently a skillful storyteller, and the lad acquired from him and his maternal grandmother considerable knowledge of tales and legends, a powerful memory, and great interest in learning. Somehow his father acquired books by the historians Nikolai M. Karamzin and Vasilii N. Tatishchev, the poet Lermontov, and Nikolai I. Novikov, as well as almanacs and collections of sacred writings. His barely literate mother encourged his love of reading, even though he exhausted the family supply of candles. In the summer of 1851, she obtained his admission to the second class of the parish school, writing, "I want to give my son a decent education."[5] In 1853, when Kliuchevskii's stutter and poor Latin, Greek, and arithmetic threatened continuation of his education and stipend, she arranged for an older student in the school to tutor him.

The Russian government, then as now, rewarded or subsidized students because they were performing a service to the state, so the future historian received a precious ruble a month for attending the parish school. When he became an outstanding student in the district school, this stipend rose to fifteen rubles a year, payable every three months.

The curricula of parish and district schools included Latin, Greek, French, arithmetic, grammar, Church and civil history, Church rules, catechism, and religious music. Even as a youngster, Kliuchevskii was remarkably observant and possessed descriptive powers. He wrote in a fine hand and never missed a class. In his first year in the parish school, he ranked thirteenth in a class of 109 in November, sixth in May, and sixth for the entire year. In his second year in the district school, he ranked between twelfth and thirty-first (Latin) in different subjects in a class of seventy in September, from fourth to ninth in January, and first or second (Latin and Greek) in May, but first in the class for the year. He remained first for the final three years, won a number of book prizes, and received *otlichnyi*, or excellent, in each course and in conduct. His Latin was so impressive that his instructor considered the pupil's knowledge superior to his own. Reading aloud in Latin forced Kliuchevskii to speak carefully and helped reduce his stutter.[6]

The Penza seminary's curriculum continued that of the district school. The patristics courses were at a higher level, and instruction in Church history in the final year introduced material about the Old Believers. Kliuchevskii studied natural history, mathematics, logic, psychology, rural economics, rural medicine, and homiletics, all presumably on a rudimentary level. German and Hebrew came in the last two years.

Memoirs of Church officials, priests, and young men who completed the district school but left the seminary, the Church's analyses, studies of the Russian Orthodox Church and its educational program, and novels alike describe life in the crowded and undersupported seminaries as grim, brutal, and squalid. The atmosphere was stifling and oppressive and control of the unruly seminarians ineffectual. Few teachers were well educated or intelligent, and many were mean and brutish. The libraries were small. Curriculum and instruction were irrelevant to the students' careers, emphasizing rote learning of subjects that inspired scant intellectual interest or spiritual enthusiasm. Even after reform, the seminaries provided little foundation in theology or philosophy: graduates acquired only the most shallow familiarity with the precepts of Christianity. Many could not write or read Church documents or qualify to teach in a parish school. In spite of efforts by the Holy Synod, reforming bishops, and rectors, the seminaries limited themselves to ensuring that graduates could read, write, and understand the catechism and Church rules and regulations. In the words of the most thorough analysis, they provided "only the haziest conception of Orthodoxy and had a decidedly secular orientation."[7]

Most seminarians were sons and grandsons of priests and lacked interest in their education or career. Many hated the seminary, which isolated them from their families, but had no alternative educational opportunity. They constituted a distinct social type, enjoying little prestige or respect. They were resented and despised by the upper classes, considered thieves and ruffians by townspeople, and scorned by the middle and lower classes. Members of a rigid caste, they were accustomed to a harsh life that promised little spiritual or temporal reward. Many graduates became admirable servants of their flocks, among those whom Kliuchevskii described as "the good people," but curés of Ars were probably even less common in Russia than in France. The history of Russian revolutionary movements demonstrates that dissatisfactions and frustrations led some seminarians into radical political movements that provided a sense of corporate responsibility and mission the seminaries failed to give.

Evidence from the seminary's archives, memoirs of Kliuchevskii's classmates, and his correspondence with Porfirii P. Gvozdev, a boyhood friend who was his rival for first-place honors, all suggest that the Penza seminary was typical. However, since Kliuchevskii was not a boarding student, he escaped the meanness and violence that marked dormitory life and conflict between staff and students over behavior after class hours. In addition, the quality of his mind and ambition combined to make him a brilliant, prize-winning student, first in his class of sixty for all but two semesters of the initial four years. Students called him Solomon or Filaret, for the then metropolitan of the Russian Orthodox Church, and members of the faculty "bowed to him" because of his "extraordinarily good progress and very good conduct."[8] His patristics instructor, Stepan V. Maslovskii, declared that a third-year Latin paper of Kliuchevskii's was the best he ever received and years later still read it to classes. The rector and most faculty considered Kliuchevskii the seminary's most able student and the one most likely to enjoy an outstanding career.

The careful analysis that faculty members made of the eighteen papers Kliuchevskii wrote each year may have contributed to his mastery of Russian and his lucid, exact style. Emphasis on analysis of texts and mastering materials the faculty thought essential strengthened his skill in critical reading and memory. The rigid order probably reinforced regular habits and self-discipline. He acquired the ability to read research materials in five languages, but he was not able to speak any.

In addition, someone lured the lively mind of the young seminarian beyond the seminary routine and introduced a glimpse into an exciting intellectual world. Although he never referred to his history instructors, one or several of them, his uncle, or some other member of the Penza community nurtured his interest in history, ancient and European as well as Russian, and helped him acquire access to an impressive literature. In the last two years in Penza, he became fascinated by the *Iliad*. Classes in Russian history led him to read Karamzin's *History of the Russian State* and Tatishchev's *Russian History*. Evenings he read other historians, beginning with the first volumes of the monumental *History of Russia from Most Ancient Times* by Sergei M. Soloviev, under whom he later studied at Moscow University and whom he succeeded. During his last year, he began the works of Granovskii and of Nikolai I. Kostomarov, who wrote mostly about Ukraine or "Little Russia." Perhaps these volumes, comments of some teachers, or classes in German led him to the works of Jacob and Wilhelm Grimm and Alexander von Humboldt, no doubt in translation.

So far as one can tell, Kliuchevskii's faith was as strong when he left as when he entered, so he did not join the young men whom seminaries drove into opposition to religion and the political and social system. Indeed, as some of his graduate students and later colleagues recognized, life "under the bells" of his father's church and the religious schools and seminary left a deep religious imprint.

However, Kliuchevskii in December 1860 requested permission to leave the seminary and seek admission to Moscow University. The most scrupulous examination of the abundant materials concerning this part of his life does not provide clear evidence concerning the reasons for this move. Militsa V. Nech-kina attributes it to radical ideas in the alleged "revolutionary situation" of that time and to radical literature from St. Petersburg and Moscow. Her hypothesis is unsubstantiated, although Kliuchevskii did have access to Moscow newspapers and journals. No single factor explains the move. There is no evidence that any faculty members, even the admiring Maslovskii, suggested that such an outstanding student should leave the seminary. No university alumnus proposed that the gifted young man forsake the life of a country clergyman for study in the principal university, almost eons away for a poor boy with a widowed mother and younger sisters whom he was helping to support. However, the atmosphere of change after Alexander II's accession in 1855, the encouragement and support his aunt and uncle provided, dissatisfaction with the seminary's intellectual fare and administration, and Kliuchevskii's sheer interest in learning seem decisive.

The "thaw" that began after Alexander II's accession was crucial. Belief that changes and opportunities were in the offing spread from the capital cities to distant towns. Kliuchevskii also obtained access to the new journals, such as Mikhail N. Katkov's *Russian Herald*, Andrei A. Kraevskii's *Notes of the Father-land*, and Nikolai N. Nekrasov's *Contemporary*, to which Chernyshevskii contributed. He may have seen issues of Alexander Herzen's *The Bell*, published in London and easily available in Moscow and St. Petersburg and perhaps in Penza as well. In addition, tutoring two young sons of an urbane landowner far less capable than he may have exercised a powerful influence. His sister Elizaveta late in life declared this the decisive factor. On the other hand, he remarked later that his tutees' father sometimes teased and often ridiculed him for dreaming of going to Moscow.

His mother, who supported his request for release from the seminary, may have encouraged and prodded him. But none of his letters to his uncle, with whom his mother and younger sister lived after he went to Moscow and his older sister married, provide testimony. His uncle retained the letters he received, but no evidence survives that Kliuchevskii wrote to his mother. Moreover, he never expressed appreciation for encouragement from her. Indeed, he scarcely mentioned her after he left Penza.

His uncle and aunt, the Evropeitsevs, may have seen a spark of genius in the young man and stimulated the great decision. When he left Penza, they gave him an enormous sum (for a rural priest) of a hundred rubles that they had saved, and assured him that they would care for his mother and sisters. He left Penza "with faith in God and hope in you." He wrote a long letter to the Evropeitsevs within a day of his arrival, declaring them "most responsible" for his being there, and corresponded frequently, especially about classes and reading, until his uncle died in 1867.[9]

In the winter of 1861–62, his first year at the university, he submitted a short story, "Pedagogical Walls," to two satirical journals, *Diversion* and *The Spark*, but both rejected it. The story was gently critical of seminary life and the administration's fear of ideas from "forbidden books." At least two characters, the rector and the inspector of students, were recognizable Penza men. In the 1890s he commented in his diary that the Church's educational institutions had been more almshouses for students than schools, and that they masqueraded under the pretense of science but produced more student blasphemy than worship.

Both as a first-year student at the university and as a scholar late in life reflecting on his seminary years, Kliuchevskii recalled some "thorns" but termed those days "the best in my life." His letters, which Maslovskii and others read to their classses, frequently inquired about his seminary instructors, including those he had not admired. The letters so impressed one seminarian that he remembered their details many years later. The rector, Father Evpsikhii, who liked Kliuchevskii and deeply regretted his leaving, retained the friendliest attitude toward him.

Growing dissatisfaction with the seminary's curriculum, scholastic approach, and teachers clearly influenced Kliuchevskii's decision. As the end of his five years of study approached and he became aware of his scholarly prowess and ambitions, prospects of life as a rural clergyman led him to consider a more challenging career. In addition, reading some of the books of Fedor I. Buslaev and Soloviev, then luminaries of the university faculty, may have provided a powerful stimulus driving him to Moscow.

Incidents at the seminary during and after the summer of 1859 led to the crucial decision. In June and again in October 1859, disgruntled students threw stones through the windows of Father Iakov P. Burlutskii, instructor in Church history and seminary inspector of students. In October, Burlutskii obtained a copy of a poem that satirized him and the aridity of seminary teaching. Investigation led to the expulsion of the students responsible, Vasilii and Stepan Pokrovskii, sons of the deacon of the largest church in Penza and close friends of Kliuchevskii. Indeed, Vasilii had tutored Kliuchevskii, and they lived together in the fall of 1861, when Pokrovskii began to study law at Moscow University. Investigators questioned Kliuchevskii about the incidents, the poems, and a satirical journal that Vasilii Pokrovskii had hoped to publish. Kliuchevskii admitted that he considered contributing, but noted that he had written nothing and that the journal had not appeared.

At about the same time, he offended Father Avraam P. Smirnov, Burlutskii's brother-in-law, a mean and unpleasant scholastic who often humiliated students. Smirnov learned that Kliuchevskii had lampooned his teaching and concluded that his essays were sly critiques. Kliuchevskii had been the leading student in his class except during his first semester and the fall semester of 1858, when he was second to Gvozdev. However, in 1859–60 he fell to tenth, in part because Smirnov rated him twelfth in the first semester and twenty-ninth in the second in a course on rural economics.

Whatever the precise reasons, on December 16, 1860, Kliuchevskii petitioned for release because of his "weak health" and "inconvenient domestic circumstances."[10] Malaria did spread in Penza in 1860–61, and Kliuchevskii apparently was so ill in the spring of 1861 that he could not travel to Moscow to attempt the May admission examinations, but both reasons proffered were no doubt spurious.

The Church at that time possessed a surplus of graduating seminarians, and the Holy Synod in 1850 had made leaving a seminary a formality, provided one obtained one's bishop's permission. Indeed, five of Kliuchevskii's classmates also dropped out that year. However, he was such a gifted student that the rector sought to persuade him to stay. Bishop Varlaam of Penza apparently was even more disappointed, reproaching him for ingratitude. He first declared that the Holy Synod rule required four years of service after graduation, demanded that Kliuchevskii repay the stipend of 66 rubles 50 kopeks, and hinted that he would deny his sister Elizaveta's fiancé's appointment as a deacon and thereby delay her marriage. Kliuchevskii apparently agreed to repay the stipend, but Father Evropeitsev persuaded the bishop to allow Kliuchevskii to resign. Varlaam granted permission four days later, the Holy Synod gave its approval February 27, 1861 "for entry into Moscow University," and the official permission was in Kliuchevskii's hands on March 22.

On February 27, just one week after the abolition of serfdom, the rescript of which Kliuchevskii copied and retained throughout his life, he applied for admission to the university. In July, he and three comrades launched "the great adventure," taking a week to travel 350 miles via Saransk to Vladimir, which he described as "so beautiful that it is impossible to describe." Then the first train he had seen, with "an engine like a horse that he did not dare to try to describe," carried him 104 miles to Moscow at an astonishing 20 miles an hour. He arrived in his new world at 8:30 P.M. on July 22, rented a corner of a third-floor room on a lane off Tverskaia Street the next day, and applied for admission to the university on the twenty-fourth. There he remained for the next half-century.

The young man who left Penza was slim, physically unimpressive, quiet, shy, and gentle. He had become accustomed to lean fare, going without meals, wearing old and shabby clothes, and walking miles to earn kopeks. As a young man and an adult, he was businesslike and serious, with little interest in political ideas or activity. He was and remained cautious, bland, and somewhat sly. But he also possessed ambition, courage, determination, and a toughness that his demeanor concealed. He was not sociable (a contemporary historian noted that he was "only verbally social"), perhaps because of the frugality in which he grew up. However, he had close friends, smoked and drank, and was a lively conversationalist in small groups. He had little interest in power, money, or achievement: his ambition centered upon learning and teaching.

Neither Penza nor his family was a concern after 1861. He never returned. When he learned in 1866 that the aunt who had done so much for him was gravely ill and his mother was dying of cancer, he remained in Moscow. He corresponded with his benefactor uncle, but did not return when Father

Evropeitsev became ill and died. After his sister Nadezhda died, he brought her two children to Moscow and helped educate them. Later, he provided support for his sister Elizaveta and her husband, who had seven children, but he corresponded rarely and saw her again only half a century later. He sent money to Mozharovka during the famine of 1891, but declined the seminary's invitation to attend its centennnial celebration in 1900. When he learned that the seminary library possessed none of his books, he sent copies of some of his publications. The 1894 report of the Penza city library (named for Lermontov) reveals that that collection also lacked his publications. Penza named the street on which he had lived for him and established a small museum in his honor only in 1991. So Penza forgot him, just as Penza and family slipped out of his life. Moreover, the family as an institution plays a minor role in his historical thought. Kliuchevskii, in brief, cut the ties to his family and home town.

Nevertheless, Penza exerted a permanent, powerful influence upon him. Throughout his years in Moscow, he remained a "countryman," living in the old Russian style to which he had become accustomed as a youngster. Penza gave him a deep appreciation of the primitive conditions of Russian life and the harsh problems peasants, provincial townspeople, and clergy endured. Similarly, his respect for the powers of nature that dominated rural life and caused his father's death and the importance he assigned colonization of frontier lands may derive from life in Penza. His skepticism and critical view of the intelligentsia also had their roots in the provincial town, as did his realism, dislike of the "undeserving rich," sympathy for the underdog, and disinterest in large ideas.

Even after Kliuchevskii had become a dedicated master of Russian with exceptional skill in creating images, his rich vocabulary did not include terms from religious writings or parables or popular phrases from the Psalms or the New Testament.

On the other hand, the schooling he acquired and the excitement about learning that Penza stimulated suggest that his education compares favorably with that of an American youngster of that time, and today as well. They imply too that our traditional view of rural Russia needs modification. Whatever their shortcomings, the Penza institutions helped him develop basic skills: clear handwriting, self-discipline, a powerful memory, a love of words and language, and exactness and lucidity in expression. They introduced him to Russian culture and to the literature and ideas of Moscow and St. Petersburg, as well as the world beyond Russia. He learned to think for himself, in spite of (or because of) the system of instruction. The blessings of Alexander II's thaw enabled an ambitious poor boy from rural Russia to attend Moscow University and begin a satisfying and even brilliant career in which he exercised a significant impact upon Russian culture and the still incomplete process of nation-building.

"I Have Started on the Road to Science"

The new spirit of Alexander II's early years had roots in the previous reign, when Nicholas I launched discussions concerning the abolition of serfdom and improvement in the judicial system. Intellectual life also began flowering under Nicholas, with the appearance of critical and radical thought its most paradoxical product. Glinka's famous opera *A Life for the Tsar* was first performed in 1836, the year in which Chaadaev's *Philosophical Letters* launched the controversy between the Slavophils and the Westerners over the character of Russia's past and the direction of its future. Gogol, Dostoevsky, Turgenev, and Tolstoy were prominent before 1855, and the poetry of Pushkin, Tiutchev, and Lermontov and many Aleksandr N. Ostrovskii plays were written during Nicholas's reign. The Malyi Theater opened in 1824, the rebuilt Bolshoi in 1825 and again in 1856 after it burned. The disaster of the Crimean War, only forty years after Russia had contributed most to the defeat of Napoleon, stimulated curiosity in history, as did European philosophy, literature, and historical writing.

The government of Nicholas I allowed and even encouraged some young men to study in Paris, Heidelberg, Göttingen, and Berlin, supported by their families or as tutors accompanying wealthy families. Many of these scholars, including Buslaev and Soloviev, added the stimulus of European training to the university curriculum. Russian scholars in the 1840s and 1850s produced tomes that reflected the new interest in history and helped create a foundation from which Kliuchevskii benefited and to which he would contribute. Mikhail P. Pogodin and Granovskii helped make history popular within the universities and among the educated public. Soloviev published the first volume of his magisterial history in 1851 and a succeeding tome each year until he died in 1879. The first volume of Metropolitan Makarii's history of the Russian Church appeared in 1851; Konstantin D. Kavelin's books and lectures helped form the "state school" of Russian history; Nikolai V. Kalachov wrote and edited volumes illuminating the history of Russian law; Kostomarov published works on Ukraine. The popularity of the historical novels of Zagoskin, "the Russian Walter Scott," and Ivan I. Lazhechnikov reflected and increased this interest in the past.

The accession of Alexander II produced great changes, especially optimism that the sleeping giant was awakening and freedoms and new opportunities were rising. The emperor's gentle leadership encouraged the flowering of the arts: Tolstoy, Turgenev, Dostoevsky, Nekrasov, Pisemskii, Goncharov, and Ostrovskii produced some of their most outstanding works in the first five years of the reign. The government relaxed control over travel and importation of publications and allowed a growing trickle of "thick" journals and newspapers. Inquiries concerning the evils of serfdom, revelations in the journals of torture and gross injustice in the judicial system, and information concerning life in western Europe informed young men such as Kliuchevskii of the new era, as a similar thaw did millions of Russians after 1985.

The rescript announcing the abolition of serfdom was the keystone of these changes, and reform of higher education, the press, the judicial system, local government, the army, and other institutions followed. Education, then and now, was a responsibility of the state, and the university was a state institution. The expansion and new spirit in higher education and the changes introduced from the top (usually the case in Russia) were representative of other transformations.

The most significant modification in higher education occurred in 1863, when the government, after studying systems in Prussia, France, and England, enlarged the freedoms that professors enjoyed, expanded faculties, increased salaries and privileges, and encouraged expansion and improvement of instruction. The superintendent of the educational district retained supervisory powers, but the university academic council became the corporate center of university life. It retained its recently awarded power to elect the rector and deans and appoint and promote faculty members, but the Ministry of Education reserved the power of approval and the right to appoint special professors.

The ministry increased university faculty from 51 to 57 and instructors at all universities from 293 to 487. Salaries rose substantially, and faculty members received civil service status, enlarged supplements for living costs (*stolovaia*) of 300 rubles a year, pension rights, and survivors' benefits for widows. The salary of a professor (*ordinarius*) became 3,000 rubles, the same as that of a major general; that of an associate professor (*extraordinarius*) 2,000 rubles, the same as that of a brigadier general; and that of an assistant professor (*dotsent*), a new rank the statute created, 1,200 rubles, the same as that of a lieutenant colonel. In short, Kliuchevskii ultimately joined a newly privileged profession in a "growth industry" that enjoyed increased autonomy, greater freedom than before, and improved benefits.[1]

The 1863 statute did not grant university autonomy, the faculty's principal concern, but making academic decisions became a faculty responsibility, not that of bureaucrats in the central administration. Faculty members were not

Kliuchevskii as a student, 1861–1865. Source: M. V. Nechkina, *Vasilii Osipovich Kliuchevskii. Istoriia zhizni i tvorchestva* (Moscow: Nauka, 1974).

interested in stewardship for student behavior, so most rejoiced when a bureaucrat under the rector assumed that responsibility, freeing them from administrative chores. However, this removed a buffer between students and the government that the faculty might have controlled, a disadvantage that became apparent when officials or police barged in when students engaged in escapades or became critical of university or state policies.

Other innovations were also significant. Of the 293 men teaching at Russian universities in 1861, 134 had studied abroad and joined their faculties since Alexander II assumed power. The most important revision, in 1855, allowed admission to all qualified students and expanded universities from six in 1856 to nine in 1881. The number of students in these years more than doubled, from 3,700 to 8,190. The government in 1857 allowed instruction concerning European political and legal systems, which enriched the curriculum and brought into the faculty such scholars as Boris Chicherin, who greatly influenced Kliuchevskii and his generation. In 1858, it permitted the faculty to give public lectures. In 1860, instruction in geography resumed, philosophy was separated from theology, the university opened defense of dissertations to the public, and students no longer had to wear uniforms (this requirement was restored in 1885). The government allowed St. Petersburg University to establish professorships in general (Western) history and literature, Byzantine literature, and modern Greek, and Kharkov University to offer the first history of the Slavic peoples. In 1862, it began to send young men abroad for advanced training for academic careers, forty-two that year and sixty-seven in 1863.

The city of Moscow, of which Kliuchevskii became a permanent resident in 1861, also underwent transformations during these years. Russians and informed foreign observers described it as a large country town of less than 400,000 that had grown slowly and haphazardly. The streets were a noisy and lively labyrinth, ancient and primitive in character, and few were paved. As late as 1914, seven of eight residential buildings were one- or two-storied wooden structures. All but two bridges over the Moscow River were wooden, and the first iron bridge was constructed in 1868. Gas lighting of streets began in 1876. Electricity was introduced in main squares in the 1870s and into homes of the wealthy in 1876. Horse-drawn trolleys appeared in 1872 and horse-drawn trams in 1889. Even at the end of the century, winter turned the city into a country village.

Moscow had one state bank in 1860, and the Moscow Commercial Bank opened in 1866. Small shops and factories were scattered throughout the city, which contained barely 50,000 workers when Kliuchevskii arrived. In the 1890s, Moscow province still counted more craft workers than factory workers. Most plants served the city and the region: in 1870, only thirty Moscow factories had national markets. Moscow trailed St. Petersburg, Warsaw, Kiev, and Lodz in introducing technological innovations. It became a railroad center only after Kliuchevskii began his studies. Lines extended to Nizhnii Novgorod in 1862, to Riazan' in 1864, Kursk in 1868, and Smolensk and Iaroslavl' in 1870. Until 1862, a merchant had to asume that shipping goods from Moscow to Nizhnii Novgorod would require ten days. Letters from Moscow to Penza took two weeks.

The city's population was almost entirely Russian and Orthodox. It grew rapidly after 1860 to 602,000 in 1871, 1,038,591 in 1897, and 1,617,900 in 1912, but 67 percent of the immigrants were from the Moscow region and were still legally peasants. In 1897, 95 percent were native speakers of Russian. In 1902, 92 percent were ethnic Russians and 93 percent members of the Russian Orthodox Church. Moscow was an enlarged Penza.[2]

Moscow in the 1860s and for years thereafter constituted the center of conservative Russian culture and patriotism. Aristocratic, patriotic, conservative families dominated social and cultural life. The merchants, just as autocratic, patriotic, and conservative and probably more religious, accepted a supportive role. The professional middle class was small and insignificant, much less important than its counterpart in western Europe and the United States. In 1882, when Moscow had 700,000 inhabitants and a garrison of 21,000, it contained 5,000 intellectuals, including 500 lawyers and teachers at all levels. As late as 1900, the city was home to only 9,000 professionals.[3]

Moscow University was 106 years old when Kliuchevskii began his studies.

Based on the Prussian model, the institution and its faculty had prestige and respectability, as professors in Germany and clergymen did then in the United States. Educated Russians considered universities an instrument of light and progress, and scholar-teachers favored servants of the nation, empowered to end privilege and bring enlightenment to all. For Kliuchevskii's generation, and that of its parents, the university was a kind of temple, its faculty "teachers of society." Soloviev, Kliuchevskii's mentor and predecessor, wrote of "the holy alliance between universities and society." One of Kliuchevskii's fellow students in 1861 saw himself as "a member of a golden order." The most popular student song praised "the glorious work" of higher education.[4] Faculty members were cloistered scholars. Few of them or students were interested in political questions, although change began soon. The critical issue was the conflict between religion and atheism, one that became political in that autocratic society.

Moscow University had become Russia's premier institution in the 1830s and 1840s, and St. Petersburg was a close second. It was about the size of a small American college in the 1990s, with 1,560 students (there had been only 821 in 1850). The renown of scholar-teachers such as Granovskii made it an intellectual magnet. A quarter of a mile from the Kremlin, across Mokhovaia, it stood at the apex of three *gimnazii* or high schools, all linked to the university and one so near that its classrooms overlooked the courtyard of the newer of the university's two buildings. Their teachers were usually graduates of the university, and many faculty had taught at one of the high schools while obtaining the degrees that qualified them for university posts.

The university was the center of a group of institutions that made Moscow the capital of education and learning: in 1890, a fifth of all Russian institutions of higher education were in Moscow. These were important to Kliuchevskii and his generation and to those whom they trained for academic careers, providing positions for graduate students and on occasion lifetime appointments. Almost all the men Kliuchevskii helped train as professional historians remained in Moscow, many at the university but others at other educational institutions, libraries, and archives. This high concentration helps explain the role that they quietly acquired in Russian cultural life.

The Moscow Ecclesiastical Academy, one of the four senior centers for training Orthodox theologians and faculty members for seminaries, founded in 1667, had moved in 1814 from Moscow to Sergiev Posad, forty-four miles northeast, but was still considered and called a Moscow institution. Kliuchevskii received his first full-time academic appointment at this university-level institution and taught there from 1871 until 1906, taking a train on Monday morning and returning late Tuesday afternoon. The School of Painting, Sculpture, and Architecture, at which he taught Friday afternoons during the last thirteen years of his life, was one of Russia's two important institutions for training artists. It began classes in painting in 1832, became the School of Painting and Sculpture in 1843, and added architecture in 1863. Nikolai P.

Kondakov and Aleksandr I. Kirpichnikov, his classmates as undergraduate and graduate students, taught there in the 1860s, as did graduate students working with Kliuchevskii years later.

Minister of Defense Count Dmitrii A. Miliutin established the Third Aleksandrovskoe Military School in 1863 on Znamenka Street and Arbat Square, three blocks from the university. Soloviev and other university luminaries lectured there during its first years. Kliuchevskii and other advanced students began their teaching careers there, Kliuchevskii as an assistant to Soloviev in 1867 and as a lecturer in 1868.

The government forbade women to study at Moscow University, so Vladimir I. Ger'e of the university's faculty of history in 1872 began the Women's Higher Courses, also called the Higher Pedagogical Courses for Women, Ger'e's Course, and Ger'e's Private School. He launched this program in the First High School building on Prechistenka Street, not far from the university or the military school, but moved it in 1876 to the new Polytechnical Museum, near what was Dzerzhinskii Square until August 1991. Courses were similar to those at the university. The lecturers were such faculty members as Ger'e and Buslaev and such promising young men as Kliuchevskii, who taught at the school from 1872 until the government closed it in 1888.

Those interested in history benefited greatly from the creation and location of libraries and archives. The government in 1862 transferred the Rumiantsev Public Museum and Library, which became the Lenin Library in 1925 and the Russian State Library in 1992, from St. Petersburg to the Pashkov Palace at the corner of Znamenka Street and Mokhovaia, facing the Kremlin. This graceful building, which now houses the manuscript division of the library, was three blocks from the university. The Rumiantsev collection was strong in old Russian manuscripts. Its book collection grew gradually until it contained 80,000 volumes in 1891 and 200,000 in 1914, making the library second to the Imperial Public Library (later the Saltykov-Shchedrin and now the Russian National Library) in St. Petersburg as an important resource. Many professors bequeathed it their book collections and papers, and it became a center for research in Russian history.

The Holy Synod Library in the Kremlin contained 2,300 manuscripts on the period before the fifteenth century. The Main Archives of the Ministry of Foreign Affairs, strong for the period before 1832, occupied the location that the Russian State Library's main building now fills, a brief walk from the university. The Moscow Archives of the Ministry of Justice were two miles away, a pleasant walk then through part of the gentry nest and open country. These possessed the largest and most important collection of sources on Russian history and became the core of the Central State Archive of Ancient Acts, now the Russian State Historical Archive. After 1851, under the administration of scholars who put their resources into good order, the materials were "the center of the world" for Kliuchevskii and his students. They brought young and old scholars together in an intellectual and social center, a kind of club for those dedicated to Russian history.

Such institutions provided employment for many of Kliuchevskii's students. Iurii V. Got'e, one of the most able men he helped train, obtained an undergraduate degree in history in 1895, began work in the Rumiantsev Museum and Library in 1898, and launched his career at the university in 1903. He remained at the library until his arrest in 1930, in the 1920s as deputy director and chief of the manuscript division. Aleksandr I. Iushkov, who made lithographed copies of Kliuchevskii's university lectures in the 1880s, worked from 1884 to 1913 as an archivist at the Ministry of Justice. There he provided advice and easy access to sources for men who had received the same training he had.

The city created other museums that nurtured cultural and intellectual activities, added to its research resources, and employed university graduates. These included the Russian Historical Museum in 1873, now the State Historical Museum, on Red Square facing the Kremlin. The handsome Polytechnical Museum in 1872 provided halls for the courses that Ger'e organized for women and the public lectures that Kliuchevskii and other scholars gave for worthy causes, such as alleviating the famine in 1891. The Tretiakov Art Gallery opened in 1881. Other museums followed: that for trade and industry in 1885, the theater in 1894, the city economy in 1896, and Pushkin in 1898.

Public lectures on anniversaries of Peter the Great, Lomonosov, Pushkin, Novikov, and Byron attracted crowds and received detailed press description. Scholarly conferences and exhibits were also important. Professor Nikolai S. Tikhonravov, under whom Kliuchevskii studied and who became a close friend, organized the first conferences for teachers of languages and literatures in 1866 and 1869. Scholars in ethnography and anthropology arranged an exhibition in 1867, and the first archeological conference took place in 1869. Kliuchevskii was interested in these sessions: he made his only trip to Kiev in 1874, when he chaired one session of the Third Archeological Congress, a ten-day international meeting of two hundred scholars at which he became acquainted with historians from other Russian cities and with Alfred Rambaud and Louis Leger from Paris.

Private individuals and the newly established city government after 1870 established reading rooms. Two founded and financed by Vikula A. Morozov and named for Turgenev and Ostrovskii were large and popular. Toward the end of his life, Kliuchevskii learned that the first volumes of his *Course of Russian History* were popular among workers who used these reading rooms.

Professional organizations and other private societies established to promote education and learning also contributed to the flowering of intellectual life from which Kliuchevskii benefited. Russia had between twenty and twenty-five such societies in 1856 and two hundred in 1880. The 1863 statute allowed universities to sponsor such organizations. By 1895, scholars attached to universities had created thirty-eight, twelve in history and related subjects and nine at Moscow University alone. The principal ones in Moscow were the Law Society in 1863, closed by the government in 1899; the Russian Historical Society in 1864 (the American Historical Association was formed in 1884); and also in that year the Archeological Society, in which Kliuchevskii was active. He was a member of other groups established to bring the new learning to the public: the Society of Lovers of Russian Literature in 1861, the Society of Lovers of Russian Art in 1863, the Society for Disseminating Useful Books in 1864, and the Committee for Spreading Technical Knowledge in 1869. In 1874 he joined the Committee for Literacy, founded in the 1850s.

The quality of the arts also helped make Moscow a lively cultural center between the Crimean War and 1914. On the Moscow scene, and throughout Russia and much of the world, Tolstoy remained a dominant force until his death in 1910. Chekhov's short stories and plays were immensely popular in Kliuchevskii's last two decades, especially as performed at the Moscow Art Theater, founded in 1898. Their pessimistic tone resembled that of the historian in his last few years, just as Chekhov's realism and simple, precise language were similar to Kliuchevskii's. The Moscow Conservatory, founded in 1866 and directed by Nikolai Rubinstein, included Peter Tchaikovsky on its faculty as a professor of harmony. This great composer's lyric works and the way in which *Sleeping Beauty* in 1890 and other ballets brought music and dance together helped elevate both Russian music and ballet to world recognition. In painting, men such as Isaak Levitan and Valentin A. Serov helped make the School of Painting, Sculpture, and Architecture as attractive to Kliuchevskii as the Bolshoi Theater's operas and symphonies.

These most visible and best-known aspects of Moscow's cultural vitality were part of a national cultural blooming. They rested upon established foundations, political and economic change that began with Alexander II, and wealthy and intelligent patrons. Families such as the Morozovs, who had acquired wealth in cotton textile manufacturing, were among the leaders. Savva T. Morozov, a patron of artists and writers, helped found the Moscow Art Theater, in which K. S. Alekseev-Stanislavskii and V. I. Nemerovich-Danchenko brought "real life" to plays by Chekhov and other playwrights. Pavel M. Tretiakov, a wealthy merchant collector of ancient icons and modern paintings, made the Tretiakov Gallery one of the world's great art museums. S. I. Mamontov, a railroad magnate, assisted composers such as Modest Mussorgsky and Rimsky-Korsakov. He also established a private opera company and made his summer residence in Abramtsevo, halfway between Moscow and Sergiev Posad, a center for musicians, painters, and sculptors. In sum, Kliuchevskii's Moscow provided an invigorating atmosphere and setting.

The university in 1861 occupied two buildings on Mokhovaia, a quarter of a mile from the Borovitskii gate of the Kremlin, just inside which was the Holy Synod's Library. Great Nikitskaia Street, now Herzen Street, separated the two university buildings. History was taught on the second floor of the new building, in the courtyard of which the statue of Lomonosov still stands, facing the Manège or riding school. The auditorium on that floor, now a library reading room, was the scene of most of Kliuchevskii's classes as a student and faculty member. The university was near the main libraries, museums, and schools, a few blocks from the Arbat, then the shopping center for the upper classes, and at the edge of the area where the nobility, many senior officials, intellectuals, and faculty lived. The section was dotted with lovely small churches, some of which survive, and was the heart of old Moscow. The university had no dormitories then and only two housing less than two hundred students when Kliuchevskii retired. Most students occupied rooms or corners of rooms in that section, which constituted a small and sedate kind of Latin Quarter.

Measuring the quality of an educational institution is always a difficult problem, but the university in recent decades had acquired a highly trained faculty, beneficiaries of the finest education that Russia could provide and of study abroad. Kliuchevskii's instructors had spent at least two years at French and German universities, spoke and read several languages, followed foreign scholarship, and acquired recognition abroad as scholars. Most reflected the enthusiasm and will to advance that Alexander II's reform years stimulated. The faculty in the sciences, such as zoologist A. P. Bogdanov and I. M. Umov in physics, in law, and to some extent in medicine, were notable in their fields. Above all, the faculty belief that scholarship was a benign science of national utility characterized the climate of opinion when Kliuchevskii began his studies. Indeed, "Bliss was it in that dawn to be alive, but to be young was very heaven."

Almost all faculty were Russian and active members of the Russian Orthodox Church: 82 percent in 1884 in all Russian universities were Orthodox, and the percentage was almost certainly higher at Moscow University, where one-eighth of the students were sons of priests. In that year, 74 of 112 teaching at the university had received their education there.[5] Most saw themselves as members of a priesthood, determined to remain free from politics and responsibility for student affairs and eager to produce scholarship of European quality. Kliuchevskii was fortunate because several of the enthusiasts with whom he studied invited students to their homes to use their libraries, discuss scholarly problems, and even study foreign languages. Buslaev and others were generous in lending books to students and assisting them through difficult financial times.

The faculty that Kliuchevskii entered, History-Philology, also included languages and literatures, theology, political economy, and art, all taught by twenty-two men. It remained the division with the smallest number of students throughout his career, although law students in particular took many courses in it and staff shrank as enrollments declined in liberal arts and rose in law and medicine. In 1909–10, History-Philology had only 25 faculty members of the total of 124. Almost all historians in this group were men whom Kliuchevskii had trained.

He and his fellows benefited from the institution's small size and physical surroundings. They formed a close-knit community because most lived in crowded rooms in that part of the city and participated in many of the same classes in the same rooms. This helps explain the intellectual vitality and camaraderie typical of Russian student groups in the nineteenth century and the explosive power that such a flock possessed when political ideas seized their minds.

Most were aware of the advantages they enjoyed and were inspired by the desire to change society. Two-thirds in 1861 were sons of nobility, high bureaucracy, or military families. Only four came from peasant families, and three were Jews. Thirty-two, including Kliuchevskii, came from seminaries and ecclesiastical academies. As late as 1903–1904, a fourth came from the nobility, 2 percent from merchants and "honored citizens," and 5 percent each from the military and peasantry. Religious beliefs had changed slightly. In the student body of 8,043 in 1907, 6,736 were Orthodox, almost 84 percent.[6]

Two days after he had arrived in Moscow, Kliuchevskii paid his admission and first-semester fees and applied for the summer admission examinations, in which he received "extremely good" grades in Latin, Greek, grammar, and literature and satisfactory grades in the other subjects. On September 1, he showed his new identity card, proceeded to the second floor of the new building, and began what he later wrote Kliment A. Timiriazev was "the best time of my life."

As far as one can tell, Kliuchevskii was a typically impecunious student and member of the class then beginning to form from sons of priests, small gentry, shopkeepers, and junior bureaucrats and officers. He was outstanding because of his abilities, intense commitment to learning, and disinterest in public issues, although most of his fellows were not the radical students of whom we read so much but were primarily concerned with learning. Homesick the first few months, he looked for letters each day and devoured them several times when they arrived. He wrote long, observant letters to his uncle, Gvozdev, and other friends in Penza. A loner, gloomy and pessimistic on occasion, he suffered often from headaches, probably migraines, but he also enjoyed playing practical jokes on friends. He was an active observer of student life, at first among young men from Penza and others who had studied in seminaries, but not a participant.

His correspondence reveals that he read avidly the principal journals and Moscow newspapers. He participated in fervent discussions of the changes taking place and the views of Chernyshevskii, Ivan Aksakov, Nekrasov, Herzen, and Dobroliubov. When Dobroliubov died in 1861, Kliuchevskii termed him "a true man" and a great loss for Russia. He appreciated Turgenev's *Fathers and Sons*, which arrived in Katkov's office at the same time he reached the city and began to appear in the *Moscow Herald* in March 1862. Many observers of Russia, then and later, thought this novel defined and perhaps even created the gap between generations. The nihilist Bazarov was Kliuchevskii's favorite character, which illustrates the attraction radical ideas and attitudes created for a staunchly conservative populist lad who had an inquiring mind.

A wealthy Penzemliak on a visit in Kliuchevskii's first semester introduced him to ballet. He enjoyed music, especially Beethoven, Mendelssohn, and Liszt, and praised Soloviev by comparing him to a composer. The Bolshoi Theater, a mile from the university, contributed to his education: he attended his first Glinka opera before he had been in Moscow three months. The theater was another pastime, appropriately, because Kliuchevskii in the lecture hall was a great actor. He wrote a friend in the fall of 1861 that the theater sometimes affected him more than a splendid religious ceremony. The Malyi Theater, adjoining the Bolshoi, was a popular diversion, with tickets only thirty kopeks. Ostrovskii was his favorite playwright, but he enjoyed Griboedov and Gogol, Molière and Shakespeare, Calderón and Hugo. In short, the young student appreciated and benefited from the exciting cultural fare the city provided.

Kliuchevskii had barely begun to enjoy Moscow's promise when a crisis threatened to close his "road to science." He had known before he left Penza that Count Evfimii V. Putiatin, Minister of Education, had in May announced a new set of regulations. The minister relaxed admissions by allowing seminarians to enter and abolished the rule that students should wear uniforms. But he prohibited student organizations and meetings, required identity cards for admission, made lecture attendance obligatory, and replaced a long-established and popular inspector of students with a severe high-school principal from Kharkov. Without warning, he raised tuition from twenty-five to fifty rubles per year (forty at universities other than Moscow) and reduced the number of tuition scholarships from two hundred to eighteen, two for the ablest and poorest students in each province, effective in the fall semester of 1861. Only the great increase in tuition depressed Kliuchevskii, but even this did not deter him.

The sudden increase in tuition led students in St. Petersburg to protest shortly after the semester began. Demonstrations that followed government refusal to reverse or delay the increase led authorities to close the university. Students in Moscow had shown no interest in the issue, although both faculty and students were upset when they learned that the heir to the throne would attend St. Petersburg University rather than Moscow. Moscow students would probably have remained passive, except for the righteous tone of Katkov's articles in the *Moscow Herald* and the encouragement that St. Petersburg students provided. Rumors spread. Most were untrue but flourished because of the severity of the regulations and the nature of Russian society. Many students concluded that the university would admit only eighteen poor students. Some claimed that the increase was designed to raise faculty salaries, that any student who attended a course outside his faculty must pay an extra fee, that the class instructor would receive this money, and that students had been arrested for lithographing and selling copies of lectures.

The governor-general of Moscow, P. A. Tuchkov, and the superintendent of the Moscow educational district, General N. V. Isakov, were sensible and civilized, understood student anguish, and sought to avoid confrontation. However, inevitably, they followed rules and regulations and refused to negotiate.

The university faculty did not have the interest, authority, organization, or leadership to intervene. Those who expressed concern placed responsibility for the demonstrations upon the student majority for allowing a noisy minority to speak for all. The Faculty Council had learned of the new regulations in June but failed even to suggest that the ministry delay the increase. Instead, it concentrated upon selecting a new faculty member in zoology and dissuading the ministry from moving the university museum to Pashkov Palace and combining the university and city libraries. In addition, the faculty in June had postponed its newly received right to elect the new rector. Poorly organized and inexperienced, the council had no leadership when students began to discuss the tuition increase. At its regular weekly meeting, three days after the first student demonstration, it declined to act. It finally allowed young and new Stepan V. Eshevskii to draft a petition that a committee of three senior faculty members and then the council would consider sending to the minister of education.

After they had failed to persuade faculty members to join, some students arranged a quiet and orderly protest at Granovskii's grave on October 4, a day on which Moscow faculty and students traditionally paid tribute to the patron of student rights. They appealed to the superintendent of the educational district, paraded to the residence of the governor-general with a petition to the tsar, which the governor-general refused to accept, and demonstrated on the night of October 11. The university administration, convinced that law students were responsible for these actions, closed the first two years of the four-year law program. In subsequent protests, some students pushed their way into the faculty lounge, discussed their complaints with unwilling faculty members, and damaged furniture.

This demonstration produced clashes with the police, injuries to some students, and the arrest of more than three hundred, one-fifth of the student body. Shopkeepers turned against students, while many women from families in the area befriended them. The *Moscow Herald* persuaded many Muscovites, including Eshevskii and Kliuchevskii, that Polish students were the leaders.

Throughout these days, the faculty remained aloof. Buslaev denounced the demonstrations as an "insult" to the professors and education. Those faculty members who commented and the faculty report in the fall declared the university a scientific institution whose activities the students were jeopardizing. Even gentle Ivan Aksakov opposed the students.

Such troubles and the proposal a few students made to close the university disturbed Kliuchevskii, who feared that either a strike or a repetition of the St. Petersburg decision would close his "road to science" and end his dream. Letters to Gvozdev and his uncle show that he attended several meetings, but only as an acute observer. He left as soon as he thought he might become involved, and he refused to sign the petition to the tsar. His letters were brief because he was afraid that officials would read them, but he discreetly urged his correspondents not to believe the press.

Kliuchevskii appreciated the interest that some students leaders had in the plight of their poorer fellows, but he was critical of both the movement and the government. Declaring that the majority had cheerfully accepted the changes, he called the incident a tragicomedy, "improper actions" by a "demagogic minority," "an affair of a few youngsters" who were "unruly and impudent." "Rowdies led by Poles," "demagogues who just want their names in golden letters for posterity" were responsible. The "insolent tone" of the petition to the tsar especially offended him. Still, he thought the government's suddenly raising tuition without explanation a serious blunder. Police "impudence" had united students against police and government, and the beatings and arrests were unjustified.

A week later, after the uproar had subsided and classes had resumed, he concluded that he was a conservative, not a liberal, "a word hateful to me in the sense of blind groping in which modern liberals participate." Grateful that "dovelike wisdom" had protected him from joining student protests, he inquired, "Isn't it true that for progress one must accept existing arrangements?"[7] This incident reflected the quietism and conservatism that marked his life. It also strengthened his resolution to concentrate upon learning and avoid actions, even thoughts, that might imperil his main interest.

Later in the fall, a faculty committee report to the minister of education criticized the government for its abrupt changes and ineptitude. It assigned responsibility for student outbursts to erosion of the inspector of students' powers after 1855 and appointment of an inexperienced inspector. In addition, the professors endorsed "liberal means and strong measures" and recommended that the district superintendent of education should retain responsibility for student behavior. This position, and the philosophy it reflects, help to explain why later student troubles expanded beyond university walls and became burning political issues.

After this threat to Kliuchevskii's career faded, poverty, a more fundamental and long-term hazard, became his major concern. His letters, his careful records, and the scraps of paper he used for notes demonstrate that money was a constant care throughout his life, as it was for many Americans affected by the depression of the 1930s. Even as a renowned and prosperous senior scholar late in life, he traveled third class to and from Sergiev Posad and reluctantly purchased a wardrobe when he accepted appointment to two state commissions in St. Petersburg. Paying three rubles a day for a hotel room there disturbed him then as much as the cost of garret space had a half-century earlier, even though the government reimbursed him.

Financial problems were acute. The trip from Penza, tuition for the first semester, clothing, and living expenses quickly consumed Father Evropeitsev's gift. Kliuchevskii could not attend the first day of class in the second semester because he lacked the twenty-five rubles for tuition. In March 1862 he obtained two small scholarships, one from the Ministry of Education and the other provided by a Moscow merchant named Demidov that added twelve rubles a month, but these did not provide full support.

He survived by finding or creating opportunities, first by transcribing lectures, writing them out carefully, in some instances persuading the professor to ensure their accuracy, and cooperating with another student in lithographing and selling the product. This was a profitable enterprise because lectures constituted the heart of most courses, and almost no courses except those in foreign languages had textbooks. Kliuchevskii's archives and those of many colleagues contain lithographs of courses they attended, and dozens of lithographed copies of many of his lectures survive. Indeed, records of the university library list copies of these lithographed courses, or "notebooks," as part of the collection.

He also helped support himself by tutoring. In his first semester, he walked four miles to and from Sokol'niki once a week to instruct a forester's son and read to his wife. For this he received fifteen rubles a month, plus a cup of tea and a piece of bread at each session. In the summers of 1862 and 1863, he tutored the children of Prince Sergei V. Volkonskii at the prince's estate near Riazan'. Later he tutored in the family of Nikolai A. Miliutin, nephew of Count P. D. Kiselev and brother of Count Dmitrii A. Miliutin, who was responsible for reforming the army in those years. N. A. Miliutin lived in a splendid house in the heart of the gentry nest on Povarskaia Street (now Vorovskaia), near Buslaev and Chicherin. He often talked with Kliuchevskii about his career, which began with studies in the 1850s that provided statistical data on population and city finance to senior bureaucrats. From 1859 through 1861, as deputy minister of the interior, he was active in preparing the abolition of serfdom. From 1863 until 1867, he held an important position in the Polish provinces, where his suspicion of Poles and Roman Catholics moderated his liberal views.

In the early 1870s, Kliuchevskii tutored two daughters of Timofei S. Morozov, an enlightened Old Believer who was a wealthy textile manufacturer, a banker, and a "Slavophil Mohican." Kliuchevskii and his family remained friends with Morozov's daughters throughout his life. One of them, Anna, married Gennadii F. Karpov, Kliuchevskii's closest friend, made stenographic accounts of his lectures, and served as a typist of the *Course of Russian History*. The two young men on occasion had tea with the Morozovs at their home, so that Kliuchevskii's work as a tutor gave him some insight into an unfamiliar kind of life and helped him widen his horizons.

In sum, Kliuchevskii's early years in Moscow were those of a relaxation of state controls; the flowering of literature, music, art, architecture, science, and the study of history; and expansion, increased freedom, and vitality in higher education. The addition of new cultural institutions accompanied the city's growth and the modernization of its economy and facilities. In this atmosphere, the seminarian overcame the challenge of moving from rural Russia into quite a different environment. He benefited from the new society's intellectual vitality, which he later represented and strengthened.

THREE

"The Guiding Stars"
The Moscow University History Faculty

Sir Paul Vinogradov, one of Russia's, and later England's, supreme scholars, entered Moscow University in 1869, eight years after Kliuchevskii. He enjoyed the same instructors and served on the same faculty, and the two were friends and colleagues for more than thirty years. At a dinner in his honor in 1925 at All Souls College at Oxford, Vinogradov recognized the Moscow institution's high qualities and contribution to his intellectual growth, especially through "the encyclopedic outlook . . . and the interconnection of the human sciences, one with another."

The university faculty encountered harrowing difficulties in its efforts to acquire autonomy and increase quality, but the institution was one of ever-growing excellence, benefiting from the age of transformation, even one of fits and starts, and the desire of educated Russians to enjoy closer relations with Europe. The intellectual qualities, professional skills, and attainments of the history faculty provided Kliuchevskii an invigorating, first-class education. His vision of a scholar-teacher's role in the nation rested upon their belief in universal science and service to society. Their study and travel in Europe and the access they provided to the ideas of some of the nineteenth century's most stimulating historians deeply affected some of his basic assumptions about Russia and the influence cultural relations between Russia and the West exercised.

The liberal arts program of the faculty of History-Philology ordinarily led into teaching, the bureaucracy, journalism, careers as publicists or literary critics, or a relaxed life for those who were wealthy and lacked ambition or talent. A career in journalism was hardly likely to attract because of Kliuchevskii's reserved nature and temperament and because such a profession was precarious. He might have found a satisfying life in the bureaucracy, especially as a researcher, but no interest or opportunity arose. He wrote with clarity and wit, and the poems and short stories in his archives reflect imagination and literary talent. But his ambition was the study of history.

He arrived at the university when higher education was expanding and academic life becoming more rewarding. Some professors invited the most able and ambitious students to their homes on occasional evenings, giving the provincial young man an enticing view of a career of which he could hardly have dreamed. Three instructors encouraged an academic career, as professors in most societies do for students whose abilities and attitude seem to designate them as teachers.

Kliuchevskii's archives and letters reveal that he attended lectures in classes other than those in which he registered, made stenographic notes, and prepared clear, well-organized outlines and summaries. Comments on instructors were astute with regard to the substance and the faculty member's point of view. They provided detailed description of lecturers: physical characteristics, facial expressions, gestures, voice, accent, and dress, demonstrating his interest from the beginning in effective teaching and the powers of observation and description that mark his art as a historian.

All of his grades in history and literature and most others were 5s, the highest. He completed his undergraduate program with an average of 4.74, second only to Aleksandr I. Kirpichnikov, a Moscow merchant's son who had won the gold medal at the Moscow First High School. Third place went to Nikodim P. Kondakov, who graduated from the Moscow Second High School, and whose father managed the property of the Trubetskois in Kursk province and then in Moscow. All three men became outstanding scholars whose careers reflect the quality of some areas of Russian academic life in the half-century before the revolution. All were elected members of the Academy of Sciences, and Russian and Western scholars alike have honored them. Kirpichnikov, whose research in French and Italian literature and art benefited from the resources of the Rumiantsev Museum, studied in western Europe on a number of occasions. He served brilliantly on the faculties of the universities of Kharkov and Odessa between 1879 and 1897 and joined Moscow University in 1898 as a specialist on Russian literature and iconography.

Kondakov obtained his doctorate in 1876. An outstanding iconographer who studied and traveled often in Europe, he taught the history of Byzantine and Russian art in Odessa from 1870 to 1888, before becoming chair of the history of art in St. Petersburg University and a curator of art at the Hermitage Museum. He "virtually founded the scientific study of Byzantine art and created the modern field of Russian archeological research."[1] After the revolution, he emigrated to Prague, where the Kondakov Seminar carried on his work. One of his outstanding students, Mikhail Rostovtsev, left St. Petersburg in 1918 and helped launch Byzantine studies in the United States, with Yale University his scholarly base.

Toward the end of his undergraduate years, Kliuchevskii chose teaching as a career. Russian history became his principal field sometime in his third or fourth year, but other subjects attracted him and widened his range of knowledge. Buslaev interested him in Russian linguistics and folklore, directed his most thorough undergraduate research papers, and may have suggested the subject of his senior thesis. Pavel M. Leont'ev was so impressed by Kliuchevskii's command of Latin and work on the Roman classics that he urged him to become a professor of Greek and Latin. But his interest in the classics waned after the first two years.

University classes took place six days a week from nine until three or four, and each student attended class from seventeen to twenty hours. Every student in the History-Philology Faculty in the first two years followed a core curriculum of the history of philosophy, theology, early Russian literature, foreign languages, and ancient, Russian, and European history. Kliuchevskii's undergraduate program was broad, from archeology and psychology to Sanskrit and statistics and Byzantine art. In his last two years, he audited courses on the history of Russian law by Ivan D. Beliaev, whose knowledge of Moscow archives was admirable, but whose Slavophil view was considered old-fashioned. He also attended scholarly, well-organized lectures on Russian civil law by Konstantin P. Pobedonostsev, then a bureaucrat in the Senate and an instructor in the Law School, but later renowned as the director general of the Holy Synod and principal adviser of Alexander III.

The instructor who most attracted and influenced Kliuchevskii during the first two years was Buslaev, but the courses he mentioned most in correspondence were those by Panfil D. Iurkevich on the history of philosophy and Father N. A. Sergievskii in theology. In 1867 Kliuchevskii considered Iurkevich a scoundrel because he supported the minister of education's reappointment of Leont'ev against overwhelming faculty opposition, but in 1861 he praised him as a stimulating scholar and a vivid lecturer. Iurkevich was so relentless in his idealistic critique of Hegel and Chernyshevskii and such an impressive speaker that some faculty members changed their schedules to hear him. Kliuchevskii forwarded detailed summaries and analyses of his lectures and articles in the *Russian Herald* to friends in Penza and produced and retained a lithographed set of the lectures.

Sergievskii's lectures on theology and essays in the *Orthodox Review* stimulated the young Kliuchevskii, who later published essays in the journal that Sergievskii and three other priests founded and edited. Sergievskii helped him recognize that the seminary had neglected the history of Christianity and increased his concern with religious issues. His lectures raised central questions about the nature of Christianity, helped reduce the "prejudice" against theology he had acquired in the seminary, and strengthened his belief that the answer to doubt lay in the study of history. Feuerbach's *The Essence of Religion* shook his faith temporarily; for the first time he recognized the conflict between atheism and Christian faith. His letters in 1861–62 were filled with expressions of doubt, and attendance at religious services his first two years at the university was irregular.

His history instructors in 1861–62 were Nil A. Popov, a Soloviev son-in-law, and Eshevskii. Popov had spent two years in Europe and was an assistant professor in his second year on the faculty. He taught a course to freshmen on the history of Europe from the Renaissance until the French Revolution, which was useful when Kliuchevskii began to teach European history at the Third Aleksandrovskoe Military School. Popov advised him on his theses and was an official opponent at the doctorate defense in 1882. Above all, he was a link between Kliuchevskii and Soloviev, who devoted little time even to advanced students. Eshevskii, who died in 1865, was a student of Granovskii and Soloviev and returned in 1861 from two exiting years of travel and study in Europe. His lectures on European history and ancient Greece and Rome brought Kliuchevskii the fruits of European scholarship: he retained notes and lithographed copies of Eshevskii lectures throughout his life. Eshevskii invited students to his home one evening a week and created a tempting vision of a scholar's life.

However, the instructor who most influenced Kliuchevskii in his early undergraduate years was Buslaev, "one of the founders of the study of Russian language and literature" and a scholar "who made the study of Russian literature a science."[2] Kliuchevskii learned early that Buslaev came from Penza and that he too had been a poor youngster who made his way by tutoring. He had traveled in western Europe with the Count S. G. Stroganov family for two years and lived with them as a tutor from 1841 to 1844 while teaching at the Second High School and preparing for a university career. Buslaev's second wife came from a prosperous Moscow family, and his comfortable home on Povarskaia Street contained a library as well as a study. In the years before 1861, he had been particularly productive, publishing a book on Church Slavonic and old Russian and a two-volume history of Russian literature and art, still valuable for scholars more than a century later.

For Kliuchevskii, Buslaev became the symbol of scientific culture and an enlightened world outlook. He was interested only in research, writing, and the arts, and had no knowledge of or concern for university affairs or public issues. During Kliuchevskii's first years, Buslaev was almost a father for his Penzemliak, inviting him Friday evenings from six until ten to use the library and on Sunday mornings to study comparative philology. Buslaev allowed him to use and even borrow ancient Russian manuscripts, some of which Kliuchevskii said were "so old they frighten me." He revealed secrets of the academic profession to the excited student by showing censors' comments on his manuscripts.

Kliuchevskii took classes with Buslaev in Byzantine and early Russian literature, Russian and other Slavic poetry, folklore and oral history, philology, old German and Norwegian literature and folklore, and comparative literature. He came to admire the Norwegian Eddas and German folktales and recognized that the lives of the Norwegian and German peoples of those times were much freer than those of Russians. Buslaev reinforced his appreciation of the Brothers Grimm, Wilhelm von Humboldt, and Ernest Renan. He also introduced him to the works of Henry T. Buckle, who was beginning to affect the views of Eshevskii and Soloviev.

Buslaev emphasized that a people's language and literature were an essential part of its history: language is "an expression of the spiritual life of a people." He taught that each society is an organism different from other societies and that history and tradition had combined to make the Russian character different. His approach to history helped turn Kliuchevskii toward the study of popular cultural life and economic and social conditions, helping to blunt the views of Soloviev and Chicherin on the central role of the state. Kliuchevskii often praised Buslaev's love of learning, emphasis upon language, enduring search for truth, patriotism, generosity, and tolerance. Buslaev widened his cultural horizons, provided insight into the attractions and problems of a university career, and emphasized that teaching was "the most holy and greatest office a man could occupy."

Buslaev's influence was seconded by Tikhonravov, a graduate of the Moscow Third High School and student of Granovskii, Soloviev, and Buslaev. Colleagues had respect for his learning, calm judgment, and skill as rector during the most difficult years under Alexander III, when he kept the archconservative Katkov under control without hazard to the university's position.

Both Western and Russian scholars have recognized Tikhonravov as a pioneer in the study of Russian literature, but he was more outstanding as a collector and teacher than as a scholar: the library he bequeathed to the Rumiantsev Museum included 11,000 volumes (more than 4,000 on the sixteenth and seventeenth centuries), 700 manuscripts, and more than 5,000 letters from correspondence with more than 900 individuals. A man of immense erudition who spoke German, English, Greek, and Latin fluently, he attracted masses of students who considered "N. S." second only to Kliuchevskii as a classroom instructor.

Tikhonravov was a conservative, patriotic Russian who had studied abroad and traveled widely. The Brothers Grimm influenced his research interests, methods, and point of view, but from Taine he learned that one must study popular life as well as political development to understand the past. Like Taine and Soloviev, and Kliuchevskii later, Tikhonravov believed that ages, eras, and periods flow into each other and that one cannot cut history into discrete sections.

Kliuchevskii began to study Russian literature of the sixteenth and seventeenth centuries and Byzantine literature with Tikhonravov. Before his junior year, he had begun to spend one evening a week in Tikhonravov's apartment on Nikol'skaia Street, near the Kremlin and the Bolshoi and Malyi theaters. Later, the two became close friends, fishing, discussing Russian history and literature, and commenting on scholarship.

Most Russian scholars who have studied Kliuchevskii and his generation have concluded that Boris N. Chicherin's influence was second only to that of

Soloviev. Chicherin, who began his brief academic career the year Kliuchevskii arrived in Moscow, came from a prosperous Anglophile gentry family in the Tambov province in the black soil region. He studied law in the most reactionary years of Nicholas I, when Western influence, especially that of Hegel, was strong. Konstantin Kavelin, one of the founders of the state school, influenced him profoundly. Chicherin concluded that the state as "the highest form of society, the leading manifestation of authority," played the central role in Russian history. After the law faculty finally approved his 1856 "overly negative" M.A. thesis, *Regional Institutions in Russia in the Seventeenth Century,* he spent three years in Italy, France, England, and parts of Germany, especially London, Paris, and Heidelberg. His classes were popular, but he resigned in 1867 when the Ministry of Education reappointed Leont'ev.

Chicherin worked to establish a rational, legal government. His view of the state's role in history convinced him that Russia could attain such a political system only through a gradual process similar to one he believed had occurred in England. Critical of both the government and students in 1861, he proposed increased university autonomy and student rights, which Russia could achieve only through "strong authority enforcing liberal measures."[3] A supporter of the reform program of Alexander II and a critic of the "revolutionary democrats," he denounced the turn toward repression and returned to Tambov to play a part in the *zemstvo* movement and promote railroad construction. The upsurge of revolutionary activities in the late 1870s and early 1880s dismayed him. In the critical months after the assassination of Alexander II, he urged the government to free peasants from the commune, end redemption payments, and invite assemblies of the land to bridge the gap between the state and society: such a benign step might lead to political participation of the most educated and responsible and then to representative institutions. Elected mayor of Moscow in 1882 under a limited franchise, he was dismissed by the tsar in 1883. Throughout the 1880s and 1890s, he was a vigorous advocate of the rights of national and religious minorities, especially Poles and Jews, then under vicious attack. He remained certain that Russia must advance toward a national legal state in a guided and slow fashion: "Unrestrained freedom leads to an enslavement of the weak by the strong." The government must encourage greater participation by educated and property-owning citizens in local, regional, and then national government and thus bring about gradual preparation for constitutional rule.

Chicherin and Kliuchevskii were in fundamental agreement on the way in which Russia might acquire effective and constitutional government, but they also differed in many ways. They were of different generations and social backgrounds. Chicherin traveled often, while Kliuchevskii never left Russia. Chicherin was strong-willed, active, dogmatic, and blunt. Kliuchevskii was determined, but quietly so, a man of the study disinterested in public affairs who avoided quarrels and confrontation. Chicherin was skeptical of religious faith:

Pobedonostsev once termed him "the great sophist of our science." But they had great respect for each other's intellect, and Chicherin profoundly influenced the younger scholar's view of Russia and the historical process.

Kliuchevskii had especial veneration because Chicherin had been a student of Granovskii and was a living tie with that popular teacher. As an undergraduate and graduate student, Kliuchevskii regularly audited Chicherin's courses. Chicherin's resignation was "one of the most difficult moments" in his life. He retained lithographed copies and notes of Chicherin's lectures and the private papers Chicherin gave him.

Like Soloviev, Chicherin described the history of Russia as that of "a country that colonizes." In the 1870s, when Kliuchevskii was completing the research and reflection that led to his doctorate, he made intensive use of Chicherin's M.A. thesis on regional government in the seventeenth century. The first three chapters of the *Boyar Council,* published in 1880 in *Russian Thought,* constitute in part a critique of Chicherin's views. Chicherin, then mayor of Moscow, attended Kliuchevskii's defense of that thesis. Kliuchevskii dedicated to Chicherin the three extensive articles he published on the *zemskii sobor* or assembly of the land between 1890 and 1892, because Chicherin's *On Popular Representation* had so affected his thinking when he read it in 1866. These essays and the pages on the assembly of the land in the *Course of Russian History* are in many ways comments upon Chicherin's ideas and extensions of them. In 1902, when Kliuchevskii was beginning the first volume of his *Course of Russian History,* his diary had twenty-four references to Chicherin and eight to Soloviev. Mikhail M. Bogoslovskii, a graduate student then, noted that Kliuchevskii spoke often of Chicherin and his work during the years he was converting his lectures into the *Course.*

Chicherin supported Soloviev's belief that "the same general laws rule the history of all mankind," derived in part from his study in Berlin of Schelling, Hegel, and Savigny and in the 1860s of Buckle. Kliuchevskii endorsed this and also agreed that each people possesses its own national idea or directing principle and has a mission that reflects its history and traditions, a view common among educated Russians at that time. Chicherin also concluded that Russia was different from western Europe because it lacked the feudal institutions from which most Western states had grown, a view that Kliuchevskii accepted. Both thought constitutional government the ideal form but were pessimistic that Russia could attain it.

Chicherin also helped direct Kliuchevskii's research to the state's institutions and law as formative factors for a society. However, Kliuchevskii noted that Chicherin studied the state and its institutions from the top and neglected the building materials from which the state was constructed, especially social classes, upon which Kliuchevskii concentrated. The subtitle of the articles in *Russian Thought* was therefore particularly important: "A Study of the History of Government Institutions in Connection with the History of Society." He found the origins of serfdom in slow growth, while Chicherin and the state school assigned its beginnings to state actions. However, he achieved these revisions with such delicacy that the *Boyar Council* constituted not a frontal attack upon Chicherin and Soloviev but a modification of and addition to their research.

Similarly, his seminal essays on the assemblies of the land, full of admiration for Chicherin, provided a different analysis. Both agreed that the rulers had called assemblies to obtain information and support from the state's servants, but Chicherin tended to see them as embryos of representative and parliamentary government. Kliuchevskii demonstrated that those called were instruments or servants of the state, not elected representatives. They came because of their official positions and constituted an advisory body, not an Estates-General or an instrument of the leading classes to restrict the state's power. Chicherin in effect agreed, but followed his hopes rather than the facts when he viewed them as the foundation of a representative system.

Another historian whose life and work reflect the atmosphere in which Kliuchevskii learned his craft and who influenced him was Ger'e, just four years older than he. A descendant from French immigrants (Guerrier), Ger'e was a Lutheran whom students thought a "Calvinist pastor" because of his dress and demeanor. Fluent in French, German, and English before he entered the university, he wrote his M.A. thesis in 1862 under Soloviev on the struggle for the Polish crown in 1733. He wrote his doctorate on Leibnitz under Eshevskii, whom he succeeded. After he returned from two years in Germany, he taught "general history," which included ancient Greece and Rome as well as European history from the Middle Ages. He began Russian research and instruction on French history, and later offered the first university course on the French Revolution.

Ger'e traveled extensively, even into Spain and Portugal, which few Russians (or Americans) considered a part of Europe. He studied the major historians, including Vico; Burke, Young, Taine, and de Tocqueville on France before the revolution; Buckle and Renan, Michelet and Gabriel Monod; Donald Mackenzie Wallace, Anatole Leroy-Beaulieu, and Alfred Rambaud on Russian history. He corresponded with French and German historians and published essays in such journals as the *Historische Zeitschrift*. Buckle and Taine in the 1860s and 1870s were for him the "twin towers" of European scholarship. Students termed the course Americans call Western civilization "Ger'e's Buckle," and he gave courses on Buckle and Montesquieu in the program that he launched and directed for women.

In his first decade on the faculty, Ger'e published an impressive number of scholarly books and articles on the relations of Leibnitz with Peter the Great and Russia, the *cahiers* that help explain the French Revolution, Abbé Mably, and European historians. Then he became a publicist, writing largely for liberal journals and newspapers on educational issues and the need for university autonomy. He completed five volumes on the three Dumas that followed the revolution of 1905 and a flood of long essays for the Brockhaus and Efron

Encyclopedia, the *Entsiklopedicheskii slovar'*, published in St. Petersburg between 1890 and 1907. The description of his archives is more than 320 pages in length, and the list of publications that his daughter compiled in 1941 fills more than 130 pages. The Russian State Library in 1990 possessed more lithographed copies of Ger'e's courses than it did those of Kliuchevskii.

Ger'e was widely known for his public service. He vigorously supported the University Statute of 1863 during the darkest days of Alexander II and Alexander III and was called "the most outspoken defender" of the university against government interference. In 1864 he founded the Russian Historical Society. He was an active elected member of the Moscow City Council (Duma) from 1877 to 1908, pressing for compulsory primary school education and improved social services for the poor. In 1889 he persuaded the council to establish a Committee on Social Needs and Benefits, which he headed for almost twenty years. Convinced that responsible citizens should help those less advantaged through private charities, in 1894 he helped create a system of overseers of the poor that improved cooperation between the city government and private charitable organizations. The service for which he was best known was founding, directing, and teaching in the Women's Higher Courses. He organized this program in 1872, managed it until the Ministry of Education closed it in 1888, and directed it again from 1900 until retirement in 1905.

Ger'e gradually became conservative (Soviet scholars termed him "a reactionary historian") and came to resemble the German National Liberals, who had yielded to Bismarck's domestic and international successes. Establishment of the Third Republic in France and the French government's attack upon the Catholic Church disturbed him. When Russia and Britain collided in the Balkans and Central Asia, he became critical of the British form of government. Then Burke, de Tocqueville, and especially Taine began to shape his view of the history of France and its revolution. He published an essay about Taine's methods in 1889 and a book about him in 1911. Rousseau's ideas loomed more and more as the cause of the revolution and the ills of nineteenth-century Europe. By the turn of the century, he considered an enlightened despotism with elected advisory institutions the best form of government for Russia. After 1905 he became an Octobrist, supported Stolypin, and praised the Third Duma. He considered the Kadets, including his former student, Professor Ivan V. Luchitskii of the University of St. Vladimir in Kiev, potential Jacobins. Even so, Kadet leader Pavel N. Miliukov, whom Ger'e feared and denounced, thought his books on the three Dumas objective and evenhanded.

Ger'e strengthened the history faculty and the university by the quality of his work and by identifying European historical scholarship, especially that of Germany, as a model and goal. Soviet and Western scholars agree that he founded West European studies in Russia and that the "Ger'e School" on the French Revolution exercised a powerful influence upon Russian higher education. But his most lasting contribution was identifying young men with potential for academic careers and providing them professional guidance.

Ger'e launched formal graduate training, introducing the German seminar into a faculty in which Soloviev and others had simply identified young men whom they thought qualified for careers as professors, suggested research subjects, and read their theses. He not only invited students to his home for seminars but encouraged the most intelligent and highly motivated women in his program to participate. Assisting students to study abroad, sharing knowledge of European archives and libraries, and introducing them to European scholars and librarians were among the ways in which he improved training and widened young scholars' horizons.

His wife inherited much of Granovskii's library and the halo of the Granovskii tie. As open, relaxed, and friendly as Ger'e was old-fashioned, demanding, and dour, she helped make their home in the gentry nest an especially comfortable setting for young men. She spoke English, French, and German well, translated Turgot and Voltaire into Russian, and educated their daughter Elena in these languages.

The list of the men whom Ger'e identified and prepared for academic careers includes Mikhail S. Korelin, who won a university gold medal for an undergraduate essay on Faust and joined Ger'e in the 1890s in teaching European history. Interested in intellectual history and the relations between literature and art, he wrote such a splendid M.A. thesis on early Italian humanism and its historiography that the faculty in 1892 awarded him the doctorate at the same time. Ger'e's successor was Robert Iu. Vipper, a prolific scholar, who considered himself a student of both Ger'e and Kliuchevskii. Vipper came to Moscow from Odessa, left his professorship and the Soviet Union in 1922 to teach in Riga, returned in 1940, and won membership in the Soviet Academy of Sciences in 1943. He died in December 1954 at the age of ninety-five, the grand old man of Soviet scholars in European history.

Another was Nikolai I. Kareev, who entered Moscow University in 1869, obtained his master's degree with Ger'e in 1877, went to France for two years, and was the first Russian scholar to undertake research on the revolution in Paris archives. His doctorate on French peasants in the last quarter of the eighteenth century won praise in France and from Marx and Engels. After serving as a Kadet in the First Duma, he published a three-volume *History of the French Revolution*, was elected a member of the Soviet Academy of Sciences in 1929, and died in 1931 at eighty-one.

A third scholar whom Ger'e trained was Luchitskii, who taught European history in Kiev for thirty years and left the university there his large library in 1918. Luchitskii worked in twenty-five archives in France, concentrating on peasants in the eighteenth century. He published in France and Germany as well as Russia, and helped train Evgenii I. Tarle, whose many works include the oft-revised studies of Napoleon and 1812, popular in the Soviet Union in the late 1930s. Tarle died in January 1955, so the Ger'e influence extended deep into the Soviet period through him as well as through Kareev and Vipper.

The greatest scholar Ger'e prepared was unquestionably Vinogradov, whom

Soviet scholars recognized and honored, although he opposed the Soviet system bitterly until he died in England in 1926. A man of many talents, including as a pianist and chess player, he taught Greek history and European medieval history from 1881 until he resigned in December 1901. He wrote on many subjects, especially English law and the history of economic and social institutions in medieval England. He spoke twelve languages fluently and taught and lectured on four continents. A member of the Russian Academy of Sciences and of the academies of most European states, he received honorary degrees from leading institutions in Germany, France, Italy, Norway, England, and the United States.

Moscow students considered him "the ideal university professor," and advanced students thought him "irreplaceable" in a seminar. He vigorously supported efforts to expand student rights, served on the Moscow City Council, and worked to eradicate illiteracy, improve high-school education, and establish constitutional government. He resigned from the university when the minister of education abruptly rejected recommendations of a faculty committee that Vinogradov had headed and arrested students who had met with the committee. He accepted the Corpus Chair of Jurisprudence at Oxford in 1903, but published articles in Russian newspapers in 1905 urging establishment of constitutional government. He returned to Moscow in 1908 as a visiting professor, resigning again in 1911 in protest over government interference. Many saw him as "a living link" between Russia and England and hoped that his presence would help introduce English political institutions.

Kliuchevskii, an official opponent at Vinogradov's doctorate defense in 1881, was a close friend and colleague. A wealthy, self-assured "Russian European," Vinogradov was more interested in university autonomy, student rights, and urban government than Kliuchevskii, but they were equally devoted to scholarship, teaching, and economic, social, and institutional history. Much influenced by Guizot through Ger'e, Vinogradov reinforced influences that Ger'e had begun in 1867. All three agreed that Russia had not enjoyed the experiences or created the institutions in its early history that western Europe had and therefore could not be expected to develop a similar political system.

While Kliuchevskii was a graduate student, evening sessions at the Ger'es' led to scholarly discussions on a variety of historical subjects, and Ger'e gradually became Kliuchevskii's informal adviser. When Kliuchevskii was under pressure from Soloviev to complete his M.A. thesis and accept an assistant professorship in Dorpat (now Tartu), Ger'e helped him defend his schedule and effort to remain in Moscow. Throughout the 1870s, when Kliuchevskii was struggling to sustain himself and his family, beginning to publish articles and engage in the archival research that led to his doctorate, Ger'e was his main supporter on the faculty. In 1872 he invited Kliuchevskii to offer the course on Russian history in the Women's Higher Courses. In 1876 he encouraged him to review a German volume on Russian history for the *Historische Zeitschrift*, and his wife translated the twenty-two pages. Ger'e probably stimulated Kliuchevskii's 1879 review of Rambaud's *Histoire de la Russie depuis les origines jusqu à nos jours.* These reviews and Kliuchevskii's comments on Mackenzie Wallace's classic, *Russia,* reflected the broadened horizons into European scholarship that Ger'e provided.

After Kliuchevskii married in 1869, the two men, their wives, and their children became close friends. The men corresponded frequently when the Ger'es traveled abroad, Kliuchevskii providing information about the university and their associates' research. Their colleagues selected him to give the main address at the dinner celebrating Ger'e's forty years of service in November 1898. The families visited frequently and discussed new books, history, and Shakespeare, whose works Mrs. Ger'e enjoyed. Kliuchevskii's son Boris began to learn English at the same time as Elena Ger'e, two years his senior, and Boris felt most comfortable in the Ger'e home after his parents died.

This galaxy of instructors eased the young provincial's participation into an academic community in which he ultimately emerged as the most outstanding of a gifted generation. From them and his associates, he acquired sound professional training, fresh ambitions, and high goals. But the individual in the faculty who exercised the greatest influence upon Kliuchevskii was the aloof Soloviev, whom Kliuchevskii termed "the pride and glory of Moscow University" and whom an eminent American scholar has described as "probably the greatest Russian historian of all time."[4]

Soloviev was in his early forties, at the peak of his intellectual and physical vigor, when Kliuchevskii first heard him lecture. He became active just at the time interest in Russian history was becoming lively and its study professional, publishing the first volume of his magnum opus three years before the Crimean War and the bulk during the thaw and Alexander II's reforms. One could hardly conceive a more appropriate time for a national history, unless it was the first decade of the twentieth century, that of the Russo-Japanese War and the revolution of 1905, when Kliuchevskii undertook his *Course of Russian History.*

Soloviev's father, a priest, had taught in a Moscow school for training secretaries and clerks. He provided his son religious instruction and taught him how to read and write Russian, German, and Latin, but nurses' tales and historical legends were perhaps even more stimulating. The young Soloviev learned Greek in high school and said that he had read Karamzin's twelve-volume *History of the Russian State* a dozen times before he entered the university. There he studied Roman literature with D. L. Kriukov, Russian history with the famed nationalist and Pan-Slav Pogodin, whom he succeeded in 1845, and European history with Granovskii. The latter introduced him to the books of Guizot, who influenced him profoundly; Soloviev called Guizot "the most eminent historian of his time."

After graduating, Soloviev traveled in Europe as a tutor, spending most of 1842–44 in Paris but attending courses in Berlin and Heidelberg and making two trips to Prague. He heard and became acquainted with several French historians, perhaps including Guizot, and leading scholars in Germany and Bohemia, and he was the first Russian historian to use Swedish archives. In short, he had received the finest training in history available in Russia, Germany, and France and acquired knowledge of western Europe. These years were profoundly important for Soloviev and Russian historical writing.

Moscow University officials quickly recognized Soloviev's brilliance: he received his doctorate at twenty-seven and was appointed a full professor at thirty. When he began to teach in 1845, he embarked on a history of Russia from its origins, which his students, those of Kliuchevskii, and many others used extensively. Thus, Rambaud's *Histoire de la Russie*, published in 1878 in its first of many French editions and translations, and Mackenzie Wallace's *Russia*, published in 1877, relied heavily on the multivolume history as well as on his textbook. Editions of Soloviev's great work appeared in 1895, 1896, and 1911. Between 1959 and 1966, the Soviet government published an edition of from 45,000 to 50,000 copies of each volume. In 1988 the Soviet publishing house Thought began producing an eighteen-volume edition of 100,000 copies of his complete works.

Soloviev and his wife were both conservative, patriotic, devout members of the Russian Orthodox Church. He was critical of the reign of Nicholas I but feared that a peasant revolt would weaken the state. According to Kliuchevskii, Soloviev's reading did not include radical newspapers or journals, which he thought harmful. He was a friend of Pobedonostsev, who became the symbol of reaction. On the other hand, he resisted Ministry of Education efforts to restrict faculty freedoms. He was dean of his faculty for two long periods and rector from 1871 until 1877, when the minister of education removed him for opposing its infringements of faculty rights.

Soloviev worked each morning from six until nine, breakfasted, spent the hours from ten to four in class or in the archives, returned home to dine and rest, and then wrote until eleven o'clock. His children were not allowed to disturb or interrupt him. Even though he added a volume each year to his *History*, between 1858 and 1861 he wrote a series of essays on the origins and history of serfdom. He was one of the founders of the Pan-Slav organization. The Polish crisis in 1863 led to a small volume on the "fall" of Poland in the eighteenth century, which he blamed on the reform movement, divisions within Poland, and "Catholic fanaticism." In 1874 he published an essay on the French medievalist Numa Fustel de Coulanges in the *Revue des Deux Mondes*. During the Balkan crisis of 1876–78, he wrote a study of Alexander I and his policies, as well as a series of articles on the Balkans for the *European Herald*.

A man of immense learning and phenomenal memory, Soloviev was interested in the Bible, Greek and Roman history, modern European history, and the past "from Herodotus to our day." His urge to learn and his ability to incorporate new knowledge were remarkable. In the 1860s, he managed to study Buckle's *History of Civilization in England* and introduce Buckle's ideas about the role of geography and climate and the universality of stages of historical development into his classes and works. Kliuchevskii has reported that his first words on meeting a friend or colleague, even a few days before his death of cancer, were "What are the interesting new books?"

Soloviev loved to teach undergraduates and was "ready to teach in a desert," but he was not an inspiring instructor. He lectured in a flat monotone with his eyes closed and later told Kliuchevskii that he did not see his students once he began to speak. Kliuchevskii, who analyzed Soloviev on the platform carefully, was impressed by "the harmony of thought and word" and his success in encouraging students to think, the most interested and advanced as well as the "lighthearted." Soloviev's views were an invisible part of the recitation: "His ideas grew organically from the facts he explained." Many absorbed the facts without recognizing the framework he used, his emphasis upon the state and its role, or the absence of periods or divisions in history.

Hegel affected Soloviev, and his views of Hegel and German philosophy were influential into the 1860s. Soloviev and his generation absorbed and introduced many basic ideas of Buckle, Taine, and Renan. Perhaps because of the amalgam of ideas from the principal Russian and foreign histories he had studied, or what Carl Becker called the "climate of opinion," he discerned unity in the historical process: Russia was inevitably a part of European and world history, and the "same general laws rule the history of mankind."

Soloviev believed that Russian culture was unique, not superior nor inferior to that of Europe but different. European countries and Russia all sought a form of rule that embodied and served the people, but Russia's system differed from Europe's. First, its geography, especially the absence of "natural frontiers," and its climate exercised a harsh and constricting impact, a judgment that Buckle fortified. Second, Russia for centuries had protected Europe from Asia, an unrecognized service that cost Russian lives and energies but allowed European culture to advance. Peter the Great then emerged as the enlightener and civilizer who drove Russia to close the gap and become a European power.

Affected by the ideas of Evers and Hegel and the spirit of the age, Soloviev viewed history as an organic development in which a regular process of change affected all societies. He charted the state's inexorable march from the primitive Slavic family through the clan to princely rule to a patristic, autocratic monarchy. Indeed, as Kliuchevskii noted in an essay on Soloviev, he frequently used the phrase "natural and necessary" to describe the relentless process through which Russian history unfolded. His classes learned that the basic social institution, the family, rested on sacrifice and that society could exist only when private interests submitted to the general welfare. Unfavorable conditions combined to force a unity of all Russian estates in a state "forced to be military, although it was not at all militaristic." Conquest played a minor role in Russian expansion for Soloviev, as for Kliuchevskii. However, both believed that the state served as "the gatherer of the Russian land."

In Soloviev's judgment, all governments, whatever their form, were representative. The state played a central and positive role, bringing classes and interests together. "Weak states cannot preserve their independence," so the Russian state had to dominate. Poland, divided and with its people neglectful of the general interest, had been doomed. Finally, formation of a strong and secure state was an impressive achievement: "Government in one form or another is the product of the historical life of a people and the best verification of that life." Consequently, Russia's centralization under Muscovy and expansion were prerequisites of survival. Ivan the Terrible and his *oprichnina* were positive steps in this process. Soloviev was an admirer of Ivan, as he was of Peter, whom "we have every right to call the greatest historical figure."

Curiously, the Church and religion played a minor part in Russian history for Soloviev, as for Kliuchevskii. The Church was a servant of autocracy, but it was far superior for Russia than Roman Catholicism or Protestantism would have been: it was both natural and national.

Kliuchevskii read the first volumes of Soloviev's *History of Russia* when he was a young seminarian, and Soloviev's presence was almost certainly part of the Moscow attraction. He audited Soloviev's lectures in his first semester, spent a precious ruble and fifty kopeks for a Soloviev volume, and wrote letters describing the scholar's physical characteristics, dress, habits, gestures, and style of speaking. However, he did not enroll in a Soloviev course until his junior year at the university.

He began graduate training with Soloviev in 1865 and visited him frequently in the older man's last days, but relations were never warm. Kliuchevskii had accepted a teaching position at a Moscow high school before Soloviev selected him for preparation for a professional career. At that time, he recommended Kliuchevskii to the Ministry of Education for a 1,000-ruble stipend, as he did again for 1866–67, but he rated Kliuchevskii second to Karpov as a promising scholar. He used both men as assistants in the military school, but Kliuchevskii's slow progress toward his M.A. degree disappointed him. In 1870 he pressed Kliuchevskii to accept appointment in the recently reorganized Dorpat University at a salary of 1,700 rubles, plus 300 rubles for living expenses, more than Kliuchevskii was earning in Moscow. He was disappointed and even angry when Kliuchevskii rejected the position, because he had persuaded the ministry and the Dorpat faculty to appoint a young man who lacked an M.A. and was not legally qualified.[5] Kliuchevskii apparently declined the position because the language of instruction was German and Dorpat lacked research resources. He may also have suspected that young men who left Moscow for provincial universities rarely returned.

Kliuchevskii began teaching at the university only after Soloviev died in 1879. He often said later that he so greatly revered his mentor that he would not have considered a position if it had been offered. When Soloviev was dying, he declined to suggest Kliuchevskii as his successor, although Kliuchevskii was the most obvious and perhaps only possible choice. However, he did not oppose when Popov nominated Kliuchevskii.

Kliuchevskii published four essays on Soloviev's life and work. Increasingly as he matured, his private and public expressions of admiration for

Soloviev were such that Aleksandr Presniakov and others considered it a calculated exaggeration. The first to analyze the corpus of Soloviev's work, he emphasized that Soloviev had made the study of history a worthy profession and that Soloviev's discoveries were not properly appreciated because they had become "conventional wisdom." In an era when railroad construction fascinated Russians, he termed him "as important as a railroad builder." In his view, Soloviev was honest, modest, realistic, and courageous, a scholar who defended academic freedom, sought university autonomy, and "never deceived a reader." He praised him "for never closing his eyes to avoid seeing the dark side of Russia's past and present. . . . He loved and respected the Russian people too deeply to flatter them and considered them too mature to tell them children's tales." His work at the university and his *History of Russia* were a storehouse: "We all begin our work with him." "A student of Soloviev," he "merely spread the light" received from Soloviev.[6]

The personal and professional relations between the two scholars were reserved. Soloviev's considering Karpov a more promising young scholar than he may have offended Kliuchevskii. The younger man occasionally indicated resentment that Soloviev had pressed him to undertake the tedious master's thesis on saints' lives. The Dorpat incident rankled both, and Soloviev in the 1870s was often critical of Kliuchevskii's seeming slowness on his doctorate.

However, the principal reasons were more fundamental. Soloviev was more than twenty years older, and their formative years differed greatly. Moreover, he was a person of great dignity and reserve who considered the position of professor one of the most elevated, particularly in a country that possessed few scholars. Devotion to research, writing, and publishing a multivolume, unified history of Russia dominated his life, and he devoted little time or energy to students.

Soloviev and Kliuchevskii also came from different backgrounds. Soloviev studied abroad, while Kliuchevskii never left Russia. Soloviev's interest in and knowledge of European history and scholarship were far greater than Kliuchevskii's. While they were both supremely able historians, their talents as teachers differed. Soloviev was a solid, unimaginative, clear, but dull lecturer: Kondakov noted that he spoke as though he were a businessman or a bureaucrat. By contrast, Kliuchevskii was an artist, an actor in the classroom. His style was full of wit and irony, as brilliant and lively as that of Macaulay, though less flamboyant. Finally, while both were conservative, Soloviev's conservatism was that of an older generation than Kliuchevskii. Thus, Soloviev refused to read Chernyshevskii, Dobroliubov, and other radical authors of the 1860s. He admired Metropolitan Filaret, who opposed the abolition of serf-dom. Kliuchevskii read the radicals with interest, although he disagreed with them. He thought that Filaret possessed a first-class mind and powerful personality but considered him a disaster for the Church and Russia.

Soloviev's contributions to Kliiuchevskii's intellectual development were substantial. The two men shared a great affection for the Russian people and early Russian history and devoted their lives to describing and analyzing that past. Kliuchevskii's concept of a university as a scientific center came at least in part from Soloviev, and he often used Soloviev's phrase "the holy alliance of the university and society." Even more than Buslaev and Ger'e, Soloviev served as a model scholar-teacher. Kliuchevskii's detailed analyses of Soloviev's classroom performance, course design, and lectures show that he followed the standards Soloviev had established. His work demonstrated the same careful accumulation of materials, tolerance of earlier ages and peoples, generosity, and modesty one finds in Soloviev.

Soloviev also helped provide Kliuchevskii's work its goal, direction, and even much basic material. In the words of Miliukov, Soloviev "provided the canvas on which he [Kliuchevskii] wrote": Kliuchevskii simply wrote a generation later and dug deeper. Pokrovskii exaggerated when he argued that some chapters of the *Course of Russian History* were popularizations of Soloviev's work, but Kliuchevskii's lectures and some chapters did follow closely those of Soloviev. They were shorter and written in a more luminous and ironic style but with the same purpose and standards. As A. A. Zimin has suggested, Kliuchevskii's views were closer to Soloviev's in the last decade of his life, when writing the *Course,* than they had been in the 1860s and 1870s.

Kliuchevskii also followed Soloviev in "viewing Russia from the inside." Their histories emphasize domestic developments and grant little attention to outside pressures, especially the Mongols, diplomacy, military struggle, ethnic and religious minorities, or revolts or uprisings. Both stressed long-term, permanent factors and resisted the division of history into sharply defined periods. Russian history was a seamless web in which every period was related to its predecessors and its successors. Soloviev was interested in "the mechanism of human society" and emphasized the primary role of the state, while Kliuchevskii paid attention to *soslovii,* or estates, on which Soloviev encouraged him to work. Soloviev avoided study of social life, but he appreciated the need to study the life of the people, the material fabric, the texture of society. Both emphasized that the *narod* or people included all Russians and that Russia throughout its history possessed particular political, economic, and social qualities. Both were eclectic: they found no single factor, such as the class struggle or external pressures, the principal determinant of the flow of Russian history, but emphasized that many complicated and interrelated elements were important, such as geography, climate, and economic conditions. Soviet scholars, who emphasize struggle, "revolutionary situations," and periodization, therefore find their understanding of the historical process deficient.

Soloviev and Kliuchevskii agreed in many analyses. Kliuchevskii accepted Soloviev's interpretation of the role of the Varangians or Normans in establishing the Kievan state of Novgorod, and the claim that the princely holdings or appanages were private property. He followed Soloviev's view of the role that colonization of the northeast played in the establishment of the Muscovite core of the Russian state and the critical role Muscovy played as "collector of the Russian lands." Both were national historians, concentrating on Russians and Russia, not on regions or groups. Both were critical of Muscovite despotism but saw the state as a unifying element that defended Europe's eastern frontiers. Kliuchevskii especially respected and supported Soloviev in raising "natural and necessary problems," and both defined the changes that Peter the Great introduced as practical necessities.

However, they also differed in some ways. Soloviev placed the state at the center of analysis and was one of the founders of the "state school." He assigned greater importance than Kliuchevskii to the rulers, whether they be the grand prince of Kiev or Peter the Great, to whom he devoted six volumes. As early as 1876, Kliuchevskii chided historians for overemphasizing the state, arguing that economic forces were more important. He studied the changing texture of society and the ways in which material factors affected social life. Why should one consider the state a progressive element? Why was a person who surrendered to the state superior to one who enjoyed independence? Beginning with his doctoral dissertation, the *Boyar Council,* which he completed, revised, defended, and published just after Soloviev's death, he gave more attention to economic and social factors than Soloviev.

Kliuchevskii overturned Soloviev's thesis that early Slav clan life gradually developed into the regular order of princely succession. He saw the Normans as armed merchants invited into Kiev to provide order and assigned a greater role to cities and trade in the Kievan period than did Soloviev. He accepted Soloviev's emphasis upon colonization of the northeast as the base of Muscovy and the Russian state, but placed the people and economic developments, not the Muscovite princes, at the center of the process. Soloviev considered Ivan the Terrible's *oprichnina* a deliberate effort to strengthen the state, while Kliuchevskii thought it a personal, unplanned assault upon the boyars. Both stressed the seamless character of Russian history, but Soloviev concluded that individuals such as some grand princes of Moscow and Peter accelerated developments and created monumental changes: for Soloviev, Peter the Great crossed the Rubicon of Russian history. Kliuchevskii found the roots of Peter's policies and actions stretching back through the seventeenth century. Earlier changes prepared the way, and many of Peter's reforms were unplanned reactions to exigencies his wars created.

They differed similarly on the origins of serfdom, which Soloviev ascribed to state actions, while Kliuchevskii emphasized that the slow maturation of economic and social forces gradually produced the institution. On abolition, Soloviev emphasized the primary role of the state and its leaders, while Kliuchevskii stressed gently ripening economic, social, cultural, and intellectual forces.

A constant thread running through Kliuchevskii's undergraduate and advanced student years was the introduction that Soloviev and his colleagues provided to nineteenth-century European historical scholarship, especially that of France and Germany. Kliuchevskii's knowledge of this work and of European history remained shallow. Yet it exercised a most important influence upon the way he viewed Russian history, especially the impact upon Russia of close cultural relations with Europe. Many central assumptions of European scholars that his mentors adopted and then passed on became a fundamental part of his view of the past. In an irony he would have relished, the patriotic Moscow scholar's learning from foreign scholars in the heart of old Russia gradually modified some of his concepts about his native land's history. This process served as an example of the Western influence upon Russia that dismayed him when he described the past since the seventeenth century.

Kliuchevskii remained a rooted Muscovite throughout the half-century after his arrival from Penza. He did not appeal when the Ministry of Education rejected his three applications to go abroad, and he expressed no envy of his mentors or associates for their travel. London, Paris, Berlin, Vienna, and the cultural ways that had fascinated the court, the aristocracy, and educated Russians at various periods since 1750 did not attract him. Distinct from many contemporaries, from Pobedonostsev and Tolstoy to Lenin and Miliukov, he showed little interest in European intellectual currents, from Darwinism to Marxism, from positivism to impressionism. Yet his education had a strong European cast and tone. In Penza he learned to read French and German, as well as Greek and Latin. His father taught him the daily readings of the Russian Orthodox Church but also read him Novikov's translation of *Paradise Lost*. When he reached Moscow, the Westerners had emerged as victors in the controversy with the Slavophils concerning the nature of Russia and its future. Moreover, Alexander II in an early version of *glasnost'* encouraged discussion of shortcomings and admitted ideas from Europe. Changes within the university and the establishment of libraries, museums, learned institutions, and journals helped produce such a lively intellectual atmosphere that he and his fellow students considered themselves Muscovites in a European world.

Near the end of his life, Kliuchevskii reminisced about those "best years," when "it was good to be young, members of a spiritual corporation united in the moral solidity of intellectual interests." Pride brought the university community together and united the university and society, while the decade echoed "the great conquests of European science and the peaceful international collision of Russian ideas and the noisy social movements of the West."[7]

It is difficult to demonstrate that the concepts of an individual or group have influenced another's views or strengthened ideas already established. Yet, evidence is compelling that a number of French and English historians stimulated the work of those with whom Kliuchevskii studied, and that they in turn passed on their influence to him. Their research and travel in France and Germany and Western scholars' multivolume histories of French, English, and European civilization, the Middle Ages, and the French Revolution created new horizons for the first professional historians interested in writing critical accounts of their country's past. Kliuchevskii and his generation were the fruitful consequences of the marriage of interest and talent with these new vistas and approaches.

Perhaps the most important way in which Kliuchevskii became interested in and to some degree knowledgeable about European scholarship was through the climate of opinion or intellectual atmosphere within the university History-Philology Faculty. Granovskii by 1855 had established an authority so extensive that the European learning he introduced and those whom he trained dominated historical scholarship for the reminder of the century. He utterly destroyed interest in Pogodin, his nationalist predecessor who retired in 1844 and lived unnoticed until 1875. Although the Soloviev and Kliuchevskii generations read Karamzin's *History of the Russian State* as youngsters and his style and views attract readers in the 1990s, the conservative monarchist exercised little influence after 1840. Kliuchevskii ignored him and Pogodin, but admired eighteenth-century scholars such as Boltin and Tatishchev. His 1872 review of Pogodin's work on the origins of the Russian state was civil but went unpublished, because the editor and he agreed that it would injure the elderly scholar's feelings without any countervailing benefit. On the other hand, his respect for Granovskii was immense: a talk on Tat'iana Day in January 1905 termed him "the ideal professor."

A Westerner who had studied in Europe and taught general or European history, Granovskii emphasized that Russia was part of Europe and that its scholarship should advance along European lines. He ignored eighteenth-century European historical work and the intellectuals whose ideas helped bring on the French Revolution. This helps explain why Kliuchevskii's instructors and his generation neglected Gibbon and rarely referred to Voltaire. On the other hand, Granovskii made the ideas of such nineteenth-century Europeans as Feuerbach, Comte, Hegel, and Renan respectable and even popular. Kliuchevskii's reading in the 1860s, typical of his student generation, included Goethe (a favorite), Humboldt, Spencer, and French and English historians, who helped open the minds of educated Russians to the outside world. He declared Heine "perhaps the greatest poet of our time."

After the ascension of Alexander II, newspapers, the "thick journals," and discussion of ideas and government actions bringing about the great reforms sharply affected the climate of opinion. Granovskii and those whom he had trained used this opportunity within the university community to introduce ideas and information they had acquired in Europe and had adapted to Russia. The faculty members with whom Kliuchevskii was most closely associated, specialists in European history, instructed him in the methods and theses of European historians whose work had impressed them, as did fellow students Kirpichnikov and Kondakov, who used European models in their studies of Russian literature and Byzantine art. Shakhov until his early death in 1877 initiated him into the mysteries of the French Revolution and French literature. Vinogradov, a fellow graduate student and colleague, contributed the understanding he acquired from studying and translating the work of Taine and de Tocqueville. All acted on the assumption, usually unspoken, that the West was different and superior, but their patriotism provided a protective coating for information and ideas they purveyed from abroad.

Thus, Kliuchevskii became acquainted with the views and techniques of European scholars, acquired knowledge of Europe and the wider world, and created an intellectual framework that extended beyond Russia's borders. He enjoyed the Greek and Roman classics as well as Byzantine art and literature. Old German and Norwegian literature and folktales, the works of the Brothers Grimm, and Shakespeare's plays fascinated him, as did comparative literature. His major interest became Russia's past, but he studied the history of Greece, Rome, and Europe since the Middle Ages with Popov and Eshevskii. European history constituted one of the areas or fields of history on which the faculty examined him for his M.A. degree in 1868. In sum, he acquired a broad but shallow foundation of a liberal education.

Except for Buckle, he was not exposed to English history or scholarship. He never read Gibbon, or even Macaulay, whose *History of England* was popular in Russia in the 1860s, although he did study Mackenzie Wallace's classic, *Russia*, published in 1877. He lacked knowledge of German history, scholarship, and philosophy and never mentioned Ranke or Treitschke. Hegel had influenced Soloviev, Buslaev, and Chicherin, but his impact waned a decade before Kliuchevskii came to Moscow. In his freshman year, Iurkevich lectured about Hegel in the class on the history of philosophy, but Kliuchevskii flatly rejected the German philosopher's determinism. His course on methodology in 1884–85 informed the class that theories do not explain. He devoted two pages to Hegel but seven to Taine. Aware of Marx, he declined suggestions to read his work. Instead, he declared that "Marxism entered our thought as mechanically as a dog sits on our laps, just as a wig lay on the bureaucratic heads of our remote ancestors."

Kliuchevskii's *kandidat* thesis, his senior paper, analyzed reports of foreign visitors in the fifteenth, sixteenth, and seventeenth centuries. His next publication, in 1867, demonstrated that Russia was primitive even in fundamental aspects of life compared to the West and borrowed even simple household items. He did not resent these adaptations or consider them harmful. Instead, he termed the architect Rastrelli "a foreigner of whom Russia can rightly be proud." Moreover, completing the book taught him that the West had begun to exert a slow but profound influence long before Peter the Great, basic knowledge that remained essential in his analysis of relations between Russia and the West.

For the class he began to teach at the Third Aleksandrovskoe Military School in 1868, a superficial course on the French Revolution, he turned to notes from his university courses and to Guizot, Taine, and de Tocqueville. The course gave him insight into diplomatic relations and the ways in which Russian participation in the revolutionary and Napoleonic wars made his country ever more a part of Europe. A comparison of the annual lithographs of this course with the many versions of his famous lectures on Russian history reveals that the former narrative neglected geography, climate, and external pressures, which the latter stressed. The former paid little attention to economic and social institutions that occupied an important place in the second. He neglected intellectuals, ideas, and religion, remarkable omissions in a course on the French Revolution, but no less extraordinary than neglect of some aspects of life in work on his own country.

However, some concepts fundamental in his mature work appear in this course. Thus, he treated Russia as a nation-state in "northeastern Europe" that possessed a distinct culture of its own, as did each Western country. He described Colbert and Richelieu as builders of France in the same admiring manner in which he described some of the makers of Russia. His emphasis upon the nation-state, a reflection of the views of Soloviev and Chicherin and the nationalism of those years, persuaded him that Catherine the Great had erred in the division of Poland, an analysis that appeared in detail in the *Course of Russian History*. Finally, the oppositional tone or flavor that runs through his major works appeared in lectures to the cadets in his admiration for the revolutionaries before 1791, constitutional monarchy, and early socialists.

Soloviev had studied with Granovskii and had joined the Westerners during the last stages of the Slavophil-Westerner controversy. A student in Paris for three years, he attended Guizot's lectures and probably met the venerated historian and statesman, as Pogodin had a few years earlier. His diary declared the French scholar-statesman "the most imminent historian of his time." Citations in his publications and emphasis upon cherished Guizot themes indicate that Guizot powerfully influenced his teaching and scholarship. The French scholar's emphasis upon social and economic factors, concept of the organic flow of history, and belief that general laws apply to all history appear in Soloviev. Kliuchevskii's memorial address on Soloviev in 1880 and his comments upon a thesis for the doctorate late in life stressed Guizot's influence upon his mentor. Viktor M. Dalin, an outstanding Russian scholar who examined the work of Soloviev and Guizot and enjoyed access to Soloviev's archives, supported that judgment, demonstrating conclusively that Guizot's conception of history had deeply influenced Soloviev by the time he published the first volume of his *History of Russia*. Dalin noted that Chernyshevskii declared that Soloviev would have been Guizot if he had lived in Paris. He also showed that Buckle's view of the role of geography and Taine's of the long, slow development of the historical process flowered in Soloviev's lectures and writings.

Buslaev, who combined Penza and Moscow foundations with an urbanity derived from study and frequent travel abroad, was a devout follower of both Guizot and Soloviev. He used Western scholarship in his work on Russian, German, and Norwegian philology, folklore, and literature and helped Kliuchevskii recognize that life in Europe was easier and gentler than in Russia. Kliuchevskii's notes on Buslaev's lectures, which he retained throughout his life, indicate that the older scholar also introduced him to Bossuet, Renan, and Montesquieu; he used their works when preparing an undergraduate paper on comparative religion. Buslaev emphasized that each national society was an independent organism that created its own culture, even its own religion, and one should study economic and social conditions and popular culture in order to comprehend another country and time. These are central themes in Kliuchevskii's work.

Chicherin, even more European in education and intellect, added German insights from Hegel and Savigny to those of Guizot and Buckle. Kliuchevskii and he shared a number of concepts: Chicherin reinforced views that the young man was developing or adapting from the atmosphere. In particular, he suggested that Russia would remain distinct from the rest of Europe but would achieve the rule of law through a process of slow, gradual change.

Ger'e, Kliuchevskii's closest associate on the faculty for more than forty years, was the most Westernized member of the university community. He taught European history and impressed upon Kliuchevskii that Russia was "the youngest part of Europe." Students termed one of his classes "Ger'e's Guizot" because he was such an admirer and follower of the Frenchman. Taine was another favorite: Ger'e published an essay and a book about Taine and considered Taine and Guizot the "twin towers" of Western scholarship. In 1874 he introduced a seminar on Montesquieu's *Spirit of the Laws*. Persuading Kliuchevskii to write reviews of volumes by French and German scholars was a visible sign of the prolonged process through which he immersed Kliuchevskii in the concepts and methods of Western scholarship.

Western ideas, especially those of Taine and de Tocqueville's *L' Ancient Régime et la Révolution*, first published in 1856, also saturated Tikhonravov, whose course emphasized Russia's "yearning for the West." Kliuchevskii learned of Western influence on Russian literature not only from his classes but also from evening walks and fishing. Eshevskii, whose thesis on the establishment of feudalism in France reflected Guizot's authority, reinforced that influence through courses on European history and relaxed conversations in the Eshevskii home concerning European scholars he had known and read.

In addition, translations of Guizot were readily available in English and Russian, and articles about him appeared frequently in the press as early as 1850. A society formed in the 1850s to encourage reading produced translations of selections from Guizot. Prominent intellectuals such as Herzen, Belinskii, and Chernyshevhskii admired his work and discussed it in newspapers and journals that Kliuchevskii read in the 1860s. Guizot's *History of England* was translated into Russian in 1868. Vinogradov, advised and assisted by Ger'e, translated the four volumes of the *History of Civilization in France* between 1877 and 1881. Chernyshevskii even applied Guizot's ideas on the relations in France between conquerors and conquered to his analysis of the fall of the Roman Empire. Shchapov studied the French scholar in St. Petersburg and Irkutsk, while Lenin read the *History of Civilization in France* in Samara. Shchapov impressed upon Kliuchevskii a number of conclusions to which Guizot and his own work had led him, particularly that Russia was a desperately backward country. Miliukov, who took classes with Soloviev, Ger'e, and Tikhonravov, used Guizot's volumes on the history of French civilization as a model for his three volumes on Russian culture.

As a student and later colleague of men who had absorbed Guizot's views and as a Muscovite alive to the intellectual environment, Kliuchevskii imbibed Guizot's judgments directly and indirectly. He studied the *History of Civilization in France* with Buslaev when he was an undergraduate and read his memoirs when they appeared in the 1860s. He cited Guizot in the course on the French Revolution. His diary during the years when he was writing the *Course of Russian History* indicated that at some stages he re-read Guizot even more than Soloviev's *History of Russia*. Comparing Soloviev and Guizot, he noted that Guizot had taught Soloviev to arrange the historical record in a systematic scheme, but that his mentor lacked Guizot's anatomical sense. Late in life, he remarked that the two greatest influences on him had been the abolition of serfdom in 1861 and Guizot, who taught him the art of social-historical analysis.

In his view, Guizot was able to "see the skeleton, the skeletal structure, the concealed framework, the stock of fundamental ideas, feelings, and interests on which lie all the variables." He compared the analysis of this "disinterested liberal intelligence" and "historian-anatomist" to those of an x-ray machine that identifies a society's concealed framework.

A number of Guizot themes or theses reappear in Kliuchevskii's work, especially his emphasis upon material factors, social institutions, interests, and classes. Guizot noted the "natural and necessary" role of custom, a phrase Soloviev used frequently that appears often in Kliuchevskii's work. His suggestions that history presented an infinite variety of developments, that "nothing is accidental," and that unifying laws govern it are present in Kliuchevskii's scholarship and are fundamental to his view of the flow of history. Some Kliuchevskii figures of speech recall his comments concerning Guizot's penetrating expositions. Thus, he compared analyzing the assemblies of the land to "studying an abandoned old building that has left no evidence of the living arrangements that indicated how people lived and thought." His statement that the *Boyar Council* reflected his interest in "the social structure of administration, rather than in the state," is almost a translation of a Guizot creed. In that volume, Kliuchevskii used Guizot's theory of the differences between conquered and conqueror in Gaul to help explain distinctions between Russian and Western political development. In this, he follows the path of the Slavophils, Pogodin, and other nineteenth-century Russian historians who compared early French and early Russian history. Guizot's preference for a "monarchy limited by a limited number of bourgeois" resembles Kliuchevskii's account of the boyar council or elected group of leading men for counsel.

Kliuchevskii's knowledge of medieval European history came from the courses of Eshevskii, a disciple of Guizot, and from reading Guizot, Fustel de

Coulanges, and other French scholars. This understanding, while not profound, persuaded him that Russia's system of rule had developed along lines distinct from those of the West because classes in Russia and Europe had evolved in divergent ways and because differences among classes in Russia were greater than in Europe. On several occasions, Kliuchevskii explained that early Russia did not possess a policy based on the relation of lord to vassal that Westerners defined as feudalism. An essay on Chicherin identified the absence of feudalism as a feature that distinguished the Russian historical process from Europe's.

Buckle's influence upon Russian historical work in the 1860s and 1870s was as visible as that of Guizot. In George Vernadsky's judgment, his *History of Civilization in England* was "one of the most discussed books of the generation of the 1860s" and "the unchallenged authority for the young people in those years." *Notes of the Fatherland,* which Kliuchevskii read regularly, published a translation in consecutive issues in 1861–62, and four other translations appeared before 1870. Mackenzie Wallace found copies of Buckle in provincial Iaroslavl' in the 1870s, and Nikolai Rozhkov read Buckle in the Ekaterinburg High School in 1880. Soloviev and Ger'e at the university and Pisarev and Chernyshevskii among intellectuals were devotees of Buckle: Chernyshevskii devoted two articles to him in the year Kliuchevskii arrived in Moscow. Shchapov, whose volumes on the religious schism impressed Kliuchevskii in the early 1870s, was so strongly affected by Buckle's work that he was called "Russia's Buckle." The distinguished Russian specialist on feudalism N. P. Pavlov-Silvanskii in 1906 concluded that Buckle's ideas had exercised great influence on Soloviev, a judgment that Zimin endorsed fifty years later after thorough analysis of the historiography of the 1860s. Each of these scholars demonstrated independently that some major Soloviev themes, such as the significance of geography and climate, the belief that "the actions of men are caused by their antecedents," the assumption that laws of human development exist and prove "the regularity of human actions," and confidence that scholars would one day discover them came from Buckle or that Buckle reinforced them in Soloviev's thought.

Kliuchevskii probably encountered Buckle's work first in *Notes of the Fatherland,* but he may have read it later in the original or in other translations, as his friend Muromtsev did in 1867 and Miliukov in the 1870s. Kliuchevskii did not accept Buckle's relentless optimism about inevitable social progress, a view Alexander Vucinich has termed "the central theme of nineteenth century social theory" which "found unusually fertile ground in Russia." However, the English scholar's views concerning the role that "climate, food, soil, and the general aspect of nature" played were all prominent in Kliuchevskii's studies, as they were in the work of Soloviev, Ger'e, and Miliukov. Buckle also emphasized that population movements were significant, reinforcing a theme one finds in both Soloviev and Kliuchevskii. The English author's view of history was also secular. He had a deep hatred for clericalism and devoted little attention to religion or churches, a pattern that Kliuchevskii adopted. Finally, his first chapter declared history a continuous and uniform process of visible regularity and rhythm that historians as scientists would one day discover and describe, a confidence Kliuchevskii often expressed in the 1890s as well as in the *Course of Russian History.*

Taine, whose major works were translated into Russian in the 1870s, also exercised considerable influence, though not so great as that of Guizot or Buckle. Kliuchevskii read some of Taine's work as an undergraduate and used the early parts of *Les origines de la France contemporaine* when he organized his course on the French Revolution. However, he probably learned most from Tikhonravov. Kliuchevskii discussed Taine's views, especially the use of applied psychology, in his course on methodology. He returned to Taine when he prepared to tutor Grand Duke Georgii Aleksandrovich in the 1890s.

Taine reinforced a quality that Kliuchevskii considered essential: recognition that one should describe historical developments in the framework of the time and circumstances in which they occurred, rather than assume the conditions and values of the historian's own years. Taine also emphasized the role that a healthy aristocracy could play as a barrier against despotic government and the significance that the French aristocracy's disintegration had played in bringing on the French Revolution. This may have helped Kliuchevskii develop his views concerning the Russian nobility's ineffectiveness in resisting absolutism. The Taine thesis that Tikhonravov emphasized is fundamental in Kliuchevskii's work: History is a seamless web, with ages flowing into each other without the sharp or dramatic breaks that many believe that heroes or apparent revolutions create.

Most educated Russians linked Taine and de Tocqueville, whose books were popular in the 1850s and 1860s. *Russian Conversation* in 1857 published a review of *L'Ancien Régime et la Révolution* within a year of its publication in Paris. Grand Duke Konstantin Nikolaevich studied de Tocqueville while engaged in committee work that led to the abolition of serfdom. Tolstoy read the volumes while writing *War and Peace* and later as well. Kliuchevskii's colleague and friend Vinogradov first read de Tocqueville when he was thirteen years old, and the French scholar stimulated his interest in the medieval roots of Western institutions. Vinogradov's interest in French history and scholarship was deep: he taught a course on the history of France in 1886–87, edited the fifth edition of a translation of de Tocqueville in 1898, and published a small book on Montesquieu the same year.

Kliuchevskii became acquainted with de Tocqueville through journals, the university curriculum, and discussion with men such as Vinogradov, and he almost certainly read some of his work. Some de Tocqueville theses appear in Kliuchevskii: changes in history, even violent ones such as the French Revolution, are part of a long, slow process that derives from a society's structural features or functional relationships. The dominant forces of recent centuries in Europe all undermine aristocracies and lead relentlessly toward democracy and social equality. Above all, each people possesses a distinct national character shaped by circumstances and traditions.

Kliuchevskii studied the scholarship of Fustel de Coulanges carefully, referred to it often, and cited it to support his views, as did other Russian historians in the 1870s and 1880s. Vinogradov valued this French medievalist, praised him in the preface to his 1892 *Essays in English Medieval History,* and urged those whom he trained to study him. Kovalevskii presented Kliuchevskii a copy of Fustel de Coulanges's *Recherches sur quelques problèmes d'histoire* in 1885. He referred to this and to *La Cité antique,* published in 1864, when preparing his study of the origins of serfdom, the substance of which reappeared in the *Course of Russian History.* Fustel de Coulanges's reliance upon materials in archives, avoidance of secondary sources, and insistence upon impartiality or the intent of objectivity are qualities in Kliuchevskii's scholarship; the French scholar served at least as a reinforcement, perhaps even as an inspiration. Kliuchevskii cited him in his course on methodology in 1884–85, as well as in his discussion of the family and tribal unions in early Slavic history in the *Course of Russian History.*

The Moscow in which the lad from provincial Penza arrived in 1861 was enjoying a cultural blossoming under Alexander II's benign thaw. The system of higher education was small and relatively new, and the university was a small college barely one hundred years old. However, its faculty contained men of high intellectual caliber and motivation convinced that the university was a scientific institution dedicated to improving society, a belief Kliuchevskii followed throughout a career lived entirely within the isolated academic community. Their sympathy and understanding for their native land and its history strengthened the affection for Russian history and culture that Kliuchevskii brought with him, as a carping and negative view would have influenced him in a different way. They provided little professional training, but selected other able young men as graduate students who stimulated his intellectual development and widened his perspectives. Their habits and values encouraged him to rely upon primary sources, seek to discover what had happened, and describe it accurately with sympathetic understanding, little theory or speculation, or praise or blame. Soloviev's effort to help Russians understand themselves by providing a unified description of the full sweep of Russian history became Kliuchevskii's goal as well, one for which he built upon his predecessors' achievements, revising and supplementing their work, as any new generation of scholars does.

Moscow and its university combined the excitement and stimulation of an upwardly mobile intellectual community with the cultural horizons, concepts, skills, and standards of European scholarship. Russian conditions, European ideas and standards, and professional talents led to the same high quality in historical scholarship that produced the flowering of literature and the arts. Kliuchevskii did not follow his associates' paths by studying abroad: just as Moscow was a kind of halfway house between Penza and Europe, his knowledge of the West was always indirect and secondhand. From these men and the circumstances, Kliuchevskii adapted a number of basic ideas that affected his entire professional life. His instructors passed on the assumption that history was an unending flow, a fabric without identifiable periods or sections. Each country was a distinct organism. None was superior or inferior, but each was distinct because of history and traditions and possessed a form of government that represented that past. Russia was a part of Europe, in it but not of it. In addition, they assumed that "the same general laws rule the history of all mankind" and that one day historians as scientists would discover the unity that underlay the historical process. From them, Kliuchevskii seized the challenge to describe the fabric of Russian history in all its shades and glories so that his countrymen could understand themselves through their past and form a national community, a nation. He and the generation of scholars who shone in the golden era after 1850 may have been as able a band of scholars as any country has produced in such a brief period. Their achievements rest upon those who were guides in the long chain of scholars and upon the skillful way they provided access to Western scholarship.

FOUR

"Years of Preparation and Change"

In the spring of 1865, Soloviev selected Kliuchevskii for training for the professoriate, a crucial decision that provided an opportunity to enjoy an academic career. The senior scholar used his prestige at the Ministry of Education to obtain stipends for each of the subsequent two years. In 1867, he named Kliuchevskii his assistant at the Third Aleksandrovskoe Military School, a high school for cadets, where Kliuchevskii replaced him the following year in an elementary course on modern European history, especially the French Revolution. This part-time position enabled him to continue research in Moscow under difficult conditions familiar to graduate students almost everywhere. It also made it possible for him to marry and establish a home and family across the Moscow River from the university, other cultural institutions, and the homes of most faculty. There he remained for the rest of his life.

In 1871, Kliuchevskii obtained his M.A. degree with a highly praised study titled *Ancient Russian Saints' Lives as a Historical Source*. The book and the five years of research work it entailed had significant if somewhat paradoxical and contradictory consequences. The voluminous but dry and unreliable materials on saints' lives and related work on theological quarrels discouraged him from further study of religious subjects. Moreover, the understanding he acquired of the Church's intellectual level supplemented his experience in the Penza seminary, and led him to assign it little attention in his teaching and the masterpiece that grew from it. In addition, *Saints' Lives* gradually turned him away from Soloviev and the state school. The state is absent from this book, and he used the mass of economic and social data collected to concentrate thereafter upon economic, social, and institutional history. Finally, his work in libraries and archives introduced him to most of those interested in early Russian history. These relationships and *Saints' Lives* established his reputation as a scholar. They also won him an appointment at the Moscow Ecclesiastical Acad-

Kliuchevskii, 1873. Photograph by P. Pavlov. Source: *V. O. Kliuchevskii. Kharakteristiki i vospominaniia* (Moscow: Nauchnoe slovo, 1912).

emy, where for thirty-five years he felt more at home than at the secular university.

Ger'e in 1872 invited him to present a three-year sequence on Russian history in the Women's Higher Courses. He used his years in these two positions to organize and constantly reshape a survey of Russian history from its beginnings and to improve his teaching skills with a variety of student groups. These teaching assignments, tutoring the sons and daughters of gentry and merchants, and honoraria for articles provided a reasonably secure livelihood while the young husband and father worked toward the doctorate necessary for a university professorship.

By the end of the 1870s, Kliuchevskii had lived in Moscow for eighteen years and had acquired twenty-six years of teaching experience, all at institutions on the fringes of university life. He had not yet attained a doctorate, although he had published two books and twenty-five articles and was well-known among historians of Russia. He anticipated no possibility of appointment at the city's only university because Soloviev had occupied the position in Russian history since 1845 and was fifty-nine years of age. However, Soloviev died suddenly of cancer, and the university selected Kliuchevskii as his successor in the fall of 1879. This appointment and his book *Boyar Council* hardly more than a year later vaulted him into a prominent position in the historical profession and established the base from which he emerged as a supreme historian.

Through his third year as an undergraduate, Buslaev and Tikhonravov were Kliuchevskii's principal instructors. An essay in a sophomore course on comparative philology that Buslaev taught revealed concern with religion, popular traditions, and legends. It concluded that nature affects the origins and character of religions and that each people develops its own god and theology, which became an important Kliuchevskii view. In a junior course on medieval literature, he completed an essay on a book by Bishop Wilhelm Durandus (Gulialmus Durandi), a thirteenth-century Dominican theologian often called "the most resolute doctor," that explained the liturgy, procedures, and symbolism of the western Christian Church. Assigned the 1854 French edition by Buslaev, the fascinated young man wrote Father Evropeitsev that its explanation of the nature of religious belief and the role of ceremonies and traditions had strengthened his faith.

Kliuchevskii attended Soloviev's basic course on Russian history in his junior year. He concentrated upon that subject only in his fourth and final year, when he wrote the required *kandidat* thesis, or senior essay, under the great scholar. *Foreigners' Tales about the Moscow State* earned Kliuchevskii a gold medal, persuaded Soloviev to nominate him for graduate work, and won praise from scholars then and a century later.

Soloviev probably suggested the topic, which was closely related to the volume he was writing, and recently published bibliographical guides included most of the materials that had appeared in accounts by English, French, Italian, and German travelers. Moreover, Kostomarov in 1861 had edited and published the first Russian translation of the travel to Muscovy of Olearius, the Duke of Holstein, in the seventeenth century. The Moscow University *News* published Kliuchevskii's research in the summer of 1866, and the university press produced it in book form. The new Society for Disseminating Useful Books, which reprinted some Soloviev works, brought out a separate edition, unusual recognition for a young man.

This first study contains visible weaknesses but demonstrates the research methods and qualities of exposition that made his later work brilliant. The guides were fundamental, but he discovered additional materials. He relied upon visitors' direct observations, paying little attention to information from secondary sources. He chose not to compare foreigners' observations with those from Russian sources, which would have made the book confused.

Foreigners' Tales is a well-organized summary and analysis of the material that European visitors, notably diplomats, provided about Muscovy in the fifteenth, sixteenth, and seventeenth centuries. It contains discriminating comments on each source and the changes from one century to another, pointing out the value of information on externals, as well as the shallow understanding of Russian customs and institutions: foreigners were ignorant of the "moral conditions" of Russian life and the motives that animated government and people. The volume compared Russian and European arrangements and traditions in a fair-minded way and indicated that each reflected the conditions in which it had developed. Kliuchevskii noted that visitors recognized that Europe became primitive east of the Oder. Unfavorable aspects of Russian life received full attention: suspicion of foreigners and restrictions, the government practice of opening and sometimes destroying correspondence, merchants' deceit and duplicity, enormous reverence for Ivan the Terrible's ferocity, widespread bribery and torture in the judicial system, and the cruel punishments allotted. He indicated that many foreigners noted the contrast between splendor and barbarism and wondered whether Russians were coarse and brutal because of the political system or whether the government was autocratic because the people were savage and barbarous.

The book also reveals that many long-term research interests, such as the expansion of Muscovy and the role of institutions, emerged early. *Foreigners' Tales* paid particular attention to the boyar council, on which Kliuchevskii published his most important scholarly work fifteen years later, and provided substantial information on state institutions and revenues. Even as a young man, he was more interested in economic and social conditions and class structures than in the central state apparatus. His attitude toward those in the empire who were not Russian appeared then too: he considered them primitive and assumed that their assimilation was a natural, inevitable, and peaceful process. Religion and the Church received little attention, although his sources were rich on both. Finally, he provided striking and illustrative portraits of individuals, and the graceful, clear style for which he became famous glowed.

Reviews then and later remarked that he devoted little attention to serfdom and the *narod* or people. As if to remedy this shortcoming, in 1867 he contributed an extensive section on the way in which the Russian people lived and worked to a translation of a volume by P. K. Kirkhmann, *Geschichte der Arbeit und Kultur*, that described German food, housing, dress, utensils, weapons, and trade. Kliuchevskii provided detailed information concerning these subjects for Russia and added a section on games that was not published. The 120 pages benefit from clear and crisp organization and are superior to those of Kirkhmann. Kliuchevskii used sources in *Russian Truth*, the eleventh-century legal code of Kiev, ancient chronicles, lives of saints, and Moscow archives for data concerning the breads, beverages, fruits, vegetables, and condiments that Russians ate over the centuries (there is no reference to meat), indicating when each food appeared and whence it came. Even though this contribution was a compilation, it demonstrates immense knowledge and skill.

The book tells us much about the young Kliuchevskii and the attitudes he held throughout his life. The preface noted that historians had overemphasized the state and neglected the way peaceful people lived. Any reader would conclude that Russia in the seventeenth century was primitive and even nobles lived in simple circumstances. The volume assists one to understand his constant criticism of intellectuals, who had no knowledge of the majority of their countrymen or the foundations on which their comforts rested. Above all, without revealing inferiority or offended national pride, Kliuchevskii showed that many items of Russian daily life came from Byzantium, the Tatars, Persians, or western Europe. In short, he discovered early and at a most elemental level that Western influence began long before Peter, and many changes from abroad arrived slowly and almost imperceptibly.

The 1870s were crucial for his intellectual formation and career and established the framework for his private life, but Soviet scholars virtually ignored the period, even though substantial data are available and they published two hundred books and articles on him. *Saints' Lives* was not published in the Soviet Union, except in 1918, when the Bolsheviks reprinted most of his volumes, and in 1980 as a photo print. Only four of the twenty-five essays he produced between 1866 and 1880, an article on the Solovetskii Monastery in 1867 and a set of three in 1872 on religious quarrels in Pskov in the fifteenth century, appeared in any of the several Soviet editions of his works until an edition of some of his essays in 1990. Nechkina's long study of Kliuchevskii devoted more space to the several months he tutored the Grand Duke Georgii Aleksandr in the 1890s than to the thirty-five years in Sergiev Posad, even though the Ecclesiastical Academy years are richly documented.

Kliuchevskii's student years, as both an undergraduate and an advanced student, were difficult. He was poor at least until 1872, and living conditions were harsh. So far as one can determine, he had no particularly close friends as an undergraduate. Even though he lived his last fifty years in Moscow, few friendships rested upon his student years. In part because of his economic position, living arrangements, single-minded concentration upon studies, and increasing understanding of Moscow's cultural riches, he was much closer to several faculty members than to men of his generation.

This period deepened the mark that Penza left and helped make him a sturdy, self-reliant Muscovite. While his mentors and graduate student associates studied and traveled in Europe, he remained fixed in Moscow. Struggling for employment that would enable him to continue his studies, walking miles to tutor a youngster, going occasionally without meals, supporting a wife and son after 1870, and carving out a professional life on the edges of the academic community also deepened his appreciation for those who had endured harsh centuries. His rejection of Soloviev's pressure to accept an appointment in Dorpat reflected the independent spirit that enabled him to move quietly away from the state school and develop ideas of his own about the course of Russian history. With little assistance from others, he also established positions in two different Moscows: the secular European university city and the Orthodox seminary in Trinity Monastery, almost another world away.

As a graduate student, Kliuchevskii developed close relationships with Aleksandr A. Shakhov and Gennadii F. Karpov, the first nine years younger and the second two years older than Kliuchevskii. Shakhov, a lively admirer of Byron and other romantic poets, was a specialist in French literature of the revolutionary years. Karpov was a dull, reactionary Russian nationalist who obtained his doctorate in 1870, failed utterly as an instructor at Kharkov University, and returned to Moscow, where he devoted his time to nationalistic histories of the seventeenth century and publication of important historical documents. These friendships with contemporaries of such different views reflect Kliuchevskii's intellectual curiosity and tact. His historical judgments might have been different had Shakhov not died of tuberculosis in 1877, when he was only twenty-seven.

Shakhov was interested in French and German literature in the eighteenth and nineteenth centuries. A brilliant student of Buslaev, he won a gold medal in 1869 for an essay, "On the Lives of Novgorod Saints." He spent 1871–72 attending lectures in Berlin, visiting Munich, and conducting research in Paris. He became a lecturer in the Women's Higher Courses at the age of twenty-three and completed his doctorate in 1875. The following year he was appointed assistant professor at the university, offering courses on nineteenth-century French literature. Long after his death, friends published two editions of his courses on Goethe, Voltaire, and French literature.

Shakhov was a superb and popular lecturer. His thesis, an analysis of French literature and the Paris press during the early years of the nineteenth century, sought to explain the characteristics of the literature and the period and to relate intellectual life to social developments of the time. It rested upon careful study of a wide range of primary sources as well as the views of French and German scholars. In his correspondence from abroad with Kliuchevskii, his comments on Johann Droysen and other German professors were as detailed and acute as those of Kliuchevskii on his Moscow instructors. They were both close to Ger'e and were the youngest members of his instructional staff, and Ger'e defended Shakhov's thesis against Soloviev's criticism of "jargon." Kliuchevskii was presenting a course then on the French Revolution at the military school, so the two men shared interests in things French. Their comrades referred to them as Robespierre and Sainte-Just or as Faust and Mephistopheles. Kliuchevskii was the executor of Shakhov's will, and his archives include Shakhov's lecture outlines and notes.

Karpov's father was an inspector in the district school in Uglich, a village in Iaroslavl' province northeast of Moscow. After graduating from high school in 1855, he studied two years in the Demidov Lyceum, which emphasized law and foreign languages, before completing a law degree in 1861. After working briefly for the Holy Synod Press, he was attracted into Russian history by Soloviev and served as his assistant at the military school. His M.A. thesis on Russian-Polish relations in the second half of the fifteenth century won the Uvarov Prize from the Academy of Sciences as the most distinguished book published in 1867 in Russian history and led to his appointment as lecturer at newly established Kharkov University. However, his doctorate in 1870, a survey of the sources of "Little Russian" history in the middle of the seventeenth century, "pleased almost no one." During his last two decades, Karpov served on the Archeographical Commission and was treasurer of the Society of Russian History and Antiquity. He devoted most of his time to research on the second half of the seventeenth century, especially Moscow's annexation of much of Ukraine, a word he did not use.

Kliuchevskii considered Karpov "a firm patriot, a true Great Russian devoted to study of his native land's struggle with its enemies," but Soviet scholars condemned him as "a Great Russian bourgeois historian" and a "martial Great Power nationalist." His *kandidat* thesis, *Essays on the History of the Russian Church Hierarchy,* held that the Church had provided the moral foundation and sense of unity during the period in which power moved from Kiev to Vladimir-Suzdal' and thence to Moscow. With the acquisition of much of Little Russia, "the former province, part of the whole, again entered into union with the whole" and resumed its natural progress. In Karpov's judgment, Novgorod's social structure and emphasis upon personal freedom doomed its independence. The Lithuanian rulers cooperated with the Mongols, against whom Moscow defended Europe. In the seventeenth century, the mass of Orthodox peasants wanted freedom from Poland, "an extremely Catholic country," and its aristocratic landowners. Above all, they recognized that it is "impossible for us to live any longer without the tsar."

Karpov's hero was Bogdan Khmel'nitskii, and he wrote two volumes attacking Kostomarov's description of Khmel'nitskii as a drunken rebel who had betrayed Moscow when negotiating with the Turks. As defender of the faith, his Khmel'nitskii reunified Little Russia with Great Russia, even though he was a "main protector of the Yids" and brought thousands of Jews into the reunion. Karpov compared him to "William of Orange, Milosh Obrenovich, George Washington, and other true representatives of their peoples, fighters for freedom and respect for the fallen against despotism, backwardness, and violence. They worked and acted in the same way and used the same methods."[1]

A resolute publisher of source materials from the archives of the Ministry of Foreign Affairs and the Ministry of Justice, Karpov produced five huge volumes of documents on diplomatic relations with Poland-Lithuania from 1457 to 1533 and completed a set of ten volumes that Kostomarov had begun on southern and western Russia from 1648 to 1664. He also edited a 1,073-page manuscript in Church Slavonic of Prince Sviatoslav and four extensive volumes on Orthodox Church songs, both for the Society of Ancient Literature in St. Petersburg.

Kliuchevskii and Karpov met when they were students of Soloviev. They received advice and assistance from Popov, were members of the Society of Russian History and Antiquity, and used the same archives and libraries. Kliuchevskii succeeded Karpov as Soloviev's assistant in the military school. Above all, they tutored Iuliia and Anna Morozova, daughters of Timofei S. Morozov, who owned textile factories and was a banker, merchant, and railroad builder. Karpov married Anna and became wealthy. Timofei Morozov and one of his nephews, Arsenii I. Morozov, financed publication of the documents he unearthed. Arsenii paid for publishing and distributing 1,200 sets of the volumes on Church songs. Anna became a benefactor of the Society of Russian History and Antiquity and other historical organizations, as her brother Savva did of the Moscow Art Theater.

The Karpovs owned property in Vladimir and Iaroslavl' provinces and in and near Moscow and inherited stock in Anna's father's enterprises. For more than thirty years, the Kliuchevskiis spent much of each summer at a Karpov dacha in Sushnevo in Vladimir. He gave the memorial address at a meeting to honor Karpov on November 18, 1890. Mrs. Karpov established an 11,500-ruble endowment to provide an award for the best book published each year on the area that Karpov called Little Russia, and Kliuchevskii served as chairman of the prize committee. His wife and he often dined with Mrs. Karpov, and she transcribed some of his public lectures and typed drafts of the *Course of Russian History.*

Kliuchevskii appreciated his friend's indefatigability in collecting and publishing documents. He shared Karpov's nationalist interpretation and emphasized Karpov's thesis that national religious unity was important in the drive to unify Russia and the Russians. Many Karpov phrases and anti-Catholic positions appear in the *Course of Russian History,* which reflects no anti-Semitism.

Kliuchevskii maintained close relations with a number of university scholars older than he and far more urbane and cosmopolitan than Karpov, but Kliuchevskii's long friendship with such an extreme conservative and apparently dull contemporary does provide additional insight into his character and the way in which he balanced apparent contradictions.

Colleagues noted that Kliuchevskii was an unprepossessing, reserved, and almost invisible person who escaped attention until he talked. His penetrating comments, graceful language, and *bons mots* attracted others, especially women, whom he charmed in Ger'e's program and in his public lectures. His letters as an undergraduate, his diary, and letters to a brother-in-law and sister-in-law in the 1870s after all were married contain comments on attractive women he saw on the streets or met at parties. Notes in his archives comment with compassion on the position that women occupied in Byzantium and early Russian history. In class he occasionally discussed differences between the work of men and women as students. His relations with Mrs. Ger'e, Mrs. Karpov, and his sisters-in-law included a good deal of teasing. They attended his courses in the Ger'e program, played the piano when he was writing, and transcribed his lectures. Some of his celebrated aphorisms and draft short stories, which comment cruelly upon women as superficial, vain, and stupid, may have reflected a form of the teasing he directed at the women he most appreciated.

His first love was an attractive young lady in Penza. However, his interest in learning was overwhelming and her health was frail, and he left Penza thinking she would not live long. In his first year in Moscow, he became acquainted with a fellow student, Nikolai M. Borodin, one of two sons in a prosperous merchant's family that lived on Great Iakimenka Street, later Dmitrov Street, across the river from the Kremlin and the university. Ostrovskii, the chronicler and critic of these patriotic conservatives and their families, was a neighbor of the Borodins and later of the Kliuchevskiis. Invited to tutor the younger son, Sergei, in Latin, Kliuchevskii visited the Borodin home at least once a week and soon became a friend of the family. One of the older daughters, Anna, lived near the Borodin home with an aunt who had married a merchant named Osip S. Dol'gov. The aunt was unwell, her husband was a drunkard, and Anna took care of the four children and served as assistant in the Dol'gov business. Several Kliuchevskii letters to Anna in 1863 and 1864 reveal that the two took long walks, discussed Pushkin and contemporary novels, and enjoyed student parties. Other references reveal that Nadezhda, one of the younger sisters, also attracted him.

However, Kliuchevskii chose to marry neither Anna, who never married, nor Nadezhda, but Anisiia, four years older than he, on January 27, 1869. The couple moved into an apartment in a house on Polianskaia Market, now Brodnikov Lane, three or four houses from the Borodins, and remained in that neighborhood for the remainder of their lives. In 1895, using the honoraria for tutoring the Grand Duke Nikolai Aleksandr, they bought a small house nearby on Zhitnaia Street, then on the southern outskirts of Moscow. The massive building where this house once stood is a quarter of a mile from today's October metro station. There the Kliuchevskiis lived quietly, with a barn and a garden, flowers, and a dog, arrangements ideal for a dedicated countryman of that time.

Anisiia Kliuchevskii was not well educated; few Russian women at that time were, but she was a friend of his friends, who considered her intelligent. She did not take part in his professional life, had no intellectual interests, and was not a research assistant, critic, secretary-typist, or even transcriber. However, their letters indicate that the Kliuchevskiis shared information about university affairs and that she discussed these matters with friends on the faculty when he was absent. Correspondence with his wife's relatives and letters and diaries of friends with notes about teas and evening parties make clear that the Kliuchevskii marriage was a happy one in a society less given to making private affairs public than is ours.

The Kliuchevskiis were rarely separated, except Monday nights during the academic year, when he stayed at the academy in Sergiev Posad, and journeys to the Caucasus in the winters of 1893–94 and 1894–95 to tutor the Grand Duke Nikolai Aleksandr, to St. Petersburg after the turn of the century for meetings, and to the Crimea late in life to rest and write. A few affectionate letters from his wife have survived, as has correspondence with their son, Boris. Mrs. Kliuchevskii's sudden death at an evening service in the parish church on March 21, 1909, devastated Kliuchevskii and Boris.

Mrs. Kliuchevskii was a member of the large and happy Borodin family and clan, which Kliuchevskii joined even before the marriage. Her mother was apparently an able businesswoman who managed affairs after her husband died in 1876. Kliuchevskii was especially fond of the Borodin sons, Sergei Borodin's wife Elena, their daughter Nadezhda, and his nieces, all of whom are buried near the historian and his wife. Kliuchevskii was the godfather of Nadezhda and signed his letters to her "Your oldest brother." In 1941 she presented valuable Borodin-Kliuchevskii diaries, letters, account books, and family photographs to the State Public Historical Library. At the same time, she presented the Karpov papers, which she had received from Karpov, to the State Historical Museum.

The Borodins were also friends of the Karpovs. Both families attended the scholar's lectures when he was a promising young man and a famous speaker as well, and the families often visited each other's summer places. This relationship and the close extended Borodin family provided Kliuchevskii a sense of family and clan that he had lacked. From this serene and untroubled nest, removed from the university and apartments of most faculty members and from the political and intellectual centers, he wrote a thoughtful account of Russia's past in a form of expression that profoundly affected the world's conception of that subject.

For Kliuchevskii, determining what had happened and explaining it in lectures and in writing were parts of one function, a coin that had two sides. In these pivotal years, he used the challenge of informing and exciting classes of military cadets, women, and seminarians, whether ill-informed, highly motivated, or "lightheaded," to nourish the skills that made him a superlative lecturer. He also used the full-year survey of Russian history at the academy and the three-year sequence in Ger'e's program to establish a sound framework and system of analysis that would serve throughout his teaching career. He borrowed, absorbed, and reshaped information from archival materials, Soloviev, and other historians in order to furnish illuminating descriptions and portraits that would distinguish a course of his own. He chose research subjects that derived from questions that his teaching inspired, deepened his knowledge and understanding of significant issues and institutions, and sharpened his students' comprehension. Many of his publications were steps to enlarge the understanding of those he taught, not to inform other specialists of new details or achieve renown. They constituted another way of instructing men and women in his classes, as well as a larger audience who did not attend educational institutions. He emphasized issues and critical analysis of economic and social factors, avoided details, and provided striking character portraits and unforgettable *bons mots*.

In short, in contrast to most American specialists a century later, his first priority was instructing. He taught and wrote for those interested in understanding their country's past: this lies at the core of his professional ethics and success.

This dedication annoyed Soloviev, who thought that Kliuchevskii's preoccupation with teaching would delay his theses, but these years of study and organizing produced an analysis and structure that were firm when he joined the university faculty in 1879 and served as the base of the *Course of Russian History,* written in his last decade. For example, analysis of the two surviving transcripts of lectures Kliuchevskii gave in 1872–73 in Ger'e's courses on the period from the sixth through the fourteenth centuries demonstrates that his views changed little between those years and when he wrote the early chapters of the *Course of Russian History* late in life. A. A. Kizevetter, one of the most able scholars he helped train, devoted much of his life abroad after 1922 to study of Kliuchevskii's scholarship. Just before he died in Prague in 1933, he completed a detailed comparison of the only surviving transcript of the 1873–74 lectures on the period from the fifteenth through the seventeenth centuries with the corresponding chapters of the five editions of the *Boyar Council* and the relevant six chapters of the second volume of the *Course of Russian History.* This showed that the printed volumes followed the lectures on all critical issues. The main changes involved reorganization of the "architecture" of some lectures, excision of lectures on the boyars' intellectual level in the sixteenth century and the origins of the table of ranks to remove distortions in emphasis, and insertion of small additions into the published works. The other revisions were stylistic, eliminating long quotations and "excursions," examples, and details. He compressed some paragraphs and even pages, expressing the substance with especial clarity as he "polished the marble." Comparison of the various versions of the lithographed lectures he presented at the university reveals the same pattern: the structure and substance remained similar, but expression became more precise and lucid.

In short, many judgments Kliuchevskii expressed in the 1870s remained constant throughout his life. Kizevetter concluded that the "world view" established then survived in his later publications. The outstanding Soviet scholar on this subject, Zimin, reached the same judgment independently forty years after Kizevetter. In the latter's words, Kliuchevskii was a gardener who constantly added flowers to an already well-cultivated plot.[2]

Kliuchevskii's first opportunity to teach demonstrates the fortuity of his coming to Moscow in 1861. Two years after his arrival, General Count D. A. Miliutin, Minister of Defense from 1861 to 1881, closed three of the four cadet schools, established several two-year schools to prepare army officers, and placed 150 youths seventeen to nineteen years of age in each class. One of the schools was in Moscow, the Third Aleksandrovskoe Military School on Znamenka Street near Arbat Square, one block from the Rumiantsev Museum and three from the university. Somehow, Miliutin hoped this school would become "a second Moscow University."

The new military schools were open to young men of all classes to democratize the officer corps (sons of nobles constituted 89 percent of the students in 1870–71 and 83 percent in 1880–81) and improve the quality of young officers. The curriculum included European history, Russian language and literature, chemistry and other sciences, and introductory military courses. Miliutin turned to university professors as instructors and graduate students as assistants and tutors. Thus, men such as Soloviev and Tikhonravov taught history and literature. Graduate students such as Karpov and Kondakov served as tutors in history.[3]

In 1868, Soloviev suggested that Kliuchevskii succeed him, and the rector assured the commandant that Kliuchevskii was responsible, patriotic, and capable. Even though his knowledge of modern European history was minimal (he had studied only Eshevskii's courses on the ancient world and medieval Europe), the opportunity to continue Soloviev's required course delighted the apprentice. He wished to work toward advanced degrees, but his fellowship had expired: the 1,000-ruble annual stipend replaced it. Moreover, he would teach only two hours a week in a building close to the research collections. Mastering sufficient European history to instruct youngsters would delay his progress, but so would any other occupation.

Kliuchevskii presented the course annually until 1883, when General P. S. Vannovskii, who succeeded Miliutin in 1881, transformed the school and others that had sprouted under Miliutin into old-fashioned cadet corps emphasizing military studies. As part of this program, he canceled Miliutin's policy of admitting non-nobles and removed liberal education courses from the curriculum and their instructors from the faculty.

The lithographed copies of Kliuchevskii's lectures after 1872 were made by Mrs. Ger'e and assistants who knew little European history and whose reporting skills were limited. Each account is about one-third the length of a lecture and contains the substance but not the details. They carry different titles: "A History of European Man" (the original title), "Europe since the Seventeenth Century," "General History," "Notes on General History," "Recent History," and "The French Revolution." Single copies for each year and four editions of the lectures given in 1874–75 and two for 1878–79 have survived. The sets for these two years are not identical, but the differences are minor. The stamp of approval of Colonel N. N. Svetlitskii, inspector of classes, at the end of each transcript suggests that all are complete and official.

Soloviev had emphasized that ideas had undermined the Old Regime and contributed to the "disorders" that afflicted nineteenth-century Europe. Kliuchevskii obtained the school's permission instead to concentrate on the origins, course, and consequences of the revolution and Russian relations with Europe. From the beginning until 1875–76, he began in the seventeenth century, emphasizing the France of Louis XIV and the Russia of Peter the Great. He continued through the French Revolution and Napoleon, with much on the origins or background of the revolution. The first semester ended after the Terror. During these years, he gradually devoted more attention to Europe and less to Russia before 1789 as his knowledge of Europe increased, but the emphasis remained on the period from 1789 through 1793.

After 1875–76, he began with a section entitled "Europe on the Eve of the

French Revolution" and devoted increasing attention each successive year to Europe in the nineteenth century, the Napoleonic wars, and Russia through the reforms of Alexander II. The last year, he examined the history of Russia more than before, with a long section on the causes of the wars not in earlier versions, a clear account of the Decembrists, and many pages on the Polish revolt of 1830. He also added materials on the Latin American revolt against Spain after 1815, expansion of the British empire in China in the 1840s, and the revolutions in Europe in 1848 and 1849.

For lectures that General Miliutin and the Ministry of Defense arranged for future army officers in the final years of the reign of Alexander II and the first of Alexander III, these constituted a remarkable series: Nechkina terms them "almost unbelievable."[4] It was not a profound course; indeed, it was shallow, badly organized, and full of errors. It emphasized narrative political history, international relations, and military affairs and treated each European state as a unit with no cultural or other connections with neighbors. It neglected the geographic, economic, social, and institutional factors his other work emphasized, except for discussion of the origins of the revolution, based on Taine. But until 1879, when the university initiated a course on nineteenth-century European history, it was the only class offered in Russia on modern Europe and the French Revolution.

Kliuchevskii was best informed concerning France in the seventeenth and eighteenth centuries, Switzerland, and the Germanys in the nineteenth century. The political structure of the Dutch Republic clearly bewildered him. He did not understand Austrian policy in the Germanys or the Balkans. He failed to explain why the revolution exploded beyond France or why the revolutions of 1830 and 1848 spread. He declared that "the English Catholic population" in Ireland lacked political rights, that nineteenth-century England's only two religious groups were Anglicans and Presbyterians, and that the Whig and Tory parties were organized entirely along religious lines.

Although *Boyar Council,* written during these years, concentrated upon the estate structure and the legal status of estates, he barely mentioned estates or classes in Europe. He failed to provide the kind of overview of Europe in 1815 that would have enabled students to comprehend developments after the revolution and Napoleon, although he had begun with a splendid description of Europe before the revolution and the *Course of Russian History* contained such reviews before and after important periods or changes.

Kliuchevskii was deeply critical of the Old Regime and fascinated by the revolution. The lectures on the reign of Louis XIV, in which "the court lolled in luxury while the people lived in misery," resembled his description of Russia before the Time of Troubles and seemed to justify the coming storm. Louis XIV's search for dominion in Europe weakened the aristocracy, which he drew from proper functions in the country, as he did the high clergy and the corporate orders. He forgot his role as guardian of the general welfare, retained the relics of feudalism, created and capriciously used armies that overburdened the poor, and brought destruction to much of Europe. But his greatest error and crime was treatment of the Huguenots, especially revocation of the Edict of Nantes in 1685. This unleashed religious persecution and misery upon loyal countrymen and drove many artisans and merchants to hostile states, where they worked against their native country. Moreover, France lost its moral and intellectual leadership, and hostility to the arrogant and stagnant Catholic Church helped bring on the revolution.

Louis XIV's successors were more harmful: they were more licentious and lacked his abilities and goals. They encouraged economic growth but denied the middle class any share of power. Their policies toward the peasants were benighted: peasants lived in better conditions than elsewhere in Europe, but the government's treatment drove them into opposition. French monarchs endorsed the reforms of Turgot and Necker but carried them out halfheartedly, unleashing popular resentment. The kings encouraged radical ideas, especially those of Rousseau, that undermined the system. In the end, demagogues, not the people, brought on the revolution. The "Old Order," in Kliuchevskii's words, was destined to collapse.

The revolution evoked the young conservative's populist sympathies and idealism. He considered it an event of worldwide importance and the early revolutionaries sagacious and benign. Robespierre, Saint-Just, and Danton, whom he called "a true street orator," excited him, and the Jacobin Saint-Just was a sentimental favorite. Colbert's mercantilism was harmful for France and its neighbors, and he viewed free trade favorably. He approved the Declaration of the Rights of Man and endorsed a system in which "even Jews," not the pejorative Yids, were equal with Catholics. Abbé Sieyes's question "What is the Third Estate?" and the new role of the Third Estate in the National Assembly were appropriate. Kliuchevskii was sympathetic to the Utopian Socialists, Saint-Simon, Cabet, Fourier, and even Proudhon: his archives contain a few pages that he wrote about Robert Owen in 1865, so his interest in the early socialists preceded this course. His favorite leader early in the revolution was Mirabeau.

But then "immoral and corrupt" Jacobin demagogues seized power over the Girondins, who sought order and freedom. They unleashed the Terror, "the horror of the revolution," an absolutism much like the earlier one, except that it was a system of personal rule without the values, institutions, and traditions that had for generations justified the Old Order. Napoleon's institutions were hierarchical, but "a more free" organization would not have been effective in France, as it would not have been in the Russia of Peter the Great. Kliuchevskii approved the changes the French introduced in Spain, while making understandable Spanish and Portuguese efforts to drive out the hated foreign rulers. "Gloomy fanatical absolutism" in Spain after 1815 drew ridicule. Similarly, he criticized the Tory government for raising taxes, passing the Corn Laws, exploiting farmers and the new working class, and persecuting the Irish. He reserved his harshest scorn for the French ultra-royalists after 1815, and Charles X he thought stupid, fully responsible for the unnecessary revolution in 1830.

Kliuchevskii emphasized the role individuals played, except for Napoleon, whose system of rule received two pages, compared to less than one for the emperor himself. "Builders," particularly Richelieu, attracted admiration. Colbert he called "a real defender of the people." Louvois received much praise for Louis XIV's achievements, and his death was one reason for the king's later errors. These lectures began to demonstrate the skill in describing individuals that help make the *Course of Russian History* so fascinating. The portraits of Louis XIV, Danton, Robespierre, Saint-Just, Paul, and Suvorov—he especially admired Suvorov—foreshadow those of later years.

In the course, Russia's role in international affairs after 1812 received increasing attention as Kliuchevskii advanced through the 1870s. The Greek uprising occupied an important position from the first year, and he strongly approved Greek nationalism. The Polish national drive for independence was a different matter. In the last two years, he devoted several pages to Poland under Alexander I, implying that Alexander's generosity stimulated romantic dreams among Polish leaders for independence and the boundaries of Poland's greatest days. He emphasized the negative effect that Russia's actions in Poland after 1830 and in 1863 exercised upon Russia's image in Europe and upon French and English policy. Russian intervention in Hungary in 1849 received brief mention, but the Crimean War was a blessing: it made evident Russian weaknesses and stimulated the reforms of Alexander II.

Discussing domestic history in the nineteenth century was delicate. Kliuchevskii skipped Paul's reign until his lectures in 1882–83, when it received thirty-three pages. These included Paul's death in 1801, but not the murder: "The oldest son of Paul succeeded to the throne." He concentrated on international affairs and war in his treatment of the reign of Alexander I, with increasing attention to 1812, twenty-nine pages in 1881–82 and thirty-three in 1882–83, perhaps to persuade General Vannovskii to retain the course. But he virtually ignored Russia's conflict with Sweden and the addition of Finland to the empire. Similarly, while his accounts after 1875 provided a factual description of the Decembrist revolt in 1825 and Nicholas I's treatment of the Decembrists, he never mentioned the "marvelous decade," the controversy between the Slavophils and Westerners, or ideas, even those of Pushkin.

The lectures failed to note the resemblance between the policies of Louis XIV toward the Huguenots and Russian treatment of Old Believers, Catholics, and Jews. The description of the Old Regime's flaws, the Terror's violence, and the destructiveness of Napoleon's wars must have appeared as criticism of a society remote from Russia and therefore not one from which Russia could or should borrow. Kliuchevskii criticized censorship in the Kingdom of Sardinia after 1815, but did not compare it with that in Russia. The course referred to British actions in Ireland, without hinting that they were similar to those of Russia in Poland. Even his comment that the Parliament's power to tax was the base of English freedom was brief and apparently irrelevant. The British Parliament and electoral reforms in Britain, the Belgians' revolt against the Dutch, Latin American rebellions, even the Greek Revolution, might have occurred in Shangri La.

This superficial and often wildly inaccurate course deserves attention because it discloses the limited knowledge and understanding that Kliuchevskii had of Europe and how little interest he showed in improving that over a fifteen-year period. One could conclude that his depiction of European injustice, intolerance, cruelty, and violence was the response of a decent person to the follies and crimes of the Old Regime and the early promise that the revolution offered for the "general welfare." One could even conclude that Kliuchevskii was a nineteenth-century liberal so far as France was concerned. But not for Russia. Europe was so distinct that his courses about it were completely unlike those on Russian history. For him and for Svetlitskii, Europe was a world apart, a series of states and a civilization whose values and political institutions were so remote and exotic that one could safely describe them, even criticize them, while remaining silent about flaws in one's native country. Policies toward minorities, censorship anywhere, and violent revolutions were interesting but irrelevant, except for Russian foreign policy. Europe was fundamentally different from Russia: no one could conclude that Russia could or should borrow from this group of states.

Even so, teaching this elementary course helped Kliuchevskii comprehend some of the basic factors, such as Europe's long shorelines and the existence of independent nations and cultures, that explain why European development differed from Russia's. The lectures also reveal that he rejected divine right but considered strong government essential for every society. He criticized absolutist government not as a form of rule but for policies the monarchs established. Everyone, especially the ruler, should submit to the "general welfare" or "civil sense." No one could read the lectures without concluding that a limited government was superior for France and presumably for all Europeans, but was not appropriate for Russia.

Kliuchevskii obtained his other early teaching experience because of Ger'e, who sought to enable women to obtain a higher education, which the 1863 reform of the universities failed to provide. In 1861, the Moscow University Academic Council voted against admitting women, which the Ministry of Education would not have allowed anyway. The ministry even forbade St. Petersburg University to continue allowing women to enter, which it had begun in 1859. The first high schools or secondary schools for women opened in the 1860s. However, interest among women from the upper classes in knowledge and preparation for teaching and other professional careers continued to grow. In 1872, sixty of the sixty-seven women studying at Zurich University were Russian.

Supported by many professors, especially historians, four hundred women in St. Petersburg in 1868 petitioned for lecture courses. The Ministry of Education the next year allowed a series of lectures for women on Russian language and literature, mathematics, and physics in cities that contained universities. Three years later, it approved a four-year experimental program, with the history of Russia, general history (basically European history), Russian and world literature, and physics the core and mathematics and hygiene optional.

The ministry in 1876 authorized these arrangements on a regular basis in university cities, the first program for higher education for women.

Ger'e was founder, director, and heart and soul of the Moscow response. His archives reveal that he obtained facilities, appointed the faculty, directed admissions, maintained records, retained the grades each faculty member awarded, and solicited funds. After the ministry closed the programs in 1888, he built an endowment of ninety thousand rubles, enabling the school to re-open when permission was granted in 1900. He taught a course each semester and invited the most able women students to participate in university seminars in his home. In 1875, he sought unsuccessfully to persuade the ministry to make the program a part of the university.

In Moscow, lectures for women began at the Third Men's High School on Liubianka Square. In 1872, Ger'e persuaded his now more liberal colleagues to seek permission to offer the courses in the two university buildings, but the ministry rejected the petition. The program therefore used the First Men's High School on Prechistenka Street, moving the next year to the Stepanov mansion nearby and in 1877 to the new Polytechnical Museum. It admitted women who had graduated from a high school, possessed a certificate from a tutor, or passed a special admissions examination: about one-half obtained admission by examination. Tuition was fifty rubles a year, plus ten rubles for each course, but gifts enabled qualified students without funds to participate.

The program provided eighteen hours of class each week. Most classes met in the morning from nine to twelve from October until late April. Most faculty were university professors, and the courses were considered equivalent to those at the university. Men such as Buslaev, Tikhonravov, and Ger'e were among the original faculty. Soloviev, rector of the university in 1872, did not participate but served as chairman of the advisory board. He also presented the opening address, which stressed that a woman's role was primarily that of mother but that women should acquire some learning and an understanding of the culture in which they lived. Enrollment in Moscow began with 70, reached 100 the second year, rose slowly throughout the 1870s, and averaged 200 in the 1880s. It jumped to 1,002 in 1904 and grew rapidly to 5,000 in 1912. After the revolution, Ger'e's courses became the core of the Moscow Pedagogical Institute. The women who fought for these courses, Ger'e, and the faculties clearly helped satisfy a genuine demand and contributed significantly to the expansion and improvement of higher education.

Kliuchevskii taught enthusiastic classes each year for three hours on Wednesday mornings or Friday afternoons, for which he received three hundred rubles, the highest honorarium that Ger'e bestowed. When the faculty chose Kliuchevskii to speak at the dinner that formally closed the curriculum in 1888, he urged his colleagues to devise new ways to provide educational opportunities for women. At the ceremony that university colleagues arranged in 1901 to celebrate his thirty years of service in higher education, former students in these courses and alumnae of the St. Petersburg program spoke enthusiastically about his contribution to their education.

When Ger'e obtained ministry permission in 1889 to organize open lectures at the Polytechnical Museum, Kliuchevskii presented a series of ten on Western influence after Peter the Great. In 1892, the Moscow Society for Teachers, an organization teachers founded in 1870 to help expand teacher training, assumed responsibility for these lectures, then called Collective Courses. They attracted 276 students in the humanities and 810 in the sciences in 1896. Kliuchevskii contributed funds to support these courses and the reopened Ger'e program in 1900. He taught Russian history that fall, but withdrew then to write the *Course of Russian History* and enable graduate students to obtain employment and experience. At least five young men who studied with him and were outstanding scholars before and after 1917, as well as Mikhail Pokrovskii, who studied with Kliuchevskii as an undergraduate and graduate student, began their professional careers in this program.

Soloviev was responsible for Kliuchevskii's position at the military school and Ger'e for that in the Women's Higher Courses. However, in 1871 Kliuchevskii acquired the faculty appointment he held until 1906 at the Moscow Ecclesiastical Academy because of the reputation he had established through his publications in the *Orthodox Review* and his M.A. thesis on the lives of saints. Selection of this theme for his first advanced degree reflected the fortuity that often occurs when scholars choose research subjects. In his case, the consequences were especially significant. Soloviev, who furnished very little guidance to the few advanced students he attracted, was aware that Kliuchevskii as a former seminarian had more interest in and knowledge of Church affairs than most young men. He suggested first that Kliuchevskii study Church landholdings in ancient Russia, for which the notes and preliminary outline that Kliuchevskii made in the summer of 1865 have survived. He then turned to the role of monasteries in colonizing northeastern Russia, in which Soloviev was especially interested. Archival papers suggest that Kliuchevskii gradually abandoned these extremely complicated themes: bishops, monasteries, and individual parishes each possessed different types of property acquired in different ways, all described in scattered and incomplete deeds and other records. Instead, he decided to analyze saints' lives as a historical source, another Soloviev proposal. This subject also awakened memories of his childhood that Buslaev had reinforced. Finally, he learned that some rich and well-organized source materials had recently become available. From this concatenation emerged a choice that deeply affected Kliuchevskii's views and career.

Kliuchevskii's father had read to him evenings from *Lives of Saints*, so he possessed an affectionate familiarity with these materials before he learned that they constituted a rich mine of information concerning early Russian history. In the fall of 1864, Buslaev had informed students that the Solovetskii Monastery, the Rumiantsev Museum, and private Moscow libraries possessed collections of these lives and that Vukol M. Undol'skii had catalogued the Holy Synod Library's large collection, which Kliuchevskii used when he prepared his contribution to Kirkhmann's *History of Social and Private Life*. He also apprised the class that the government in 1854 had moved another depository, the

Solovetskii Library, from the White Sea Island where the Crimean War exposed it to destruction or seizure by the British fleet, to the Kazan Ecclesiastical Academy, where Afanasii P. Shchapov had catalogued it in 1857. Kliuchevskii's archives contain forty pages of notes from Buslaev's lectures on the Solovetskii collection and a ten-page list of lives he had copied from the Holy Synod catalogue in the summer of 1865.[5]

Eshevskii supplemented Buslaev's information. He had taught at the Kazan Academy from 1855 until 1858, gave a lecture in 1857 describing the collection, used the materials while writing an article on the role of monasteries in colonizing northern Russia, and helped assign Shchapov to catalogue the Solovetskii Library. Indeed, Shchapov published a helpful essay on these sources, which also stimulated Kliuchevskii's interest in the intellectual level of ancient Russia and the reasons for the seventeenth-century schism.

Soloviev obtained permission from the Ministry of Education and the Holy Synod for a research trip enabling Kliuchevskii to study the Kazan archives. There he proved so "serious" that the archivist allowed him to work in the collection after the archive closed. The material from this expedition and work in the Holy Synod Library led to a thirty-three-page article in 1867 in the Moscow University *News* on the economic activity of the Solovetskii Monastery, one of only four he produced in the 1860s and 1870s that Soviet editions of his work have included. It constitutes a coherent description and analysis of the monks' achievements. These men, who displayed diplomatic skills in enticing aid from Novgorod merchants and later from Muscovites, succeeded in building parishes, developing economic enterprises, especially the salt trade, attracting natives and Russians by their successes, and organizing colonies. They helped populate the White Sea shore and islands, drove off Germans and Swedes, provided "enlightenment" and "moral authority" for those they attracted, and added the wilderness area to the "Russian world." The article strengthened Kliuchevskii's understanding of the harsh conditions in which early Russians had lived and persuaded him that Russians in the Solovetskii area had gradually absorbed the Karelians and other Finns who had lived there or were drawn to it. This theme of the peaceful absorption of non-Russians was prominent in his description of the colonization that marked all Russian history.

The young scholar's goals shifted as he widened his search to the Imperial Public Library (now the Russian National Library) in St. Petersburg, the Iosif Volokalamsk Monastery Library, the library of Trinity Monastery in Sergiev Posad, and private collections in Moscow. Indeed, Elpidifor V. Barsov's arrival in 1870 from the Olonets Seminary with materials that Kliuchevskii had not seen helped delay completion of his volume until late 1871.

This pioneer study consumed five years. Shakhov thought the subject unworthy and urged that Kliuchevskii move to a more important topic, but both scholarly and popular reviews of the book were favorable. The outstanding Soviet specialist on Russian monasteries praised its thoroughness, accuracy, and insight. Dmitrii S. Likhachev, dean of specialists on Old Russian literature, a hundred years later lauded Kliuchevskii for describing the process through which saints' lives developed into literary forms. When the Academy of Sciences in 1980 published a photoprint of the volume, the editor, Valentin I. Ianin, praised its meticulous research. However, he did not include it in the nine-volume edition of Kliuchevskii's work that the academy published between 1987 and 1990. It is one of the few Kliuchevskii publications Lenin did not own: at least, it is not in Lenin's library in the Kremlin.

Kliuchevskii's archives contain five thousand pages of closely written notes on five hundred lives of 166 saints in a variety of scripts in Old Church Slavonic, many very difficult to decipher. Kliuchevskii organized his theme in an ingenious way, dividing the lives by eras and types, writing chapters on types of biographies as well as on some individual lives, and incorporating discussion of sources. He used this combination of substance and historiographical comments throughout his career, especially in the *Course of Russian History*. Identifying the author and the date the manuscript was written was a considerable achievement. Placing the biographies in chronological order revealed the changing pattern of the art form, as well as the various scribes' revising, borrowing, and embellishing. From this, Kliuchevskii concluded that the lives, designed for reading on holy days, had gradually become an important literary form. However, in the process they had lost their freshness and reliability as historical sources, except for economic and social data, because many biographies were revisions of other lives written in other times and places.

The thesis represents Kliuchevskii's talent for locating primary sources and extracting valuable data and insights from apparently lifeless material. Moreover, in an age before xeroxing, he was indefatigable and exacting in comparing dozens of scattered manuscripts. The research constituted a training school because it involved philology and archeology as well as other sciences. Demolishing the originality and sanctity of saints' lives without offending Orthodox Christians reflected his diplomatic adroitness: the grace and dexterity with which he removed the encrusted truths from legends disarmed most critics.

The knowledge that Kliuchevskii obtained from this study constituted a foundation for all his scholarly work, as Aleksandr Presniakov's excellent analysis demonstrated. The study informed him concerning the religious ideals at the heart of the monastic movement, the effect that Christian values exercised upon literature, education, and life, and the role that monasteries played in colonization and spreading the gospel. It also reinforced his understanding of the role of geography and climate: he wrote a friend in 1868 that the research had strengthened his "faith in the Russian people, whom so many doubt will ever amount to anything." Matvei K. Liubavskii was inaccurate when he concluded that the peasant was Kliuchevskiii's hero, but he did place the monk and the peasant, the icon and the ax, at the center of Russian history. His understanding of living conditions and the struggle for survival of most Russians in the country's past were central to his analysis.

Saints' Lives produced other significant effects, some paradoxical in their incongruity but all central. First, poring over the mass of economic and social data he had collected subtly turned him away from the "state school." Instead he concentrated upon the "structural materials" of history and economic and social institutions. Research on saints' lives and other related religious subjects and his Penza experience also convinced him that the Church's low intellectual level had undermined its influence on Russian life and that the schism had further reduced its role. The book not only solidified his recognition as a scholar among churchmen but led to his lifetime appointment to the faculty of the Moscow Ecclesiastical Academy, one of the bases from which his influence radiated after 1871.

From the time he began advanced study of history, Kliuchevskii showed the same avidity for research and writing as for teaching. While providing instruction at three different institutions and establishing and reshaping his famous course, he published essays that won scholarly recognition. In addition to the M.A. thesis, he published twenty-five articles in the 1870s and devoted eight years of archival study to the *Boyar Council*, the scholarly book that solidified his position in the academic community. He divided a third of his publications in that decade about equally between studies of historical scholarship, collections of archival materials, and contributions collectors made. These reflected his preoccupation with source materials, those responsible for them, and teaching a survey course on Russian history. The other review articles and essays dealt in one way or another with the role of the Church and religious institutions, especially monasteries.

The articles concerned with history appeared in *Critical Review*, a short-lived Moscow journal that Soloviev and other university faculty members founded. Almost all the others were published in the *Orthodox Review*, founded in 1860 and edited by Sergievskii, university professor of theology, to disseminate materials about religion and ecclesiastical affairs and quietly propose reform of the Church and an increased Church role in public life. In the 1860s and 1870s, it devoted particular attention to religious life in Europe and reviewed the most important Western theological literature. Ten Kliuchevskii review essays and articles appeared in it between the fall of 1869 and the fall of 1879, more than in any other journal. Perhaps the clearest evidence of the change of his intellectual interest in the mid-seventies is that the journal published only three of his articles, all book reviews, after 1874, and none after 1879.

Kliuchevskii's first review article illustrates his religious concerns and their relation to moral behavior and nationalism. It was a fifty-two-page analysis in Ivan Aksakov's *Moscow* in June 1868 of a large volume of readings from biographies of saints, sermons, interpretations of the Holy Scriptures, and writings of the Eastern Church Fathers. The tome was the first of a twelve-volume set, one for each month, compiled by Makarii, Metropolitan of Moscow in the sixteenth century, and reprinted by the St. Petersburg Archeographical Commission. Kliuchevskii ridiculed the expensive, poorly organized edition, which contained many inaccuracies, no table of contents or index, and an uninformative preface. The waste and incompetence annoyed him because "after the Bible, the *Monthly Readings* are the most useful book for educating our people, directing our intellectual development," and defining the Russian view of the world. Inexpensive sets would build "our moral strength and self-confidence" by showing that Russians had built a vast state while warding off invasions from the East and propaganda from the West. "Perhaps we would understand ourselves and our future more fully if we knew and valued better our past moral strength."[6]

The following year, he demonstrated exacting knowledge of early Russian history with a devastating review and then a rebuttal of the author's defense of a six-hundred-page doctoral thesis on Byzantine influence on early Russian education: the work had no plan, did not use lives of saints or other primary sources, ignored old Russian literature, chronology, and geology, was uncritical in its use of secondary sources, and was full of errors.

The book on the lives of saints and its by-products were Kliuchevskii's last publications on religious issues, except for a flurry of book reviews and introductions late in the decade and splendid commemorative talks in the 1890s on anniversaries and on the causes and consequences of the religious schism. The early 1870s therefore marked a shift of interest to economic, social, and institutional factors, analyses of institutions such as the boyar council, *zemskie sobory* or land assemblies, and serfdom, and essays on scholarship and education.

The reasons for this crucial transfer are difficult to identify: perhaps the major ones were the boring character of research on saints' lives, growing awareness of the low level of Church intellectual life throughout Russian history, and interest in the "structural materials" of history as he acquired economic and social data and became more professional. The shift occurred just when he was outlining the course of lectures on Russian history, so it profoundly affected his interpretation: indeed, the course almost ignored the Church after the seventh century.

The final consequences of *Saints' Lives* derive from the process of research and Kliuchevskii's articles in the *Orthodox Review,* which introduced him to most of the collectors, librarians, archivists, scholars, and publishers interested in early Russian history. He learned much from these men, who were eager to discuss their intellectual concerns and impressed by his learning, research skills, and cogent writing and speaking. The foundation of his reputation in the Moscow intellectual community rests upon these years and relations.

University regulations provided that each M.A. candidate publish his book and defend it before two official opponents, the faculty, and the public. Moscow had no commercial publishers and only twenty printers, and Kliuchevskii had little money. Probably through Morozov, Soloviev, or others he had met while on research, he became acquainted with Kuz'ma T. Soldatenkov, a rich Old

Believer merchant whose estate at Kuntsevo was a haven for those interested in early Russia. Soldatenkov in 1856 had begun collecting books and maps and subsidizing publication of research works in Russian history, as other wealthy men collected art or supported the Moscow Art Theater. He supplied funds for publishing the *Chteniia* or *Readings* of the Society of Russian History and Antiquity, as well as volumes of documents, folklore, legends, and folk culture. He enabled Kliuchevskii to meet the university requirement by publishing three thousand copies of *Saints' Lives,* an unusually large number.

A crowd of faculty, students, women, bureaucrats, intellectuals, army officers, and priests attended the defense, at which Kliuchevskii, superb on such occasions, described his research and conclusions. Soloviev and Popov, official opponents, and Buslaev, Tikhonravov, and Barsov raised questions or made comments. Ger'e and other university and academy faculty saluted him after the session, and some observers remarked that they had not attended a more satisfying exercise.

A series of fortuities then assisted him to spend the rest of his life in Moscow. Following a review of religious education after the death of Metropolitan Filaret in 1868, the tsar had approved a program for training theologians and faculty members for the fifty-eight Orthodox seminaries at the academies in Moscow, St. Petersburg, Kiev, and Kazan and the academies and seminaries together for training teachers for Church schools. Thus, the academies became the equivalent of universities and the seminaries of *gimnazii* or high schools. Since the revised curricula added Russian civil history, the Holy Synod authorized the academy to appoint a well-trained scholar with an M.A. in that subject.

Among those whom Kliuchevskii's defense impressed were Aleksandr F. Lavrov, professor of Church law and librarian of the academy, and the rector, Father Aleksandr V. Gorskii, who had met Kliuchevskii in archives. They considered him ideal for the appointment: a former seminarian, a devout learned young man trained by Soloviev, and an experienced and gifted teacher. Kliuchevskii thought the position splendid: he wanted a post at the university level, saw no opportunity at the university, and was comfortable at the academy in the Trinity Monastery, which possessed a splendid library and archive. In another fortuitous development, Mamontov in 1860 had built a railroad through Sergiev Posad that enabled him to reside in Moscow and teach at the academy.

Lavrov nominated Kliuchevskii on May 23, 1871. Kliuchevskii submitted his thesis on June 8 and presented a lecture at the academy the next day. The academy faculty by a vote of ten to one recommended his appointment as a *privat dotsent* or lecturer, with a salary of one thousand rubles and a housing allowance of three hundred rubles a year. After he had successfully defended his thesis in January 1872, the academy unanimously named him a *dotsent* or assistant professor, with a salary of two thousand rubles and the same living allowance.

He taught at the academy from 1871 through 1906, except for 1902–1903, when he obtained leave to begin the *Course of Russian History.* His fame rests on his teaching at the university, but for thirty-five academic years he spent Mondays and Tuesdays at the academy, his first academic home and spiritual center. His long career on the faculty of a religious institution within a national shrine near Moscow provides concrete evidence of the important role that the entwined Church, religion, and nationalism played in his life and thought.

The academy during Kliuchevskii's early years on its faculty enjoyed a golden age. Changes introduced in 1870 brought a new spirit, an enlarged faculty, student body, and library, and prestige among Moscow intellectuals and in the Church. Gorskii's annual reports extolling the faculty's scholarly achievements resemble those of an American university president. The institution grew from 94 students in 1870 to 360 in 1888, but the Holy Synod decided in 1883 to reduce enrollment in all academies. It enrolled no more than 200 during the last fifteen years of Kliuchevskii's career. An average of 16 obtained M.A.'s in history or theology each year in the 1870s and 9 in the 1890s: he commented carefully upon 146 M.A. theses.[7]

Kliuchevskii taught a course on Russian civil history to second-year students, lecturing from eleven to one on Mondays and Tuesdays. A colleague, originally Father Evgenii E. Golubinskii, taught a parallel course on the early history of the Church, so Kliuchevskii concentrated upon the Church role in the "internal historical life of Russia," emphasizing the Church's helping the state to build civil order but not discussing the effect of state connections upon the Church. Later, he told Iurii Got'e that he paid less attention to the Church at the university than at the academy: perhaps he thought that university students were not interested in religious issues. Got'e, who helped edit the 1937 Soviet edition of the five-volume *Course*, noted that the pages on monasteries and Western influence on the religious schism were fuller and more detailed than were his university lectures. Perhaps Kliuchevskii recognized the imbalance and sought to correct it in the published version.[8]

Appointment at the academy enabled him to teach his favorite subject to classes of highly motivated students, many of whom audited each year they attended the institution. Their letters as alumni reflected appreciation, especially for his teaching them "to love Russian history." When the academy staged a two-day celebration in October 1896 to honor Kliuchevskii's twenty-fifth year of service, many former students, including several bishops, returned. One of his first students and the outstanding member of the 1896 class were among speakers at the dinner on the initial evening. The following day, students carried him from the monastery hotel to the auditorium for his class.

Academy salary and allowances were the same as those at the university, so Kliuchevskii had a secure and comfortable position after 1871. He became an associate professor in 1880 and a full professor in 1882. The academy allowed him to live in Moscow, teach on Monday and Tuesday, hold defenses Monday afternoon, and avoid administrative responsibilities: minutes of the Academic Council reveal that he rarely attended. He was able to leave Moscow on the 9:00 A.M. train from Iaroslavl' station on Mondays, return on the 5:00 P.M.

train on Tuesdays, remain close to his beloved libraries, archives, friends, and family, and accept other teaching appointments. The trip was pleasant, and the total cost each week, including a room in the older of the monastery's two hotels, was less than four rubles.

The greatest advantage, however, was that Kliuchevskii felt at home at "Trinity," or "S.P." He loved Moscow but enjoyed a respite each week and wrote and spoke with affection of Trinity. The monastery, one of Russia's richest, was a quiet religious and rural oasis, soaked in history since the fourteenth century. The monastery and academy libraries both held manuscript treasures: correspondence with the rector revealed that Kliuchevskii possessed several manuscripts in 1907 that the librarian had allowed him to take home in 1893. Above all, the monks, priests, and students shared his values and interests. The faculty, especially the historians and theologians, many of whom were highly educated, accepted him warmly and made Monday evening discussions a most pleasant part of his mature life.

One of his earliest and closest associates was Gorskii, whose erudition and personal qualities impressed Moscow intellectuals. Fifty-seven years old when they met, Gorskii had organized and catalogued the monastery and academy libraries. He had published five volumes of manuscripts from the Holy Synod Library, was well acquainted with the collections of the other Moscow libraries and archives, and held high standards for students and scholarship. His generosity toward the Old Believers, campaign against dogmatism, and insistence that faculty and students seek objectivity were positions that Kliuchevskii shared. They also agreed privately that the Church would benefit if it could separate itself from the state and reestablish the patriarchate.

Another member of the group was Golubinskii, five years older than Kliuchevskii and a physical symbol of monastery and academy history. His father had taught philosophy at Trinity from 1818 until his death in 1854. Golubinskii graduated that year and resided his entire life in the family apartment. He completed his doctorate in 1880 under Kliuchevskii's direction and as Kliuchevskii's first "student" occupied a special place in his affections.

Golubinski knew French and German well, recited French, German, and Russian poetry to support his views, greatly admired Gibbon's history of the Roman Empire, and was well informed concerning nineteenth-century Germany history and philosophy, especially Hegel. He haunted the same Moscow libraries and archives as Kliuchevskii, and his knowledge of Russian history, especially of the Church, was so great that many called him a "living library." Kliuchevskii's admiration of his resourcefulness in locating source materials and his critical analysis was widely shared. Golubinskii was elected a corresponding member of the Academy of Sciences in 1882, won its Uvarov Prize in 1888, and became a full member of the Academy in 1903. Pobedonostsev and the Holy Synod criticized his four-volume *History of the Russian Orthodox Church* until the middle of the sixteenth century for its overly skeptical analysis, but Soviet scholars praised the "bourgeois liberal Westerner" for the "wealth of factual information" he provided.

Kliuchevskii valued the generous, quiet, and modest gentleman as a vivid representative of the best of the past, a deeply conservative but tolerant, old-fashioned fundamentalist. He found in him many values that he admired in the clergy of ancient Russia. Evenings with him provided insight into the past that he could not obtain from manuscripts.

Two other men who helped make Sergiev Posad refreshing were students who became academy faculty members and able scholars. Kliuchevskii was especially close to Father A. P. Golubtsov, whose background resembled his own: his father had been a poor priest with five children in the countryside near Kostroma, and his mother was illiterate. Young Golubtsov had to walk one hundred miles to reach his seminary, and he suffered throughout his life from poor health. He was also brilliant: Kliuchevskii marveled at the clarity of his mind, Golubinskii awarded his senior thesis an A+, and Soviet scholars have shown respect for Golubtsov's erudition. His M.A. thesis was a splendid study of Orthodox-Catholic religious disputations in the middle of the seventeenth century, and his doctorate in 1899 was a four-volume study of the ecumenical *sobory* or councils. Kliuchevskii in 1898 nominated him for a position at the School of Painting, Sculpture, and Architecture, at which they both taught the last thirteen years of their lives. The two men were especially close in these years, and Golubtsov died just a week after Kliuchevskii.

Sergei I. Smirnov was perhaps Kliuchevskii's favorite among all the scholars he trained. An immensely intelligent but unassuming young man from Iaroslavl', Smirnov attracted attention because of his perspicacity and fluid and graceful writing. He became interested in subjects that occupied Kliuchevskii at the turn of the century: the clergy in ancient Russia and the influence that Christians gradually acquired over morals and attitudes toward justice. Smirnov's M.A. thesis on the clergy of ancient Russia and his doctorate both illustrated the Church's civilizing impact on ideas and ideals. Smirnov later became a Byzantinist, concentrating upon Byzantine educational and "social disciplinary" activity and moral outlook. Probably because the academy's treatment of Kliuchevskii in 1905 and 1906 so annoyed him and perhaps also because his own resolute criticism so angered the rector, he left the academy in 1908 to become a lecturer in the university history faculty. There he wrote a two-volume thesis on the clergy of ancient Russia, under the direction of Mikhail M. Bogoslovskii, a favored student of Kliuchevskii who succeeded his master at the academy and the university and considered Smirnov one of the most erudite men he had ever met. Smirnov's thesis won him the Academy of Science's Uvarov Prize in 1915, a year before he died in 1916 at age forty-six.

Kliuchevskii was a devout Muscovite. He loved the city and taught and wrote the history of his native land as a citizen of its old capital. He acquired renown as a professor at Moscow University, and his famous *Course of Russian History* blossomed from the lectures he gave there for more than thirty years. Moscow was central, but Trinity was just as important. For Kliuchevskii, "S.P.," the academy, and Trinity Monastery were as much a part of Moscow as they had been for more than six centuries. His commitment to Orthodoxy and research on *Lives of Saints* brought him to the academy, and his classes there constituted the foundation for the course at the university, much as his years at Trinity provided the intellectual and spiritual foundation for his fame. Sergiev Posad and Moscow, Church and state, past and present, were inseparable, intertwined parts of his life and scholarly work.

FIVE

The Breakthrough
The *Boyar Council*

Russian and foreign observers have all considered the years 1879–1881 critical in Russia's political history. Nechkina even termed them "the second revolutionary situation." The reaction of those in government and the informed public to the humiliating diplomatic defeat at the Congress of Berlin in 1878 so weakened the position of Alexander II that he appointed General Mikhail T. Loris-Melikov minister of the interior to establish a program to win support from the educated elite. The assassination of the once-popular tsar on March 1, 1881, and the accession of Alexander III led to a bleak period of reaction that contributed to fissures within the political public and the growth of radical and revolutionary forces.

These years were crucial in Kliuchevskii's career. In the summer of 1879, Soloviev learned that cancer of the liver would prevent his return to the university. Shortly after Soloviev's death on October 4, the superintendent of the educational district and the Ministry of Education approved the dean's and Academic Council's nomination of Kliuchevskii to the premier academic position in Russian history. On December 22, the council of the academy nominated him for associate professor, giving him two full-time positions (and salaries) and two part-time appointments as well. Thus, Kliuchevskii obtained a permanent base at Moscow University and economic security when he was thirty-eight years old.

Related to this achievement was a scholarly triumph. In its first issue in January 1880, *Russian Thought* published the first of a series of eleven articles by Kliuchevskii on the boyar council, an important state institution, especially in the fifteenth and sixteenth centuries. He revised and expanded these essays through the seventeenth century in a book published early in 1882 that received high approval and is still considered "the beacon guiding his successors."[1]

News of Kliuchevskii's nomination and appointment upset university students: his positions at the seminary and military school suggested that a conservative faculty and government were promoting an obscurantist. Some suggested protesting but decided to delay until after the first lecture, on November 28. Kliuchevskii, who termed such a talk "the most difficult in a professor's scholarly life," prepared with especial care. University and seminary faculty and students crowded the main auditorium to hear him follow tradition by describing and analyzing his predecessors' contributions. His artistry as a lecturer and the warmth with which he dedicated his life to continuing Soloviev's work made the lecture a stunning success, almost a sensation. That talk, an introduction to Russia before Peter the Great that continued where Soloviev had ended in the spring, and *Boyar Council* were turning points in his career, and to some extent in scholarship on Russian history.

On September 29, 1882, Kliuchevskii defended his doctoral thesis in the crowded auditorium. Tikhonravov, the rector; Count P. A. Kapnist, superintendent of the educational district; I. I. Krasovskii, the vice-governor; Chicherin, mayor of Moscow; several members of the Church hierarchy; professors from the university, seminary, and St. Petersburg University; hundreds of students, and other citizens attended. The students greeted Kliuchevskii's appearance with an ovation. His account, official critics' comments, and the learned discussion carried the session for four hours, and the applause lasted ten minutes. The editor of *Russian Antiquity* noted that he had not seen such an attentive audience in twenty-six years in Moscow, and assigned two reviews to the book. The weekly *Voice* declared, "Not for years, perhaps never, have the walls of our alma mater witnessed such noisy and unanimous enthusiasm as that with which the large audience of the public and students greeted the elevation of Mr. Kliuchevskii to the doctorate" and the rise of "an already established star of Russian science." Following the defense, the faculty unanimously nominated him for promotion to extraordinary or associate professor, and the academy made him a full professor.[2]

The subject that Kliuchevskii chose for his doctoral thesis, the boyar duma, was the council of high-ranking noblemen, serving men of the prince who filled special administrative needs as they arose and who in the fifteenth century became advisers on non-court affairs as well. Historians had concentrated upon the state's structure. For some, such as Karamzin, the state was Russia. Few had noted the existence of the complicated and almost invisible council. The boyar class was always small and the council's composition difficult to determine. Kliuchevskii noted that it lacked a chancery and archives and did not occupy an important place in historical records. Even the meaning of words used by and about the council lacked clarity, in part because boyars were practical administrators without clear ideas concerning political responsibilities.

In his view, the boyar class played an important role in the Kievan period from the tenth through the twelfth centuries, aiding the princes as administrative assistants, senior advisers, counselors, and military officers. The class gradually united with the local aristocracies in the prince's service. As popula-

Kliuchevskii, Moscow, 1895. Source: M. V. Nechkina, *Vasilii Osipovich Kliuchevskii. Istoriia zhizni i tvorchestva* (Moscow: Nauka, 1974).

tion and power shifted to the Moscow-Volga region, the boyars as large, independent landowners continued to serve the prince as free assistants. In Moscow in the fifteenth and sixteenth centuries, in which Russia became a centralized state, the one hundred boyar families who formed the highest rank of the service aristocracy and from which the tsar chose the council occupied the highest positions in the civil and military administration. In the seventeenth century, after the council had failed to use the Time of Troubles to increase its authority and establish limited government, it gradually lost the power it had shared with the prince or the tsar. Peter the Great abolished it when installing the Senate in 1711.

As reviewers and the faculty that approved his promotion recognized and the first readers appreciated, *Boyar Council* was a history of Russia from the tenth century to the empire under Peter. It emphasized the growth and operation of a central state institution with origins in Kiev that played a crucial role in the unification of Russia. It analyzed the role that interests and classes played in that development.

Kliuchevskii considered the council an invisible "administrative spring," the "flywheel that put the administrative mechanism into order."[3] In his view, it helped plan the economy, assess taxes, make personnel decisions, determine foreign policy, and wage war. It often reviewed and revised policies and sometimes made decisions in the tsar's absence. Above all, it helped establish order and unify the state, a point emphasized more strongly in the third edition than in the first or second. Even so, no one appreciated its role because "we see only its results."

This volume reflected his concentration upon economic and social interests, classes, and change. He did not mention the boyar council in the first quarter of the work, but instead described the background from which it rose. He was interested in the "social structure of administration," "social materials," and "concealed internal connections" that formed the system, rather than the state's structure. His description of the way in which the state administration operated in the seventeenth century is remarkably lucid. In modern American terms, he studied "state building," rather than the rise of Muscovy or the Russian political system or why that system was different from Western systems.

According to Kliuchevskii, the origins of Russia derived from the formation of armed merchant cities along the Dnieper and its tributaries. He compared the society that emerged to an organism, each river a spine in an organized neural system. The cities replaced the family, clan, and tribal organizations that had developed as the eastern Slavs in the sixth century moved from the Danube and then the eastern slopes of the Carpathian Mountains to the plains of the upper Dnieper in the seventh and eighth centuries. These armed themselves against the Pechenegs and other tribes that raided convoys engaged in trade with Byzantium. They formed regional centers ruled by a military-trading aristocracy, who called in the Varangians or Normans for defense. Thus, foreigners founded the Kievan state. Economic ties gradually became political foundations, uniting tribes and areas, and cities appeared prior to a princedom. The prince's council or *druzhina* from the beginning was a "necessary condition of good princely administration." The prince turned to the boyars for counsel or for administrative assistance for practical reasons. Cooperation was not a political right but was useful for both and survived from Kiev until the seventeenth century, although locations and vocabulary changed.

Kliuchevskii concentrated upon the boyar council in Kiev and northeastern Russia, thus defining the geographical areas he thought important. The Lithuanian pattern of administration was similar to that of Kiev and Muscovy until the fifteenth century. However, Novgorod and Pskov were outside the mainstream of Russian history and were of limited duration and significance. As work by Soviet and other scholars has shown, his account of these cities was one of the weakest parts of *Boyar Council*.

From the tenth through the twelfth centuries, the *veche*, the town meeting or general assembly, met in the Kievan principalities to choose a prince and decide all questions, including going to war. Merchants and capitalists created the institution, and the boyars were a separate military and administrative group that grew from the old city officers who ruled under the princes. With the arrival of the Mongols in the thirteenth century, the popular assembly declined rapidly, except in Novgorod and Pskov, where it dominated until Moscow annexed

Novgorod in 1478 and Pskov in 1510. There the merchant-capitalists did not develop a corps of serving landowners or a regular princely line. In a slow and gradual development over two or three centuries, about which Kliuchevskii did not provide much information, the prince became a hireling chairman of a group of city officials. The *veche* became an oligarchy, a rival to the council, an anarchistic, strident, sham democracy dominated by oligarchic families. Moreover, "the administration of free cities was generally not distinguished by simplicity" and produced "no exact order of things."[4] The council's functions and authority fluctuated but gradually declined because it was isolated from the prince and the elected representatives of the *veche* as well.

Kliuchevskii attributed the character of Novgorod and Pskov institutions to geographical location, which the coming of national unity discounted. His neglect of these cities and of an institution that many observers consider a nascent form of representative and democratic government suggests that he thought Moscow the inevitable successor state to Kiev, "the mother of the other cities of Russia," and autocracy the natural form of government after the sixteenth century. For him, Novgorod's loss of political independence was "a sacrifice that the general welfare of the land required."[5]

Curiously, *Boyar Council* provides almost no information concerning the gradual transfer of the center of political authority from Kiev to the northeast. The reader simply learns that this momentous change occurred, with no explanation and no account of migration or physical transfer of population. In appanage Russia, northeastern Russia or the Moscow–Upper Volga region from the thirteenth to the sixteenth centuries, the princely holdings or appanages (*udely*) were small and rural rather than relatively large and centralized, as in Kiev and in later Muscovite Russia. In Kliuchevskii's account, the history of administrative institutions during this period was therefore complicated. Successive divisions of princely possessions among male heirs converted some holdings into small districts in which the prince combined the functions of a ruler with those of a landowner. Often, the appanage was more a private manor than a political unit, so the appanage prince was "more seignior than sovereign."

Each prince possessed personal power only in his appanage and felt himself more an owner than a ruler. The boyar council of administrative aides became a court council in an administrative system that Kliuchevskii declared a copy of the old Kievan patrimonial estates. It was similar to that of later Muscovy, but in different circumstances. The boyar was a serving man of the prince, a court adviser on non-court affairs. Each boyar was able to choose and leave his prince. The appanage court was the primary seed from which all Muscovite administration grew and the base of Muscovite central administration.

The fifteenth and sixteenth centuries constituted Kliuchevskii's favorite period and the one about which he was best informed. According to him, Moscow continued the appanage administrative system. In a slow and unplanned way, the Moscow princes, aided by the boyar class, slowly formed the Great Russian state that included all the Great Russian people. From the fifteenth century, the prince ruled with his boyars, his court council, on court issues as well as non-court subjects. The boyar council in a way served as a natural and necessary link between prince (later tsar) and land. It began to see itself as the guardian who ruled the Russian land *with* the prince, who was never one of them. The princes were busy liberating lands from Mongols and fighting raiders in the south, so neither they nor the boyars had time for theories. Indeed, they lacked political consciousness. But the joint labors of the prince and an aristocratic administration led to an enlarged and unified state. After the 1550s, "the Moscow boyar council represented all the Russian land. It consisted of numerous families, the clan heads of which gathered in Moscow not just from all corners of Russia but even from those areas where Russia 'smelled weak.' "[6]

Gradually, the Moscow princes, later tsars, began to rule through a class of servants freely bound to them and to change the substance but not the form of the state. Service became a requirement because of external pressures and the drive to establish unity, and length of service became more important than genealogy. The administrative mechanism became increasingly certain and steady, bureaucratic, and "ordinary." For local and regional administrators over finance, diplomacy, and ever-growing lands, it also began to use men from families that had not contributed boyars. Two parallel groups of administrators thus grew, one of boyars and the other of clerks and bureaucrats. In the sixteenth century, the boyars sought release from service duties, and the latter gradually acquired responsibility and power.

After demonstrating that "the boyar council built the Moscow state order with their own hands, but not in their own interests," Kliuchevskii sought to determine why the boyar class had rejected the power it had used so effectively, gradually withered, and decayed. Why had the boyars simply wanted to remain the prince's advisers? Why had they constituted "an aristocracy without a taste for power"?[7] In substance, although he did not so indicate, he was interested in the reasons the boyar council did not lead to some form of shared or limited authority and why Russia became an autocracy.

Typically, his response was multicausal. The aristocracy were not conquerors or "triumphant warriors": they did not resemble aristocracies of the West, but had been conquered. The character, spirit, and attitude toward power of the descendants of William the Conqueror differed from those of Rurik, who were accustomed to being ruled rather than ruling.

In addition, the boyars, especially in Muscovy, where their powers slipped away, lived "under the tsar's hands," not on their estates. Their service responsibilities gradually required duty at the center, without the right to leave. The boyars became "free slaves" in a weak political, juridical, and moral position. As state power became more united, the boyars became simple serving citizens ever more distant from the village: "The sixteenth-century village was one of the main reasons the Moscow state was not aristocratic."[8]

The boyars did not possess a charter, chancellery, or archives. They lacked a sense of corporate solidarity and responsibility, as well as a leader. They had no inherited offices or positions, no sense of their interests or the nation's interests, no feeling that they constituted a group or an estate, as Western nobles did. Their power did not rest on possession or merit, their intellectual level was low, and they failed to develop a political philosophy or a plan for a state structure. Preoccupied with ancestors and interested in defining class relations rather than in advancement, they concentrated upon genealogical interests, intrigue, and freedom from service duties. As defense needs led the state to concentrate upon military strength, the boyars and their council became more observers than participants.

Finally, Kliuchevskii emphasized the role that colonization played in undermining the boyars. This theme, absorbed from Soloviev and central in the *Course of Russian History,* has greatly influenced the views of many scholars, Russian and foreign. Its corollary, Kliuchevskii's thesis that an economic crisis swept Muscovite Russia in the second half of the sixteenth century, was another seminal idea that later scholars have praised highly. Briefly, he concluded that gradual exhaustion of the land and oppressive taxation caused peasants to flee from the central areas to the south and southeast. This decreased the value of the boyars' privileges by depriving them of labor, eroding their position from below. It also blinded them to the weakening of their position from above until Ivan the Terrible attacked them with the *oprichnina,* a kind of private state, and was a primary cause of the Time of Troubles.

Kliuchevskii followed Soloviev in concluding that Ivan the Terrible's policies derived from his concern over the succession, rather than a struggle for power against an aristocratic group. Like many other scholars, he concluded that the supremely suspicious Ivan sought to destroy the boyars' authority by using a police state against those whom he considered seditious. The *oprichnina* was simply a development of established institutions. Neither side had any political ideas or prepared plan of state organization, and both recognized that they shared many interests. In short, in his view, Ivan's desire for power was personal. He did not intend to create new institutions, although he did recognize that the state's new needs and goals made a different political order and state organization essential. In the polished words of Kliuchevskii's later classic, the collision between Ivan and Kurbskii was one of "political moods, not modes of political thought."[9]

The Time of Troubles, especially the boyars' fumbling incompetence in trying to create an aristocratic state, was proof that his analysis was sound. It gave the boyars a temporary taste for power, and Vasilii Shuiskii briefly and futilely tried to establish a system in which the highest aristocrats would rule. However, the boyars and the council were so muddled and defensive about their interests as a class that they failed to create a state order acceptable to them. The people, not the boyars, conquered both anarchy and the Poles who tried to take advantage of it. The *zemskii sobor,* or assembly of the land, not the boyar council, was the instrument of recovery.

In the seventeenth century, the council slowly drifted into decay. It gradually lost its share of power and became a weapon in the hands of the tsar, the national leader of the united Russian people. After codification of the laws in 1649, it was only a consultative institution. Peter the Great abolished it as an administrative instrument, replacing it with a council of available advisers, a kind of council of ministers, that converted the tsar's decrees into law. Thus, an institution that had constituted "a basic fact of the history of the Moscow state" and had contributed to creating and directing that state faded into insignificance, replaced by forms that Peter the Great and his successors thoughtlessly borrowed from the West.

The *Boyar Council* is an impressive and powerful book, particularly as the doctoral thesis of a cautious and conservative man. It solidified Kliuchevskii's reputation as a scholar, not only in his time but for the future as well. It devised new methods of research and new conceptual approaches to a baffling institution on which evidence was available only in scattered bits. It made thoughtful judgments about an important class and institution that helped direct and administer an unwieldy state.

Kliuchevskii's account of the way in which Russian government operated for ten centuries rested upon analysis of the council personnel, "the building materials" and "social structure of administration," and relations between government and society. It modified and supplemented the views of Soloviev, Chicherin, and the state school. Some scholars consider it a declaration of independence from Soloviev, who had emphasized the state's vertical structure and neglected the people and social classes. Kliuchevskii denied that the volume was an attack upon the state or historic-juristic school, "of which I am one," but declared that all historical analysis is by nature revisionist and that he built upon earlier research, as all scholars do. However, for him "the building material is more important than the building itself." He was as interested in the people as in the state, especially in leading groups that expressed themselves as social classes, and he was the first Russian historian to emphasize classes and class interests.

Boyar Council concentrated upon the way institutions work, the slow manner in which families and family alliances rose and declined in authority, and the significance of population transfers, all he thought more difficult to analyze but more significant than leaders, reigns, and wars. He also emphasized economic, social, and institutional factors. His demonstration that economic factors play a central role in social and political development affected many others, especially the outstanding scholars he helped train and hundreds who attended his classes. Men as different as Petr Struve, a leading liberal intellectual, and Georgii V. Plekhanov, considered the first Russian Marxist, have testified that *Boyar Council* convinced them of the significance of economic factors before they heard of or read Marx. It contributed to the "climate of opinion" that led conservatives such as Liubavskii, liberals such as Miliukov and Kizevetter, and radicals such as Nikolai A. Rozhkov to emphasize economic and social forces in their analyses. It helped make Kliuchevskii a predecessor of the Marxist historians, some of whom, such as Rozhkov and Pokrovskii, he helped train.

Using the vast canvas of ten centuries, Kliuchevskii emphasized the role that historical forces and established institutions exercised upon the flow of the past: "History explains history." Institutions, values, customs, and traditions are far more important than individuals, decrees, or ideas. The people and their state are not the work of a handful of princes or tsars or the pressure of external forces but the result of a slow, undramatic, almost invisible organic development. In his judgment, many skilled observers had concluded from studying the state and its operations rather than its "structural materials" that innovation and reform existed where only modifications had occurred. He suggested instead that the origins of Russia's political institutions lay in Kiev and that later changes in the state's forms and practices were only nominal or technical. The appanage system of the fourteenth century was an exact copy of the old boyar *votchina*, and the Moscow state formed its central bureaus from "the administrative deposits" that had accumulated from earlier centuries. Ivan the Terrible's *oprichnina* was not a new instrument but the natural outgrowth of an institution that had matured during the sixteenth century. Similarly, Peter's changes had deep roots in the past. Using instruments, people, and ideas from the boyar council, he introduced minor modifications in the seamless web of history to meet changing circumstances.

So many scholars have relied upon *Boyar Council* in their research, analyzed it, accepted some judgments, and disagreed with other insights that its historiography would constitute a major enterprise. Those who have built upon it have enjoyed access to far more primary source material than he. They also benefit from his preliminary work when they examine issues to which he could devote only fleeting attention, and they have devised new research techniques and methodologies. Nevertheless, *Boyar Council* remains a respected basic book.

One source of lively controversy has been Kliuchevskii's conclusion that the council was active in Kievan Russia, supporting his thesis that the origins of the Russian state and people lay in Kiev, not Moscow, and that Ukrainians and Belorussians were Russians. Many argue instead that the council appeared only in the fourteenth century. Kliuchevskii also neglected a number of issues or factors that later historians have included. Thus, he did not examine any impact that Byzantine practices and administrative traditions exercised. He did not mention serfdom. He ignored the Church, except for a short chapter introduced into the third edition in 1902. The Mongols play no role, and he barely mentioned Poland-Lithuania. These factors were absent from most of his analyses. He knew little about Byzantium. Serfdom became a central research issue for him only in the 1880s. He did not refer to it in the *Boyar Council,* because he found its origins in the sixteenth century. He paid little attention to the Mongols, the Church, and religion in any major work after the early 1870s.

The subjects that most aroused his contemporary critics and Soviet scholars were his view on the origins of the Kievan state and his conclusion that the boyar council shared power with the prince or tsar. This second judgment led some scholars to infer that he found the seeds of constitutional government in the council.

His statements on the founders of Kiev were typically cautious: he emphasized that no one could determine scientifically which theory of the early Slavs' life was correct. After summarizing the evidence and interpretations, he concluded that the founders of the Kievan state were Norman, Varangian armed merchants engaged in commerce, not Slavic agriculturalists who had moved into the fertile Dnieper valley from the eastern slopes of the Carpathians.

Many materials discovered later support the Normanist thesis. On the other hand, some Soviet scholars accumulated evidence to sustain the view that the founders of the first eastern Slav state were Slavs. Boris Grekov in particular contended that Kliuchevskii exaggerated the role of trade in the formation of the Kievan state. Instead, he collected vast quantities of information to demonstrate that agriculture was central in the Kievan economy and that the founders of Kiev were basically agriculturalists. This is an important point in the Marxist interpretation of history: the establishment of a state in the ninth or tenth century by a class of armed merchants would destroy one of the symmetries central to the Marxist faith.

Some Russian and Soviet scholars have concluded that *Boyar Council* was a veiled criticism of the autocracy and advocacy of limited government. Most Western specialists agree, seeing Kliuchevskii as a secret constitutionalist who preferred constitutional government to the autocracy and used this book as a weapon. Ironically, Russian observers since 1987 have reasserted this theme and lavished praise upon him as a "liberal." Thus, Konstantin Kedrov in *Izvestiia* in January 1988 termed him "Our Contemporary," a product of the 1860 reforms who opposed the autocracy and recognized that "the establishment of freedom is the eternal, unceasing process of history." *Boyar Council* was "a manifestation of relatively independent political thought."

In the 1890s, Vasilii I. Sergeevich, a St. Petersburg professor, stated that Kliuchevskii suggested that the council limited the tsar's power. Almost a century later, an American specialist, Robert O. Crummey, added that Kliuchevskii's eagerness to find limits on arbitrary power and identify roots of wide participation in state affairs affected his choice of source material. Crummey contended instead that the prince and tsar used the council as an advisory group only when they chose, and that the council possessed no administrative or other authority.

In her massive study, Nechkina described Kliuchevskii as a "bourgeois liberal" who wrote the *Boyar Council* as an argument for constitutional government under the influence of the 1879–81 crisis. In her view, he interpreted the council as "a constitutional institution" that exercised wide political influence in the fifteenth and sixteenth centuries, ruled jointly with the tsar, and legislated. In the interregnum during the Time of Troubles, it served as a temporary government and concluded a pact limiting Shuiskii's authority before he assumed the throne.

Nechkina also charged, with some plausibility, that Kliuchevskii modified his views, or at least his expression of them, after Alexander III became ruler. Thus, she suggested that he omitted from the book the "liberal" preface published in *Russian Thought* in January 1880 because the political temperature under Alexander III made it dangerous. In addition, she noted that two undated draft prefaces in his archives were more forthright in their criticism of the nobility ("its history is the history of a social disease") than was the published preface. Similarly, he did not mention the council's constitutional character when defending his thesis in September 1882, eighteen months after Alexander II's death. Instead, he described the volume as a history of the council's role in forming and administering the state.

Boyar Council is an account of eight hundred years of Russian history through analysis of one institution, not a tract implying that the council provided the historic base for constitutional government. It described Russia in the fifteenth and sixteenth centuries as "an absolute monarchy with an aristocratic administration." The tsar ruled Russia *with* the council, the members of which were important officials and landowners to whom he turned for advice on occasions he chose. The council cooperated with the prince or the tsar in administering the country as a useful middleman between the ruler and people. It acted with the tsar, under his actual or nominal chairmanship, and without him when he was absent. The ruler's obligation to serve the general welfare was a primary restriction against absolutism, and he also shared power with the boyar council. In short, Russia had been an autocratic state, but not absolute. Its government was not representative or democratic. However, "society," by which he meant the boyars through the sixteenth century and an indefinable ever-growing group in later periods, participated, not in the Western sense and certainly not through universal or even limited elections. Instead, those shared authority who exercised functions of importance.

Full discussion concerning Kliuchevskii's judgment of the autocracy's place in his definition of Russia and of its role in Russian history occurs in chapter 12. However, analysis of those works that describe *Boyar Council* as a political treatise or as advocacy of constitutional government for Russia will serve as an introduction to his goals and qualities as a historian. It will also shed light upon the conditions in which he worked. In addition, it will testify to the consistency of his judgment that the autocracy had been and remained at that time a "natural and necessary" system of rule for Russia.

Like many, perhaps most, historians who work in societies much freer than Russia in the last third of the nineteenth century, Kliuchevskii sought to determine what had happened by thorough analyses of all primary materials available and to describe it clearly and accurately. He also believed firmly that neither one's political views nor one's philosophy of history had a place in historical scholarship. Endorsing or advocating particular systems of rule or policies, applying theories to the past or future, and participation in governance were totally inappropriate. The historian should try to understand other peoples and other times. He should describe, not praise or condemn.

Kliuchevskii was not entirely successful in his efforts: no historian is, perhaps most especially those who claim that they are scientific. But his grade was high. All observing him should follow his injunction and try to recognize that his judgments, made in different circumstances in much different times, were objective, and to separate his views of Russia's past from others' political recommendations. None of us will succeed, as he did not.

Review of *Boyar Council* and the circumstances in which he completed and published his essays and book seems to suggest that those who conclude that Kliuchevskii was discreetly advocating constitutional rule were correct. Thus, the years in which Kliuchevskii completed, published, and defended his thesis did not constitute a time in which a Russian could discuss political ideas freely, in particular advocate a constitutional or limited form of government. Except for passage of the military reform of 1874, which Kliuchevskii late in life praised almost as highly as the abolition of serfdom, the period during which he did research on the boyar council was bleak for those who hoped that Alexander II would resume the reform program. Defenders of the old system became increasingly vocal as government and society drifted apart. Russia's failure in international politics further discouraged those who hoped for reform. Military victory in the Balkan Wars, the apparent diplomatic victory achieved in the Treaty of San Stefano, and the humiliating loss of most gains at the Congress of Berlin in 1878 increased antagonisms in the court and among others interested in domestic and international politics. However, appointment of Loris-Melikov as the tsar's principal adviser created rumors in 1879 and 1880 that the general might propose an advisory council. This led to sanguine expectations that Alexander would establish a system that would close the gap between the ruler and the leading elements of society. The assassination of Alexander II on March 1, 1881, and Alexander III's establishment of repressive policies ended the sanguine period and produced a long era of repression.

Kliuchevskii completed the *Boyar Council* during the final hopeful months of Alexander II's reign, published sections before the assassination on March 1, 1881, revised it as a book during the early months of Alexander III, and defended it eighteen months after reaction had begun. His essays on the council appeared between January 1880 and September 1881 in *Russian Thought*, a new journal that became popular with "liberals" and radicals. Its founder, Sergei A. Iur'ev, was a respected liberal. Viktor A. Gol'tsev, editor from 1885 until his death in 1906, was "a true knight of constitutionalism" throughout that period, and a member of the Kadet or Constitutional Democratic Party when he died. The journal published articles by leading proponents of constitutional government, such as Sergei A. Muromtsev and Kovalevskii. Lenin read it in the 1890s, commented upon some Kliuchevskii articles there, and submitted a manuscript to it for publication in 1893. The police and conservatives considered it "tendentious" and even seditious. Police files contain occasional reports on Kliuchevskii because he knew its editors well and published more articles in it after 1880 than in any other journal. Irate opponents of change were especially upset by an essay by someone other than Kliuchevskii in the February 1881 issue that declared that Russia must proceed beyond abolition and other reforms to the rule of law: "Without freedom of the individual, without freedom of conscience, without freedom of speech, the fruits of civil freedom are unthinkable."

Additional evidence supports the imputation that the ordinarily prudent historian was more critical of the autocracy and supportive of change before Alexander II's assassination than after. At the end of the traditional introductory lecture on his predecessor on December 5, 1879, Kliuchevskii declared Peter the Great's reforms of limited significance because the tsar did not comprehend that "Russia must become free if it is to become wealthy and powerful." A week later, he forwarded the first two articles on the council to the editor of *Russian Thought*. A January 12, 1880, talk on Tat'iana Day, the university's principal holiday, noted that Soloviev had termed study of the autocracy one of archeology, even paleontology, not history. Moreover, Soloviev had said that enlightenment led to self-knowledge. In Kliuchevskii's view, such understanding "must lead to independent action." Three days later, his first article condemned the efforts Russians had made for more than two centuries to introduce foreign forms. It suggested that Russia's leaders consider establishing "a constitutional laboratory" to study ways of using modified early Russian institutions, such as the council, to bridge the chasm separating government and society and fortify the contemporary reform effort. He eliminated this proposal from the book published just two years later, after the assassination of Alexander II.

No one can read the *Boyar Council* and its account of the sharing of power between the prince and the council without concluding that Kliuchevskii did have a benevolent attitude toward limited government. However, neither before nor after the tsar's assassination did Kliuchevskii use his articles or the book to advocate that Russia establish constitutional government or adapt other Western institutions: Instead, consistently in all his work, he counseled that Western institutions were inappropriate and even absurd to Russia. He urged that Russians seeking improvement consider native instruments that had served well when the state was "an absolute monarchy with an aristocratic administration," an autocracy behind a facade. The ruler's powers were limited only by the need to share authority with officials, who never sought privileges or attempted to establish representative institutions. The system helped ensure the nation's survival, independence, and reunification in a hostile world. When the boyar council failed to respond effectively in the Time of Troubles, the assembly of the land, not a foreign institution, rallied the country. In sum, Russians should learn from history and improve institutions and practices that had served well in the past.

PART TWO

The Moscow University Professor

SIX

A Professor's Life

The lives of academicians ordinarily attract little interest. Kliuchevskii was no exception. As Platonov wrote, "One could say that he had no 'biography'; all his life took place in Moscow, with books and manuscripts, reading lectures and working in his study."[1] His only interest was "the work of my life, Russian history," but his professional qualities and account of Russian history attracted thousands into interest in history and created a sense of Russian nationhood. To comprehend the magnitude of this achievement, one must understand the institutional arrangements in which he worked, quite different from those with which Americans are familiar, and the circle of friends and colleagues of the community in which he "swam like a fish."

Although some earlier Russian rulers promoted education to strengthen the nation, few nineteenth-century leaders supported this policy. The French Revolution and Napoleonic wars persuaded even the most conservative rulers that the state must train a small number for its bureaucracy and army, but also that expanding education would endanger established values and institutions. They sought enlightenment and advancement but not the critical attitude at their base, because they recognized a dilemma that has tormented authoritarian states in the twentieth century. In the words of Uvarov, "They wanted education without danger, i.e., a fire that will not burn."

When Kliuchevskii arrived in Moscow, Russia had only six state universities with a total enrollment of 4,000 students. When he joined the faculty in 1879, the number of universities had grown to nine and that of students to somewhat more than 8,100. When he died, universities registered 34,000 students, of whom 9,000 were in Moscow. Technical institutions, special programs for women, new commercial schools, and Russia's first private university doubled that figure. Even so, Kliuchevskii was a member of an elite group in a system of higher education inadequate for Russia's population and role in the world. The United States, for example, had 355,000 students enrolled in 1911.

Among the changes introduced in Alexander II's early years, the 1863 statute on education expanded modestly the six universities, opened admission to talented young men from outside the aristocracy and the higher levels of the bureaucracy, increased faculty salaries, and added the rank of *dotsent* or assistant professor. The state allowed instruction in political economy and European history. It also granted the universities more self-government, but not autonomy or independence. Ministry of Education officials retained jurisdiction over the student body, which the faculty did not want, as well as censorship of publications and observation of classes. It also preserved authority over appointments and promotions, although it allowed the faculty to submit nominations.

In 1884, the state tightened controls. The ministry acquired authority to appoint administrators and faculty directly. It restricted admission through the "cooks' children" ruling and restored the requirement that students wear uniforms. Finally, it removed the fiction of faculty autonomy, intervened in one of the faculty's most cherished functions, determining the curriculum, and even exercised the right to inspect course content. Thus, the university had required that each student in the History-Philology Faculty complete the two-year survey course of Russian history that Soloviev had introduced and Kliuchevskii continued, and that law students take one year of that sequence. The 1884 statute made history a "secondary subject," reduced the course to one year, and required it only of History-Philology students. Enrollment in that faculty declined by 30 percent from 1884 through 1887, one of the ministry's goals, and in 1899 constituted only 3.9 percent of the university total. Kliuchevskii, his colleagues, and most students accepted these changes and other such actions because they considered scientific learning Russia's best hope for political and social progress.[2]

In spite of the restrictions, Russian universities before the First World War produced scholarship of high quality in a number of fields of study, including history. But some scholars whom controls irritated withdrew into inactivity and "internal migration." Others sought refuge in an ivory tower. Still others, such as Chicherin and Vinogradov, resigned or were discharged.

Kliuchevskii joined the academic profession because his interest in learning and teaching was as intense as that of Dostoevsky in writing or of Repin in painting and because he considered that increasing his countrymen's knowledge of their history would renew the sense of national unity that had begun to wane in the seventeenth century. Even as an undergraduate, he recognized that most Russians were indifferent to their history and "were only beginning to understand our past." Moreover, "the yoke of the political and moral humiliation" of the Crimean War and the Treaty of Paris were mainly responsible for even that feeble start. "Calamity much more than books teaches a people history," for men "seek to understand how and why changes have occurred" only in troubled times. "History equals power. When it is good to people, they forget about it and ascribe prosperity to their own actions; when things go badly, they begin to feel the need of understanding the past."[3]

Kliuchevskii chose to satisfy his purposes as a scholar by discovering the

A Professor's Life

Kliuchevskii lecturing at the School of Painting, Sculpture, and Architecture. Painting by L. O. Pasternak, 1909. (Among the students is the artist's nineteen-year-old son, Boris Pasternak.) Source: M. V. Nechkina, *Vasilii Osipovich Kliuchevskii. Istoriia zhizni i tvorchestva* (Moscow: Nauka, 1974).

reasons for Russia's unique development and communicating his knowledge widely to formal students of all kinds and anyone who could listen or read. Even as a young man, he concluded that an instructor should combine two functions in one as scholar-teacher. He should advance science toward understanding the general laws of history, which he did not attempt to define, by the "separate study of Russian history." Above all, he should encourage everyone to understand his nation's past in order to make Russia a nation as well as a state. The course on methodology added that knowledge of other societies, even India, would help a Russian to understand his country and identify ways to improve it. A lecture at the School of Painting, Sculpture, and Architecture in 1897 declared history an art and that "the highest good of art is to improve man . . . for beauty is a servant of virtue." In a more homely fashion, Kliuchevskii compared history to a stomach ache: awareness of pain creates interest in a cure. Analysis of the "laws of a local society's movements, that is, its mechanics, can teach how best to avoid mistakes and to build a better society." People should understand the reasons for their country's failings, just as a runner who falls examines the terrain so he will not stumble again or a doctor examines a patient to determine the causes and cures of an ailment. In sum, a historian helps create national consciousness and the sense of community fundamental for a nation's progress.

Kliuchevskii's dedication to making Russia a nation also had origins in the service creed of Granovskii, who helped create a community of European-trained men devoted to serving their country and science by teaching and research. Soloviev strengthened the Granovskii dedication to national service and appreciation for those who had preserved records. He sought to lift Russian historical scholarship to the standards of Europe and to raise national consciousness by describing the Russian past as a whole, rather than by writing monographs on one period or theme.

Kliuchevskii considered himself a member of the knightly order of Granovskii, whom he revered as a seeker of truth, servant of science, teacher, and lecturer. Granovskii's commitment to duty to society, not the state, was such that Kliuchevskii termed him a saint, "the prototype of the ideal professor" and "a symbol of social resurrection."

Kliuchevskii had a profound appreciation for the historical profession's unsung heroes, those who compiled chronographs and chronicles, collected materials, and organized libraries and archives. They were part of a great chain dedicated to educating and uniting their people: an architect designs a building, but many workers construct it. Public lectures and essays on scholars and scholarship emphasized the continuities of Russia's past and the need to honor all those who nourished a knowledge of history. Perhaps the most revealing essay concerning this quality was his review of a volume describing the manuscripts that V. M. Undol'skii had collected during his short life (1815–1864). A staff member of the archives of the Ministries of Foreign Affairs and Justice and a volunteer librarian for the Society of Russian History and Antiquity, Undol'skii had also organized and catalogued the manuscripts in the Holy Synod Library and begun the same task in the Rumiantsev Museum. While an undergraduate, Kliuchevskii had come to know and value him: few libraries then had descriptions of their holdings.

Undol'skii never earned more than 750 rubles a year. He lived in an unheated apartment and ate only two meals a day in order to purchase prized manuscripts. Yet he collected 1,348 manuscripts, including 110 lives of saints, more than 900 early Church registry volumes, and 1,422 other volumes, a library for which the Rumiantsev Museum in 1866 paid his heirs 25,000 rubles. The essay tells us much concerning Kliuchevskii, who described Undol'skii in loving detail as a quiet hero, one of the "good people," a selfless laborer who served Russia, just as did a monk, a peasant on the frontier, or a ruler.

I. N. Boltin, a dedicated collector and amateur historian in the reign of Catherine the Great, to whom Kliuchevskii devoted a quarter of his lectures on historiography, was another particular favorite. He lauded Boltin's effort to produce a coherent account of all Russian history. But he particularly approved of his insistence that Russians understand the origins and nature of human societies and institutions, especially their own: "The eternal goal of the study of national history is strengthening the moral principles of Russian life." Russians could understand themselves only when "the direction and purpose of our past are part of our national consciousness and when that has become a basic part of people's thinking," when one generation transfers knowledge to another through children's sayings and the lessons that mothers and nurses transmit. "Our history is still relegated to archival shelves, and we have only begun to move from these depositories to scholars' work tables. Far to go."[4]

For Kliuchevskii, Moscow and the university were intertwined and formed the world's intellectual center. However, neither he nor his associates felt the affection for the university that an American faculty member, especially an alumnus or alumna, usually possesses. Instead, service to "science" and society through teaching was central: the university was only an instrument. Moreover, he was more comfortable at the academy than at the university and showed more warmth toward it than toward his alma mater, principally because the university was controlled by the Ministry of Education. In addition, the institution provided none of the facilities, even offices, lounges, or dining room, that might have made it an intellectual and social center. Like his colleagues, he prepared lectures and wrote essays and books at home, coming to the institution briefly only to teach.

A civil servant, Kliuchevskii was not active in the efforts to acquire greater faculty authority or introduce instructional changes. Moreover, teaching in other institutions weakened his loyalty. He spent every Monday and Tuesday in Sergiev Posad. Until 1883, he taught three hours Wednesday mornings at the military school, from which he walked to the university nearby. From 1872 until 1888, he taught in the Women's Higher Courses, usually on Wednesday afternoons. After 1898, he spent Friday afternoons in the School of Painting, Sculpture, and Architecture. Thus, the university was his main institutional base after 1879, but it was one of several competing for his time, energy, and affection.

Kliuchevskii attended the Academic Council only when student disturbances created problems. He was dean of the History-Philology Faculty from September 1887 until March 1889 and pro-rector of the university until December 1890, when the rector accepted his plea for early release. In these positions, he was basically a clerk, arranging schedules for classes and examinations, reviewing rules for the library, and considering student applications to transfer from one faculty to another. Late in the 1890s, he served on a committee that discussed construction of student dormitories, and in 1901 he was an active secretary of a faculty committee appointed to study student unrest. Actually, his most visible and important extra services were memorial talks he gave for men such as Soloviev, Buslaev, and Tikhonravov and addresses at university ceremonies honoring Pushkin and other luminaries.

For Kliuchevskii, the university meant lecturing to large numbers of students taking notes assiduously in a hushed and crowded auditorium. He taught five hours each week at the university when he was an administrator and six at other times. The survey of Russian history was his favorite, one he taught in modified form in the Women's Higher Courses, at the academy, and at the art school as well. Ordinarily, this class at the university met twice a week for two hours. It enrolled about four hundred students, but many more audited, so the largest university auditorium was always full. The advanced classes for juniors, seniors, and graduate students attracted two hundred, although he devoted them to highly specialized subjects, such as the code of 1550, terminology, methodology, estates, and historiography. Graduate students ordinarily attended this rich course two or three times.

Faculty members, like Soviet scholar-teachers later, were carefully selected senior civil servants and members of a closed guild. Although many by 1900 were dissatisfied, they were among the economic elite after the 1863 statute raised salaries and provided casualty and disability insurance, generous pensions, and survivors' benefits. After thirty years of service, they received a pension identical to their salaries, plus an additional 1,200 rubles a year if they continued to teach. Senior members chose and trained their successors: each could nominate an undergraduate senior whom he thought qualified for the professoriate, obtain a state scholarship for a year or two, and launch the young man toward an academic career.

As a youngster in Penza, penurious undergraduate, graduate student, young husband and father, and honored senior professor, Kliuchevskii had a profound concern about money, one that his wife and their son shared. After 1871 he taught at two, three, and even four institutions simultaneously because he enjoyed lecturing and considered it a public service, but also because he felt insecure economically. He was as upset to pay three rubles fifty kopeks in 1905 for a hotel room in St. Petersburg, even though the state reimbursed him, as he had been to spend five kopeks in 1865 for a bun for lunch. He was forever frugal, walking rather than taking a trolley or cab, traveling to and from Sergiev Posad in a third-class coach, dressing simply, and wearing old clothes when he worked at home. With reluctance he acquired a frock coat when he tutored the Grand Duke Georgii Aleksandr. He purchased a home only in 1895, using the 3,600 rubles he received for each of the two periods he tutored. The Kliuchevskiis enjoyed many dinners and parties in friends' homes, as well as summers in friends' dachas. The only references to the Kliuchevskiis' entertaining are informal seminars and occasional invitations to members of the Society of Russian History and Antiquity to the their home after meetings. The Kliuchevskiis did not own or rent a dacha.

Appointment papers, university annual reports, university and academy archives, miscellaneous letters, and the Kliuchevskii account book from 1888 through part of 1898 together enable one to determine with some confidence his income from teaching and total income for the final twenty-five years of his life. Income from his academic appointments rose from 1,000 rubles for 1868–

71 to 2,800 for 1872–78, 7,600 for 1885–88, 7,900 for 1888–91, and 9,100 for 1901 through 1906, when it declined to 6,100. But university teaching produced other income. From 1884 until 1901, he received a ruble for each student enrolled in his courses. The account book, which is not complete for any year, reveals that he obtained at least 400 rubles annually from this source. However, his classes were always full, and in 1894 he received more than 1,100 rubles, so complete accounting would no doubt raise the average addition to at least 1,000 rubles. He received an additional 600 rubles when he served as dean of his faculty in 1887 and 1888, and 1,500 rubles annually the following two years, when he was pro-rector.

Books added substantial royalties. He received several hundred rubles each year in royalties from *Boyar Council,* even ten years after publication of the first two editions of 1,000 volumes each. In December 1888, he received 70 rubles 40 kopeks and in November 1891, 100 rubles from the book on saints' lives published in 1871.

Public lectures were another source of income. The account book records that he received 490 rubles in December 1889, probably for talks at celebrations the university organized. Russian journals paid authors for articles, and Kliuchevskii produced more than sixty after 1880. He received 423 rubles for the series of three essays on the assembly of the land published between 1890 and 1892. The following year, *Educational Herald* offered a hundred rubles for an essay. *Questions of Philosophy and Psychology* paid forty rubles for each proof sheet or typographical unit of his essay "Western Influence in the Seventeenth Century." This filled eighty-four pages in three issues, so Kliuchevskii received approximately 2,000 rubles for that paper.

He also collected royalties from the outline that he began to publish in 1899. The *Course of Russian History* almost certainly produced the largest royalties of any Russian scholarly work during his lifetime. Unfortunately, no figures have survived. The first volume in 1904 sold 10,000 copies within a month and reached its fourth edition of 10,000 in 1910. Three other volumes appeared before he died, the second in three editions. Boris, who began service as his father's research assistant in the 1890s and became an energetic and effective business manager, made the Kliuchevskii home on Zhitnaia Street a center for distributing it and reprints of other publications, so Kliuchevskii acquired a substantial amount of money annually from these sales.

Other sources provided additional income. The state paid a thousand rubles and expenses for participation in the 1905 Peterhof meetings. He probably received a similar fee for serving on a commission to review censorship regulations. The account book reveals that the Kliuchevskiis received at least 1,200 rubles in interest from stocks and other property each year from 1888 through 1898, and presumably from some years before 1888 and after 1898. Thus, his annual income as a teacher-lecturer-writer-rentier during the last twenty-five years of his life was at least 10,000 rubles and probably substantially more: the apparently complete record for 1890 was 10,301, and his income was almost certainly higher after that. Average wages in Moscow at the turn of the century were 300 rubles a year. In 1906, 72.1 percent of civil servants received less than 2,000 rubles, 25.3 percent obtained from 2,000 to 5,000, and only 2 percent received more than 5,000. Kliuchevskii was therefore a most prosperous man.

Moscow University during Kliuchevskii's lifetime was barely larger than many American colleges a century later. It enjoyed a central location near the Kremlin, leading archives and museums, the main theaters, and concert halls. It was at the edge of the comfortable, bucolic section in which merchant families such as the Morozovs, senior bureaucrats such as Pobedonostsev, respected old families such as the Aksakovs, and many faculty members—but not Kliuchevskii—lived. The institution and its faculty enjoyed splendid isolation from the state administration, the social groups surrounding it, and the remote worlds of factories, workers, and peasants. After the mid-1870s, Ger'e and other civic-minded scholars gradually opened a breach in this wall by election to the Moscow City Council and work in public service programs. In the last two decades of Kliuchevskii's life, Miliukov, Kizevetter, and other members of their generation helped form political groups. Even Kliuchevskii began to leave the shelter occasionally, as the famine, the drive against illiteracy, tutoring the Grand Duke Georgii Aleksandr, and new intellectual interests engaged him. His acquaintance with Fedor Chaliapin, meeting Serov, Leonid Pasternak, and other artists at the art school, and encounters in the highest levels of the St. Petersburg administration in 1905 brought him outside the university circle briefly. However, he was never close to the government or in the "ministerial group." In short, the university formed a restricted intellectual and social community. His close family life and weekly visits to Sergiev Posad formed other closed "islands." This isolation deeply affected his definition of Russia and the world and his conception of history.

His protected existence had a number of other origins, the most important of which was his nature as a loner and his intense dedication to his craft. In addition, while Russia's rulers, the university administration, and the faculty considered the university an important institution for instruction, none of them thought it an intellectual center or wanted it to be one. Students could enter the two buildings only with a pass. Guards on occasion even made Kliuchevskii identify himself. The university offered no public lectures, and the governor-general's permission was necessary for open lectures elsewhere. The conservatory was nearby but was an independent institution. The Bolshoi and Malyi theaters were less than a mile distant but had no connections with the university. Neither the university nor any other educational institution provided plays, choral performances, or athletic contests that might have brought town and gown together.

Even in the capital cities, faculty members were so few in number that they had no corporate or estate sense and created few organizations, even clubs. No relations existed with scholars in other cities, and organizations such as the

Moscow Archeological Society that brought academics and amateur scholars together remained few and small after they appeared in the 1860s.

Moreover, they considered themselves members of a special class, even caste. With some noisy exceptions, they were servants of science and seekers of truth, not intellectuals who assumed competence to advise or lead society on contemporary issues. A few wrote occasional articles for the so-called "thick journals," but these essays were not devoted to current issues and certainly not to state policies.

The university's neighbors and other educated Muscovites appreciated and respected the faculty and the luster it brought the community, but considered the university a closed institution, walled off from society. Moreover, Moscow's journalists, writers (such as Tolstoy), artists, and intellectuals paid little attention to the university in an arrangement of mutual indifference. With few exceptions, intellectuals maintained their own circles, as scholars did, at least until the barriers began to crumble at the turn of the century.

Even the new scholarly organizations were closed corporations. Their small membership consisted largely of faculty, graduates employed in other educational institutions, libraries, and archives, and a handful of learned collectors and amateur scholars. They did not serve Moscow or the nation, except in a precious, antiquarian sort of way, important though that was. Moreover, each university was part of a regional educational district under a superintendent appointed by the Ministry of Education. It had vertical ties with the ministry but no relationships with other universities.

Each university replaced retiring members and expanded its faculty by appointing men whose undergraduate and advanced instruction it had provided. Thus, Kliuchevskii and his colleagues had received their degrees from Moscow University. In some cases, they had graduated from the same high school, and in many cases they had known each other from their undergraduate years. Those who taught history at the university when he died in 1911, as well as those who taught at other Moscow institutions of higher learning and high schools and staffed the libraries, archives, and museums, were Moscow University graduates.

In spite of his talents and reputation, Kliuchevskii never presented a talk at St. Petersburg University or any institution outside of Moscow and Sergiev Posad. There is no evidence that the university invited visitors to give lectures: each institution was an island unto itself and limited instruction to regular classes. Kliuchevskii knew well the publications of K. N. Bestuzhev-Riumin, the specialist in Russian history in St. Petersburg, who had studied at Moscow University with Soloviev, but there is no evidence that they met or corresponded. Kliuchevskii became an acquaintance and then a friend of Bestuzhev-Riumin's successor, Sergei F. Platonov, a scholar known especially for his research on the Time of Troubles, only after he served on a committee that awarded Platonov an Academy of Sciences prize in 1890. Except for Platonov, his only tie with the capital was Nikolai P. Barsukov, whom he met when Barsukov joined the staff of the Holy Synod archives in 1870. After Barsukov became archivist of the Ministry of Education in St. Petersburg in 1883, Kliuchevskii and "my Petersburg correspondent" exchanged information about scholarly matters, especially the location of documents.

None of the men and women closely associated with Kliuchevskii was a Samuel Pepys or Boswell. Dozens of memoirs about him and his diary, correspondence, and essays about friends provide abundant evidence about his work habits and intellectual and social circles, which professional colleagues dominated, but little about his inner life. In some ways, he saw himself as an outsider because of his Penza background, early poverty, and concern with financial security. Moreover, he was a reserved, skeptical, and often melancholy person who maintained an invisible barrier against friends and associates. After a half-century in Moscow, his home, dress, and style of life were those of a rural priest who had somehow become a learned professor. His total commitment to learning and disinterest in travel abroad also set him aside. From the time he married, he lived in a merchant and manufacturing section of the city, across the river from the university and his colleagues. His acquaintanceship with immediate neighbors and knowledge of merchants and workers were minimal, and he was not even close to his parish priest. Small gatherings of three distinct groups of friends, the priest-scholars at the academy, the Borodins and Karpovs, and a small circle of university faculty constituted the core of his social life.

A workaholic, Kliuchevskii ordinarily engaged in teaching and research, writing, and rewriting sixteen hours a day, working at a small desk in his study, in which he slept. Summer provided an opportunity to work without interruption until late afternoon, when he enjoyed walking in the countryside with his son, his dog, and friends who were interesting conversationalists. On such occasions, he tested *bons mots* and aphorisms and often became as lively and stimulating as in the classroom. He had little interest in the outside world, and read Moscow newspapers irregularly. His hobbies were those of a solitary man and included few games. Instead, he enjoyed listening to music, attending plays, gardening, and fishing—not hunting, which he considered a destructive sport of the nobles.

The only organizations that Kliuchevskii joined were scholarly, and most were related to the university. He was an inactive member of the Russian Historical Society, which Ger'e founded in 1866. He participated regularly in the monthly meetings of the Moscow Archeological Society, the Society of Lovers of Russian Literature, and the Society of Russian History and Antiquity, all of which he joined in 1874.

The Society of Russian History and Antiquity, the organization that most engaged him, best illustrates the way in which learning dominated even his social life. Founded in 1804, the Society had helped preserve Russian culture as a club of about one hundred men interested in history and collecting documents. Its office and library were within the university, and members included historians, folklorists, lawyers, and doctors from the faculty as well as librarians and archivists from outside the university community. In addition, Alexander III was an honorary member and contributed financial support for its publications.[5]

Thus, Sergei A. Belokurov studied with Kliuchevskii as an undergraduate and after 1886 worked in the Moscow Archives of the Ministry of Foreign Affairs, where he assisted Kliuchevskii and his students. A collector and active member of the Society, in 1913 and 1914 he published in its *Readings* an immense amount of archival material about his revered mentor and friend. Similarly, El'pifidor Barsov, a quiet archivist, had the same background and early education as Kliuchevskii: his grandfather and father had been poor rural priests. He had graduated from the St. Petersburg Ecclesiastical Academy and taught at the Olonets Seminary before joining the staff of the manuscript division of the Rumiantsev Library in 1870. He served as secretary of the Society from 1881 until 1907 and was an active editor and publisher of documents.

Soloviev sponsored Kliuchevskii for membership in the Society, as he later endorsed those whom he trained. He attended almost all meetings over a period of more than thirty years, and *Readings* published some of his most important papers. From 1893 until 1906, he served as an active and enlivening president: he made the sessions scholarly and transformed the annual *Readings* into a series of books.

The Moscow Psychological Society was the most innovative scholarly organization that attracted Kliuchevskii. His active participation in its meetings and contributions to its journal, *Questions of Philosophy and Psychology,* reveal his interest in new approaches to scholarship and the ways in which the walls that sheltered him and the university were crumbling. Professor Iakov K. Grot, assisted by Kovalevskii and Muromtsev, founded the Society in 1885 to introduce new ideas and a critical approach to philosophy. With the aid of the Abrikosovs, a wealthy merchant family, Grot began publication of the journal in 1889, when Kliuchevskii became a member, and created a national and even international organization. All members were interested in philosophy, psychology, and European ideas. Most were positivists; some in the 1890s claimed to be Marxists and some had no religious faith, but five members of the Ecclesiastical Academy faculty also joined.

Kliuchevskii, most of his friends, and some historians whom he had trained were active participants, but the Society was one of the first scholarly organizations that brought faculty, intellectuals, and artists together: S. N. Bulgakov, N. I. Berdiaev, Tolstoy, Merezhkovskii, Chicherin, and Vladimir Soloviev joined university associates at the university library one evening each month. William James and Thomas G. Masaryk accepted honorary memberships. The journal's circulation doubled to 2,000 in 1892 because it published an article on Nietzsche and a critique of religion by Vladimir Soloviev in an issue for which the censor rejected an essay by Tolstoy.

After Kliuchevskii presented a brilliant lecture on the artist's view of surroundings and dress at the School of Painting, Sculpture, and Architecture in 1897 and joined the faculty, he became acquainted with painters such as Serov, whose birthday party he attended in 1900. Serov spoke affectionately at a ceremony honoring Kliuchevskii's retirement from the university in 1901. Pasternak's 1909 portrait of Kliuchevskii lecturing there was one of Kliuchevskii's favorites and one of the most attractive that have survived. His last lecture was at this school, and he corrected student papers from it in the final days of his life.

Nechkina's detailed description of Kliuchevskii's life and work devoted two pages to his brief acquaintance with Fedor Chaliapin, the great bass, more than to his thirty-five years of teaching at the academy. However, this encounter illustrates that Kliuchevskii left the familiar circle only on brief and infrequent occasions. Summer dacha life with the Borodins in Vladimir province in 1898 led to his meeting Chaliapin, whose performance in *The Maid of Pskov* he had especially appreciated. Chaliapin, who studied the characters he was to portray and the circumstances in which they lived, spent two long afternoons walking with Kliuchevskii, acquiring such insights that he attributed much of his success as Godunov to Kliuchevskii. He invited him to a special benefit performance and a dinner afterward at the famous Testov restaurant, at which Kliuchevskii spoke and from which all sent greetings to Chekhov. However, this episode served as just a dramatic interlude. In short, the rarity and brevity of his forays into the world of art and music demonstrate how contained and placid his life was.

The academic circle in which he lived consisted of highly educated, cultivated men, often with spouses of equal intellectual vitality and intelligence. Almost all these men and their families lived near the university, between what are now Herzen and Kropotkin streets, with Arbat Square the focal point. The professors walked to their classes and archives, and the families easily visited each other's homes. Kovalevskii and nine others lived in one apartment building on Mokhovaia, adjacent to the university itself. On some evenings only men participated in long discussions, but often wives were present and active. Most of the men had devoted their lives to the study of some aspect of Russian history and culture. Some, such as Ger'e and Vinogradov, traveled abroad frequently. All, particularly the scientists, had been affected by Western modes of thinking and ideas. Positivism exercised a considerable influence, even though few had studied Comte. In short, this circle was steeped in Russian history and deeply patriotic, but was also knowledgeable concerning the European world.

These men and women were civic-minded, involved in women's education, reducing literacy, and alleviating the effects of famine. Most were unpolitical until the turn of the century, when some began to flirt with political action, generally but not always as liberals. Some, especially the librarians and archivists, were thorough conservatives. Others, such as Ger'e, became Octobrists, moderate conservatives. Some, including Muromtsev, became Kadets. None became radicals of either the left or the right, although some of their students did. All remained friends.

Kliuchevskii had especial respect for learned older men. Those with whom he was closest from his undergraduate years were the scholars with whom he had studied. As older colleagues passed on, their successors on the faculty assumed their places. Bogoslovskii, Kizevetter, and Liubavskii became especially warm associates. In the last decade of his life, they entertained the Kliuchevskiis and enjoyed occasional Sunday afternoons on the Kliuchevskii lawn. In 1907, Kliuchevskii began informal meetings in his home on Wednesdays, called "Shakhov Evenings," in memory of his friend of graduate student days. These relationships helped establish in them and others the concept of "the Kliuchevskii school" and provided a support system during the difficult years after 1917.

Kliuchevskii's circle extended beyond the history faculty to a few others interested in Russian culture, such as Dmitrii N. Anuchin, a highly cultivated anthropologist and geographer well informed about European music and art who taught the first Russian course in physical geography. Sergei A. Usov, a geologist interested in numismatics and early Russian church architecture, was another valued friend, for whom Kliuchevskii wrote an especially affectionate memorial. They were the only scientists who were close associates: Timiriazev, the eminent botanist, had known Kliuchevskii as an undergraduate and young faculty member. However, they drifted apart and into different circles, perhaps because Timiriazev lacked interest in history, his research drew him away from the physical center of the university, and he became a radical.

Specialists in law and medicine and their families also entered the circle. Most were liberal politically, but Nikolai P. Bogolepov, professor of Roman law, whom some called "the stone face," was a devout conservative. He served two terms as rector, became superintendent of the educational district in 1895, and was appointed minister of education in 1898. Kliuchevskii and he were friends throughout the nineties, and Kliuchevskii was one of those who comforted his widow after his assassination in 1901. Ironically, Bogolepov's stalwart blindness to student complaints and Kliuchevskii's correspondence convinced the historian that even faculty and students in cooperation could not change the university system.

SEVEN

The Outside World Intervenes

Kliuchevskii had made his way from the Russian equivalent of a log cabin. As an observant and ambitious young man, he had learned about the restrictions upon academic activity from life in the seminary and from watching some of his most admired mentors leave the university. After he had won his position at the Ecclesiastical Academy and succeeded Soloviev at the university, he had achieved as much security as a prudent, able, and renowned Russian civil servant could expect.

Yet the unassuming, ordinarily perceptive scholar seemed unaware of many conditions of Russian life. The three separate and quite distinct circles in which he lived, the Borodin clan–Karpov nest, Sergiev Posad, and the university, and his growing economic well-being sheltered him from Russian realities. The universe beyond the Russian community which Poles and Jews inhabited constituted a remote cosmos, while the areas in which Georgians, Uzbeks, Yakuts, and others lived were totally unknown to him. By nature reserved and cautious, comfortable only among close associates, friends, and family, he buttressed his isolation by avoiding official functions and responsibilities. He never served on a Ministry of Education committee or attended an Academy of Sciences meeting. He read Moscow's daily newspapers only in crises, and in the early 1870s stopped reading the great Russian literature of his era, except for Chekhov plays late in life. He despised Tolstoy, who had lost his faith and his mind, and compared his creativity to that of a puddle reflecting a pale moon on a dark night.[1] Perhaps because of his systematic regime as a teacher-scholar, and perhaps because of her character and personality, his wife in her own way enjoyed a sequestered life, cut off from the heart of the university community.

However, in Kliuchevskii's last two decades, the outside world gradually intruded into his sanctuary, disrupted his serene existence, and ultimately shook his confidence in the country's stability and even survival. The causes of this slow metamorphosis were multiple and interrelated. His deepening awareness of the transformations making the West ever more free, prosperous, and powerful and of the decline of religious faith together posed the greatest threat to Russia's cultural integrity since the seventeenth century. The autocracy's visible ineffectiveness in responding to these challenges and to Russia's economic and social problems intensified his unease. But his gradual understanding of the growing unrest in a neglected part of the university, the student body, contributed most sharply to dismantling the web of security that had protected him.

Life was not so tranquil and pleasant for students as it was for faculty members. Most students accepted hardship passively because arrangements at home had not been superior and they felt a camaraderie in poverty. They endured also because these were years of preparation for improved positions and bringing the fruits of science to their country and countrymen. But their material conditions were difficult, as in many countries then and even today, except for those from Moscow or who lived with relatives, who amounted to fewer than half the total. Most lived, as Kliuchevskii had, in a corner of a room in a garret or in a crowded rooming house. The university offered no cafeteria. In 1896, fewer than 1,200 of the 4,147 students received small state stipends. A Moscow doctor calculated that the average student lived on soup and bread and survived on twenty-five rubles a month. A friend of Kliuchevskii, A. I. Chuprov of the Law School, in that year completed a study revealing that about 2,500 were in dire need. The Ministry of Education in 1896 provided 300,000 rubles for building three dormitories for 450 students and permitted formation of a committee to stimulate private support on which Chuprov, Vinogradov, Anuchin, and Kliuchevskii served. Bogolepov presided at a public meeting in December 1897 to encourage contributions. Members of the Morozov family gave 15,000 rubles to the drive, which indicated that the ministry, faculty, and Moscow community were finally beginning to recognize the students' plight and take belated action.

More important than the students' economic situation was their growing resentment of restrictions and the brutal way inspectors and beadles monitored their behavior. The 1884 decree required students to wear uniforms. Inspectors checked passes at the university's two gates, and beadles in the halls and classes observed behavior. Each student had to obtain permission to attend a class outside his program or faculty. Students had to submit notebooks for inspection, promise not to participate in demonstrations, and obtain permission to absent themselves from class.

Students lacked the fraternities, singing, dancing, and theater groups, intramural and intercollegiate athletic contests, and parties that bind American students to classmates and institutions. "Circles," based on regions from which students came to Moscow, rooming arrangements, or political views served as centers of student intellectual and social life. The only organizations allowed were orchestral and choral groups and, after 1905, self-help regional groupings (*zemliachestva*). Many students therefore lacked the affection for their institution that animates an American alumnus or alumna, although close friendships formed in these circumstances often lasted throughout their lives.

The faculty in 1863 had willingly surrendered responsibility for monitoring student behavior to the ministry. Most members concentrated upon scholarship and their social lives, neglecting students, a pattern familiar at many American universities a century later. However, by 1890 Vinogradov, Chuprov, and others became active out of sympathy for young men enduring needlessly the same difficult conditions under which they had studied. They provided advice and defended student efforts to establish self-help regional organizations. Many later supported the new Kadet party after the students' plight had convinced them that political action was vital. Some of their graduate students, such as Miliukov and Kizevetter, helped found that party and presided over it after 1905.

Kliuchevskii knew as little about the students' situation as he did about workers until student disorders after 1887 informed him of these aspects of life below the surface of the university. The accumulation in his archives of newspaper clippings about student incidents throughout the country suggests that his understanding and sympathy gradually rose. He became interested in improving students' economic situation and their powers on issues directly affecting them.

Kliuchevskii's introduction to the students' plight began in the fall of 1887, when a student angered by the expulsion of 127 students from St. Petersburg University struck an offensive beadle, was expelled without trial, and was sent to the army for three years. The protest that followed led to the expulsion of sixty-three students and the closure of both universities for two months. Timiriazev led a small, ineffectual faculty protest. The offending students were not in Kliuchevskii's faculty. There is no evidence that he resented or opposed the ministry's decisions, but he regretted Maksim Kovalevskii's departure from the faculty. Moreover, his archives reveal that he collected information about the incident, a signal that the outburst was a revelation for him.[2]

Kliuchevskii was the unwitting spark for the next incident. At the monthly meeting of the Society of Russian History and Antiquity on October 28, 1894, a week after Alexander III's death, he read a short paper praising the late tsar as a great peacemaker. "In Memory of the Late Emperor Alexander III" was quite unlike his carefully constructed and often rewritten scholarly articles: it dealt with contemporary affairs, provided no evidence for its rotund judgments, and was sentimental concerning the Society's patron. It lauded the tsar's interest in history and support for the Society and absolved him from responsibility for undoing some of Alexander II's reforms, which it ascribed to those around him. It also saluted him for revising the European view of Russia.

The Society published the talk in its *Readings*, which only its hundred members received, but radical students lithographed two hundred copies. According to the most credible reports, from three to six students from the law and science faculties then whistled at Kliuchevskii in class on November 30. The majority applauded Kliuchevskii, who ended the slight interruption by saying, "I do not understand. I know only that I am responsible to maintain the freedom of teaching and you to follow me in achieving this."

The incident quickly escalated into an affair that divided the university community for six weeks. Presumably, some students considered his speech intolerable. Others resented his abandoning his classes in early December for four months to tutor a grand duke in the Caucasus. However, the basic cause was resentment at restrictions and the authorities' refusal to allow regional associations to collect material support for especially needy comrades. The faculty were largely indifferent, but some understood and quietly endorsed the students' right to organize and to have a university court, not the administration, adjudicate complaints. The administration was divided: the rector, the pro-rector, and their aides were decidedly hostile, while Kapnist, the superintendent of the Moscow educational district, was sympathetic to the students.

In any case, the fledgling grouping of student regional associations on December 2 respectfully urged the rector to release the three students he considered responsible for the whistling and had abruptly expelled. The police then rather gently arrested 119, most of whom they released soon, but the university expelled forty-four.[3] Ger'e on December 10 drafted a petition to the governor-general, which forty-one faculty members signed, that declared the incident a university affair and that the police should not have entered. It urged him to free those arrested and suggested that university courts, including judges and others from outside the university community, should adjudicate charges concerning student behavior. The university should allow student organizations, and the ministry should permit expelled students to continue their education in another university. Kapnist privately supported the petition and urged Ger'e to calm the students so that the governor-general would act favorably. However, a series of meetings revealed deep divisions within the faculty and between the majority of the faculty and the rector. This persuaded Kapnist that the faculty petitioners were mainly responsible for the students' behavior and the bitter disagreements within the faculty.

Count Ivan D. Delianov, Minister of Education, was appalled by the affair and refused to review the expulsions, although all but eighteen were later allowed to return. On February 15, he discharged and expelled from the city two instructors, Miliukov and P. V. Bezobrazov, one a former student of Kliuchevskii and the other a son-in-law of Soloviev. Miliukov, whom Bogolepov termed "the rector of the student movement," had been the primary drafter of the December 10 petition, although he was not formally a member of the faculty and should not have participated. Only the combined efforts of Kapnist and the rector dissuaded Delianov from dismissing Ger'e and three other faculty members, but he did issue them private reprimands and scolded the others who had signed the petition.

This affair remains minor, but it advanced Kliuchevskii's understanding of student problems. None of his colleagues criticized his talk, although some must have felt it silly. He privately criticized Nicholas II's February 1895 address, which denounced as "senseless dreams" efforts to make the government democratic and open, and he skillfully evaded an official request to write a biography of Alexander III. Two years later, he joined those urging construction of student dormitories. Above all, he became deeply involved in faculty actions during unrest in 1899 and 1901.

In 1899, the tsar's assignment of fractious students to the army produced disorders at St. Petersburg University and many expulsions. This led to a student strike in Moscow and expulsions there as well. On this occasion, Kliuchevskii repeated classes that the strike closed, invited students to his home to discuss complaints, and joined colleagues who called upon the rector to urge relaxation. He was so aroused by the expulsion of Aleksei I. Iakovlev, a gifted Marxist who had impressed him as a freshman in 1896, that he persuaded the rector to arrange his return. He corresponded with Iakovlev in jail, guaranteed his behavior, and provided financial assistance. The two remained close until Kliuchevskii died. Iakovlev was an able and honored scholar until his death in 1951, and his archives are one of the richest resources on Kliuchevskii as a teacher.

After the troubles had abated, Bogolepov, then Minister of Education, sought advice. Kliuchevskii's carefully crafted letter suggested that state policies had so demoralized the university community that resentment affected new students as soon as they arrived. The forlorn and helpless students needed only paternal guidance. The ministry should therefore remove inspectors and beadles. It should end dismissals without explanation and allow students to defend themselves before a university court chaired by a jurist without ties to the university. The letter produced no effect.[4]

When troubles broke out late in the winter of 1901 and police arrested five hundred students for demonstrating, Kliuchevskii accepted appointment to a committee of senior faculty members that Vinogradov chaired and wrote the core of the report "On the Reasons for Student Unrest and Measures for Restoring Order to University Life." From interviews with students, faculty members, and officials, he became familiar with student economic circumstances, the rules, prohibition of student organizations, and the need to end police intervention and establish a university court. Although he had been a faculty member for more than twenty years and knew that some young men, like him, had benefited from small scholarships, he was stunned to learn that the university had few resources for students in need and had dismissed sixty-nine students unable to pay fees.

The committee devoted several meetings to identifying the issues and discussing remedies. Ger'e and Vinogradov obtained student views in class sessions, and Vinogradov invited student comment upon preliminary proposals. The committee also held open discussions for students and faculty: three hundred students attended one of these meetings. The recommendations included permitting students to audit lectures, removing the inspectors, allowing student organizations, and establishing a court. The group submitted its report to the superintendent and the minister of education, who came to Moscow for that purpose on November 3. The superintendent two weeks later blocked publication of the report, and the minister shortly afterward rejected it.[5]

Dismissal of this study, which the great majority of the student body and the faculty endorsed, demonstrated the state's obtuse policies in higher education and the inability of the most honored and respected university professors to overcome barriers of bureaucratic ignorance and suspicion. Kliuchevskii felt betrayed, returned to a new edition of the *Boyar Council*, and obtained the first research leave of his career to begin writing the *Course of Russian History*.

Noting that only five of the previous fourteen university years had been quiet, he became increasingly despondent about Russia's future. Most of his colleagues on the committee were equally despondent. Vinogradov resigned from the university in disgust, even though a large majority of the faculty signed a petition urging him to remain and 1,500 students signed another such plea. Kliuchevskii's withdrawal from his brief concern with university affairs and Vinogradov's departure were vivid symbols of the government's lack of wisdom, the alienation and "brain drain" it inflicted upon the land, and the gradual disintegration of Kliuchevskii's university community.

Information from his diary and letters provides additional information about his increasing dismay. Thus, in 1891 he compared Russia to a medieval knight, who seemed powerful but was easy to topple. His confidence in the autocratic system remained unshaken, but in 1895 he remarked, "Nicholas II will end the Romanov dynasty; if he has a son, he will never rule." A long 1898 memorandum in his archives described Russia as tottering at the brink of a precipice. Five years later, he noted that first the rulers, then the intellectuals, and finally everyone had recognized that the system was rotten and that Russia's leaders were useless ornaments, scarecrows, or dinosaurs. A little later, he observed that the dynasty was coming to an end and a new Time of Troubles was approaching. Bloody Sunday, "our second Port Arthur," in January 1905 led to a diary note that Nicholas II would be the last tsar, a comment he repeated the following day in a lecture celebrating Tat'iana Day. However, he did not attack the form of government or hold it responsible. Instead, he told students that autocracy was indestructible and that overthrowing the autocracy would bring no improvement: the system was not the cause; sensible policies would have prevented a crisis. An updated aphorism late in life declared Russia the lowest animal in the international zoo: it continued to move even after it had lost its head.

During these years of increasing gloom about affairs within the university, his old circle of friends began to discuss the unrest and other manifestations of disaffection beyond their universe. This did not lead Kliuchevskii into political activity, but many in his group did become engaged and shared information and judgments with him. Some became liberals and advocated constitutional government. This band included Vinogradov; Muromtsev, who resigned from the law faculty in 1894, helped found the Kadet Party, and was president of the First Duma; and Prince Sergei N. Trubetskoi, a professor of philosophy elected rector of the university in September 1905. Others, such as Ger'e, active for years in the Moscow City Council, joined the conservative Octobrists.

In the early 1890s, Kliuchevskii also began to venture beyond his familiar fellowship, at first among a group of about a hundred colleagues and others who shared interests. Thus, monthly meetings of a "little island of freedom," the Moscow Psychological Society, brought him into contact with intellectuals and artists, atheists, Marxists, followers of Comte or Nietzsche, and members of the Orthodox Church, all aware of the country's ills and concerned about resolving them.

As Kliuchevskii's alarm grew, he participated in the quiet political discussions then allowed and served as a government adviser. None of these muted activities had any effect, but they ended his isolation and reinforced his judgment that those who ruled were blind and stupid and a catastrophe was approaching.

Although police maintained informal surveillance of Kliuchevskii from the time he began contributing to *Russian Thought,* officials recognized that he was conservative and loyal. Senior administrators arranged for him to tutor members of the tsar's family, first the Grand Duke Georgii Aleksandr during the winter months of 1893–94 and 1894–95 and then members of the family of Grand Duke Sergei Aleksandr.

The next opportunity involved membership in a discussion group that D. N. Shipov, a liberal leader in Moscow local government, formed in 1900 to respond to a memorandum that Witte had published on autocracy. Kliuchevskii became involved because two friends who were members knew that he believed that the government must close the gap separating it from the community by appointing or allowing election of recognized leaders to an advisory council. Most members became Kadets, but seven of the twelve founders of the Octobrists participated.

Shipov expected that the group would endorse a statement outlining the country's problems and suggesting reforms, including a broadly elected advisory council and increased local self-government. He also hoped that outstanding citizens from all parts of Russia would sign, making the document a powerful national declaration. However, the participants could not reach agreement. Some wanted to enlarge the powers of local government. Others urged that public institutions elect representatives to the Council of State. Still others sought a constitution. The group disintegrated late in 1901, but several participants kept him informed of their ideas and activities.

This effort had barely collapsed when V. K. von Plehve, secretary of state for Finland, a deeply hated minister of interior whom Kliuchevskii had despised, requested a paper on Russia's problems. The June 1902 memorandum, for which Kliuchevskii received two thousand rubles, reiterated his main thesis: state and society were isolated, quiet private grumbling had grown into disaffection throughout the society, and the public was becoming increasingly restless. The government should establish an advisory council of sensible senior officials and well-informed community leaders. This suggestion, which he noted was common among responsible men, resembles those of Loris-Melikov in 1880–81 and discussions in the Shipov group. But it exercised no influence, and Kliuchevskii later declined von Plehve's request for a memorandum on Finland's historical position within the empire. These functions were only specious government efforts to utilize Kliuchevskii's prestige and to persuade some leaders of opinion that genuine reforms were under way. They are important only because they represent the government's response to the growing crisis and his willingness to provide advice, the appropriate action of any citizen.

The Russo-Japanese War and turmoil in 1904 and 1905 drew Kliuchevskii into advisory work in the highest St. Petersburg councils. The first occasion, welcomed because it affected access to information, was a February 1905 invitation to join a commission to review censorship regulations. The group, which met thirty times, consisted largely of conservative journalists and churchmen. Kliuchevskii's denunciations of Church censorship were especially severe. He vigorously opposed all restrictions, urged that the courts exercise authority whenever the government thought review necessary, and declared that only limitations to defend "state security" were justified.[6]

Kliuchevskii then became an observer and to some degree a participant in preparing the short-lived August Manifesto. On February 18, 1905, the tsar announced a plan to summon "the better people for preparatory elaboration and judgment of legislative proposals," while at the same time "unfailingly preserving the Fundamental Laws of the Russian Empire." Someone at court suggested that the historian would constitute a useful ornament in meetings to discuss this advisory council. He accepted the invitation and an honorarium of a thousand rubles to review a draft manifesto that Minister of Interior A. F. Bulygin had prepared. Indeed, he immediately drafted a memorandum discussing systems for choosing a council. This concluded that neither the land assembly nor Western constitutionalism was appropriate, but an advisory group of experienced men resembling the boyar council would be effective.

Kliuchevskii knew only two participants at Peterhof and was the only one not a member of the imperial family or bureaucratic elite. His comments provide an excellent summary of his political beliefs. He supported the autocracy vigorously. However, the aristocracy, which had made significant contributions earlier, had lost connections with the nation, was disorganized, and no longer constituted an effective administrative support. The Church he did not even mention. In their stead, Russia needed an elected all-class representative advisory assembly or Duma to restore national unity, inform the ruler of popular needs, and reduce "the errors and imperfections of Russian life." Demonstrating that Peter the Great, Catherine the Great, and Alexander II had understood public needs, he declared that the government must know "the disposition of the country . . . which only the Duma can provide." Voting should not be by estates: most Russians would interpret such elections as "creation of a state Duma to defend the class interests of the aristocracy," an "unjust and dangerous" notion that the tsar was the symbol and tool of a class. Peasants should enjoy a large share in the indirect electoral system: they would vote for "competent persons who understood the interests of the rural population" and would defend peasant interests, which were those of society as a whole. However, he accepted and presumably endorsed an electoral system that disenfranchised the opposition by denying the vote to all those under twenty-five years of age, most educated urban residents and workers, nomads, and most non-Russians. Four years later, his account of these years acknowledged the folly of such an electoral system.

On July 30, he participated in the meeting that Pobedonostsev chaired to draft the manifesto, of which six versions were then at hand. There he sought to soften irritating edges by shortening references to the war, removing phrases that referred to "internal troubles," and ending the manifesto with a positive, ringing declaration about unity and power.

The August Manifesto on a consultative Duma that emerged from the five July meetings at Peterhof, over which Nichlas II presided, constituted one of the government's last opportunities to deal with discontent before the 1905 revolution broke. Events that fall swept it away.

Kliuchevskii's other actions during the period from 1904 through 1906 are difficult to evaluate because the rate of change was great. Above all, he was a novice in political affairs and understandably confused and discreet. In the fall of 1905, he resigned as president of the Society of Russian History and Antiquity because he feared that the government would ask the Society to take an official position on the political crisis. When Witte requested historical data on the concept of autocracy, he pled ignorance and proposed another scholar. His archives contain materials from active liberal and conservative friends, but he remained passive, even in university affairs, from which he had withdrawn after the fiasco concerning student disorders in 1901.

However, he honored student strikes and signed a January 1905 petition describing the country's educational needs. Early that fall, when the government issued "Temporary Rules" allowing the faculty to elect the rector and departments to choose their chairs, he signed a petition to protest the minister of education's retaining authority to approve faculty appointments. He considered the October Manifesto inadequate by the time it appeared and feared another Time of Troubles, especially as he watched striking workers from the nearby Sytin printing plant parade by his home.

In his judgment, responsibility for the revolution belonged to the government, but he was critical of the revolutionaries as well: they and the new parties thought politics a game and did not understand national issues. He had contempt for the striking workers and considered the Moscow uprising late in 1905 an explosion of hooligans, the ignorant, and the idle. But Russia would regain stability because the structure of society remained unchanged. The crisis had revealed only that popular "moral aversion to injustice led to yearning for just and responsible government." The insurrection resembled a dose of castor oil: it cleaned out society and made a new beginning possible, but proffered no acceptable alternative.

Kliuchevskii's criticism of the government and sympathy for those who sought improvements persuaded some Kadets and observers that he sought constitutional democracy. The most important but still unconvincing evidence for this conclusion was his relationship with Miliukov, a Kadet leader. In 1892, he had alienated Miliukov by blocking the proposal granting him the doctorate when he defended his M.A. thesis and the M.A. Ten years later, when he learned that the police had arrested his former student, he innocently wrote von Plehve and Count Sergei D. Sheremet'ev, a geologist friend who was a member of the Council of State, urging release of "a clumsy, naive academic liberal" and "inexperienced fire-eater" who often acted thoughtlessly. Moreover, his wife was the daughter of a Moscow Ecclesiastical Academy colleague and had been a student of Kliuchevskii.

After Nicholas II freed Miliukov, he and Kliuchevskii resumed friendly relations, and Kliuchevskii invited him to serve as an adviser for the Peterhof meetings. Each night, Miliukov came to his hotel room for an account of the session and to discuss strategies. After publication of the manifesto, Miliukov used documents that Kliuchevskii had shown him and their discussion to write an article in *Law*, for which he was arrested. Kliuchevskii, this time fearful, urged release of his "former student and old acquaintance with whom he shared an interest in Russian history," not a radical or underground agitator but a critic of extremist political parties. He asked D. F. Trepov, chief of police, to return the papers found in Miliukov's rooms: "They were not given to him by me, but I did not request their return because I was confident he would not misuse them."[7] Somehow Kliuchevskii regained the documents and escaped involvement in the affairs of Miliukov, whom the police released after a month.

Kliuchevskii was equivocal and unclear concerning the representative system of government established by the October Manifesto in 1905 and modified by the fundamental laws in May 1906. On one hand, he recognized that significant change was necessary. But he regretted that the new arrangements provided for a representative Duma or legislature rather than an advisory council, such as the boyar duma. He joined no political group: such an action would have violated his deepest conviction. He had such scant knowledge of Russia beyond his little circles that he thought the country lacked intelligent men who could do more than advise seasoned bureaucrats. The vast corpus of archival material contains almost no references to the *zemstvo*, the local government institution allowed limited powers after 1864. Many of Kliuchevskii's liberal contemporaries, and many Western historians, considered this a school preparing hundreds of Russians to contribute to governance on a regional and national level. In his judgment, limited experience in local government since 1864 had not prepared anyone to help rule: "No one learns to swim in a puddle across which a sparrow can walk."[8]

He did endorse some Kadet positions in conversations with Miliukov, and he apparently voted Kadet in elections for the First Duma in 1906: he may even have stood unsuccessfully with combined Kadet-Octobrist support from Sergiev Posad. In April 1906, he stood for election to the Council of State as representative of the Academy of Sciences and the universities, voted for himself, and won. He then chose not to serve, declaring, "I can only sympathize: I cannot participate," because of his political beliefs, the inability of a professor as a state bureaucrat to express opinions freely, and his unwillingness to leave his family for St. Petersburg. However, desire to complete the *Course of Russian History* was no doubt the most important reason.

Kliuchevskii was uneasy after 1906 because of the existence of political parties, stereotyped imitations of foreign models unrepresentative of Russian tradition. All parties claimed to rest upon political principles but represented private interests and destroyed national unity. Their maneuvers and speeches resembled useless arm-waving. Legislative sessions constituted a game of blind man's bluff. Having a group represent Polish interests in a Russian legislature especially affronted him. He was even more critical of the Black Hundreds: "There is no Russia now, only Russians."

Kliuchevskii's views of the Duma gradually changed to moderate approval as a barrier against chaos, although he remained fundamentally hostile. The government was "a rabble of dilettantes and reactionaries," so the First Duma became a practical alternative to revolution, "a low price for bloodless pacification of the country."[9] He considered the First Duma speeches moderate and even sympathized with those who signed the Vyborg Manifesto urging Russians to boycott their government. Replacement of a liberal legislature by a reactionary one was not a misfortune: "perhaps" Russians were acquiring a political education and would reject both extremes, choose a legislature that represented national concerns, and seek the national welfare, not party goals. By July 1906, he concluded that Russia needed an institution that had some popular approval. "Practical patriotism" required one to support the Duma. However, no responsible person should join the government: education remained the most effective way to help. Following his own advice, he turned away from observation of political life and concentrated upon writing, leaving decisions to the forces of change that had always been decisive.

The Scholar

Kliuchevskii studied and taught when scholarly research on Russian national history was at an early stage and the censor was powerful. Few undergraduates displayed interest in their country's past, and the reading public was small. His generation lacked access to research materials, theories, techniques, and equipment that later scholars have enjoyed. Moreover, a scholar's work did not end with writing, but extended into arranging publication and distribution of his completed manuscripts. A professional association and its services and stimulating conferences of specialists were several generations distant.

Still, historians enjoyed some advantages, especially budding awareness of history. The popularity of historical novels by Lazhechnikov and Zagoskin stirred interest in the past. Tolstoy's *War and Peace*, written and published in the 1860s, raised curiosity to a new level. Men such as Buslaev stimulated interest in folklore and early literature. In 1859, an institute for training archivists was established, modeled upon the great Ecole des Chartes in Paris. The first historical atlas appeared in 1865, the same year as a splendid collection of Russian songs. Several of the "thick journals" that blossomed under Alexander II devoted attention to history. New libraries, archives, museums, theaters, conservatories, and other cultural institutions were transforming Moscow into an intellectual center that honored learning and turned public lectures and exhibitions into civic celebrations. Finally, those who trained the Kliuchevskii generation had studied with Europe's masters, so that he benefited from Western techniques and standards. Yet this training was so new, casual, and relaxed that the scholarly traditions, habits, and jargon that restricted originality in conception and style of much later scholarship did not affect him. Indeed, he and his small generation resemble in many ways the amateur scholars and early professionals who made historical literature popular then in the United States.

A prolific scholar-teacher for half a century, Kliuchevskii modified his research interests as he sought to understand the past. In the first eight years, he concentrated upon subjects involving religion or the Church, and the *Orthodox*

Review was the principal publisher. During the decade after his M.A. degree on saints' lives, he devoted most of his energies to articles and the book on the boyar council, his most significant scholarly work. From the beginning of graduate study in 1865 through 1890, he spent much of his time in archives. During his last years he labored just as relentlessly, but he relied upon notes compiled earlier for more than fifty publications, including superb studies of the land assemblies and the religious schism. He published the first tome of the *Course of Russian History* in 1904 and the fourth in 1910, but these and the posthumous fifth volume were the product of constant reworking of classes he had taught since 1871 and of all his publications.

In his three decades at the university, he produced four major revisions of *Boyar Council* and at least one substantial article each year but three after 1879. Several were in fact small books on subjects as complicated as the origins of serfdom. Many were by-products of his seminar. Most dealt with education, the impact of the West, and historiography, interrelated concerns that widened his knowledge and that of his advanced students. Others were analyses of the life and work of historians, links in the great chain of those who had increased knowledge and were themselves essential elements of that past.

During the early 1880s and in the 1890s, he completed manuscripts of seven advanced courses and graduate seminars, most of which were published after his death. Beginning in 1899, he published an outline-textbook for his survey, annually adding materials on contemporary developments. He also left the texts of ten public lectures on Western influence on Russia after Peter the Great, presented in 1890–91 but published only in 1983.

Kliuchevskii's knowledge was prodigious, his memory exacting. Definition of the data he considered significant was catholic, and he seemed to assume that relentless, probing study would lead to full understanding. From childhood, he read constantly and intensely, measuring the meaning of each word, probing the author's point of view and conclusions, and adding tested new information and ideas to the organized stock. His scholarly publications and comments on student reports and theses are filled with detailed information concerning a wide range of history. Colleagues called him "a walking library" and learned not to dispute with a man of such erudition.

Yet he was ignorant of or discounted some aspects of Russian life. He told students early in the academic year that he ignored "the intellectual and moral aspects" of the past: this helps explain his omitting the substance of the moving essays on saints and "good people" from his major works. He analyzed the work of a number of great writers and drew upon his knowledge of literature, especially Pushkin, when he attacked the nobles for their dismissal of Russian culture. Yet his survey of history and the great volumes that grew from his famous course neglected literature and ideas. Although he enjoyed Western and Russian music, he was as blind to the role of music, art, and architecture as he was to national minorities.

Other imperfections were also significant. In effect, he ignored the Mongols.

His treatment of nobles concentrated upon eighteenth-century aristocrats in Moscow and St. Petersburg who succumbed to French influence. Those who remained faithful to their culture and served their society loyally received scant attention. The thousands who resembled the country squires of Henry Fielding's eighteenth-century England are also absent, so that his analysis of the aristocracy is almost a caricature. His animus toward intellectuals was equally strong, and they play no role in his account of the past.

Similarly, he was unfair to the Church and churchmen. He concentrated on their obvious flaws but neglected the silent service of men such as his father and gave insufficient account to the circumstances in which they worked. He paid inadequate attention to the Church's contribution to early Russia's cultural triumphs, "allowing Moscow to crowd out of his account five centuries of an ancient way of life which was incomparably richer than it in culture and spirituality."[1] He simply omitted the Church and religion from the *Course*, much as many contemporary scholars ignore religion in their analyses of America's past. This was due in part to his knowledge of the Church's low intellectual level and administrative lethargy, personal disappointment at its contemporary weaknesses, and the influence of the secular world in which he worked in Moscow. But it also reflected his definition of culture, which exalted achievements in written expression and neglected spiritual triumphs and artifacts.

All Kliuchevskii's teaching, but especially the seminars and advanced classes through which he attracted and trained his successors, illustrates his methods and values as a professional scholar. The lectures in the first four years at the university on the use of early sources identified the difficulties scholars encountered when studying a different age. Beginning in the fall semester of 1884, he introduced successive courses on terminology, the methodology of historical research, and social structure, none of which he repeated or published because they did not satisfy his standards. The twenty-four lectures on methodology reflected clearly his positivist approach to history, rejection of philosophy of history, and conviction that a national society constituted a historian's subject. He should examine its origins and nature as a form of community that emerged as ever larger associations supplanted the family, clan, and tribe. Ultimately, scholars would compare the different forms of community to help others discover historical laws.

He had begun notebooks on terms and collecting dictionaries of juristic expressions as a freshman and devoted six years to preparing the seminar on terminology. Its eleven lectures demonstrated his devotion to precision upon accurate definition "of the terms one encounters in our historical sources," especially those for economic processes, social classes, institutions, and currency. The Soviet scholar who prepared these lectures for publication eighty years later declared them still the most useful dictionary of early Russian terminology.

The seminar on estates completing this trilogy constituted an almost unique analysis of primary sources and scholarly work on social structure before

1765. It is a history of Russia through its classes, as *Boyar Council* analyzed national history through that institution. Based upon research in the archives of the Ministry of Justice, it described the origins and significance of the rights, privileges, and obligations of four social classes. Russian and Western scholars engaged in unraveling the mystery of social and political history before Catherine the Great point out flaws, particularly his finding boyars and estates in Kiev, but make extensive use of his "immense learning."

Kliuchevskii's research and conviction that historical writing was an essential element of a nation's growth turned him toward advanced courses on historiography, which he designed to acquaint apprentices with their profession's roots and its role in their country's development. He began with Byzantine chronographs and demonstrated how Russian compilers using their information gradually adopted "the Byzantine world view." Detailed information on the chronicles then explained how chroniclers gradually broke free from the Byzantine mold and developed "a Russian world outlook." The course was especially rich in materials from the lives of saints, but it also pointed out that scholars should extend their research beyond official documents, for knowledge of tales and legends was essential for understanding the past.

He encouraged Miliukov, a graduate student who became an instructor in 1886, to introduce the first course on Russian historiography, ten years before Charles Seignebos and Charles-Victor Langlois introduced such a course at the Sorbonne. Miliukov taught the class in alternating years with Kliuchevskii until the minister of education dismissed him in 1895. Kliuchevskii then alternated the course on "scholarly opinions about the past" with one describing and analyzing basic sources. Three of his students continued the class after his retirement.

These instructional exercises represent a basic element of Kliuchevskii's scholarship, his constant effort to make every subject he touched understandable as part of the long stream of Russian history. They paralleled his studies of the boyar council and estates and the survey course he was teaching then at three institutions. He emphasized their importance by declaring that Russia and its historiography had advanced hand in hand. Historians were as important as rulers and critical events because their depiction of the past defined man's understanding, helped shape national consciousness, and of course became a part of history.

Kliuchevskii's analyses of historiography illustrate his scholarly qualities with exceptional clarity. The well-organized lectures and articles reflected enormous knowledge and careful reflection. Designed for would-be scholars, they described briefly the historical period and its scholarship, the impact of the age upon the accumulated knowledge and of scholarship upon the age, the relationship of the historical work to earlier efforts, new elements introduced, and the most important studies. They also analyzed scholars' goals, the problems or issues reviewed, sources used and neglected, and interpretations. Soviet analyses recognized their quality and the importance that Kliuchevskii assigned to historiography as a part of the national record.

Kliuchevskii's research showed imagination in locating materials, and his judgments reflected keen insight. Many of his works, especially *Boyar Council, Ancient Russian Saints' Lives as a Historical Source,* and those on prices in the fifteenth and sixteenth centuries, the origins of serfdom, the land assembly, and historiography remain valuable more than a century later. Nevertheless, contemporary critics noted neglected sources and disagreed with some interpretations. Russian and Western scholars who have utilized materials and analytical approaches unavailable to him have identified additional imperfections. But even specialists who have criticized his judgments on issues such as the role of trade in early Russian history or the nature and purpose of Ivan the Terrible's *oprichnina* consider his scholarship substantial and his conclusions sensible.

Kliuchevskii everlastingly sought to raise the quality of his work. Dispassionate and accurate description was his goal, but he failed often, as do the most resolute and able. Perhaps the most fundamental flaw was his blandly viewing his country through the eyes of a Muscovite: he considered that the Ukrainians and Belorussians were Russians and that their inclusion in the Russian state was a "natural and necessary" form of manifest destiny. He failed even to consider other views of this crucial question. In addition, his view of the role of harsh internal circumstances and external pressures, respect and even reverence for the past, and affection for Russia gave his account such a conservative tone that some thought that it signified approval, not just acceptance, of the political system.

Kliuchevskii's understanding of the seventeenth century was profound, but that of the following century unbalanced and of the nineteenth century fragmentary and disorganized. On historiography, to which he devoted much of his last twenty-five years, he neglected the defenders of the established system as well as radicals, perhaps because both were passionate and therefore not scholarly.

Curiously, although he was an early student of legend and folklore and some have declared him a historian of the people, neither the peasants nor the workers received attention. He grew up in rural villages, but there is no evidence that he knew any peasants or was informed concerning agriculture, rural crafts, or peasant life. He confessed ignorance of the working class, although the section of Moscow in which he lived contained many factories and merchants' and workers' homes and the Borodins were a merchant clan. He seemed oblivious to the industrialization of Russia that was taking place before his eyes. In short, knowledge of his homeland, even contemporary Russia, came from archives, his study, and a small circle of friends, mostly academics, not from observation, travel, or even the newspapers he read.

His account neglected revolts, the army, and weapons, and his course on terminology even excluded military terms. The role war played in the rise and expansion of Muscovy received little attention: expansion, which he called colonization, was an inexorable and peaceful process, with few exceptions or casualties, except in the reign of Catherine the Great. Cultural relations with Europe were more important than diplomatic relations and conflicts. He included some of the causes and consequences of wars with European states, but not battles or human losses. Even the conflict between Russia and Japan that took place while he was completing his famous volumes received little attention in them or in the textbooks that he produced for students during and after that war.

The qualities of his scholarship are far more impressive than the flaws, particularly when one considers that he taught and wrote in an early period of Russian historical study and was a generalist trying to provide a coherent, faithful account of the entire course of the past. First, he saw research, teaching, and writing history as a noble and creative activity, one that helped his countrymen understand themselves and come together as a nation—an important social function that American specialists a century later have forgotten in their emphasis upon writing for each other about details and means of interpretation. He saluted his predecessors, who had begun the process of determining what had happened, passing along to successor generations the responsibility to deepen and widen that knowledge.

He also stressed that historians must approach their subject without preconceptions or biases: "History must be itself, not try to become philosophy."[2] One should be eternally alert concerning the point of view of the chronicler, collector of documents, and scholar: they were often uncritical or careless and had perspectives of their own. Like Gibbon, Kliuchevskii was distrustful of enthusiasm or passion. One finds neither romanticism nor alienation in his work. The strong emotions he displayed against the eighteenth-century nobility were an exception.

His insistence on critical detachment and a determined but inevitably not fully successful effort to escape the assumptions of his time are especially clear in comments upon other historians and would-be scholars. Tendentiousness, "unthinkable in the academic world," was the most common complaint he directed against both student reports and scholarly books: they judged rather than observed. He admired Boltin for being candid without idealization or condemnation, but criticized Lomonosov for allowing nationalism to color his judgment. Karamzin encouraged interest in Russian history, but his dramatic moralizing led Russians to love their past rather than understand it. Overtly and uncritically political, he was not a historian but a writer of great cultural significance. Although Kliuchevskii had strong populist sympathies, he rejected the Slavophil view that the people were a source of wisdom.

In short, historians should recognize that each country and age possesses virtues and flaws that reflect logical and temporal conditions that scholars should record without praise or blame: "If we hope to understand the life of other men, we must first of all be just . . . and recognize that we at that level of development would not have acted differently." Thus, early Russians used the knout and other brutal devices to punish, sometimes even to determine innocence and guilt. One should describe these practices, not condemn them, as scholars from other cultures and later times should describe, not ridicule, practices of nineteenth-century Russia. *Boyar Council* warned that one "should not interpret ancient times in modern terms" by concluding that seventeenth-century leaders sought the same political institutions that nineteenth-century intellectuals preferred. Similarly, those in the 1880s analyzing Iurii Samarin's ideas in the 1850s on voluntary division of land for freed peasants should remember that he wrote before abolition, not twenty years after the great act. "The historian is an observer, not an investigator." He should "honestly and benevolently enter the feelings and needs of others."[3]

Kliuchevskii attained integrity, an essential quality, through prudence in hazardous circumstances: he was a civil servant engaged in a field that an oppressive government considered sensitive and in which no attractive opportunity existed should the Ministry of Education discharge him. Observations in Penza, Buslaev's apprising the young undergraduate of the censor's role, and the shattered careers of Shchapov, Kostomarov, and Chicherin instructed him of the state's authority and actions. The Ministry of Education's revision of the university curriculum (even of his basic course), treatment of student disorders, and dismissal of Miliukov and a son-in-law of Soloviev from the faculty reinforced his caution. He therefore avoided involvement in academic administration or public affairs, respected the blurred boundaries that identified hazardous issues, and spoke and wrote with disarming irony. But he intervened to secure the return of the expelled Marxist student Aleksei I. Iakovlev to the university and was forthright on university committees on student disorder. In 1905, he accepted appointment to two St. Petersburg committees, which he considered a required public service, and spoke with vigorous candor in both groups.

Russian and Western readers in the twentieth century marvel at his honesty. His M.A. thesis was the first demonstration, for its conclusion that ancient saints' lives had little value as historical sources dismayed many devout Christians. His account of the nobility's Gallomania and actions after 1765, comments on the Church and churchmen, descriptions of Peter the Great's fumbling administrative reforms and the costs of building St. Petersburg, and analyses of Catherine the Great's policies in Poland demonstrated frankness and helped explain his appeal. Yet his analyses were usually so judicious and fair-minded that political leaders as diverse as Witte, Pobedonostsev, and Lenin not only devoured his publications but helped make them available to varieties of reading publics.

The knowledge that Kliuchevskii commanded was inevitably limited, but he ventured far beyond archival documents and publications to study the total community. His approach resembles that made popular by Marc Bloch, Lucien Febvre, and the *Annales* school, first in France and then elsewhere, after 1930.

Like these men, in the words of one of their most prominent and respected disciples, he concluded, "There is no unilateral history." Study of the past "should break out of the walls in which so many have enclosed it." In the same way as Fernand Braudel, he saw the nation as "a bundle of realities" that one must analyze from every angle, seeking and "using facts like fuel for a fire."[4]

Thus, he was a rooted Muscovite who rarely traveled beyond the Moscow region, but his publications reflect thorough knowledge of the geography of European Russia. He visited important sites and drafted maps while writing. His work utilized archeology, diplomatics, linguistics, numismatics, and paleography. When preparing the third edition of *Boyar Council*, he studied statistics.

Knowledge of religious rituals was essential because they were visible representations of the most profound moments and deepest traditions of a people's past. Tales, legends, and oral traditions were a corrective for cold analysis. "Almost like a phonograph record," they served as "indices of the turning points of national life." They informed the historian what the people thought, essential insight otherwise almost impossible to acquire.

Scholars should also understand that words and concepts have different meanings in different countries, places, and social classes. Thus, a review of von Bernhardi's *Geschichte Russland* in 1876 noted, "To understand one's neighbor, one must comprehend the words and gestures with which he explains himself and the customs and circumstances of his life to his contemporaries, as well as to us, their descendants and observers."

Seminar students learned that statues, paintings, and musical instruments were important artifacts and that dress and furniture contributed insights. Thus, Kliuchevskii used the literature, art, and furniture of early Russia to demonstrate that piety ruled then. In the same country late in the nineteenth century, apparently similar aspects of life and culture revealed that religious faith had faded and that people lived for themselves, not the community. Most art and literature had become individualistic, even autobiographical. Apparel had been utilitarian and practical, but men and women in the late nineteenth century dressed to impress: women's dress was "the alphabet of life" a historian must master to understand a society. Kliuchevskii applauded an early work of Platonov on the Time of Troubles because the St. Petersburg specialist devoted the volume to tales and legends from that time, recognizing that "everything is important" when one studies the past.

Just as Kliuchevskii was an early practitioner of a multidisciplinary and interdisciplinary view, so he saw the history of Russia as an organic whole. He sought to produce a coherent account of the entire past, not monographs on minor issues or short periods for other specialists. He was concerned with what Braudel called "la longue durée, . . . the deep currents of history, of those living waters on which our frail boats are tossed." He sought to examine social structures, determine causes, and provide reasoned explanations. Thus, *Boyar Council* set out to analyze "the structural materials or the concealed internal strengths that held the structure together," not the structure itself.[5] In short, one could understand one's country only by mastering the full sweep of its past, the sum of which was greater than the total of its parts. Directing his talents to that conception of history is a secret of his success.

Unremitting reliance on research in primary sources, particularly in archives, was another distinguishing quality, one not unique then and a convention a century later. However, the popularity of the works of Karamzin and Pogodin, the success of gifted popularizers and political interpretations, and the role of novels that touched upon history made his insistence upon original sources crucial at a time when the Russian historical profession was being formed.

Few bibliographies, secondary studies, or even guides to archives existed, so Kliuchevskii plunged directly into primary sources, following veins as they appeared, as archivists or others suggested them, or as questions arose. Colleagues noted in disappointment that he consulted their works only to identify primary materials: one informed observer noted succinctly that "he did business only with history, not with historians."[6] His dictum for students was "Go to the sources," for only grueling research enabled one to locate the keys and understand a different era. In the archives, scholars must examine all materials, whether they be scattered and disorganized sources on local administration in the seventeenth century or hundreds of repetitious saints' lives, because one could never know where a valuable nugget or insight might appear.

Sustained hard work was a central characteristic. Utterly single-minded in concentration upon study of the past, Kliuchevskii was even more indefatigable than Soloviev, who was renowned for working sixteen hours a day. Libraries and archives were open only six hours a day, and no instruments existed to reproduce materials. Therefore he copied by hand hundreds of documents and compiled detailed notes on thousands of others. He wrote comments and summaries, marked passages in the margins of books, and filed articles from newspapers in envelopes. He used pocket notebooks to record sudden ideas or *bons mots* that came to mind while he was fishing, walking, or chatting with friends.

None of his public lectures was a casual, informal chat: he devoted weeks and even months to their preparation, dictated drafts to Mrs. Karpov or one of the Borodins, and revised them again and again. He gave graduate students little direct guidance but expected them to work untiringly: vacations and holidays did not exist for scholars. Commitment to work without stint was an academic's first responsibility: "He who is not willing to work sixteen hours a day does not deserve to live."[7]

His legendary perfectionism constituted an important teaching instrument and was central to his scholarly achievements. He was ever alert to additional data concerning subjects on which he had published. Thus, by the end of his life he had collected more than fifty pages of materials and put together an eleven-page supplementary bibliography for improving the volume on foreigners' legends published when he was an undergraduate. The third edition of *Boyar Council* in 1902 added massive revisions and five chapters to the second edition nineteen years earlier, and the fifth in 1909 added other changes. A review of the posthumous first edition of his course on estates noted that he had compiled thirty pages of information and corrections after the 1886 lithographed version. He rewrote endlessly and then revised the proofs from the printer. After he had devoted five months to revising the proofs of the first volume of the *Course of Russian History,* he wrote comments in the margins of the published book. In his last years, when he was desperately concentrating upon the final two volumes, he prepared new editions of the first two.

His analyses of undergraduate papers commented in detail upon the research, organization, and conclusions and suggested materials the student should have investigated. He expected advanced students to demonstrate imagination in locating sources, clear understanding of terms, careful thought, and clear exposition. Comments on M.A. and doctoral theses were most detailed, persuading listeners at defenses that he had spent days studying the manuscript and investigating potential source materials. His judgments were so precise and severe that some advanced students, including Miliukov and Pokrovskii, abandoned graduate training after he had dissected their M.A. theses. His book reviews and comments at public defenses not only helped establish his reputation but also raised research standards among apprentices and senior scholars.[8]

Kliuchevskii's perfectionism was such that Iakovlev exulted when he found a factual error while preparing the 1937 edition of the *Course of Russian History* for publication. The others who helped edit those volumes and those who prepared for publication the eight-volume edition published between 1956 and 1959 and the nine-volume set that appeared after 1987 professed the highest admiration for his accuracy. Russian and Western scholars who have examined and used his most specialized works, even his M.A. thesis and the manuscript from his first seminar on *Russian Truth,* have all expressed strongest appreciation for the absence of error.

Kliuchevskii's archives contain a large number of unpublished manuscripts, many of which friends and publishers thought ready for publication. These vary from his final lecture on Pushkin to the series on Russia and the West after Peter the Great. A volume of more than four hundred pages published in 1983 incorporates some of these materials. The last Soviet edition of his works and a 1990 volume of essays on important historians and other individuals include others. But his archives contain at least twenty more, as well as transcripts of courses that did not meet his standards and that scholars have not yet edited.

Discussion of two publications will illustrate the level of excellence he demanded. His course on methodology and terminology led to a comparison of the price of bread in the sixteenth and seventeenth centuries with that from August through October 1882. In this he used numismatics and metrology in evaluating evidence in "an experiment with materials on the history of prices, with full explanations of the difficulties" encountered. No one since has sought to undertake such a study. However, reviewers then and historians a century later have lauded the analysis as a classic, especially for locating sources. The calculations he made on seventeenth-century prices have proved so accurate that scholars still use them in studies of economic history.

Iushkov and two other graduate students produced a transcript of Kliuchevskii's seminar course on social structure in the first semester of 1885–86. After Iushkov had transformed his shorthand notes of each lecture into a script, he and his associates reviewed and revised that version. Iushkov then spent several hours each week with Kliuchevskii, amending that week's lecture. Even after Iushkov had incorporated his suggestions, Kliuchevskii denied permission to lithograph because he wanted to introduce changes, but he finally allowed Iushkov to produce two hundred copies. After these quickly became rare and valuable, Kliuchevskii refused permission to produce additional numbers.[9]

Just as his first lecture at the university attracted a packed auditorium and launched his renown as a classroom teacher, so his first appearance at an M.A. thesis defense was an instructional session on scholarly standards and values. The candidate, Vasilii I. Semevskii, had been denied an M.A. in St. Petersburg and dismissed as an instructor: he was a populist and an advocate of Darwinism, and his thesis criticized the terms of the abolition of serfdom. Kliuchevskii, who thought scholars should be apolitical and did not share Semevskii's approach to the peasant question, nevertheless accepted him as a graduate student and presided over the grueling M.A. defense in February 1882. After St. Petersburg had dismissed Semevskii again in 1886, Kliuchevskii agreed to direct his doctorate on the peasant issue in the century before 1861. At the defense in February 1889, he recognized the candidate's immense learning and the high qualities of the thesis. But he criticized its polemical tone, lack of organization, overreliance on memoir literature, and concentration upon the process of abolition.

On the other hand, he withheld his comments from publication to preserve the young man's prospects for an academic position. He voted for the degree and nominated the study for the Academy of Science's Uvarov Prize, which Semevskii received. Scholars then and a century later have recognized Semevskii as the outstanding Russian specialist on the peasant question.

Kliuchevskii's technical qualities as a historian, some of which must appear unexceptional to Americans a century later, as a coherent system of scholarly conduct were innovative and raised the level of Russian scholarship. Application of these principles and the felicity with which he wrote ensured him a high place in Russian culture. They also explain the magnetic attraction he has held for all generations of Russians and the alluring alternative and quiet reproach his *Course* offered to Soviet scholarship, which neglected some of the canons of scholarly behavior and distorted much of the past.

His courses on historiography, sixteen essays on historians, and as many articles of reminiscences and book reviews together describe his view of the historical profession and his place in it. Even late in life, when he had achieved national renown, he saw himself as just a link in a long national chain of hundreds, even thousands, who had contributed to the many functions involved in scholarship. His modesty, admiration, and appreciation of Soloviev grew as he matured, as did his appreciation of his other mentors. Moreover, from early in life, he urged recognition of all those who had engaged in collecting, organizing, preserving, and cataloguing the raw materials on which his craft depended: they were all part of a great chain of learning and an important thread of national history. Preserving his papers, even notes scribbled on the backs of envelopes, reflected his reverence for the past and his appreciation of the careful preservation of all records. An especially pithy comment noted that an architect plans a building but that construction involves many workers.

Kliuchevskii's clear definition of purpose also set him aside from Soviet scholars and in a different way from most American historians a century later. His goal was to increase his countrymen's knowledge and understanding of their national past so that they might come together as a nation. He was not a specialist who sought to produce original insight into a relatively minute segment of history or a striking new interpretation of an event or an individual's life. In his entire career, he unveiled few great discoveries (very few scholars do). Instead, he sought to put together a dispassionate and accurate account of Russia's long national past, an immensely difficult task. He was convinced that no theories, scientific or complex, explained what had happened. He avoided or muted debates about the Slavophil-Westerner controversy or other such issues that excited, and still excite, many historians, and he rarely attacked others' versions of parts of the past. Instead, he excelled because of the qualities he skillfully combined.

Convinced that the record of the past is many-sided and that many factors shaped his country's history, he adopted a multicausal approach that often included summaries of others' views of particular events or trends. The *Course of Russian History* is therefore complex and full of nuances and subtleties, ironies and paradoxes. It is difficult to categorize him or summarize Kliuchevskii accurately, even though his expression was precise and clear. Convinced that no one could be certain that he had ascertained the truth, he was forever seeking new information, reflecting, and revising. He would have agreed that "truth is the daughter of time." One of the many paradoxes of his career is that he attracted so many others into the study of Russia's fascinating but baffling history that he established a school that carried forward his standards and approach.

More important than his excellence in all these principles and professional attributes was his uncanny insight into the historical process and his artistry as a writer: these two qualities gave his work its permanent distinction and ensured its impact upon the historical profession. The masterly analysis of the way in which institutions operate and change that made *Boyar Council* such an achievement was but an early illustration of these special skills.

In this volume and other works, his analyses were more subtle than the common sense or intuition they appeared. He continually sought to determine why something had happened and "could it have been otherwise?" In *Boyar Council*, this relentless probing uncovered the role that economic factors play in social and political change. This innovative analysis of social classes and the "building materials" and "social structure of administration" produced insights that were often profound and always stimulating. They especially encouraged students and readers to reflect on Russia's past, led advanced students and later generations into new searches, and exercised deep influence upon the way Russian scholars studied history. His other publications and lectures helped pave the way for the acceptance of Marxism by many intellectuals.

Kliuchevskii's artistry as a writer was more visible or obvious than his analytical skills. It also reflected conscious work to improve great natural talent: he honed his skills to become a master of prose style and one of Russia's greatest writers. In many ways, the words of J. B. Bury about Gibbon apply to him: "a singularly happy union of the historian and the man of letters" and "perhaps the clearest example that brilliance of style and accuracy of statement are perfectly compatible in a historian."[10]

Kliuchevskii had innate gifts as a writer and flirted with *belles-lettres* throughout his life. His archives contain short stories, poetry, satirical essays, and analyses of some of Russia's greatest writers and playwrights that he considered insufficiently polished for publication. One story illuminates his childhood in Penza. Others analyze characteristics he thought feminine. He left dozens of burnished aphorisms, usually reflections upon the nature of humanity, scholarship, and society. Together, these items and his published work reflect the artistic sensitivity of a scholar who enjoyed working with words.

Part of the secret of his style was reverence for the Russian language, which he considered a principal instrument of culture and the core of Russian civilization. He studied Russian constantly, analyzing words and their history, enlarging his vocabulary, and re-examining the works of Pushkin to improve his mode of expression.

A superb stylist, he combined simplicity of expression and a rich vocabulary with devout attention to grace and clarity. Composing was a pleasure, but rewriting he enjoyed even more. He continually revised his works in a relentless search for accuracy and lucidity. He labored to create aphorisms that would enable students and readers to understand and remember critical insights: "It is easy to write and talk in a heavy style, but to talk or write lightly is difficult." "The search for a word is a search for a thought." He constantly "polished the marble."

Even the position of a word or phrase in a sentence demanded infinite care, and he would test its sound before reaching a decision. The impressive rhetoric was the product of long searches, tests of alliterations and rhythms, and dedicated craftsmanship: success was "molten gold." When a colleague suggested that he published little when one considered his unremitting labor and immense knowledge, he replied, "In history, one should never hurry." Kizevetter's analysis of the progressive versions of the transcripts of the courses on the French Revolution showed that Kliuchevskii labored constantly to make lectures concise and clear. Over the years, he reduced the length of quotations or produced lucid summaries. He tightened narrative accounts. Sparkling phrases replaced sentences and even paragraphs. Comparing the lectures on Russian history that he gave early in the 1870s to those six, eight, or thirty years later illustrates his craft in selecting succinct quotations, providing transitions and summaries, and above all increasing elegance and lucidity. He introduced remarkably few substantive revisions: most modifications affected language and style. When he transformed transcripts into the *Course of Russian History,* he used sets from the early 1880s as the base. He incorporated some new knowledge but concentrated upon clarity and grace of expression.

Contemporaries remarked that he was "an artist before he was a historian," or defined him as "an artist with a feeling for truth" whose pages "read like a novel." Miliukov declared that his portraits were "forever ingrained upon the mind" and that his artistic skill set him aside from others. Platonov concluded that he "united a powerful mind, a wealth of learning, and poetic perception." Sergeevich, a conservative critic, complained that his deft writing concealed his thought. Pokrovskii agreed: he wrote as skillfully as Turgenev, but his scholarship was shallow and his "talent exclusively artistic."

Immense learning, professional discipline, dispassionate and discriminating analysis, common sense, affection for his country, and precision of thought and language lie beneath Kliuchevskii's eloquence. But he also developed an almost intuitive insight into Russian history. These skills and his talent in expression brought the past to life and provided analysis more important than the artistry. They carry his achievements far beyond the triumphs of a compelling lecturer and writer into an account that helped shape the view millions have of Russia and its history.

PART THREE

Explaining Russian History

NINE

The Origins of Russia and the Russians

The debate in the 1830s and 1840s between Slavophils and Westerners over the nature and destiny of Russia had apparently ended with the Westerners' triumph, but Kliuchevskii was aware that the issue had arisen in the seventeenth century and remained alive. Indeed, the intellectual atmosphere of his Moscow combined conservative Orthodox Russian nationalism and liberal, secular, questioning European thought. This controversy and the careful thought with which he organized his survey course in the 1870s ensured a central position for these crucial questions in his work. Moreover, whether his account was accurate or not, his definitions were, and remain, relevant. Thus, his placing Russia in a European framework and identifying Russians as Europeans from its very origin was as salient in the structure and substance of his account as the Soviet Russians' placing their country at the head of an international movement. Similarly, his assuming that Russia's origins lay in tenth-century Kiev and that the Ukrainians and Belorussians were Russians, a Russian "manifest destiny" approach, remains significant a hundred years later. His determining that circumstances made absolutism and then autocracy natural and necessary shaped the view of thousands of students and readers, abroad as well as in Russia. An analysis that describes the past as accurately but emphasized the long roots of constitutional and democratic government in the Bible, the boyar council, and the assembly of the land would have established a different structure and approach. Finally, his conclusion that the Russian Orthodox Church had exercised little influence in Russia's early centuries and that its "poverty of intellect" and the religious schism had baneful consequences exposed the weaknesses of one of society's pillars.

From the beginning, Kliuchevskii described his country and its people by making Russia a part of Europe and comparing its circumstances with those of Western Europe. He also portrayed and analyzed their origins and early centuries and the effects that location, geography, the autocratic system of rule, and the Church had exercised. In his account, the Church's shortcomings and relative insignificance and the various strains upon the autocracy, some caused by policies of the autocrats themselves, bear a remarkable resemblance to information now available concerning the weaknesses and problems that overwhelmed the Communist Party and the Soviet state at the end of the twentieth century.

In the Slavophil-Westerner debate, the Westerners saw Russia as a formless, backward, underdeveloped country that possessed no cultural distinction and had to borrow from the West to become a modern, civilized state. For the Slavophils, on the other hand, Russia was an organic, harmonious, agricultural nation with a distinct, superior civilization that its leaders should preserve from foreign contamination. The national church's role in creating and strengthening the state and people and their liturgy, architecture, music, and art had helped establish the country's unique character. The Slavophils also venerated the long-suffering *narod*, the Russian people whose folk wisdom preserved the state and culture in difficult circumstances. Finally, they found special virtues in native institutions, such as the commune or *obshchina*, which reflected the traditional Russian attitude toward collective action in a harmonious organic society.

Kliuchevskii's treatment of the controversy helps clarify his views concerning the nature of Russia. He ridiculed the dispute, terming it a false antithesis and minor affair involving two or three Moscow drawing rooms and their encounters with police. The rivals were "two attempts to study heavenly bodies under a microscope. Both are wrong, one to the right and the other to the left, but neither looks straight."[1] Instead, like Dostoevsky, he insisted that every intelligent Russian was both a patriot who loved his country and culture and a Westerner who continued the process of introducing European technology that had begun in the tenth century.

His definitions accepted some tenets fundamental to each. Like the Slavophils and many European liberal nationalists before 1870, he saw the world as a bundle of nation-states in each of which a nationality formed "a national union with a single culture" within relatively well-defined boundaries. As an undergraduate, he wrote that each society was an independent organism in which a people created its character and culture, even religious beliefs. This concept remained central: "Every society has its own nature and form." Each state possessed its own national group, rights, and responsibilities. Thus, Russia should include all Russians but no Poles, and an independent Poland should include all Poles, but only Poles. No national aggregation was superior or inferior to another, for each represented a "combination of factors" that history and tradition had formed into a whole. No state had the right to overrun or destroy another. However, the gradual absorption of small national groups or the peaceful blending of a small group into a large one was proper and inevitable. Thus, especially compelling pages describe the absorption of Finns and their culture in northeastern Russia by those Russians who moved from the Dnieper in the thirteenth and fourteenth centuries.

With the Westerners, Kliuchevskii considered Russia part of the European cultural community and state system long before Peter the Great. However, it was in Europe, but not of it. Europeans encountered a different world as they moved east. On occasion he referred to Russia as "the youngest part of Europe," "northeastern Europe," or "Eastern Europe," terms he may have acquired from Buslaev, who used them often.

In Kliuchevskii's judgment, Russia was as much a part of Europe as the Netherlands but was on its fringes. His undergraduate study of foreigners' impressions of Russia before the eighteenth century taught him that Europeans recognized this in the fifteenth century; they were more critical of Muscovy than of the Tatars because they considered Russia a European state that should observe European standards of behavior. However, Russia's position was complex because it had to preserve distinctive qualities against powerful external influences while participating in the life of the larger community.

On occasion, Kliuchevskii defined Russia by comparing it with Europe, but in a different fashion than had the Slavophils and Westerners. First, Europe consisted of a series of independent states. Each possessed its own language, population, and national character, but all shared a larger common culture. This he assumed but did not define, largely because of the inherent difficulty of defining a culture and civilization so old, rich, and varied. Europe's heart consisted of France, England, and Germany, in that order. He rarely mentioned Italy, Spain, Portugal, or the Scandinavian states. He appeared to assume that the Habsburg monarchy was either a state in which one people and culture had absorbed or were absorbing others or a confederation in which Germans, Czechs, Slovaks, Hungarians, and other nationalities were independent and free. The Balkans were a part of Europe geographically but not culturally: he discussed the area only when it became a source of conflict between Russia and the West.

The fundamental causes of distinctions between Russia and the West were location and geography, not religion. In emphasizing these factors, his choice of subjects and methods as a scholar most resemble those of Fernand Braudel, whose writing on the history of France and the Mediterranean world has profoundly affected many twentieth-century scholars. The first volume of Braudel's *L'Identité de la France*, entitled *Espace et l'histoire*, contains a chapter entitled "How Geography Created France." Braudel's account of the high cost of defending French frontiers, a traditional one among French scholars, is similar to Kliuchevskii's analysis of the pressures that Asia and the steppe placed upon Russian society. If Kliuchevskii had given his famous third chapter a brief caption, it would have been "How Geography Created Russia." Similarly, he would have entitled his celebrated twenty-first chapter on the rise of Moscow "The Advantages of Moscow's Location."

The first two chapters of the *Course of Russian History* constitute a chronicle of the effect that natural features exercised upon Russia and his country's immunity to foreign ways and ideas in early centuries. The introductory lecture each year stressed that geography had played an important role in early Russian history, reduced in modern times by advances in transportation and communications. In the 1890s, he urged (unsuccessfully) that the university require each history student to take a new course on Russian historical geography.

In Kliuchevskii's view, Europe was a small area with lengthy shorelines. Its bays, harbors, and river basins provided access to the world and its cultures. Mountain ranges and river valleys created distinct national communities. These made Europe a congeries of peoples and states sharing a culture and other bonds that justified their being referred to as Europe or the West, although each possessed individual qualities. Holland's rich, flat land, access to the riches of Europe and the open seas, and wealth from distant colonies helped explain why that country differed from its near neighbors and from Russia as well. In addition, Europe was blessed rather than harmed by nature and was "sheltered by an advance guard and a rear guard." It benefited also from colonies, which helped its people attain "progress in industry, trade, social life, science, and the arts."[2]

In part because of these formative elements, Europeans developed a lively culture based on individual rights and political structures in which the chosen government system served the population in an easy and friendly way. The West therefore was freer and richer than Russia. By the late nineteenth century, its peoples had established constitutional monarchies or were moving along a path toward constitutional and representative government.

On the other hand, Russia filled much of the vast flat region between two geographical areas that shaped two different cultures. Europe occupied the small western end of the great Eurasian plain, Russia the middle, and Asia, on which Kliuchevskii turned his back, the other large extremity. "A neglected state between Europe and Asia, between forest and steppes, far from the educated old world, battered by a harsh life, rapacious neighbors, and the West," Russia had sacrificed generations, "fertilizing the Don and Volga steppes with Russian blood" and "defending the eastern gates of Europe from Asia in guard service, always thankless and forgotten."[3]

Its distance from warming seas guaranteed a climate of extremes and little rainfall. Much of Russia had been forest, so creating clearings, living in hamlets overshadowed by dark areas, and frequent moving because of overused soil had kept Russians poor. Slow, meandering rivers in some areas countered these forces by providing a wide horizon and a sense of community, but they did not open Russia to the world. The small shoreline except in the frozen north in effect isolated the country.

For Kliuchevskii more than for the Slavophils and Westerners, the origins of Russia and the Russians formed an important part of his definition. Writing about centuries of which little was known, he placed the genesis of the Slavs on the northeastern slopes of the Carpathian Mountains in the sixth century. Those later known as the western and southern Slavs moved into the territories they have since occupied, while the eastern branch migrated into the western edges of the boundless and almost uninhabited Euro-Asian plain and the Dnieper valley.

After the eastern Slavs had settled in the Kievan region, they combined with the Varangians, or Vikings from Scandinavia, who acquired control over some of western Europe and the western Mediterranean at the same time they established trade connections between Scandinavia and Byzantium. In Kliuchevskii's judgment, they founded the Kievan principality when Slavs invited them to provide military power and leadership against Pecheneg raids from the steppes. Thus, Varangian explorers and armed merchants, "an alien ruling class over a dependent population," established the city of Kiev and the Kievan principality. Indeed, his course on estates declared that the word *Rusi* in the tenth century was not an ethnographic or geographical term but referred to the governing estate, the Varangians. These invited rulers and the eastern Slavs then combined over a period of two or three centuries to form the Russian nationality. The people and culture of Kiev were Russian, that part of the European plain became Russian, and the Kievan principality was the first Russian state, the mother state of Russia and "the foundation of Russian history." Moreover, popular recognition of Kiev's role in establishing the national culture explained the affection that Russians felt for Kiev.

Kliuchevskii acknowledged that he was not a specialist on this period or these issues and that the strongest evidence for his conclusions was linguistic. He ridiculed those who squabbled over the identity of the founders of the state and people. No one had sufficient information to make a sensible judgment; whoever they were, they had helped establish the state that became Russia. He gradually reduced the number of pages devoted to these issues in the successive lithographs, but he kept them under review, devoted a detailed lecture to them in his historiography course, and drafted unpublished essays on them late in life.[4]

A subsidiary conclusion was that the Russians were from the beginning European: explorers and merchants from Europe combined with peaceful Slavs to form the state and people in a territory that possessed no cultural tradition or even ruins on which to build. For generations, the only connection with the advanced outside world was the thin commercial line connecting Scandinavia and Byzantium, one perpetually threatened and ultimately cut by marauders from the steppe. Educated Russians almost inevitably turned westward, as a sunflower follows the sun.

Kiev was not only the first Russian state but also "the cradle of Russian nationality." As the center of a genealogical federation, it also became "the mother of the other cities of Russia." Above all, in ninth-century Kiev rose "the idea of the Russian land," the crucial conviction that Russians shared a common fatherland, culture, needs, and goals. Kliuchevskii's nationalism was more territorial than ethnographic: "the idea of the Russian land" was the most important bond that held Russia together. The *Russian Primary Chronicle* was an especially venerated source, because the thirteenth-century chronicler emphasized Kiev's role as a legend and symbol of the "national idea of unity."[5] The princes and boyars in particular, but the *narod* as well, kept the vision alive throughout the period when the Russians divided into three groups and during all subsequent crises.

In the thirteenth and fourteenth centuries, social disintegration of the slave-owning Kievan society and raids from the steppes broke up Kiev and dispersed the population. In Kliuchevskii's view, the groups who separated them and their descendants remained forever Russian. One aggregate remained on the right or west bank of the Dnieper River, spread westward into Galicia, and by the fourteenth century was called Little Russian. The second group migrated northeastward to the Moscow region of the Oka and the upper Volga, a move he ascribed to internal divisions before the Mongols appeared. By the sixteenth century, it had absorbed the Finns in that area and formed the Great Russians. These migrant settlers proved their Kievan origins by bringing with them the epic poems and names of the villages they had left behind, much as seventeenth-century English settlers carried their values and village names to North America.

As early as the twelfth century, Andrei Bogoliubskii in the remote northeast proclaimed the unity of all Russian land. Between the twelfth and sixteenth centuries, national priorities gradually became greater than local ones. The Great Russians in the northeast established a new order of princely rule and a spirit of national self-confidence. From this foundation, they slowly began accumulating strength and gathering all Russians. Then, aided by popular acceptance of "the idea of the Russian land, . . . the most deep and secret strength of the Russian people," and "armed with the strength of the united state, they returned southwest to the Dnieper to rescue the weak part of the Russian *narod* from foreign influence and rule." This emphasis upon gathering Russians represented the same irredentist nationalism that drove the Germans, French, Italians, and others of Kliuchevskii's time to bring into political union all members of their nationalities and all territories to which ancestors had a claim.

In Kliuchevskii's judgment, the drive for regaining hallowed territory and attaining unity was a central feature of Russian history. Early in the famous survey, he declared that "the history of Russia is that of a country that colonizes" and that "colonization is the fundamental fact of our history."[6]

In the long, arduous, but peaceful reunification process, the Great Russians first filled the region from Smolensk west to the Dnieper, which he termed "northwest Russia," but which now constitutes Belorus and part of Ukraine. His terminology course created the impression that much of that area was uninhabited until the Great Russians arrived from Moscow and that the Belorussians and Belorus did not appear until the sixteenth century. Moreover, he apparently considered the Belorussians a product of the westward-moving Great Russians' cultural absorption of "the pagan and semibarbarous Lithuanians" between 1400 and 1600, much as the blend of Russians and Finns formed the

Great Russians. In fact, although he admitted that the word *Belorussian* appeared late in the fourteenth century, he did not define it in the course on terminology or use it until late in life.

Treatment of the Ukrainians was summary: he simply considered them Russians. He did not use the word *Ukrainian* and rarely referred to them as Little Russians. In his judgment, the term *Little Russian* had appeared first in a 1347 reference to Russians who lived on the right or west bank of the Dnieper. Muscovite Russians so dominated his view that his M.A. thesis on the lives of old Russian saints utterly neglected the noted saints of Kiev.

The Lithuanians emerge as a minor people, absorbed as the Finns had been earlier. He ignored their long history as a distinct nationality who had formed an independent state and then as part of the Polish-Lithuanian Commonwealth became subject to Polish cultural influence. The union of the Polish and Lithuanian states at the marriage of Jagiello and Jadwiga in 1386 was "an artificial alliance of two alien and even hostile states" that shared no common interests. The Poles and Lithuanians together then subjected West Russia, which the Great Russians liberated in the gathering process.

The only significant resistance to Russian reunification came from Poles, who claimed territory that Kliuchevskii considered Russian. However, the anti-Russian policies of the Polish nobility who became predominant in the 1569 Union of Poland and Lithuania at Lublin drove many Russians south and created a breeding ground for insurrection. In the seventeenth century, these "godless and stateless" Cossack Russians united under the Russian national and religious banner to help rescue the Little Russians, former Lithuanians who had become Russian, and others from Polish kings, nobles, and priests. The Treaty of Andrusovo in 1667 ended this stage of the long conflict with Poland and won for Russia the Smolensk region and much of the territory on the east bank of the Dnieper north of Kiev. It also justified the tsar's title, "Autocrat of All Great, Little, and Belo Russia, Lithuania, Volynia, and Podolia."

Kliuchevskii recognized that the conflict between the Russian Orthodox Church and the Ukrainian Catholic Church, or Uniates, played a part in the relationship between Russians and Little Russians after the sixteenth century, but he considered the dispute national, not religious. His descriptions of the formation of the Uniate Church were clear, but not even the most assiduous reader would learn why these Little Russians later resisted rejoining the Russian Orthodox Church. He simply assumed that all Uniates were Russians who should and would one day rejoin the Russian Orthodox Church. But the goal of the gathering process was the return of national groups to the nation, not of religious groups to the Church.

The fundamental elements of this account are his assumptions that the concept of Russian nationality appeared in the early centuries and that the Ukrainians and Belorussians considered themselves Russian and were Russian. He ignored the existence of separate Ukrainian and Belorussian nationalities and cultures and those who proclaimed it: in his judgment, these peoples were

Russians. They shared history, nationality, and culture with the Great Russians, who were twice as numerous as the Little Russians and Belorussians combined and who had absorbed them or incorporated them into a unified Russian nationality and state. In short, identifying Russians was a simple process. The Russian state under a kind of "manifest destiny" included all Russians, and the "return" of Little Russians and Belorussians to "the Russian land" was "natural and necessary."

In Kliuchevskii's eyes, "the gathering of the Russian lands" was not complete when he died. Millions of Russians (actually Ukrainians) lived under Austrian rule in Galicia, a part of "the Russian land" under foreign governance. A central concern of foreign policy in the nineteenth and twentieth centuries was "the struggle for those parts of the Russian land that the Moscow state had not yet regained." "Natural boundaries" constituted a separate issue, but acquisition of Finland and Bessarabia in the nineteenth century had enabled the state to attain those goals. Of other boundaries, even of expansion in Central Asia and the Far East, he wrote nothing. His Russia was European Russia, the state that included the Russian people, the three capitals, Kiev, Moscow, and St. Petersburg, and above all "the Russian land."

That part of Kliuchevskii's definition of Russia and Russians that incorporated Belorus and Ukraine and absorbed Belorussians and Ukrainians was one shared by Soloviev and most other nineteenth-century Russian historians. Kliuchevskii simply expressed it more lucidly and effectively than they. Moreover, his account affected professional historians, beginning with those whom he helped train and those who produced textbooks and other popular volumes, so it remains a thread in the past's tapestry that remains vivid a century later.

Kostomarov posited a rival definition to this classic nationalist one even when Kliuchevskii was an undergraduate, but the tsarist government dismissed him from university appointments and prohibited publication of many of his writings. However, a growing number of Ukrainian historians, most notably Mykhailo Hrushevs'kyi, and the Ukrainian nationalism they helped stimulate bloomed in the half-century after Kostomarov died in 1885. This flowering, which became visible a generation or two later than Russian nationalism, was part of this powerful movement that has swept the eastern part of Europe and other parts of the world as well in the past century.

Ukrainian and Belorussian scholars, in part because many have been professional searchers for the truth but also because they are nationalist, and many other twentieth-century specialists on this simple but also immensely complicated subject have rejected the Russian nationalist definition of the Russian people and the lands they occupy. For example, they suggest, with considerable justice, that Ukrainians possess a distinct language, culture, and history, older than and different from that of the Russians. Different nationalities created Kiev and Moscow: Kiev was and remains the mother and center of Ukraine and the Ukrainians. The origins of Russia and the Russians lie in the Moscow region in the fourteenth century, not in Kiev.

After the Ukrainians failed to establish an independent state in the chaos following the First World War, Stalin in 1930 began to crush Ukrainian and Belorussian nationalism and scholarship. Under his prodding, Soviet scholars used archeological, linguistic, numismatic, and other forms of evidence to "prove" that the creators of the Kievan principality were Slavic ancestors of those who came to be known as Russians, and indeed were the first Russians, and that Kiev was the first Russian state. Some, led by B. A. Rybakov, even discovered a Slavic tribe called "Rus" in the Kievan area before the ninth century. In their view, the Ukrainians and Belorussians are fraternal descendants of this tribe who separated after the disintegration of Kiev and reunited in 1654.

Ukrainian and Belorussian nationalism continued to smolder even under Soviet rule until they burst into flame after 1985. Ukrainian scholars began to publish research about Kostomarov in the early 1980s. Kiev University in 1989 reprinted Kostomarov's autobiography and began a new edition of Hrushevs'kyi's works. These revivals and the establishment of independent Ukraine and Belorus as the Soviet Union collapsed have demonstrated the force of nationalism.

Russian, Belorussian, Ukrainian, and other specialists and publicists will continue research and discussion on whether Kiev was "the mother city of Russia" or the first capital of Ukraine and the cradle of the Ukrainian people. Kliuchevskii's works, those of others who share his views, and the writings of men such as Rybakov will serve as instruments for Russian nationalists, as scholars in each country seek to locate evidence that sustains positions they have chosen. But political developments within these countries and relations among them will no doubt be decisive, at least in the short run.

Kliuchevskii, Miliukov, and others were critical of Soloviev's defense of "unpardonable despotism and petty tyranny" and comments upon minorities, especially Jews. None of Kliuchevskii's published works mention Jews, although examination questions inquired about their economic role in West Russia. The course on the French Revolution praised the 1791 grant of equality to Jews, and he wrote letters to newspapers praising two liberal Jewish editors as Russian patriots. He ignored the vehement anti-Polish and anti-Semitic campaigns of men such as Dostoevsky and Katkov. Moreover, while Karpov, his closest friend for a quarter of a century, was openly anti-Semitic, only a handful of comments in Kliuchevskii's first two years of teaching at the military school, in draft papers, and in his diary refer disparagingly to Jews or refer to them as Yids.[7] In sum, the Jews of Anatevka, Odessa, and Moscow were beyond his circles: they simply did not exist.

For a nationalist historian in Moscow intensely interested in Western influence, Kliuchevskii devoted surprisingly little attention to Poles and Catholicism. There is no evidence that he was acquainted with any Poles or Catholics. An 1861 letter assigned responsibility for student demonstrations to Poles. His diary later in the decade blamed the Polish revolt of 1863 for ending the reform period. Unpublished 1896 lectures on Alexander II declared that émigrés had planned the 1830–31 and 1863 uprisings and denied that either had popular support or national content. His descriptions of Alexander Wielopolski and Ludwig Miroslavskii contain gibes: the former was "a real Pole: taciturn, educated, although without talent, not stupid but malicious, like all Poles," and the latter "a representative of democrats and communists." A diary entry in the 1890s ridiculed the "complicated sickly-savory-sad music of Chopin."[8]

Even the course on the French Revolution contained only a few lines on Polish history and the Polish revolution of 1830. The *Boyar Council* barely mentioned comparisons between the rise and decline of the council in Russia and similar institutions in the Kingdom of Poland or the Polish-Lithuanian Commonwealth, which he termed "the northwestern area" or "West Russia." Neither Poland nor the struggle between Catholicism and Orthodoxy over "the borderlands of Europe" occupied a central role in his account until late in life. On the other hand, several pages in the 1909 textbook for his course described the Balkan conflict as a Russian effort to free fellow Slavs and Orthodox Christians from Muslim rule. Hostilities between Russia and the Ottoman Empire were between two cultures, one Orthodox Christian and the other Muslim.

His published works rarely refer to the Catholic Church and Catholicism, but occasional unpublished comments were vicious. Thus, an 1868 diary entry noted that scholasticism did not save the "prodigal daughter of Christianity" from the "blasphemous papacy, with its doctrine of visible supremacy and infallibility," nor from "the abomination of religious fanaticism . . . the eternal shame of Catholicism." His archives contain a fragment on Dostoevsky that referred to Catholicism as "an un-Christian faith" that bred socialism, but that may have been a summary of Dostoevsky's views, not of Kliuchevskii's. They also include a draft paragraph dated March 4, 1910, that referred to "the backward nonsense of Catholicism." At the same time, he admonished Russians who ridiculed Catholic doctrine on purgatory but failed to condemn the Orthodox Church's emphasis on devils.[9]

Neither Kliuchevskii's published works nor his private papers refer to Church and state policies after 1881 that discriminated against ethnic and religious minorities, even though the Moscow press must have made him aware of these programs. He never referred to the prohibition against publishing in Ukrainian, Belorussian, and Lithuanian or the suppression of national and social unrest in the western borderlands. He apparently assumed that everyone in Russia was or should be Russian and Orthodox and accepted state policies to ensure conformity. In this, he reflected the conventional nationalism of his milieu and that era of European history.

On the other hand, ignoring the realities of state policy toward non-Russians and non-Orthodox was in part deliberate. For example, he frequently summarized interpretations of events or individuals that differed from his, but he failed to mention rival versions concerning the origins and character of the Russian state and nationality and the nature of the colonization process. From his student days, he was aware of the Ukrainian interpretation of the early centuries, which his close friend Karpov vigorously denounced. Later, he learned that other scholars recognized that the Ukrainian and Belorussian peoples possessed their own languages and cultures and were distinct from the Russians. He read some of Kostomarov's early work while a student in Penza and heard Soloviev criticize his views when he came to Moscow. He cited Kostomarov works in undergraduate papers, heard Kostomarov's highly praised paper in 1874 in Kiev, and discussed Kostomarov's views in his study of the land assemblies. Kostomarov's autobiography must have attracted his attention, because *Russian Thought* published it in 1885, a year in which two of the journal's issues included Kliuchevskii essays. His archives even contain a draft paper he wrote on Kostomarov's talent as a storyteller. However, Kliuchevskii's works ignore Kostomarov's view that Ukrainians were a distinct nationality, the Ukrainians possessed an independent culture, the history of Kiev was an integral part of Ukrainian history, not Russian history, and no genetic ties existed between Kiev and northeastern Russia.

Kliuchevskii's instructors, friends, and acquaintances and almost all his students were Russian. He considered all the young scholars he trained Russian, although one was Ukrainian, another had a Ukrainian mother and a Serbian father, and a third was Belorussian. He knew no Poles, Balts, or Germans and only two or three Jews. He did not visit regions where more than scattered numbers of non-Russians lived, and even those he no doubt assumed were being absorbed, as the Finns had been earlier.

Late in life he recognized the shallow character of his knowledge and encouraged two young scholars he trained to study the peoples of western Russia. One, Matvei K. Liubavskii, was a Russianized Belorussian born in Riazan', and the other, Vladimir I. Picheta, was a Russianized Ukrainian twenty years younger. Throughout their lives, which extended to 1936 and 1947, respectively, they considered themselves guardians of Kliuchevskii's "sacred legacy" and tried to pass on his values and skills. Both considered Kiev the foundation of Russian history and the history of Russia one of colonization and expansion from the center. However, their gradual awareness that the Lithuanians, Belorussians, and Ukrainians possessed histories and cultures of their own contributed to their modifying Kliuchevskii's definition of Russia and the Russians. But the scholarship of these two men and the complicated and tortured political history of this issue under Soviet rule is another subject.

The distinctive qualities that Kliuchevskii attributed to Russians formed another element of his definition. His assumption that Russians, and others as well, possessed a character of their own was one held by many nineteenth-century nationalist historians. Macaulay, Michelet, and Treitschke are only three who identified qualities that made their countrymen distinct and superior. Indeed, the additional assumption or article of faith of many, especially in well-organized states, that their people's qualities made them superior to others, remained common until after the First World War and still survives in some areas. Hitler's policies and his pronouncements on the superlative qualities of the Germans and the inferior and corrupting ones of Jews, Poles, and others demolished the pseudoscientific claims some nationalists had made, as well as their respectability.

Kliuchevskii's knowledge of the country's past and his nationalism led him to find distinctive qualities among Russians, although some of the most important did not exalt the national character. This critical attitude reflects the realism that marks his work and distinguishes his nationalism from the more aggressive type that many of his European contemporaries displayed.

Kliuchevskii's interest in the character of individuals and his relentless probing for explanations of the processes behind historical change led him gradually into curiosity about psychology and, ultimately, national psychology. Thus, his description of Ivan the Terrible in 1872 emphasized Ivan's consciousness and behavior. In the course on methodology in 1884, he told students that history was "a popular-psychological study" or a study of the "historical personality of a people." He praised Boltin for demonstrating that study of others' histories helped one identify Russia's national character, and he occasionally cited Taine's judgment that "all historical events are psychological phenomena." The early pages of the *Course of Russian History* compared Russia to a human being suffering from a nervous ailment, an analysis that one scholar termed a psychological portrait of the Great Russians. As Marc Raeff has noted, his articles discussing the nobility emphasized the psychological effects of their social-political position.

Moreover, his interpretation of Western influence upon the religious schism was almost exclusively psychological. Most of his last articles on individuals such as Afanasii Ordin-Nashchokin, Pushkin, and Nikolai N. Novikov reflected concern with what he considered fundamental aspects of national character. They related the individual's career to history and national character by analyzing family origins, education, moral and intellectual qualities, and philosophy, as well as the period and milieu.

In his last two decades, Kliuchevskii was an active member of the Moscow Psychological Society and published essays in its journal, *Questions of Philosophy and Psychology.* At a dinner in his honor in 1902, the Society's president praised him as "one of Russia's most profound thinkers and original psychologists." The vice-president, his friend Trubetskoi, described him as "a psychologist who taught history."[10]

Kliuchevskii's description of Russian national character differed from that of the Slavophils because it rested on his understanding of the effect that circumstances and historical development had exercised. The first two volumes of the *Course of Russian History* constitute a chronicle of the effect that these had exerted to form the Russian character, whether in Kiev on the banks of the Dnieper, in fifteenth-century Pskov, in the northeast, or in Galicia.

No people could select a culture other than the inherited one, just as no man could choose to become a tenor rather than a bass. Russians were different from others, as Germans, Poles, all peoples were distinct, because of the circumstances in which they lived and their historical backgrounds. Over centuries, a society could change through a slow and gradual process, but fundamental transformation was impossible. Folklore and linguistics taught that many Russian words, customs, and foods were of foreign origin, as were everyday instruments of domestic life. However, these increments were a natural, even inevitable part of the historical process in which one culture slowly absorbed slight additions from another, as a flower changes color through the seasons, but not form or character.

While Russians possessed a distinct temperament and capabilities, individual Russians enjoyed qualities that distinguished them from others. Moreover, Russia had well-defined classes: its peasants were quite different from its nobles. French peasants were distinct from Russian peasants, as English nobles were from Russian nobles. But all Russians shared certain common features, as did all members of other nationalities.

The most notable Russian characteristic was easy acceptance of absolutist rule. This posture, huge social fissures, and class antagonisms nourished an obsequiousness already deeply rooted that laid the foundations for the serfdom that emerged in the seventeenth century. This servile attitude and serfdom together were "a sacrifice that our country was forced to make in the seventeenth century in its struggle for safety and external security."[11]

Moreover, the state's domination grew and freedom declined as Russian territory expanded and relations with the ever more powerful West became closer: he noted an inverse relationship between territorial expansion and freedom. Serfdom reached its peak, or nadir, at the time Catherine the Great pushed the country's boundaries westward.

Reticence, self-control, resourcefulness, and endurance were other distinct elements. A section in the first volume of the *Course of Russian History* entitled "The Psychology of the Great Russians" emphasized that "no people in Europe is capable of such intense work for a short time as the Great Russians, but it seems, too, that no people in Europe is so unaccustomed to sustained, measured, constant labor."[12] He found a remarkable degree of moral consistency in his countrymen and thought no people less spoiled. Russians were also resolute. The essay on Saint Sergei noted that "one of the distinguishing characteristics of a great people is its ability to rise to its feet after a fall." Such fortitude or toughness under pressure or attack constituted "the deepest and most secret strength of the Russian people."

Russians were also peaceable: colonization was a nonviolent process, not conquest or imperialism, and wandering was an individual adjunct of that quality. In Soloviev's words, the Russian people "were forced to be military, although they were not at all militaristic." Moreover, local rulers, not their people, caused the little resistance that did occur. The Great Russians' assimilation of Finns, Lithuanians, and others was tranquil and untroubled. The Belorussians and Little Russians or Ukrainians eagerly accepted Great Russian leadership in the gathering of the Russian people, demonstrating that patriotism was a deeply rooted national quality. However, Kliuchevskii ridiculed the suggestion that Moscow was, would be, or could be the Third Rome: messianism was not an element of the quiet, inward-looking Russian character.

The Time of Troubles, serfdom, and the religious schism in the seventeenth century solidified Russians' basic characteristics. They also added a sense of melancholy, as informed Russians became aware that their state, once independent and self-assured, was losing its cultural integrity. This gloom, almost despair, deepened in the nineteenth century when recognition of Western superiority shattered Russian self-confidence. Kliuchevskii's essays on Pushkin and Lermontov sought to demonstrate how pessimism and loss of nerve had sunk into Russian consciousness. Leskov and Chekhov represented a further stage of these qualities. For Kliuchevskii, a twisting road going nowhere became a symbol of Russian character.

The Flow of Russian History

The chief cause of history appears to be history.
—Archibald Cary Coolidge

Kliuchevskii had no interest in or knowledge of philosophy, confessed that his mind was feeble when confronting abstractions, and rarely used philosophical terms or even words such as *nationalism* and *patriotism*. He considered his brief effort to construct a philosophy of history a failure: the study of history was an art, not a science. History "must not be philosophical if it wishes to remain history." In short, he would have rejected Hayden White's dictum that there is "an irresistible ideological component in every historical account of reality" and that every historian develops a philosophy of history, although it may be inconsistent and unclear.[1]

In the 1884 course on methodology, he used Bossuet and Hegel as targets when he declared that no philosophy of history could explain what had happened and what was likely in the future. Late in life, both his diary and the first two chapters of his most famous volumes reiterated that position, concentrating then against the Slavophil interpretation. He accepted evolution but emphasized that continuity did not mean progress. Men moved neither forward nor backward, and no political system or period of time was superior to another. Moreover, "progress in some spheres of life is accompanied by losses in others."

Although he did not read Comte or any of the positivists nor mention positivism, his methodology resembled theirs. Thus, he believed that a probing analysis of all materials would produce an accurate account and lead toward discovery of the laws of history. In the words of his successor, "His mind always needed concrete factual material, as a fire needs fuel. For him, facts seemed to take the place of logical constructs. That is why he was organically incapable of setting himself the task of extrapolating the entire course of Russian history from any kind of abstract principle."[2] However, as Braudel has pointed out, "Narrative history is not an objective method, still less the supreme objective method, but is itself a philosophy of history."[3]

In spite of his skepticism concerning philosophy of history, Kliuchevskii found a clear, coherent, even deterministic pattern in Russia's past. In his judgment, gradual change was an "eternal law" of human life. Each element or "reality" in every society was in a constant process of change, and each alteration in each element produced modifications in the other structural materials. Indeed, the principal factor affecting all histories was the permanent process produced by the "complicated interaction of shifting bundles of building materials." These generated slow and gradual changes within society in a course that was not logical, rational, moral, providential, or predetermined, but natural and "national psychological."

Continuity and change were both evident throughout history, but change gradually reshaped the most ancient institutions, customs, and values, as successively superseding concentric circles form when a stone falls into water. Kliuchevskii often used "natural and necessary," a phrase popular with Soloviev, who inherited it from Guizot. Sometimes he substituted "sociological determinism," particularly when he referred to the effects geography and economic conditions produced. He noted that "the history of humanity is an endless series of facts, completely independent of personal will, apparently even independent of individual consciousness. In this it resembles nature." Thus, Rurik had no alternative but to establish the Kievan kingdom, just as a tenor had to remain a tenor even though he might prefer to be a bass. The scholar's function is to analyze and describe the flow of history: "To know one's history is to understand why it was so and the consequences to which earlier periods inevitably led. This is why someone who understands the past is not always a historian."

All events are products of "the laws of the interaction of historical forces," part of the general historical process through which all society moves, for "the same general laws govern the history of mankind." These laws were hidden to his generation and its immediate successors, who were collecting the raw material on national histories from which scholars would one day create a science of history, based on a combination of geography and sociology. But one general historical law was already apparent, the gradual disappearance of social inequality in every society: "Political community begins with distinctions within society that gradually disappear as history moves on."

The process of history, "the external reflection of natural changes in society's social structure," has few sharp breaks, saints, heroes, or devils and lacks a beginning and an ending. The record is organic and continuous, unspectacular and gradual, flowing like a river, sometimes spilling over the banks. "Inherited administrative deposits," not the judgment or will of men such as Ivan the Terrible or Peter the Great, over the centuries transform institutions, habits, and values. "The past does not move forward without influence. Only the people have gone on, but they have left everything to us as inherited property. . . . We are in great part their content and feelings. . . . Consequently, the history of our native land is our biography. . . . The object of history is the historical process."[4] Changes that some label reforms are "the products of all the previous history of a people" and grow from widely recognized needs. Peter the Great's Northern War was a powerful engine of reform, but reform would have occurred without that war. Often a society appears to advance. At other times, it seems to retreat. But where one historian sees advance, another sees retreat because judgments are subjective. Education is an important cause of change, because its effects are gradual, but efforts to hasten or direct change through "violent interruption of the established political tradition" rest upon the illusion that man can control the flow. Such attempts inevitably fail. Reconstruction after a failed endeavor is slow and painful, but the stream of history invariably returns within established banks, of course affected by the interference and violence.

In sum, Kliuchevskii assumed that providing a historical account of an institution constituted both a definition and an explanation: "History is the main cause of history." The past was a seamless web in which every development was the consequence of previous events in new conditions. Every era quietly ripened into its successor. Examples abound to demonstrate this. Thus, the original harsh circumstances gradually lost authority as man acquired mastery over some geographical elements and reduced the effects of climate. Pressure from the steppe and Asia declined as Russia became stronger. "National religious unity" had constituted a major force until the religious schism in the seventeenth century, after which the autocratic state assumed leadership of the drive for national unity that gradually became secular.

Boyar Council traced the slow, undramatic, and organic rise and decline of an institution from the tenth century until late in the seventeenth century, the councils first helping to manage small princedoms and later helping to direct the Moscow state. The volume emphasized the role of families and family alliances, the immense power of customs and traditions, and the continuous way changing elements and combinations transformed the institution. The departments and colleges of later tsars simply modified the council as it faded away.

Kliuchevskii's studies of social structures and the rise and decline of the land assembly analyze similar processes. He divided Russian history into four periods, but "the idea of the Russian land" and colonization linked the segments and helped each period grow into its successor. Even the organization of the *Course of Russian History* reflects this approach. Few chapters have precise headings or titles, and the paragraphs and chapters flow into each other.

His treatment of historiography, the rise of the state and the autocracy, and the origins and abolition of serfdom illustrates the role that gradual change played as well as his eclectic explanations. Indeed, the process through which he created the course on historiography served as an unplanned model of the way transformations occurred in history and of his effort to record it. In its first year, he taught students how to use primary sources. He then added lectures on the first collectors and editors of documents and on eighteenth-century amateur historians. Finally, he moved back in time to the first Russian historians, who appeared during the Time of Troubles. In sum, he showed that Russian historiography had developed at the same pace as the nation's history. It was an essential part of the national past, one of the "bundles of realities" that underwent constant modifications and transformed other elements of the country's constitution. Historians were as important as rulers: they reflected the laws of history, influenced other elements of society, and enabled a people to understand itself by explaining its origins and development. The twelve lectures and essays on contributors to historical scholarship were part of that instructional campaign, as were the ten he prepared on anniversaries and the abolition of serfdom. Similar lectures and articles commemorating the birth or death of scholars, saints, rulers, and writers sought to make Russians aware of the continuities that bound past and present.

In Kliuchevskii's judgment, the origins of the state lay in primary or natural unions. The secondary or artificial union known as the state gradually replaced the tribe, as the tribe had succeeded the family and clan when changes made them inadequate instruments. The foundations of the state and nationality lay in Kiev, which also produced the crucial "idea of the Russian land." The early Russians divided geographically, but Great Russian leadership brought the Great Russians, Belorussians, and Little Russians together in a unified state and people. As this process gathered momentum in the fifteenth century, Muscovy, "the Great Russian national state," became the defender of national interest in an inexorable series of steps. Ideas, except for "the idea of the Russian land," played no role. He compared Moscow to an anthill, a huge, lifeless collective body "without any traces of individual happiness," from which emerged a powerful, unified Russia.[5]

The foundation was faith in national unity, which legitimized the centralized power's replacing the contractual agreements and freedoms of the appanage centuries. Location and geography were significant. Moscow's early isolation offered protection, and its position at the center of a river network provided commercial advantage. The *pomest'e* system contributed: the ruler granted land to those who agreed to fulfill obligatory military service against Asia, the steppe, and the Germans. The land of northeastern Russia was so poor that the nobles tended to gather around the ruler, who rewarded them with grants from conquests, making them "the earliest shareholders in the Russian state."

The rulers' part in Moscow's rise was minor. Indeed, the mediocrity of its princes, more products than causes of its success, was an important reason for Moscow's emergence and rise. Their promotion of Moscow's growth through Mongol grants, purchase, and seizure of property contributed quietly to the state's gradual eminence. The system of succession also kept the land together. Constant migration and colonization then helped fill the huge, poor, and sparsely populated land over which the center gradually tightened control.

The same eclectic description of Moscow's emergence as the capital also explained the rise of the autocratic system. Kliuchevskii almost derisively eliminated Novgorod and Pskov as possible centers or as precursors of another form of government than autocracy. Location, geography, social disunities, and the power of nationalism together condemned them to become permanent and indistinguishable parts of a Russia ruled autocratically from Moscow.

Maintaining control over expanding territory and defending open boundaries tended to concentrate power. Indeed, Russia's defense of Europe against Asiatic pressure was responsible in part for autocracy. Kliuchevskii demonstrated in detail that Moscow continued to use the boyar council and land assembly until their melding in the seventeenth century made autocracy the natural and apparently inevitable system of rule.

The crucial period for enthroning the state and establishing autocracy was that between the mid-sixteenth and mid-seventeenth centuries, a plateau that both separated and joined early and modern Russian history, with the Time of Troubles a hinge. It included part of the reign of Ivan the Terrible, the Time of Troubles, and the years until the religious schism. During that century, the autocracy and serfdom together became dominant forces, with roots extending deep into Russian history. One of Kliuchevskii's most famous phrases applies to the period after 1613: "The state grew fat, the people grew lean." Neither Ivan's reign nor the Time of Troubles nor any other individual or event was a turning point: they were all parts of the seamless web, of the constant undramatic flow.

During the plateau century, Russians gradually recognized that the state was more important than the dynasty. As the national will emerged late in the Time of Troubles, they accepted an unencumbered state as the instrument for achieving the general welfare. The boyar council gradually lost its share of government. The land assemblies, which had helped create the sense of nation, faded because they too proved unnecessary. By the middle of the seventeenth century, Russia was no longer the absolute monarchy of Ivan the Terrible tempered by an aristocratic administration. Instead, it gradually became an autocracy, the "natural and necessary" consequence of a process that flowed from historical circumstances. During a period of about a half-century, the new dynasty slowly established a firm grip on power, the structure of society changed, the nobility began its ascent, and westward expansion advanced.

Kliuchevskii also emphasized the role of unremitting, slow change in articles on serfdom and Peter the Great's poll tax and in summary accounts in the *Course of Russian History.* The essays unfolded slowly and gradually: their organization and style seemed examples of the historical law. Their dispassion reflected his scholarly approach: he revealed his feelings only in denunciation of the nobles but provided no information on the sufferings of millions of serfs.

Most Russian historians of serfdom before 1917 supported his analysis. More recent scholarship has saluted him for assigning economic factors major responsibility and declaring the economic crisis in the second half of the sixteenth century critical. However, most scholars in the twentieth century have rejected his "brilliant attempt" to identify the gradual growth of peasant indebtedness as the primary cause of serfdom, in part because new sources have provided additional insights. Instead, they ascribe enserfment directly to "the primacy of the role of state power," expressed in a series of state actions. The most thorough analysis of the "dread institution" termed the culminating step the 1649 Code, "the greatest legal act directed toward the final enserfment of the peasants."[6]

The roots of Kliuchevskii's interest in serfdom lay in the abolition decree of 1861, which he proclaimed the most important event in his life. The university classes he attended devoted little attention to serfdom or the decree, and the slow growth of his engagement was almost a symbol of the way history unfolded. Teaching a survey course of Russian history in Ger'e's program renewed his understanding of its central significance, and he began to collect documents on its history. Research on the boyar council then elucidated some of serfdom's causes and effects, particularly upon the declining role of the council and land assemblies and the establishment of autocracy.

Even while Kliuchevskii was desperately laboring to complete the *Boyar Council,* he reviewed Iurii Samarin's 1857 proposals concerning abolition and responded to Samarin's son's rebuttal. In 1881 he wrote that serfdom "was prepared by centuries and molded by the unsatisfactory conditions of our life" and that dismantling it would be an equally slow process. For example, abolition had not touched 15 percent of the serfs twenty years after the edict.[7] The seminars on *Russian Truth* and *Pskov Truth* gave him insight into the peasant's position before serfdom. Finally, a book he read in 1884 by Professor I. E. Engelmann argued that a series of state decrees in the first half of the seventeenth century and the 1649 code had established serfdom. This "state school" thesis collided with Kliuchevskii's judgment that Russian history was complicated, so he set out to demonstrate that serfdom derived from imperceptible changes without exact and clear definition of time.

In his judgment, the fundamental reason for serfdom's rise and long survival was the low level of cultural and political life: the peasants' freedom was "one of the sacrifices" necessary to ensure the nation's survival. The immediate reasons were primarily economic, for growing indebtedness caused peasants to drift into serfdom through long-term servile residence, agreements, and contracts. Poverty, inflation, and continuous borrowing forced thousands to default on their financial obligations and abandon the right to move. The turmoil and dislocation created by the Time of Troubles, foreign intervention, and the financial burdens of wars in the first half of the seventeenth century hastened serfdom's spread and the state's formal acknowledgment of it. The state accepted and perhaps promoted the process, but it did not initiate it and certainly did not decree it. Indeed, the state lacked the authority and competence for such momentous action. It simply accepted serfdom and established its boundaries: the 1649 Code was "belated recognition of what life itself had already enacted."

After 1649, serfdom expanded and deepened. It protected the treasury and landowners, who received responsibility for collecting state revenues from peasants fixed to the land. The owners' powers over the peasant's person, work, and even posterity then grew gradually. Peter the Great's detailed poll tax to support a peacetime regular army gave serfdom a "double foundation" by amalgamating its forms and blending slavery and serfdom. Conditions worsened after Peter. The "third formation" in 1762 and Catherine the Great's policies provided Russia the most deeply rooted and vicious form of serfdom Europe had ever seen, just when the last "justification" of serfdom had disintegrated. For Kliuchevskii, the poll tax darkened Peter's image, while the history of Catherine's Russia was that of serfdom.

The institution affected every aspect of Russian life. It corrupted the nobility, who became a slothful, worthless class wasting their time on petty disputes and their funds on luxuries. Living dissolute lives in an artificial social regime, they formed a cancer feeding on their fellow citizens. Set apart from others, they became politically indifferent, although they should have served as society's leaders. Joining the state in determined resistance to change, they served as a brake against advance.

The economic consequences were disastrous. Serfdom led owners to exploit the peasants rather than the land. It wrecked the natural distribution of labor and capital, undermined entrepreneurial spirit, and destroyed incentives to create capital. The predominance of backward agriculture kept Russia mired in a stagnant rural economy without the active urban classes that provided initiative in other societies. Instead, enterprising non-Russians dominated Russia's weak industry and internal trade, leading many to despise energy and enterprise as foreign qualities. The state became a hungry debtor, and retrogressive taxes crippled the economic system. Russia spiraled downward economically and became "a colossus on serf legs" at a time when European states were becoming more productive, prosperous, and free.

The effects extended far beyond deadening arrangements binding the peasant to the land. Serfdom weakened Christianity and lowered further a civilization already humble. The character and quality of education remained at the lowest level in Europe. A form of "civilized barbarism," serfdom placed injustice and cruelty at the heart of Russian life. It determined the character of Russian culture by tilting every aspect of existence away from freedom and responsibility toward passivity and arbitrary rule. This strengthened the submissive attitude that Kliuchevskii considered a central aspect of the national character and political system. More than any other factor, serfdom destroyed the slim possibility that the land assembly might grow into an effective representative assembly: how could a serf society remain Christian or a serf participate in representative government? In addition, making noble landowners tax collectors ensured that peasant dissatisfaction would turn against the state rather than the landowner. This helped Kliuchevskii understand why the violent assaults upon the nobility in the seventeenth century became rebellions against the state a century later.

From the time he began teaching, Kliuchevskii planned to make 1861 the culmination of his course: abolition completed the process of estate formation and class landowning that had begun in the tenth century. When he died, the pages on the reign of Catherine the Great in the *Course of Russian History* satisfied him as much as anything he had ever written. However, the section on the period after 1796 was scrappy and unfinished. He had commented, sometimes in detail, on early criticisms of serfdom and had drafted essays on approaches to abolition that men such as Kiselev had considered. But he described the steps that led to abolition only in the last article he drafted, published first in 1958. This unfinished essay was unusual because it provides a detailed factual account, especially for the years after 1835, but contains little analysis of the issues engaged or the forces pressing for and against action. Similarly, the materials on the period after 1861 consist largely of details, with little analysis.

Even so, the abundant materials on abolition and its aftermath express clearly the thesis that change is constant and slow and that abolition was the result of the same process that had brought an end to slavery. Alexander II needed almost six years to reach a decision and prepare the decree. Fifty years later, Kliuchevskii judged that little change had occurred.

According to Kliuchevskii, the first criticisms of serfdom and suggestions for abolition appeared late in the seventeenth century. Eighteenth-century imperial rulers snuffed out comments, but men such as Speranskii under Alexander I and Konstantin D. Kavelin under Nicholas I proposed study of ways to abolish it. Nicholas I recognized that serfdom weakened Russia as a power, but he did not comprehend the problem's magnitude. Lacking a concept of the national interest and the resolution to confront the nobles, he established secret committees to study serfdom but introduced only minor revisions. He "approached serfdom as though he were a doctor who treated his patient's scabs individually, moving from one scab to another only after ointment had completely healed the first."

After the Crimean War, men of good will such as Samarin proposed liberation with a garden plot for each family, gestures that showed they considered serfs the owners' private property, guests, or lodgers. For them, serfdom was a legal issue, not a central national problem rooted in history that would disappear no more quickly than it had risen. In short, even liberal reformers of good will did not comprehend the cancer that "remained in our customs like a mortal illness."

Slow or stagnant economic growth, an incompetent government staffed for centuries by urban bureaucrats, and steady population growth were among the most significant causes of abolition. While Christianity had contributed to eliminating slavery, Kliuchevskii assigned it no credit for abolition, demonstrating indirectly that Orthodoxy no longer exercised much influence. His failure to mention Radishchev or the impact of Western ideas or models reflects the minor significance he assigned intellectuals and ideas, as well as his limited understanding of the West's impact in the nineteenth century. The immediate cause, but only the immediate cause, for Alexander II's tardy initiative was the increasing number of ever more vigorous uprisings. "The nobles feared the peasants, the peasants hated the nobles, neither had any confidence in the state, and the state feared both."[8]

Because of the government's failure to comprehend and resolve the long-term causes, the problems responsible for abolition worsened after 1861. Population pressures raised land prices. The artificial and destructive commune denied peasants the advantages of freedom and drove the most able and ambitious into hostility. The economy remained stagnant, the population inert, and the cultural level low. Resentment of inequalities and injustice rose. On the other hand, Stolypin's program to dismantle the commune after 1906 was too drastic. Only a long period of slow, steady change would remove the old distortions and recent poisons. Kliuchevskii in his last months doubted whether Russia had time or the will to avoid an explosion.

In Kliuchevskii's judgment, change occurred slowly because the nature of humanity, traditions, and external forces exercised restraints. The motive forces were complicated and mysterious, but education and foreign influence had become significant in modern times. However, the fundamental causes of successive modifications in all societies were "the human spirit" and "physical nature." Within his native land, the principal volatile structural material was migration or colonization, an elemental force that helped produce mastery of the land and bind Russia together. Like Soloviev, he declared it the principal visible source of change running through Russian history.

Another crucial element in the "bundle" of materials was economic: "Political facts grow from economic facts." Every historian should begin his analysis by concentrating upon economic and social factors. Economic elements, the social interests and groups that created them and then reflected them, and administration were among the principal building materials that constituted a society: they were "more important than the building itself." No community could survive unless individuals were willing to sacrifice their interests to the general welfare: the conflict between private economic and general political interests is constant at every institutional level. Whenever private interests, in the form of a family, tribe, or class, refuse to sacrifice for the common good, a new political system arises in which private and general interests achieve some balance.

Thus, an armed merchant class helped establish the state in Kiev, replacing the tribe, just as economic factors had led to the clan's superseding the family and the tribe's replacing the clan. Economic elements were mainly responsible for the rise of Moscow and autocracy, the origins of serfdom, and its abolition. Economic and social transformations since 1861 constituted the fundamental reasons for the revolution of 1905. The 1909 edition of Kliuchevskii's outline history barely mentioned the Russo-Japanese War: it was only the immediate cause of the revolution. He assigned more significance to completion of the Trans-Siberian Railroad and the Stolypin land program than to the cataclysmic events of 1904–1905. This epitomizes his relegating political systems to a secondary role. They reflect a society. They are responsible neither for backwardness nor for achievements.

On the role that rulers and prominent leaders played, he was ambivalent. He considered social processes decisive but recognized that rulers affected the character and timing of change. History recorded no miracles or miracle workers. He saluted Peter the Great for his sense of duty and service but declared that no one, even a tsar, could exercise significant influence, except through promoting education. The aristocracy's contribution before 1762 in building and helping administer the state won praise, as did rulers and peasants in their assigned places. But he despised the nobility after 1762: they were an undeserving privileged class freed from responsibility at the same time serfdom reached its peak. Many then betrayed their country by abandoning service to society and state. Some became more French than Russian. Moreover, individuals' efforts to divert or direct the flow of human affairs were almost inevitably unsuccessful and destructive: Russia's autocrats caused heavy damage when they tried to force or hasten change.

Dozens of Kliuchevskii's aphoristic statements as well as analyses of trends and events minimize the importance of individuals. Leaders were "lamp posts that light the path to change in times of peace and on which people hang errant rulers" in times of trouble. A society's moral level depends as much on its separate members as the temperature depends on the thermometer. Similarly, "Life is like a church procession. Those in the front ranks should not conclude that they lead the others." Princes are drops of water, products of conditions, not agents of change. They represent economic and other forces that thrust them to the forefront as figureheads and symbols. Muscovy's early rulers did not enlarge the state: it grew because of factors beyond the control of such mediocrities. Peter the Great's achievements were due to his recognizing and responding to natural needs at the appropriate time, not foresight, energy, or genius. The changes for which many gave him credit had been under way for more than two generations. In fact, reforms are "the product of all the previous history of a people" and are simply natural responses to long-recognized needs.

On the other hand, Kliuchevskii recognized that practical leaders often contributed to directing and even creating peaceful change in stable, well-governed societies, such as England. He also assigned some individuals an important place in the flow of Russian history, particularly in the period after 1500, when more information was available concerning individuals, and individuals played more distinctive roles than earlier. While he assigned responsibility for the fundamental aspects of Russian history to the inexorable flow of impersonal forces, he awarded much of the liability for dynastic crises, wars, and extravagant waste to individual rulers, as though they were aberrations from the historical process.

Kliuchevskii may have given increased prominence to particular persons as a teaching device. His artistry in character analysis and storytelling provides some of the most engaging and informative sections of the *Course of Russian History,* as it did in the classroom. His most effective lectures and essays described the role particular individuals had played, not so much as men or women who constituted turning points but as individuals who reflected the spirit of an age. The essays on Pushkin, Lermontov, Boltin, and Saint Sergei were illustrative of this technique. Analyses of rulers and men such as Dmitrii M. Golitsyn and Speranskii also provided insight into the forces pressing for continuity and change. Thus, the immensely gifted Golitsyn failed to limit the powers of Empress Anna because no accretions from other necessary economic and political changes existed in 1730. Kliuchevskii devoted seven chapters in the *Course of Russian History* to individuals and only two to the Church: the Russian editor of the most recent edition of his works termed his masterpiece "a gallery of portraits" and in 1990 published a volume of Kliuchevskii essays entitled *Historical Portraits* in a printing of 2 million copies.

Using individuals as an instructional technique was especially obvious in the courses in the military school and in Ger'e's program. Kliuchevskii's description of the origins of the French Revolution demonstrated that France had benefited greatly from the wisdom of discerning builders such as Richelieu, Colbert, and Louvois. These men helped create a strong government that maintained close ties with the country through the aristocracy and Church. However, Louis XIV drew the aristocracy and high clergy into Versailles, abused absolute power, abandoned responsibility to promote the general welfare, and wasted national resources trying to conquer Europe. He unleashed destructive religious persecution, drove some of the nation's most productive men and women abroad, and united much of Europe against France. His successors were even less intelligent. They ignored the rising middle class who created much of the national wealth, drove the prosperous peasantry into rebellion, launched halfhearted reforms that further alienated those they were seeking to aid, and encouraged demagogues.

Kliuchevskii found paradoxes everywhere that illustrated the workings of "the eternal law of change" in the flow of history. At the time "the state grew fat and the people grew lean," millions of individuals, most of them invisible, were producing changes beneath the surface that led to gradual transformations. A long draft statement in his archives described the haze of the gloomy sixteenth and seventeenth centuries through which one could envision the forms of Peter the Great and Pushkin, shining like lighthouses on a rocky coast. In the earlier period, the state fulfilled its basic functions, external security and internal order, providing the conditions necessary for cultural progress. Sheltered by the state, millions of tireless men and women and small

groups kept society operating and produced the nation's culture. They constitute the creative force of the nation, the quiet motor that drives the other mutually dependent variables or "realities" that form society. "This energy, this
creative work does not derive from inspiration from above, like snow falling on
one's head: it is the product of successive work-loving generations who adapt
themselves to national circumstances, morals, and life."

Kliuchevskii produced as many brilliant lectures and essays on "quiet heroes" as he did on dramatic rulers. The role of the "good people" was less
visible than that of leaders but more discernible than that of the peasant population, who were a quiet part of the flow. Their patriotism and faith helped the
nation survive and created its culture. They fed the poor and built churches,
helped create the national character, and made Russia a sound society. Those
in the great chain who produced the historical record were among those unassuming and invisible contributors. When historians utilized the product of
other unsung heroes to provide their countrymen an account of the past, they
established the national consciousness that would one day help establish a
nation.

Kliuchevskii either neglected or ridiculed individuals who sought to impede
or hasten change but who were not legitimate rulers or among the faceless millions who contributed silently to the processes that underlay transformations.
He devoted little attention to uprisings and revolts, thereby enraging Soviet
Marxist historians. He rejected those who sought to prevent transformation as
well as those who attempted revolution. He ignored reactionaries, such as
Pobedonostsev and Katkov, who attempted to freeze the political system, and
radicals of all kinds who wanted to quicken the process. He ridiculed those
who believed that influencing state policy or overthrowing a system of government to create a "better world" was an appropriate function for those who had
enjoyed some education. Inaction had historically proved far more fruitful than
vigorous attempts to improve the human condition. Indeed, the more forceful
the effort, the less likely was progress. An American of his day would have
regarded the United States as a rapidly changing society in which sweeping
modifications constituted the only constant. Kliuchevskii viewed Russia as subject only to slow, gradual change, not as a land in which one could safely introduce revisions.

Intellectuals occupied the lowest rung in his assessment throughout his life.
He scorned them, criticized use of the word *intellectual*, and despised most
those who praised them as sources of benign change. As an undergraduate, he
carefully separated himself from contemporaries who considered themselves
intellectuals, whether radicals or conservatives. Although Soloviev's course on
the French Revolution had assigned much responsibility to Rousseau and Voltaire, Kliuchevskii ignored those men and their ideas when he taught it. Only
in the early 1880s did he suggest that "theories without substance" had helped
demolish a social order that had served France for centuries. In these lectures,
he termed Speranskii a "Voltaire in Orthodox theological garb."

From that point, his published works and even more his unpublished essays and highly crafted aphorisms excoriated intellectuals. An early lecture announced that the survey course excluded them and ideas: their place was in biographies and studies of philosophy. They failed to recognize that society was a living organism with its own language and ways. Not realizing that reason is a method of thought, not a way of life, they used logical concepts, artistic forms, and limited personal experience to explain history. They were "educated fools," a noisy, publicity-seeking handful of political ideologues who sought self-aggrandizement and rapid social change, the source and substance of which they did not understand. Lazy and ignorant of a homeland they despised, "the colored Russian dolls of Western civilization" were superficial and unpatriotic demagogues, more foreign than Russian, who produced alluring but dangerous proposals for "milk and honey socialism." While claiming to be individualistic, they herded together and rushed like blind lemmings from one extreme to another. "Poor in spirit, collecting the fruits of wisdom as they fell from the windows of European temples or grain falling from the European trapeze that had no place for them," they reminded Kliuchevskii of leaves falling from a tree: "They felt sorry for the tree, which did not miss them and instead grew other leaves." His famous work failed even to mention the names of Russia's most prominent intellectuals.

Except in essays on writers that exposed the nobles for succumbing to Western influence, he neglected ideas. They were toy windmills turning in whatever direction the wind blew. They played a role only when economic and social conditions transformed them into accepted beliefs and they became an essential element of the national culture. In fact, an idea resembles a spark or a flash of lightning, ephemeral and useless until harnessed as electricity, when it acquires enormous power. Abstract ideas were especially abhorrent, particularly those suggesting that people are born free or that a social contract exists. Human history is independent of human will. "Life must create its own forms, using inherited materials."

Men and women of good will and unknown heroes of all sorts, including historians, exercised significant influence within a process in which structural materials and psychological factors created interactions and alterations. History reflected flux, and the rate of change appeared to increase in modern times. Thus, the rise and fading of institutions and the waning position of the Church indicated that apparently permanent organizations were temporary elements bobbing in the flow of history. Kliuchevskii informed a class in 1886 that there had been times and would again be periods without estates or classes. A decade later, he noted in a public lecture on Alexander II that one day the land assembly might reappear. He also suggested that even the unflagging migration or colonization that distinguished Russia's past might not be permanent. Increasingly close relations between Russia and Europe, of which it had been a part from its beginnings, hastened change. Moreover, just as serfdom and the autocracy had developed in long, slow processes and abolition had begun the end of serfdom and the servile mentality, so autocracy might disappear as part of the endless, even "natural and necessary" flow of change that characterized history. But the successor system, whether constitutional or some other form of governance, would also be transitory, a part of the eternal flow.

Kliuchevskii crafted a philosophy of history in the sense that it grew from his scholarly values, approach to source materials, and even love of gardening. It carries elements from many individuals, especially Soloviev, and groups, including both the Slavophils and the Westerners. It also reflects the current or climate of opinion of his years. Perhaps, most important, even though it is organic and eclectic, its emphasis upon an inexorable flow may have helped lure some students and leaders toward Marx's iron law.

ELEVEN

The Church and the Religious Schism
The Dilemma of Relations with the West

Kliuchevskii recognized that Russia had been a part of Europe from its origins. His work in early Russian history showed that his native land had managed cultural relations with Europe skillfully until the seventeenth century, absorbing household utensils and architecture with advantage and without visible harm to its cultural integrity. The effort then of a small number of reformers to restore the accuracy of the liturgy by borrowing minor corrections from the West led to the schism that unveiled the Church's weakness and seriously damaged religious and national unity. It also exposed the cruel dilemma: Could Russia borrow from the West without having foreign influences dissolve the qualities and institutions that made his country unique and independent?

The West's superiority in power derived from its freedoms and the opportunities that private initiatives enjoyed. Russian failure to adopt Western ideas and methods, even minor liturgical corrections, would widen the gap and in the long run challenge Russia's independence. On the other hand, borrowing techniques inevitably imported the values responsible for the advantage. This established a clear threat to cultural integrity and national unity. Moreover, Russia could not catch up by borrowing: it acquired the tools and products of Western processes just as the West discarded them as it continued to change. Thus, Russia was always becoming what the West had been. But if it adopted the qualities that made the West different, it would abandon the culture that made Russia distinct.

Kliuchevskii's analysis of Russian history after the schism in the second half of the seventeenth century increased his understanding of the issue, especially as he realized that foreign ideas and ways had penetrated many at the highest social levels. Thus, his undergraduate thesis published in 1866 noted that Europe became more primitive and backward as one moved eastward. His undergraduate courses, discussions with faculty members, and the experiences of friends who traveled all described a culture freer, more prosperous, and more attractive than the one he knew. The humiliation that the Berlin Congress inflicted so soon after the enthusiasm and triumph of the Balkan crisis revealed that his native land had not overcome the weaknesses that the Crimean War had laid bare. Lectures on the French Revolution recognized the West's greater prosperity but explained that circumstances had forced Russia to grant priority to state-building rather than economic development. The decade of research on the boyar council and reflections upon the reasons it had not developed along the same lines as apparently similar Western institutions provided another example of the differences. His seminars admitted that political freedoms helped explain Western prosperity and strength, but noted too that European society had been "politically pulverized" and inequalities prevailed.

Research in the 1880s deepened Kliuchevskii's apprehension, particularly because he recognized that the most fruitful years of the boyar council and the rise of serfdom had both occurred in the golden seventeenth century. This suggested that the "most depraved institution" appeared when the most benign old ones were fading, and that Russia was stagnant or moving backward. This anomaly became more striking with Peter the Great, the most relentless and forceful Westernizer, who ended the boyar council, introduced the poll tax, and combined slavery and serfdom. The apparent contradiction, a Westernizing tsar who strengthened absolutism and its instruments, awakened him fully to the dilemma and dangers.

Public lectures on Russia and the West in the Polytechnical Museum in 1890–91, prepared for publication in 1896 but published only eighty years later, were especially clear. These ten lectures on the years from the death of Peter the Great to the end of the eighteenth century flatly recognized Western superior wealth and strength and described Russia as a backward state whose people were born to follow others' lead. Accepting help was a moral duty. "Any patriot must become a Westernizer, and Westernization must become another manifestation of patriotism as Russia uses Western examples to improve itself." Insistence that his son master English, French, and German and his son's interest in Western technology, particularly the automobile, reflected his judgment about the need to borrow.

In Kliuchevskii's opinion, the roots of the quandary lay in Russia's being part of the West, though only on its fringe. In addition, the West began to change rapidly in modern times, while modifications in Russia continued at a slow pace. By the seventeenth century, France and England had developed centralized state structures, national cultures, and dynamic economies. These reflected and also led to technical innovations, mobilization of labor and capital, and enriching discoveries in other parts of the world. Russia then had established a centralized state and national culture, but lagging intellectual and economic development and foreign invasions diluted its strength. It therefore confronted a cruel dilemma, similar to that which helped destroy the Soviet Union and that many peoples and states have encountered in the twentieth century. As statesmen around the world have learned, maintaining national independence and cultural integrity while borrowing from and "catching up" with more prosperous and stronger members of the European community of states constitutes an almost impossible assignment.

Kliuchevskii appreciated that Russia had enjoyed and benefited from contact with the West: "It is the air we breathe." Moreover, "European life is a necessity for us: Its culture is the highest form of human development: to be a cultured man or people means to master the culture of Western Europe." On the other hand, "Not all fresh air is healthy."[1] After the seventeenth century, many Russians began to recognize Western superiority and Russia's apparent shortcomings, and the government advanced beyond borrowing science and living comforts to importing institutions, ideas, and values, quickening the national historical process. In his judgment, such actions violated patriotic responsibility and moral duty. Adapting others' ideas, laws, and institutions, the roots as well as the fruits of a different culture, destroyed the nation's spiritual life.

To Kliuchevskii, the small changes introduced in the seventeenth century brought about a fanatical and violent reaction that splintered the Church and the society of which it had been a pillar and shoved the Church into a political and cultural backwater. This made him increasingly critical of the Church and churchmen and pessimistic about the country's stability and survival. It shook but did not destroy his religious faith, although it may have made him less open and active as a believer than he would have been.

Studying the dilemma that had led to action that weakened the Church helped him understand quickly the similar quandary confronting the system of government and the character of Russia as a state and society. This also shook but did not destroy his deeply held assumption about the system of governance. In addition, it made him increasingly aware of the government's shortcomings and the threat that its failures raised for integrity and unity. The policies of Peter and his successors created even more serious hazards than the liturgy reforms had caused because they touched directly the system of rule and involved every level of society. Worse, the repressive measures that the autocrats adopted to hasten change and crush opposition gave rise to greater division, even dissolution, than the schism had, and turned Russia further backward. Those who sought change, including the autocrats themselves, had already been corrupted by Western influence, and those they alienated included most of the most educated and powerful elements of society. This led him to conclude that another Time of Troubles was imminent.

Finally, Kliuchevskii almost certainly recognized that he was a personal representative or symbol of the dilemma. His limited knowledge and understanding of the West, from French and British historians to European economic progress, deeply affected his religious faith and political philosophy. It also influenced the framework and spirit through which he viewed his Church and its history, the Russian system of rule, and the full sweep of Russian history. Thus, he was a sample of a process that dismayed him and that he considered a threat to Russian culture and unity.

In summary, Kliuchevskii thought that Russia could not survive if it isolated itself or resisted change. But he wondered whether it could maintain its independence and cultural integrity when its leaders sought strength and prosperity by encouraging massive borrowing and when many became more foreign than Russian in their ways. Can one graft a branch from a deciduous tree onto a conifer without fatal consequences for the conifer? Can one nation emulate another's "morals, attitudes, customs, ideas, and social relations" without undermining its own structure and values? Would not the regressive measures adopted to enforce borrowing and repress the hostility it caused move Russia further from the foundations in freedom that had produced the Western metamorphosis? Notes in his archives reveal that he appreciated the dilemma and danger when an undergraduate. Twenty years later, he told students that borrowing techniques was simple because they were the products of "human personality." However, transferring values and institutions was hazardous: they represented a total society and carried dangerous infections for a culture. In the *Course of Russian History* two more decades later, he described the dilemma in detail.

Determining the character of an individual's religious convictions is difficult, even when the primary sources are rich. So far as one can determine, Kliuchevskii's faith from childhood through maturity remained firm. A quiet, unemotional member of the Church, he believed that "to live is to love, to treat one's neighbor as oneself," and accepted and acted upon the doctrines of Orthodoxy without hesitation or doubt. He attended services faithfully, read scriptures every day, and honored religious obligations. Miracles were a reality, and his home had cherished icons in every room. His wife was devout, as were his sisters and the members of his wife's family. Letters throughout his life and his diary reflect a profound concern with faith and the reasons for which people believe.

Many remarked that everything about his dress, posture, hairstyle, and voice reminded them of old Russia and its clergy: Struve, a leading liberal intellectual, observed that Kliuchevskii was "bone from bone of the Russian clergy" of earlier days. Fedotov, an eminent Orthodox theologian and historian, saw him as an embodiment of the sixteenth and seventeenth centuries and thought his pages on those years "almost autobiographical." Colleagues in Moscow as well as St. Petersburg officials considered him a true believer and a stalwart supporter of Church and state. In January 1906, he declined to join a conference planning a Church council to reform the Church and re-establish the patriarchate because he wished to concentrate upon completing his masterpiece, but he remained interested, encouraged his friend Trubetskoi to participate, and read carefully the papers that Trubetskoi brought him.

In Kliuchevskii's judgment, man was weak but neither doomed nor perfectible. Each religion represented "local" or national conditions. Western faiths differed from the Russian state religion and each other because of local circumstances, but the distinctions were minor because the Christian religions share a common core. In particular, religions did not determine the principal characteristics that separated societies or constitute the primary cause of conflict between societies.

Orthodoxy "liberated man from the idolatry of happiness," made him a member of a close community, and instilled a sense of the need to work and of duty toward family and country. It was a democratic religion, in which all were equal and the fortunate and successful accepted an obligation to assist the poor and ill. It taught scorn for the undeserving rich and sympathy for the poor and disadvantaged. Some of Kliuchevskii's most eloquent lectures and essays were moving paeans to saintly men and women for their contributions to Russian culture.

Orthodoxy was more appropriate for Russians than Catholicism or any form of Protestantism because it occupied a central position almost from the beginning of Russian history, helped create national unity, and softened and civilized Russian culture. Indeed, all Russians should be orthodox Christians: "An educated Russian man cannot be an unbeliever." The word *freethinker* was a pejorative. Even as a senior scholar teaching at a secular university, Kliuchevskii recommended that students read saints' lives because they taught the importance of personal relations with God, exalted tradition and duty, and helped create a foundation for Russian values. In sum, the disruptive and even violent religious-political explosions of the second half of the twentieth century would have appalled him, for he was as Erastian as Macaulay, or even Voltaire, in his appreciation of the quiet support that religion furnished society.

Until he entered the university, Kliuchevskii had received his education in Church institutions. No bright lad could have observed the character and plight of the clergy or the quality of the seminary in which he spent more than four years without becoming critical of the institutional Church. The men under whom he studied at the university were devout Christians, but the atmosphere there was as skeptical and secular as that in Penza had been Orthodox. The beliefs and values he had assimilated at home wavered in his first two years in Moscow, but four years of class with Buslaev confirmed his belief that nature and circumstances helped each people shape its own theology and religious institutions, as it did its literature and folklore, and that Orthodoxy was an essential part of Russian history and culture. Courses with Popov and Soloviev showed him concretely how Russian history and the Church were interrelated. In short, his religious convictions and their nationalist framework remained firm and perhaps even gained strength by the time he had completed undergraduate study.

Nevertheless, his beliefs appear cultural and traditional, inherited and absorbed, rather than rational or doctrinal. He declared that one must accept the historic achievements of Christianity and recognize that religion reflected "not the needs of the soul but the memories and customs of one's youth." An essay in his third year as an undergraduate noted the importance of ceremonies and holy objects in strengthening faith. In a review then, comments on these elements, the Catholic Church's cruciform shape, and women's head coverings suggest that he was more interested in such aspects of religious life than in theology. Similarly, as a mature scholar, he considered long-established rites a fundamental part of any faith: they provided the emotional cement that held generations together. Religion was a matter of faith, not logic, and rested upon rituals and symbols which helped meet man's most pressing psychological requirements and maintain stability in times of personal and national crisis. They were especially important for fulfilling "the spiritual needs of simple people," for whom they were the main source of knowledge of God.

"The basic furniture of religious life," ceremonies preserve religious truth in the same way a photograph does. "Strip contemporary man of his inherited rites, customs, and conventions, and he will forget everything and start again from the beginning."[2] Kliuchevskii wrote far more about ceremonies than about doctrines or beliefs: they sustain the great moments of a people's history and faith as a phonograph record reproduces a voice. After his wife's funeral, he remarked that the liturgy's familiar words had been especially comforting. Although he was ordinarily mild, he reproached intellectuals who failed to recognize the psychological role that rituals exercised for the uneducated. He denounced Tolstoy's and Vladimir Soloviev's attacks upon Christianity and its symbols because they provided no substitute, except a cold rationalism beyond the ken of their compatriots.

Legends were also important, whether they concerned saints such as Sergei or secular leaders such as Peter the Great, because all truths require substance, as symphonies need themes. He respected those who adhered to deeply held beliefs and traditional rites that expressed their faith: old ways reflected essential values. He was therefore sympathetic to the Old Believers, although he prayed that they would return to the Church. He considered Peter the Great a pious man who revered and regularly honored Orthodox rites, except for fasts, but whose policies erred because of his inability to comprehend the indispensability of rites.

Like many pious Christians, Kliuchevskii was deeply concerned about his flaws and those of his compatriots and Church. His father's struggle to survive and acquire a tolerable position, disappointment over the behavior of the priest who succeeded his father and of other priests he knew, and experience in the seminary made him critical of the Church and its leaders: they had lost contact with life. While a student, he declared orthodology a swindle and the Church a theater with a religious repertoire. The almost universal dislike of the intelligent but reactionary Metropolitan Filaret until his death in 1869 strengthened Kliuchevskii's anticlericalism. Especially in his last twenty years, he was privately critical of the institutional Church and a strong proponent of the separation of Church and state. These numerous penetrating comments provide the emotional fire that underlay his cool published treatment of the Church.

Discussions at the academy with informed and shrewd scholarly colleagues reinforced his criticisms, which touched every aspect of the Church's organization and activity, or inactivity. On one occasion he termed the Church "a cassocked division of state administration." Those who believed shared no sense of community. The Church was arrogant and negative in its policy toward science and all things intellectual. The bishops' intellectual level was abysmal in "ignorant self-conceit," and they barely knew each other. The academy rectors who succeeded Gorskii after 1875 were unimpressive, and the level of theological study and instruction was perilously low. Some, especially Evdokim early in the twentieth century, were incompetent and irresponsible scoundrels. Diary comments after Kliuchevskii resigned from the academy in the fall of 1906 were especially bitter: in 1910 he urged abolition of the hierarchy. In the fifth volume of the *Course of Russian History,* he noted caustically that the Church had provided Russian areas six times as many clergy per capita as non-Russian districts, with no appreciable effect.

Monks were "those who had taken the ranks of angels." He admired clergymen who devoted their lives to their flocks and paid tribute to the clergy's role in preserving elementary education in the early centuries, but he devoted little attention to them in his major publications and omitted them from his university course on estates. The low intellectual quality, civil cowardice, hypocrisy, and drunkenness of many clergy appalled him: they constituted "a parasitic estate" who taught their flock not to know and love God but to fear the devil. Most rites they conducted were "holy ashes." Many priests could not even maintain order in the services they celebrated. Even Peter the Great had to intervene to establish discipline during religious ceremonies.

The Church's educational institutions were not genuine seminaries or schools; they neglected essential doctrines and emphasized fear. The Church provided no food for the mind and did not stimulate thought or raise the basic issues that should consume every Christian. "Instead of theology it produced theological mastery of rites, regulations instead of a creed." The seminaries' efforts to place theology on scientific foundations resembled dressing a doll of God in contemporary costumes. At a time when the majority lacked faith but yearned for it, the Church was a dead mechanism unable to provide instruction. Kliuchevskii's diary contains frequent laments about the status of Christianity. He found no genuine faith: Russians go to Church once a week as to the bath and are interested only in worldly goods and comforts. They admire and envy the sentiments of the old faith but do not share them. They reminded him of a lecherous old man who admired young girls but lacked the capability to love them. One could no longer hear church bells in the city. Religion had become only a memory or habit inherited from childhood. "Let the dead bury the dead," because there cannot be a Russian Christian Church.

Except for his cultural commitment to Orthodoxy and his understanding of the contributions that its rites continued to make to Russia's survival and culture, Kliuchevskii shared many of the intellectuals' criticisms of the Church. He became most censorious in his last fifteen years, after his detailed analysis of the causes and consequences of the schism. Late in the 1890s, he drafted a memorandum entitled "Belief and Thought" that outlined proposals to meet national problems he considered critical. The views in these unpublished papers are consistent with those in essays published in the 1890s, comments in his diary, and positions he advocated in St. Petersburg in the winter of 1905 on the committee to review the censorship. Thus, the Church must recognize the problems that contemporary life created, end its self-imposed isolation, and play an active role. It should call a *sobor* or council to re-establish the patriarchate. Church and state should end censorship and allow religious freedom. The Church should admit that both its leaders and the Old Believers had erred and persuade the Old Believers to return to the fold. It should then bring together all Orthodox Christians and Slavs (presumably except the Poles) in a unified institution. The parish should serve as the Church's primary unit, with responsibility for all primary education, and should constitute the basic unit of local government. Each religious group could maintain its own middle schools, but higher education of the most talented should be the state's responsibility.[3]

Historians, of course, disagree concerning the Church's place and the character of its influence. In spite of Kliuchevskii's training and beliefs, publications, and years at the Moscow Ecclesiastical Academy, in effect he assigned religion and the Church to a ghetto. The *Course of Russian History* was the modified version of the class he organized during his first years at the academy, after he had completed his M.A. thesis on saints' lives and while he was undertaking research on theological quarrels in Pskov. He began designing the *Course* at the same time he presented his most effective public lectures on Saint Sergei, charity, and religious education, wrote the essays on the religious schism, and commented first in his diary and then publicly upon the character of the Church and the status of religion. Yet religion and the Church are absent from his central publications, as though he lived in a secular society in which religion was insignificant. The phrase "Holy Russia" did not appear in Kliuchevskii's publications, nor did the slogan "Orthodoxy, Autocracy, and Nationalism." This is striking because the course he taught on the French Revolution devoted substantial space to Huguenots, Jesuits and Jansenists, Anglicans and Methodists, and the revolution's assault upon the Catholic Church.

In his account of the past, the Church from the beginning was a secondary part of the state. Fledgling Kiev in the tenth century was already sufficiently established to master Church influence as it entered gradually from Constantinople, absorb the Church itself, and make it dependent, as it was in Byzantium. As years passed, harsh circumstances strengthened the prince's powers and combined with "the waves of Russian life" to incorporate some churchmen into the state's staff and transform the Church into a state institution, a dependent relationship that it readily accepted. This meek surrender, a basic reason for the Church's failure, also left Russians without the protection that Western churches established against civil power. Kliuchevskii's review of an academy student's paper noted that no church under an absolute government had acquired significant religious or moral influence.[4]

Kliuchevskii rejected the basic Slavophil doctrine that the Church had played an important role in Russian history and culture. His works ascribe only a modest role to the Church, except for its essential service in helping to establish early national unity, introducing the values of Christianity, and dispensing some elementary education. The *Course of Russian History* and his other major publications barely mention the conversion of the Grand Duke Vladimir in the tenth century. Kliuchevskii introduced Byzantium and the Church into the record by discussing *Russian Truth,* a thirteenth-century legislative collection based on Byzantium written rules and codes that churchmen had compiled over generations for ecclesiastical courts that served as a guide for princely courts as well. These pages rested on a university seminar he taught on *Russian Truth* throughout the 1880s and 1890s "to acquaint listeners with the literature of the documents of ancient Russian law and the historical, legal, and other institutions of ancient Russia." He incorporated more than fifty pages from this seminar into the *Course of Russian History,* so the first significant reference to the Church and its role slipped into his major work indirectly. His principal publications contain no reference to his favorite saint, Sergei of Radonezh, who founded Trinity Monastery and was an important factor in strengthening national unity in the fifteenth century. The spiritual aspects of the Church's history and its contribution to architecture, art, and music are also absent. Peter the Great's abolishing the patriarchate and establishing the Holy Synod to administer the Church received no attention, and neither did Catherine the Great's sequestering Church property. Fedotov described this position best when he asserted that both Soloviev and Kliuchevskii were "so overwhelmed by the fact that the Muscovite kingdom was the creator of the Russian Empire that they have allowed Moscow to crowd out all the five preceding centuries of an ancient way of life which was incomparably richer than it in culture and spirituality."[5]

Kliuchevskii assigned the Church little direct influence on Moscow's triumph over other princedoms and the rise of Muscovy to authority, although he recognized that the transfer of the metropolitan's cathedral to Moscow early in the fourteenth century was a critical step in Moscow's rise. Each cleric defended his own prince's interests, so the Church was as divided as the princes were. The Church blessed and complemented the political order, but less so than in Western Europe. It exercised only random and disorganized influence on civil affairs, and churchmen did not enjoy an important role in the princes' councils. The boyar class was far more important in forming and administering the centralized state than was the Church.

In Kliuchevskii's major publications, the monasteries' success in colonization and landholding constituted an important contribution to Russia's consolidation: the *Course of Russian History* contains more than forty pages on this topic. However, this achievement and spreading Christianity among the Finns and others whom Russia absorbed were not that of the Church but of restless monks (seventy-four of whom became saints) and small groups fleeing the church, so they could work and pray by themselves. Moreover, the expansion of the network of the monasteries and the wealth that many had acquired led to debate about their functions and the wealth that the successors of those who renounced the world had accumulated. Kliuchevskii's remark that "the riches of the Church are the riches of the poor" suggests that his sympathies were with those who sought salvation through flight and isolation, rather than those who had amassed wealth.[6] Similarly, his 1872 essays on the Pskov religious quarrels revealed the poverty of intellect among churchmen in the fifteenth century. The course on the French Revolution showed that Western religious groups, however mistaken their beliefs and intolerant their behavior, were far more active and intellectually alive than were Russians. For him, one of the clearest distinctions between the Western churches and the Russian Orthodox Church was that the former founded many institutions of higher learning and the latter none.

Until the second half of the seventeenth century, the Church was influential because it contributed to national unity. Russians might not have succeeded in creating a unified state if several religious groups had risen in early Russian history or the schism had occurred before the seventeenth century. Kliuchevskii noted with relish that none of the three holy men, Saints Sergei and Stefan and Tsar Alexei, who had contributed most to national unity, were natives of Moscow or the Moscow region: they represented different sections, and their contributions in bringing Russians together were a symbol of the Church's national role. Russia's greatest heroes included the monks who recorded the chronicles, preserved libraries and archives, and kept alive knowledge of the past. Sermons such as those by Stefan of Perm' in the fourteenth century transmitted the essential rules of moral life and civilized behavior. The lowly priest and dedicated parents together created a "Christian abode" in which moral ideals prevailed. Parish schools provided a year or two of basic education and prepared children for life. The patrimonial family, priest, and parish school maintained civilized behavior at a rudimentary level, but one that transmitted guidance toward salvation, essential spiritual and civil rules, practical virtues, and elementary literacy. "Keeping the faith" and maintaining the tiny flame of civilization in a primitive country were crucial for survival. Kliuchevskii despised intellectuals who did not respect the significance of this early "non-book learning."

In the past, the clergy's emphasis upon morality and virtue in private life had "placed a stamp upon the Russian soul" and helped create the national character. Thus, the lives of saints with which millions were familiar nourished the spiritual strength that helped the Russian people achieve "national unity in a single culture." Daily readings filled "the most important and useful needs of simple people" and constituted an essential part of the nation's spiritual foundations. The Church was feeble, but religious life was powerful, because of Christian emphasis upon service, loving one's neighbor, and helping the poor. The founder of Trinity Monastery was a great Russian not because of the string of monasteries he launched, but because he contributed to national unity and moral education as the "Beneficent Educator." The two titles that Kliu-chevskii gave this lecture on Sergei were "The Splendid Inspirer of Russian National Spirit" and "The Significance of Saint Sergei of Radonezh for the Russian People and State." Tsar Alexei, the "good people" who gave their pos-sessions to the poor, and printers and booksellers such as Novikov who devoted their lives to spreading Christian values through education helped create the nation.

Kliuchevskii stressed the benign effects of charity upon the giver and praised the early Church for emphasizing personal involvement in good works. Hunger was a tool of moral education: the poor were as necessary for a coun-try's welfare as ill people for a clinic or hospital. Peter the Great's opposition to private charity was an error: the state's assumption of responsibility for social welfare destroyed the moral benefits of personal involvement. Noting that the Church in his lifetime played a minor part in charity, even in alleviat-ing the famine in 1891 and 1892, Kliuchevskii added that the flaw was benign: it encouraged individuals to act in ways that benefited them as much as it did those whom they helped.

Religion also exercised civilizing influence upon public life, a subject to which he directed a number of his academy students. Christianity informed the ruler that God ordained him to punish evildoers and show mercy to the poor. It taught people how to act and sustained a sense of humility and duty. Chris-tianity and the early Church exercised a profound effect upon the status of women, which before the tenth century had been equivalent to that of horses. They helped end abduction, made marriage indissoluble, and established women's right to property. Church legislation on marriage strengthened the family. The juridical and moral relationships it established made the family a community that transmitted cultural values from one generation to another and established a civil society.

Christianity also contributed to the disappearance of slavery in law by 1723, a long process, as almost all important developments were. Churchmen "nib-bled" at slavery by insisting that it was a temporary and unnatural condition. They concentrated upon practical actions, such as freeing slave children of a master at his death, establishing that slaves had the right to own property, op-posing the sale of baptized slaves to pagans, and allowing slaves to make legal agreements and purchase freedom. In short, morals transformed juristic norms and rules. Ending slavery constituted "one of the brightest features of [the Church's] activity," one that "alone was sufficient to place the Church among the main resources on which our society was built."[7]

However, the Church was not a direct participant in the slow but continuous series of small changes that led to the abolition of serfdom. It had accepted serfdom and owned serfs, many hierarchs and clergymen had defended it, and Metropolitan Filaret had even opposed abolition. Neither the Church nor any of its leaders confronted serfdom directly, emphasized the sanctity of each in-dividual, or defended human rights. The process of abolition triumphed be-

cause Christian doctrines concerning mercy and compassion gradually modified "the climate of opinion" and directed the attention of Christians, especially
those with economic power, toward the least fortunate. Dramatic gestures were
not so important as the "softening and civilizing" values that readings, sermons, and concession produced. Greek and Roman juristic concepts, slowly
suffused by notions of the dignity of the individual and the obligations of
Christian love, introduced a civilized view of serfdom and the millions of
humans subject to it. They helped to create distinctions about the status, rights,
and responsibilities of serfs, to "chip away" at the most barbarous practices,
such as the separation of family members for sale, and to forge the consensus
that Russia must somehow abolish the institution most responsible for its backwardness.

In Kliuchevskii's view, Catherine the Great's "enlightened ignorance" prevented her from comprehending the Church's keeping civilization alive for
centuries. She damaged the nation and its culture even more than Peter the
Great had, because she did not understand the national religion and traditions.
Introducing European concepts and utopian dreams and assigning prominence
to intellectuals delayed abolition and weakened the Church's benign influence.
Impressing upon a country's aristocracy principles foreign to the nation's experience broke the moral connections with their homeland without which they
could not survive. Education must begin by teaching love of one's country, but
her "hothouse plan for Russia's northern forests" and cold, schematic Voltair-
eanism seduced the nobility from national traditions. Nineteenth-century intellectuals dreamed and schemed to perfect the nature of man and create a superior society over which they, the elite, would preside, but they failed utterly
to comprehend the Church's early service in preserving some sense of civilization.

Several factors help explain the contrast, perhaps contradiction, between the
devout believer who produced lectures and essays on religious themes and
the classroom teacher and author who presented a damning picture of the
Church, lamented the decline of religious faith, or worse, omitted religion and
the Church from his account of the past. Perhaps because of the education
Kliuchevskii received or his intellectual interests, his knowledge of religious
literature and doctrine was shallow. He was always more interested in rites and
ceremonies than in doctrine, and religion was almost a part of folklore. Even
his religious writings do not include citations from the scriptures, references
from other religious literature, or popular sayings from the Bible. He was a
consummate craftsman, worked interminably to ensure grace and clarity of
expression, and was a skillful creator of aphorisms. Yet he used no familiar
concepts, epigrams, or even vocabulary from religious literature. His vocabulary was less rich in religious terms than Stalin's.

Kliuchevskii was not well informed about Church history. At the university,
the classes in which he studied used literature as a source of information concerning social and economic history, but ignored religion and the Church.

When he was a graduate student, the only aspects of Church history his essays touched on concerned property, the monasteries' role in colonization, and saints' lives as historical sources.

Other factors may have turned Kliuchevskii from assigning major roles to religion and the Church. Thus, studying the lives of the saints had proved such a dull and time-consuming subject that he and his friends resented Soloviev's suggesting it. The months devoted to the essays on theological disputes in Pskov proved so tedious and fruitless that he undertook no archival research on religion or the Church after 1872. Instead, he used the economic data from this research on subjects that fascinated him, such as the boyar council, the land assembly, and serfdom. Other graduate student associates directed their energies into Byzantine and Russian art and literature for the same reasons: these subjects excited their professional curiosity.

Circumspection also contributed to his neglecting religion and the Church. From the time he entered the Penza seminary, his income came from the state. He enjoyed no alternative means of obtaining an education or continuing the only career that attracted him if he should lose his academic positions. A tactful, cautious, noncombative person, he sought to avoid quarrels and confrontations, particularly with Church and government officials. The only unpleasant incidents in his career occurred at the academy in 1905, when he resisted the rector's suggestion to cancel a class and retired in dismay after a series of misunderstandings.

Tolstoy, who did not know Kliuchevskii, was contemptuous of his religious essays and denounced him as "sly." Nechkina, who devoted much of her long scholarly career to Kliuchevskii and to directing the work of others on him, concluded that he was duplicitous: he did not write what he believed because he feared government penalties and restrictions. Such an interpretation may have seemed logical because of the conditions under which Soviet scholars wrote. However, none of the many other Soviet historians who studied Kliuchevskii have suggested this interpretation. Moreover, Nechkina applied this thesis not to his treatment of religion and the Church, which she, too, neglected, but to his political beliefs as she defined them.

Nevertheless, the views of Tolstoy and Nechkina contain an element of truth. Kliuchevskii was prudent, but timid men and women are common in academic communities. On the other hand, while he did not criticize the political system or the Church frontally, he was remarkably frank. Any reader of his work in the last part of the twentieth century must marvel at his descriptions of Russia's weaknesses and failures and the shortcomings of its leaders. Russians in particular must read his analyses with amazement because he was so open about flaws and failures similar to those that Soviet scholars concealed in their account of Soviet history. Indeed, his honesty has been a main reason for his immense popularity.

Paradoxically, his service at the academy contributed significantly to the neglect of religion and the Church in his major works. From 1871 until 1906, the academy was his primary censor. He limited the Sergiev Posad survey to civil history because one colleague presented a parallel course on the history of the Church and another a course on the schism and the Old Believers. The course he taught at the academy after eight years became the foundation of the university class he began in December 1879. Unfortunately, no transcript of his academy lectures has survived, so comparing those lectures with the university lithographs is impossible. However, he concentrated upon secular society at the university, omitting Church history, the schism, and the Old Believers because of the pattern established at the academy.

However, almost certainly, the major contributing factor was his accepting the secularism that was part of the university atmosphere. Chernyshevskii and his associates exercised a far more important place than the metropolitan or any churchmen. Kliuchevskii's mentors and colleagues, except for the Lutheran Ger'e, were Orthodox men of deep religious faith, but none considered religion a vital force in society or assigned the Church an important role. Soloviev neglected religion and the Church in his courses and in the monumental *History of Russia*, which Kliuchevskii used heavily. Buslaev and he ridiculed the Slavophils, who exalted the Church's role. Buslaev considered early Russia a primitive, stagnant culture without intellectual curiosity, aesthetic vision, or literary talent, in which religion was powerful only among the ignorant masses.

In sum, as a number of scholars have noted, Kliuchevskii in these aspects remained a man of the 1860s, a pious Christian in an increasingly secular urban society whose faith occupied an isolated place in his life. The way in which he separated the profoundly moving essays on individual Christians from his teaching and major books, his anticlericalism, and his assigning religion and the Church a minor role reflect commitment to a view of the world that separated religion from life. The wave of criticism of the Church among pious clerical and lay leaders, which grew sharply after 1890, only strengthened these views. Thus, the Russian part of one of his aphorisms applied neatly to him: "The West has a Church but no religion, while Russia has a religion but no Church." In Fedotov's words, he sacrificed his spiritual views to the "social command" of his time.

Kliuchevskii often lamented the weak imprint of religious values upon Russian life, but his major works and university courses illustrated that same quality. His approach demonstrated the impact that Western secular thought exercised upon the "poverty of the intellect" that marked devout conservatives struggling with the familiar dilemma. It also identified one of the Old Regime's major weaknesses, its inability to utilize the faith of the Church's millions of members, even its most prominent adherents, in its support.

In Western Europe or the United States, a talented and devout scholar of his generation would have become an outstanding scholarly cleric or devout lay professor, combining an appreciation of the role that religion and churches have played with the techniques of scholarship. In the battle in Russia between the two fires he mentioned in the 1860s, "science" triumphed and religion lost in a conflict that revealed one of the major tensions of his life, one of the curious qualities of his scholarship, and one of the characteristics of his generation.

Kliuchevskii saw history as a constant flow, without any significant leaps forward or backward or sharp turning points. However, the period from the middle of the sixteenth century through the schism in the second half of the seventeenth century was crucial because the fracture of the Church and society shattered national religious unity and precipitated the decline of the Church and religious faith. Western influence, which had begun long before the schism, increased sharply afterward and by late in the nineteenth century had begun to destroy the integrity of Russian culture.

After 1890, about half of Kliuchevskii's published articles and many unpublished manuscripts discussed the interest scholars had shown in the West and its effect upon their views of Russian history. Stepping out of the ivory tower of the university to help those suffering from famine, which he believed unknown in Europe for generations, deepened his understanding of Russia's backwardness: "Each century we fall twenty-four hours further behind the world." Draft papers in his archives are far more devastating than his published work. Russia was weak in part because of the division between the educated few and the ignorant majority. Russians seem to rely on the will of God rather than their own resources, which society crippled. The country has no "thinking people" or leaders, and Russians are servile before authority. On the other hand, Western culture rests upon the enormous intellectual and moral resources of free societies. Ideas ferment constantly because Europe encourages imagination and creative minds. Each generation there is more productive and rises higher than its predecessor in an upward spiral of advance.

This awareness is muted but nonetheless evident in the *Course of Russian History,* which describes Russia until the second half of the seventeenth century as a confident, independent country with a national culture. The changes that began in the West in the fifteenth century were such that by 1740 Kliuchevskii's native land culturally and in every other way trailed the European powers. Moreover, the Russian government from that point lost self-confidence and began to fear its people.

In the discussion concerning Russia's nature and destiny and its relations with Europe, Slavophils and Westerners, and many other observers as well, placed the turning point in Peter the Great's reign. Kliuchevskii rejected this, in part because he denied that individuals exercised significant impact, but also because he did not consider Peter's reign a sharp break. Instead, Russia had easily managed the relationship until the seventeenth century, when a series of developments with roots in earlier centuries transformed the West. The changed qualities of the two areas and Russia's inability to assimilate as skillfully as earlier produced the religious schism, a hinge that produced profound effects.

Kliuchevskii's diaries and comments on contemporary developments in the last two decades of his life reflected the concern over the survival of Russian culture that led to his essays on the religious schism. Half the aphorisms crafted during these years stressed the importance of knowing one's history and the harmful effect of foreign ideas upon a hollow culture. Russia's poets were only the more eloquent heralds of the disaster.

The first sharp reference to Europe's fateful influence was the "Letter of a Frenchwoman," written in April 1886, a few months after *Russian Thought* published his articles on the origins of serfdom and just before it produced those on the poll tax published a century later. This was a private expression of rage at those who failed to recognize that Russia is not France and who betrayed their native culture by becoming more French than Russian. It ridiculed St. Petersburg society for assuming that people are the same everywhere and that reason can govern. The capital's social leaders, Westernized Russians whose bodies were in Russia but whose minds and hearts were in France, loved books, especially novels, but despised learning. They considered Europe a workshop producing ideas and institutions that Russians could apply to their homeland as easily as one could don a French wig.

An 1880 talk at a university dinner to celebrate the unveiling of the Pushkin statue declared that Pushkin's poetry, novels, and historical work offered insight into the declining role of the nobility between Ordin-Nashchokin and Onegin, "who grew up convinced that he was not a European but was obliged to become one." Seven years later, Kliuchevskii read "Eugene Onegin and His Ancestors" at a meeting to commemorate the fiftieth anniversary of Pushkin's death. This talk was a detailed chronological catalogue of the nobility's flaws and failures from the middle of the seventeenth century. It drew from the poet's work, much of which he knew by heart, but also cited the eighteenth-century playwright Sumarokov and satirist Fonvizin as well as Lermontov, Turgenev, Gogol, and Goncharov.

Kliuchevskii recognized that nobles were "an honorable class that has long served our land" and that Pushkin's analysis of Onegin was a "local poetic chronicle" of several varieties of nobles. But these "songs of a dying order" revealed that many nobles were products of an educational program that had turned first to Europe's workshops and harbors for practical benefits to the nation. Borrowing had descended through fashions and furniture to destructive antireligious ideas. The nobles benefited from the guards' role after Peter the Great and from an arrangement with Catherine that provided "an indulgent and pleasant existence" and "overwhelming and unjust dominance over Russian life." This enabled them to live "intellectually from the West's hands and physically from the labor of the serfs." Europeans saw them as "Tatars disguised as Europeans, and Russians considered them Frenchmen born in Russia." In short, the descent from Ordin-Nashchokin to Onegin produced a hollow man who had lost his soul and become "a man without a country."

Four years later, the famous essay on the fiftieth anniversary of Lermontov's death suggested that the poet was pessimistic because he realized that Russia had abandoned the ideals and qualities that had made its culture distinctive and had adopted European ways. In Kliuchevskii's view, Lermontov's gloom was typical of his generation and reflected a national melancholy. This had become part of the Russian national character and helped distinguish Russia from ebullient, self-confident Europe. Five years later, the article on Fonvizin contributed a more censorious depiction of the nobility and Catherine. It stressed their stupidity, perfidy, and criminality, which grew from the arrangements Catherine had made with them over the bodies of millions of serfs. An unpublished essay written in the fall of 1897 continued the pattern by adding "primitive" but arrogant antireligious intellectuals to the nobility as agents of Western poisons.

The broadest analysis of the Western impact appeared in ten lectures in 1890–91. Mainly a critique of the nobility under Catherine, they emphasized that the roots of the fatal attraction lay in the seventeenth century. Europe was moving upward, while Russia, struggling to recover from the Time of Troubles, was recovering "Russian land" and rescuing millions of Russians from Polish rule. Under these circumstances, foreign ideas easily penetrated Russia's "half-baked order." These talks recognized European superiority: Europe was a train and Russia a cart. Moreover, Russians had to adopt European techniques if they were to live as well as Europeans. Alas, though, Peter's practical engineer and artilleryman became Elizabeth's courtiers. They in turn became Catherine's men of letters, "fools stuffed with European ideas" who "lived as Russians but thought as Europeans." Some surrendered their values as they swooned before Western techniques. Others doubted God's existence. Still others resented and resisted Western penetration. But the consequences were disastrous because many Russians were fatally infected.

The culmination of almost two decades of research and reflection on this theme appeared in a set of three 1897 articles on the origins and consequences of the religious schism. These long essays, which carried the subtitle "A Psychological-Historical Essay," supply more details on this subject than Kliuchevskii's lectures or the relevant section in the *Course of Russian History*, but the substance is the same. Even the journal he chose to publish the articles describing the reasons for the decline of the Church from its fourteenth-century height to the schism revealed the depth of his concern, and the milieu in which he wrote. They appeared in *Questions of Philosophy and Psychology*, a positivist journal devoted to introducing European ideas, founded in 1887 by literary scholars "to bring Russia back to its senses" and reconcile intellectuals with their "native religion and healthy national ideals." The articles suggest that the Church was culturally dead and commended those who looked to the West for intellectual sustenance. They also indicate that he had moved from a conservative, civilized circle in Moscow and the academy to a moderate liberal, equally civilized, patriotic, but secular group in its view of man and the world.

In Kliuchevskii's judgment, Russia attained a high plateau between the middle of the sixteenth and seventeenth centuries. The Time of Troubles constituted a demoralizing midpoint, and serfdom, almost constant war, and revolts made the seventeenth century among the most destructive in history. On the other hand, every age encounters crises, and the country ultimately produced effective "natural and necessary" responses. The boyar council and land assemblies were active during these years, and Muscovy progressed in gathering the Russian people and regaining control of "the Russian land." Above all, Russia enjoyed national-religious unity and confidence, both crucial for any society.

At the end of this splendid era, Tsar Alexei and his chief minister provided wise leadership and a sensible reform program. The pious Alexei revered tradition but used Western learning to strengthen the country. His minister developed a vision of the national interest and policies for improving education, promoting industry, introducing European work habits, and expanding trade. He sought to decentralize the administration: Russia needed less government, not more. Moreover, Ordin-Nashchokin comprehended that friendly relations with Poland not only reduced pressure on the frontiers and helped Russia open a Baltic door to the West, but constituted a step toward Slavic unity. In short, his program rested on traditional foundations.

The process of absorbing ideas and instruments that had prevailed from Kiev through the sixteenth century broke down in the seventeenth century because the West continued to advance while Kliuchevskii's homeland moved from effective assimilation to succumbing to Western influence. Paradoxically, the subtle but devastating change in outlook from "becoming aware of another country's and environment's superiority to trying to emulate its morals, attitudes, ideas, customs, and social relations" reached a turning point under the pious tsar. Moreover, it advanced through the Church, a silent and even dormant part of the system. The clergy, who had been cautious and effective carriers of foreign ideas, suddenly split into two groups, incompetent advocates and hostile opponents of change. As a result, millions of devout Christians who revered the past turned against their Church and state, destroying national-religious unity and creating a permanent spiritual crisis.

The immediate cause of the conflict was borrowing authentic materials from abroad in order to correct deviations from Greek liturgical texts and rituals that had become traditional. The proposed changes, or return to correct texts and procedures, did not involve dogma but concerned translations from Greek, the way in which Jesus' name was spelled, and minor points of ritual, such as the number of fingers one should use when making the sign of the cross. When Patriarch Nikon assumed leadership of this drive early in the 1650s, his dictatorial tactics drove thousands of devout conservatives who revered the infallible formulae and practices into protest against men they considered agents of the Antichrist. Expulsion of many pious believers as heretics by a Church council in 1667, the same year as the Treaty of Andrusovo and Ordin-Nashchokin's removal, and the persecution and martyrdom that followed created an Old

Believer movement outside the Church that united with other dissatisfied groups against the state.

While borrowing corrections for the liturgy was the visible cause of the schism, the fundamental reason was Russian intellectual backwardness and disdain for learning. This reflected the intellectual weakness of the Church, which glorified ignorance, elevated simplicity over knowledge, emphasized formulae and rites, and encouraged casuistry. When Nikon and others turned to clergymen from Constantinople and Kiev to help eliminate the irregularities, men and women who saw the program as a Latin plot unleashed a paroxysm of rage against them and the outside world.

In the essays and the two-chapter summary in the *Course of Russian History*, Kliuchevskii assigned responsibility for the unstable foundations of the glorious fourteenth century, Russian intellectual backwardness, the schism, and the seventeenth-century calamities to Russia's acquiring Christianity from Byzantium rather than the West. First, the Church had been such an ingrained part of the Byzantine state and was so feeble intellectually that it did not affect state policy, except when the patriarch was an outstanding individual with close relations with the ruler. Even the weak new state converted the Church's functions into state responsibilities by the fifteenth century.

Second, the Orthodox Church did not bring with it the Greek classics. Instead, it transferred the exaggerated Byzantine emphasis upon moral purity, acceptance of revealed truth, and devotion to ritual and ceremony. In Byzantium, thought meant temptation and sin and truths became dogmas. Orthodox Christians were taught not to reason, but to believe everything and everyone, blocking independent intellectual development and making them slaves to any ideas encountered. Russian clergymen from the beginning lacked interest in intellectual activity and at every level failed to achieve the stature and significance that Western clergymen exercised. The Church and religion therefore had little effect upon the dominant political and social groups, even though Russia's leaders were formally Christian. Moreover, over centuries the quality of the clergy's education declined from the original miserably low level. Many priests were not interested in their work, and the clergy deteriorated into almost total insignificance. Some responsible clergymen sought refuge as hermits. Others devoted their energy to founding monasteries and helping the state expand.

Paradoxically, some of Russia's greatest saints contributed to the disaster through some of their greatest achievements. Thus, by stimulating a religious and patriotic renaissance in the fourteenth century, Saints Sergei and Stefan of Perm' helped produce unity under Moscow. But they also contributed to the state's expansion, the Church's accumulation of wealth, and the bizarre pretension that Moscow was to succeed Byzantium as the Third Rome. This arrogance laid the foundation for a sharp division or schism within the Church and then to an almost insane anti-Westernism.

Kliuchevskii was forthright in criticizing religious arrogance, probably because he was by nature modest and considered humility a cardinal virtue of all religious faith. He never used the term *Holy Russia*. He thought especially offensive the suggestion of some churchmen that Russia was the Third Rome destined to bring salvation to the world because "it was the best and last place of truth."

> The chronic ailment of the Russian religious community was its certainty that Russian Orthodoxy was the only true religion in the world, its conception of God the only correct one, and that the creator of the universe was identical with their own Russian God who belonged only to them and was unknown elsewhere, and that the Russian Church had replaced the universal church. Complacent and content with these tenets, the Russians regarded their own purely national ceremonies as sacrosanct and inviolable, their own religious view as the norm, and their knowledge as the true knowledge. Moreover, fanaticism increased as their attitudes came into conflict with official state policies.[8]

After Constantinople fell in the fifteenth century, the primitive Russian Church suffered from the delusion that it was an adult religious organization, successor to Byzantium, guardian of the truth, and even the messianic Third Rome. Blinded by ignorance and conceit, Church leaders turned their backs on the Bible and the Byzantine East and reduced their intellectual horizons to the isolated Russian land. They scorned the efforts of those Greek churchmen who reached Moscow from fallen and therefore despised Constantinople and sought to correct the visible deficiencies of the Russian liturgy. The Greek and Russian churches, "two brothers," therefore quarreled rather than cooperated over the modest role they should jointly have undertaken.

The Church might have taken advantage of the state's feeble powers during the Time of Troubles to regenerate itself and its authority, but that crisis instead exposed its weakness and further crippled it. The rise of Poland and Sweden, the loss of Russians in the West to the Ukrainian Catholic Church, and the Thirty Years War in Europe contributed to further debilitation. Russia was as unprepared for the challenges the seventeenth century posed as a ship drifting into an unknown sea.

The final blow was the schism, which would not have occurred except for the Church's intellectual failings. Renewed efforts to purify the liturgy and strengthen the Church began early in the seventeenth century. When Patriarch Nikon, "the most powerful and remarkable Russian" of that century, led a determined reform campaign from the top, pious but totally ignorant men and women revolted against the Western influence they perceived behind the changes.

In Kliuchevskii's view, all honored the old beliefs, but Russian society was torn by its perception of itself and the outside world. One group praised simplicity over wisdom. Exalting ignorance and fearing education, fanatical Old Believers called themselves "the survivors of ancient Russian piety" and the only true Christians. In their perception, rites, the "basic furniture," became the center of belief, and to pray fervently meant to believe rightly. They refused to recognize the changes that had occurred in their practices over the centuries. Certain that they possessed "a national monopoly of religious truth," the schismatics opposed corrections even before Nikon began his organized effort, on the assumption that they were defending antiquity against Latinity: all change was a Latin plot. They used the danger Western influence posed to strengthen the mechanical formation of religious life that had already stifled expression.

The other group used intellect, honored science, and venerated learning. Thus, two levels of receptivity, two visions of the world, and two psychologies that shared much in common competed. All, even the reformers, were suspicious of the West and changes that seemed to reflect alien influences. A handful sought to borrow practical elements, but even they recognized the difficulty of separating the fruit from the roots from which it grew. The others refused to try to overcome stagnation but saw God as a miracle worker, revered the past and its forms, and became almost insanely fearful that Latin ideas would poison the pure well of Orthodoxy. They sacrificed their lives to preserve their inherited faith. Concluding that no one could achieve salvation within a Church led by infected pilots, they sought to sink the ship. A paralyzing Great Fear swept the country. Both sides became so dogmatic and morally blind that they undermined the social order and national welfare.

These essays emphasized the schism's "psychological circumstances" and the way it spread alarm against Western influence into every aspect of life. Russia in the seventeenth century was "a primitive, ignorant, and monotonous country," its learning "alphabetical" in character. An "incomplete building" marred by serfdom and deep class divisions and administered by an autocracy in the tsar's hands, "Russia was incapable of forming a lively and productive society." The schism not only illustrated this backward character but worsened it: "Under Byzantine influence, we were slaves of a foreign belief: under Western influence, we became slaves of foreign thought. Thought without morals is stupidity: morals without thought is fanaticism."

The schism destroyed the self-confidence that had sustained Russia and produced disagreement over the country's nature and destiny. It created alienation between ruler and ruled and between the Church and many believers, so that Russia was as divided within itself as it was from Europe. By weakening interest in and affection for religion and the past, it brought about a precipitate decline of faith. For the small but crucial number of Russians who were educated, religion, the Church, and the clergy meant backward antiquity, opposition to progress, and a ghetto for the ignorant. This contemptuous attitude and Russia's traditional indifference to scientific study and intellectual activity together explained the susceptibility of intellectuals to the Enlightenment's utopian ideas. In short, the Old Believers, who represented the absolute denial of Western influence, paradoxically ensured its full triumph in the eighteenth century.

Many leading Russians recognized the West's supremacy and the need to borrow, but the populace remained anti-intellectual and hostile to all change, especially any connected with Europe. This fear and the bitter religious and political dispute between an intellectually decrepit Church and the state delayed Russia's adopting modern science. By weakening an already feeble institution, the schism increased the Church's dependence upon the state and its isolation from the informed public. Later the state "fastened" science onto Russian life, but the implant did not thrive because strength comes only from gradual growth from within, not from imposed programs.

The clash between Church and state and their supporters weakened the foundations of the religious unity that had enabled Russia to survive and had endowed it with a cultural and political order equal to that of the West. This and the foolish disputes over trifles reminded Kliuchevskii of the Pskov quarrels three centuries earlier that first enabled Poles to increase their authority in western Russia. In the seventeenth century, the schism allowed Uniates and the Catholic Church to lure millions from Orthodoxy, a disaster from which he concluded that Russia had not recovered at the time of his death. Following the schism, the Western influence that had been an immediate cause poured into the vacuum that the schism had left, corrupted many of the nobility, and destroyed the cultural integrity that had made Russia distinctive. Russia's relations with the West occupied a central place in his account, especially for the period after the seventeenth century, when the history of Russian culture became "the history of Western culture in Russia."

Finally, the schism fortified the differences that separated Russia from Europe. Russia remained a credulous society based on unthinking faith in external observances and traditional formulae, while Europe respected learning and relied upon critical thought. Europe's tradition of nonconformism helped produce a confident, lively, and productive society in which "gradual leveling" ensured stability, reduced inequalities, and encouraged advance. It made Europe a society of innovative and enterprising citizens that produced material advantages and comforts in an upward spiral. Russia, on the other hand, fell into a downward spiral because of its poverty of intellect, the schism that grew from it, and the further decline that followed the separation. The intensified social inequalities and exploitation of the culturally unarmed populace lengthened the downward trend. As the divide between Russia and the West grew, the tsars and court nobles led enforced campaigns to reduce the gap, a tactic that widened the fissure within the Russian community as well as the gulf between Russia and Europe. The dilemma became even more complicated and tragic when forceful rulers sought to compel the transformation of their society along Western lines.

TWELVE

The Autocracy and the Autocrats' Policies
The Dilemma of Relations with the West

> The closer we approach Western Europe, the more difficulty we encounter in acquiring freedom, because the instruments of West European culture fall into the hands of a few in the top layer of society. These men have used Western techniques for their own advantage, not that of the country. This has deepened social inequality, exploited the culturally unarmed masses, lowered the level of social consciousness, and increased class antagonism. It has prepared the people for revolt, not freedom. The main responsibility for this lies on thoughtless administrators.[1]

> The more we have made use of the fruits of Western civilization, the more we have diverged from Europe's fundamental striving for equality and freedom. As we have mastered West European forms of political and civil life, the character and structure of our state have become more Asiatic and less European. Thus, our political structure has been in inverse proportion to the stock of knowledge and ideas we have received from the West.[2]

The quandary that relations with the West raised for the Russian system of government affected Kliuchevskii's political philosophy and treatment of the state and government policy as much as it did his religious beliefs and discussion of the Church. Western ideas and values had deeply penetrated his mind, if not his habits and way of life, so that he represents and reflects the same dilemma as his Church and state. In fact, relations with the West and the quandary they raised formed a central thread in his work and emerged as an especially important theme in his teaching and writing about modern history, especially about Peter the Great, Catherine the Great, and their successors.

Soviet leaders and historians confronted the same dilemma as the Russian government and Kliuchevskii's generation. They ultimately failed because the challenge proved overwhelming and their responses resembled those of Peter the Great. Relations with the West constitute the same delicate and baffling problem for the leaders, peoples, and scholars of many countries throughout the world in the twentieth century as they try to cope with the cultural and other resources of Europe and the United States and at the same time preserve their cultural integrity and independence.

While many Russian and foreign scholars have paid some attention to Kliuchevskii's political philosophy and the place he assigns the state in history, their analyses have concentrated upon the *Course of Russian History* and the other works that dealt most directly with governance, such as *Boyar Council*.

His political views were far more subtle and discreet than his religious values, but analysis of his lectures, writings, letters, and archives, those of his closest associates as well, and his actions—and inactions—allow one to determine his basic values. These beliefs affected his view of Russian history, as much as and perhaps more than did his religious faith, if only because the system of government had been more important than the Church in modern times. It was not only the principal "representative" of the Russian people, but it was also the instrument most involved in and affected by cultural relations with the West.

Kliuchevskii sought to decipher and explain the past and thought that neither theories nor philosophies had a place in historical scholarship. As he frequently asserted, observers should always consider the circumstances in which a scholar worked. Thus, two of Kliuchevskii's gifted contemporaries, in a country and milieu more free than his, declared that everyone was born either a little liberal or a little conservative. In Kliuchevskii's Russia, the nature of the political system made these terms almost meaningless. The literature of political philosophy was slim and offered little diversity, and Kliuchevskii's university studies did not include Western political philosophies. Little of the European scholarship he read dealt with political thought. He had no understanding of political participation or the problems a political leader confronted in achieving and maintaining control.

His knowledge of political systems rested almost entirely upon his command of Russian history and observations from living in a service state. He was far more interested in the social materials and structure of administration than in the system of governance. Moreover, he displayed little interest in participating in making decisions at any level, from the history faculty to St. Petersburg. Like many such passive observers, he hoped for, but did little to achieve, "a more just order of society." Some scholars have misinterpreted occasional wistful expressions of desire for change as liberalism. They were far from that.

Kliuchevskii accepted a deanship at the university most reluctantly and succeeded in escaping its responsibilities before his term ended. His interest in government at any level was so low that he rarely criticized the bureaucracy, a favorite target of most educated Russians. Friends and associates recognized this passivity: Ger'e and Vinogradov did not request participation or even support for their activities in the Moscow city government or discuss programs with him. The only occasions on which he expressed an active concern with state policy came in times of great change, as in the confident early 1860s, or in turbulent periods, such as 1879–81 and 1904–1906. Even then, the span of solicitude was brief, and he quickly returned to the study. In sum, his concept of one's role in society was vastly different from that of most Western scholars a century later.

Both as an undergraduate fresh from the countryside and as a venerable senior scholar, Kliuchevskii concluded that forms of government reflect circumstances and traditions: history provides legitimacy, and he accepted and supported autocracy as part of the national inheritance. Each system of rule was representative, and elections were only one of many ways to establish a system of rule that represented the state's and society's interests. The effectiveness of a form of rule depended on the good sense of its leaders and their advisers, not on the system of governance. Because of local circumstances, autocracy was as "natural and necessary" for Russia as other forms of government were for other societies in different circumstances. It had combined with the Church to establish national unity, and utilized instruments such as the boyar council to administer and expand the state.

No form of government was perfect or permanent; but solidarity of government and people was essential, especially for a country perpetually confronting grave threats. The most effective arrangement was "a well-organized state" that brought government and people together, ensured security, and created conditions under which "civilizing activities could thrive and culture bloom." A satisfactory form of rule could be autocratic, oligarchic, aristocratic, democratic, even socialist. However, it must rest upon national unity, provide resolute leadership, encourage participation and support from the most able, satisfy national needs, and enable the populace to live in peace. Indeed, "Every society has the right to demand of those in power, its stewards, 'Rule us so that we may live comfortably.' " In his judgment, a satisfactory system could be autocratic if it were enlightened. The ruler should be a gardener, not a mechanic.

Comparing Kliuchevskii's views on the purpose and nature of government with the opening words of the American Constitution illuminates his values sharply. For example, neither establishing Justice nor securing "the Blessings of Liberty" was among the functions he allotted the state. Moreover, he was so committed to study of the past and so convinced that Russia was in permanent peril that he ignored the Posterity so attractive to those who wrote the Constitution. His engagement with history and his apprehensions ensured passivity about both the present and the future.

Russia first attained national unity by combining state and religion. After the schism, it utilized state and national culture. Since the fifteenth century, the autocratic state had played an indispensable role in regaining "the Russian land" and gathering Russians in a national community, "natural and necessary" state-building functions in distinct Russian conditions. Other forms of governance had fulfilled similar but less demanding requirements in different circumstances in other parts of the world. Before criticizing any form of government, one should compare it with possible alternatives.

While autocracy had been essential, it had made Russia a state rather than a nation of people connected by ties of blood, language, religion, customs, and sense of national purpose. It constituted an odious political system, a form of government that one could accept "only when the individual who exercises this unnatural power devotes himself unsparingly to the general welfare, accepts advice from the most competent, and provides equality outside the political realm." Tsars were often as useful as scarecrows. Some had been monsters and others were grossly incompetent. In the nineteenth century, autocratic rule had failed dismally to recognize national needs or carry out changes beneficial for the country as a whole. Even more important, tsars since Peter the Great had failed to resolve the dilemma that relations with the West raised. Russia's situation at the turn of the century was more complicated and hazardous than ever before.

Kliuchevskii accepted autocracy, as he would have any rigorous form of rule, for another reason than traditions determined by circumstances. As a Christian, he assumed that man was weak and dependent upon others from birth. "Man is not born free. . . . States rest on submission of the individual will to society, of the private good to the general welfare."[3] The family, clan, tribe, estate, and ultimately the state surround and protect individuals and groups, with the state more decisive as history advances. A deep-rooted sense that Russia and Russians lived on the edge of obliteration was crucial throughout his life: survival was a significant achievement for a person as well as for a nation. Even in the 1860s, when he was most optimistic, Russia resembled "some kind of naked being without a name, without an inheritance, without a future, without experience, like a frivolous girl without a dowry, condemned by fate to sit by the sea and wait for a bridegroom."[4]

Kliuchevskii's Christian beliefs and nationalism reinforced his conviction that the place of each individual was secondary: Everyone should serve his fellows and the nation. In his case, responsible work as a scholar-teacher constituted the first duty, next to caring for his family. Education in Granovskii's sacred order was a form of service "in the quiet court of humanity," as well as an effective way of improving the lives of his countrymen and making Russia a nation. Each member of that order should work to his utmost ability, whatever the circumstances, however competent the government. Kliuchevskii so honored this credo within and beyond the university that he thought that contributions beyond one's official duties should be unobtrusive and even confidential. Thus, he endorsed a May 1899 memorandum on state policy toward the university that ten colleagues sent to the minister of education. He did not sign it because it was not confidential, but with the others' assent he wrote a private letter of support.

Kliuchevskii was also convinced that one should not seek to expand one's role beyond its natural boundaries or persuade associates to change their views. Serving others did not grant the right to change them. Thus, he did not attempt to convert his wife into a scholarly associate, as Mrs. Ger'e was for her husband, or to deflect his son's fascination with motorcycles. Discussion of politics, especially advocacy or criticism of a political system, had no place in a university: In class, one should teach, not preach. He ignored the political views and activities of graduate students who worked with him. Each chose his research project and worked with full independence: he accepted their "human personality," a phrase he used often. He did not endeavor to establish a doctrine, organize the Russian or even the Moscow historical community, or improve the university. Properly, men "high above and far away" established state policies: they served in their place as he and a peasant did in theirs. Suggesting government actions, except when senior statesmen requested advice, was unthinkable.

Those he most admired were quiet heroes, such as book collectors, librarians, and archivists who accepted their positions in society and devoted their lives to creating and preserving depositories of knowledge for later generations, activities that received little recognition or reward. Novikov and Granovskii were members of this group, educating students in love of their country and the essential moral virtues, which included the homely one of supporting oneself and one's family. Kliuchevskii's favorite ruler was Alexei, "the gentle tsar, the finest man of ancient Russia," a pious and humble ruler interested solely in eternal salvation and his country's welfare. On the other hand, Pobedonostsev, the deeply unpopular director-general of the Church, was a disaster because he "despised everything, both what he loved and hated, both good and evil, both the people and himself."[5]

The essay that best reflected these views was "The Good People of Ancient Russia," which sang the praises of men and women, rich and poor, who gave their goods and lives to their fellows and country. He compared them to miners of precious metals. Russian women received special affection, even veneration, for they were "born with sympathy for the poor and needy." He saluted Peter the Great for his sense of duty and service. The aristocracy's contribution before 1762 in building and helping administer the state won praise, as did rulers and peasants in their assigned places. But he despised the nobility after 1762: they were an undeserving privileged class freed from responsibility at the time serfdom reached its peak. Many then betrayed their country by abandoning service to society and state. Some became more French than Russian.

For Kliuchevskii, the peasants were "a bleak mass," concerned solely with survival, unable to contribute in governance, and apparently not interested in trying to improve their economic situation, except in wild, blind revolts. But he admired the Russian people for persevering against nature and nobles. Moreover, he valued the ordinary Russian's common sense and declared many illiterate countrymen sensible and intelligent: instinct was a more certain guide than education and intellectual attainment.

Inherited and traditional, "an alliance formed to attain the general welfare," or national interest, the Russian state was designed specifically "to maintain external security and preserve internal order." Moreover, the title "autocrat" had a different meaning in 1498 than centuries later. Originally, it signified that Muscovy was an independent state whose ruler was "sovereign of 'the Russian land' " and "head of the independent Russian Orthodox Church." Later, the tsar was the symbol of national independence and represented the state's interests in international affairs.

In Kliuchevskii's judgment, circumstances and traditions were decisive: the French Revolution had proved that no people can create a durable state based on abstract principles. Freedom was "a hard-bought thing" that peoples could achieve only after economic and social progress had created proper circumstances. It began at the top with the upper classes and descended gradually, just as the sun's rays first touched the mountain peak and slowly proceeded down the slopes as the sun rose in the sky.[6]

In the course on the French Revolution, he suggested that a constitutional monarchy was the most effective system of government for France, even though it suffered serious weaknesses. In his diary in 1868, in a university lecture in 1886, and again in the final volume of the *Course of Russian History,* he declared discreetly that constitutional monarchy was the most satisfactory form of government, "the most complete form of public power." A well-organized state resting upon the free individual, who possessed both rights and responsibilities, it established an executive authority in which "the prince is tamed." It provided firm leadership, wise counsel, and rational rule. However, such a system was feasible only after nature and economic evolution had created the necessary foundations. All parts of Europe were moving toward such a system of governance, some nations earlier and more systematically than others. But the permanent character of change revealed that constitutional rule would not be the final system of governance.

In Kliuchevskii's judgment, Russia had lacked the necessary bases for constitutional government throughout its history, in the sixteenth and seventeenth centuries, when Speranskii tried to promote a kind of constitution under Alexander I, and in 1905 as well. The enormous forces of history and tradition made the "plain, heavy, but durable" Russian state less advanced, even backward, in material and cultural resources than Europe. "An incomplete building," Russia trailed the West in constructing an equitable society that encouraged or even tolerated independence and lively thought. But it was not inferior in any way, it was simply different. And, like other countries, it would continue to change.

As a student in the glowing reform years of Alexander II, Kliuchevskii concluded that the abolition of serfdom would lead gradually to disintegration of the autocratic state and freedom and equality before the law. He was also hopeful that Alexander II's other reforms meant progress toward improved living standards, a livelier and more lofty culture, and expanded access to education.

He even included reduced interference in university affairs and public life. Russia was apparently establishing a system in which a well-informed government would rule a freely united society.

This confidence gradually dissolved after 1865 but revived in the last years of Alexander II's reign, when Kliuchevskii hoped that the ruler would turn to the most responsible members of society for counsel. After the accession of Alexander III in 1881, the sense of assurance melted. Kliuchevskii's research then emphasized the differences between European and Russian institutions. As the 1890s advanced, he became more aware of the spread of Europe's transformation and critical of the inefficiencies of Russia's form of rule. Discussions with friends, turmoil among the students, some involvement in university and public affairs, and the violence of 1904–1906 multiplied his pessimism. After 1906 he returned to passivity, still convinced that the law of permanent change remained in operation.

The early tone of cautious optimism was understandable. The reforms enabled him to make the great ascent from Penza. He enjoyed the confidence of youth in ever-improving circumstances in a university community that was a visible beneficiary of change. Even dour Soloviev was confident that autonomy presaged further advantages for scholars and therefore for the country as a whole. Buslaev, Ger'e, and Tikhonravov transmitted the ideas of Guizot, Buckle, and other Western scholars, who "scientifically" predicted that new knowledge would change the world. The faculty considered Russia a part of Europe, indicated directly and indirectly that the West was more civilized and advanced, and suggested that Russia would inexorably become more European. Even the *Orthodox Review* concurred, informing readers concerning European intellectual and religious developments and urging reform of the Church.

The university "lions" of the day recognized Kliuchevskii's potential and welcomed him into the select academic community. Achievements as a teacher and scholar promised that his future, like that of his country, would be bright. His personal life helped make this a happy period: marriage and relations within the Borodin clan provided a serenity that suffused his view of the world.

Further, Kliuchevskii's interest in and knowledge of Europe were greatest during those early years in Moscow. His courses with scholars who had studied abroad, relations with the Ger'e family, and friendship with Shakhov made Europe attractive, even a model. Teaching about the French Revolution and his research together demonstrated that the Russian "level of enlightenment and sense" was far beneath that of the West, but that Russia, as a segment of Europe, would follow the apparent long-term Western trend toward limited government. In words from Miliukov's M.A. thesis, this would be "an inevitable consequence of an inner evolution basically the same in Europe and in Russia which external conditions had delayed" in Russia. Such a system of rule was not superior: it simply reflected changed circumstances. Russia should borrow materials and techniques from the West, but not ideas. Neither ambitious intellectuals nor other groups should press toward limited government. Similarly, neither bureaucrats nor others should seek to delay it. The rulers' wisdom and the subjects' patience would determine whether or not the change would occur peacefully. In a homely but effective aphorism, Kliuchevskii remarked that a wise countryman who was lost simply dropped the reins and allowed his horse to find the way home. Nature triumphs.

Except for the military reform of 1874, which Kliuchevskii praised almost as highly as the abolition of serfdom, the 1870s were a bleak period. He was ignorant concerning the *zemstvo* movement and ridiculed those who thought that Russians active in local government had acquired the experience for participation in the central government. Moreover, defenders of the old system became increasingly vocal as government and society drifted apart. Russia's role in international politics further depressed him. Military victory in the Balkan Wars, the apparent diplomatic victory achieved in the Treaty of San Stefano, and the humiliating loss of most gains at the Congress of Berlin in 1878 increased antagonisms in the court and among others interested in domestic and international politics. However, the appointment of Loris-Melikov as the tsar's principal adviser created rumors in 1879 and 1880 that the general might propose an advisory council. This led to sanguine expectations that Alexander would establish a system that would close the gap between the ruler and the leading elements of society.

Kliuchevskii completed *Boyar Council* during the final hopeful months of Alexander II's reign, published sections before the assassination on March 1, 1881, revised it as a book during the early months of Alexander III, and defended it eighteen months after reaction had begun. His essays on the council appeared between January 1880 and September 1881 in *Russian Thought*, "the professors' journal." Its founder, S. A. Iur'ev, was a respected liberal. Viktor A. Gol'tsev, editor from 1885 until his death in 1906, was an advocate of constitutional government and a member of the Kadet or Constitutional Democratic party when he died. The journal published articles by leading proponents of constitutional government, such as Muromtsev and Kovalevskii. Moreover, as indicated earlier, Kliuchevskii was publicly critical of government policy during the period before Alexander II's assassination. This has led some observers to conclude that *Boyar Council* was a nineteenth-century liberal tract proposing a limited monarchy.

However, these observers transpose the values of other years upon Kliuchevskii's scholarship. *Boyar Council* described Russia in the fifteenth and sixteenth centuries as "an absolute monarchy with an aristocratic administration." The tsar ruled Russia *with* the council, the members of which were important officials and landowners to whom he turned for advice on occasions he chose. The council cooperated with the prince or the tsar in administering the country as a useful middleman between the ruler and people. It acted with the tsar, under his actual or nominal chairmanship, and without him when he was absent. The ruler's obligation to serve the general welfare was a primary restriction against absolutism, and he also shared power with the boyar council. In short, Russia had been an autocratic state, but not absolute. Its government was not representative or democratic. However, "society," by which he meant the boyars through the sixteenth century and an indefinable ever-growing group in later periods, participated not in the Western sense and certainly not through universal or even limited elections. Instead, those shared authority who exercised functions of importance.

Kliuchevskii may have selected the boyar council and the land assembly to suggest that these two institutions had limited the power of the central government. However, *Boyar Council* is an account of eight hundred years of Russian history through analysis of one institution, not a lament that Russia differed from Europe or a tract implying that the council provided the historic base for constitutional government. Neither in *Boyar Council* nor elsewhere did he advocate that Russia establish a constitutional monarchy: he urged only that Russian leaders consider instruments that had served effectively in the past. Even the introductory essay in the issue of *Russian Thought* that excited Nechkina condemned the efforts that Peter and Catherine had made to introduce Western institutions. Constitutional monarchy and democratic government had developed in circumstances different from those Russia had enjoyed. Moreover, *Boyar Council* criticized the boyars' efforts to create an elected monarch during the Time of Troubles. Its quick failure proved that it was foreign, worst of all Polish, and irrelevant. Russia could not and should not borrow: it should "grow" its own instruments.

In the 1880s, after he had completed his work on the council, Kliuchevskii concentrated upon his survey course, new seminars, and the origins of serfdom. His lectures on estates in 1886 criticized European political systems for "pulverizing" their societies. He ignored the *obshchina*, or commune, which the Slavophils had proclaimed the basic democratic peasant institution, one that Westernization had destroyed. He also paid little attention to the *veche*, or assembly, that had flowered in Novgorod and Pskov and in which some scholars found democratic roots or a kernel from which limited and then democratic government might grow. He occasionally referred to them with affection, but for him the two cities were "wreaths of beautiful white foam in the form of free communities" that "the slow, heavy tide of the turgid Russian sea" rolled up on the beach. There the light and vaporous materials quickly vanished as they yielded to the inexorable thrust for national unity. He described their absorption and loss of liberties in almost the same words he used for serfdom, "a sacrifice that the general welfare of the land demanded."

In the late 1880s, Kliuchevskii devoted months of research to the sixteenth- and seventeenth-century land assembly, which some considered a potential foundation for representative, democratic government. In 1891–92, *Russian Thought* published three long articles on this institution that he considered among his most important and included in the first volume of selected essays.

Some have suggested that he selected the assembly as a subtle way of advocating limited government, but examination of the essays and the pages on the land assembly in the 1886 course on estates and in the *Course of Russian History* demolishes that judgment. Instead, he demonstrated that it was an instrument of the central government, "extremely poor and colorless even in comparison with the French Estates-General, the least strong of Western representative institutions." "In Russia, popular representation came into being not to impose limitations on authority, but to define and strengthen it. This was the essential difference between Russia and western Europe." When students suggested an analogy between the assembly and the *zemstvo*, he reprimanded them sharply for "cheap liberalism."[7]

Kliuchevskii established that the assemblies between 1566 and 1653, the first and last ones, had no legislative or other powers, sought none, and did not create a base for political action. Moreover, the assembly had no historical connection with the *veche*. The ruler called it when he needed advice and support. He appointed the members and imposed participation upon reluctant participants as state service, a burden they jettisoned as soon as possible. They brought no instructions, demands, or list of needs to Moscow and did not engage in general debate or raise questions other than those the ruler called them to discuss. Boris Godunov might have transformed the assembly into a national representative assembly, but chose not to. Even if he had, Russia lacked the social base necessary to make such an assembly a permanent institution. None of the assemblies attempted to transform itself into an instrument of legislative power, even in 1613, "the first truly representative gathering in Moscow." Then they were a "source of power and necessary base of order" called to end the Time of Troubles by electing a new tsar. In the following decade of permanent crisis, it might have acquired rights or guarantees for itself or established a permanent national assembly, as English and French barons had in similar situations. Instead, the assembly sat passively while Tsar Michael and his father, Patriarch Filaret, struggled to establish a stable government.

Why did these assemblies act so lethargically and disappear, leaving no institutional foundation for later groups? Basically, Kliuchevskii provided the same multicausal response given to explain the withering of the boyar council. But his research in the 1880s led him to add serfdom. How could a society based on serfdom develop a representative system of government?

According to a legend Kliuchevskii cited, Peter the Great recognized the dilemma that relations with the West raised and planned only temporary borrowing: "Europe is necessary for a few decades and then we must turn our backs to it."[8] However, the man of action's momentum led to an orgy of infectious borrowing that became permanent and deepened the eternal dilemma. The closer Russia's relations with the West, and the more Russia's rulers borrowed and altered the society they sought to strengthen, the greater that popular resentment grew. To achieve the transformation the rulers deemed vital against resistance from the conservative, hostile populace, they were forced to increase the state's authority. As this process strengthened the state, the divergence between the old and the Europeanized society, the people and the state widened. State power and expansion were in inverse proportion to freedom. In a double irony, imported elements undermined the state they were designed to strengthen at the same time growing despotism destroyed the possibility that Russia would develop the attitudes and institutions that made the West alluring and powerful.

The dilemma appeared most clearly with Peter the Great, who fascinated Kliuchevskii. He did not interpret Peter as the Slavophil devil who broke decisively with the past nor as the Westerner genius who catapulted his homeland into Europe. Indeed, the pages on the historiography of Peter mentioned neither those who accused the tsar of destroying Russia's ancient institutions and values nor those who acclaimed him as the great enlightener or civilizer. Instead, Kliuchevskii saw the years after 1613 and all of Russian history as a continuum. Peter maintained and expanded the tradition of adopting European ideas and practices that began in the tenth century but became destructive after the sixteenth century. Even men as sensible as Alexei and Ordin-Nashchokin contributed to the debate. Influenced by the West, they sought simultaneously to reconstruct the old and build a new system: the law code of 1649 was an attempt to preserve the past's fruits as a foundation for a brighter future, but recognized and strengthened serfdom. Social inequalities widened and caused such bitter dissatisfactions among the lower classes that revolts were frequent. Worst of all, the religious schism, ignited by inept borrowing and the fierce reaction it instigated, destroyed Russia's precious unity.

Kliuchevskii devoted twelve pages of his master work to Prince V. V. Golitsyn, principal adviser during Sophia's regency in the 1680s and an immediate predecessor of Peter in turning to the West. Golitsyn, a well-educated Westerner of good sense, was especially attractive because Russia regained Kiev while he was in a position of authority. Recognizing that adopting foreign ideas and ways by "an ancient and complex country" required great delicacy, he concentrated upon educating Sophia and her senior collaborators about the need for care in introducing change. He was an exceptionally wise statesman, but the schism had smashed the defenses before he became a senior adviser.

Peter combined continuity and change. His physical stature, energy, and brutal tactics led contemporaries and historians alike to exaggerate his role and the changes he introduced. He was not a radical revolutionary who wanted to create a new society but led a generation who sought to rebuild Russia on its old foundations. A man of action who gave little thought to long-term consequences, he utilized instruments at hand to achieve immediate goals. He was outstanding in part because he gave highest priority to the country's general welfare, which he thought rested on secure frontiers on the southwest and northwest. He also pledged to obtain a foothold in the Baltic that would give Russia secure access to Europe. Finally, the tsar sought status for Russia as a

European power. To achieve these goals, he centralized administrative controls, strengthened the armed forces, promoted industry, located funds to support these enterprises, and borrowed ideas and techniques.

Kliuchevskii devoted an introductory chapter in the *Course of Russian History* to the tsar's character and personality, one many consider a masterpiece. These pages and the essays on Peter represent a significant shift in his interpretation of the motive forces of history. Although he had recognized the importance of the character and personality of men such as Nikon, he had previously emphasized the role that economic, social, and institutional factors played. However, his brilliant psychological portrait of Peter assigned a significant role to his education, family relations, marriage, and personal characteristics. In his judgment, Peter was an intelligent, energetic, and ruthless man who introduced changes without plan or consideration for the people, whom he saw only as taxpayers. A ruler who by force of will placed his stamp upon the people and the age, he was also the harbinger of an era in which individuals, especially rulers, played a central role.

Of all Peter's instruments, Kliuchevskii considered his concept of the national welfare and awakening national self-consciousness the most fruitful. Convinced that strengthening Russia was his primary obligation, he refused to yield to conservative opposition or surrender responsibility to "inevitable historical processes." Instead, by example and force he tried to harness all national energies to the state as the bearer of the national interest.

Absolute power was another essential instrument. Kliuchevskii considered autocracy "odious in principle" but conceded that Peter at least sacrificed himself as well as his countrymen. He abolished the boyar council, on which Alexei had often relied, but utilized its personnel. He concentrated authority in his hands or assigned it to trusted and carefully monitored collaborators. While Kliuchevskii lamented Peter's system of rule, he admired the emphasis upon duty and service: this almost justified autocratic rule.

Many scholars have asserted that Peter reached power determined to transform Russia, and Soloviev added that the tsar also responded to a popular demand for change. However, Kliuchevskii's Peter was an almost reluctant agent of change who reacted to external developments. The stimuli for his makeshift policies were military requirements, the desperate need to support conflicts that he launched or into which he stumbled. One change led to another: enlarging and equipping the armed forces led to new taxes, social changes, modifications of the administrative structure, and then another wave of new forms of taxation and alterations. Consequently, many pages on Peter's reign described administrative reorganizations.

Peter's ambitions and ways of resolving problems led him to expand the centuries-old practice of borrowing, even from his principal direct antagonist, Sweden. In his judgment, Peter adopted only instruments immediately useful: he did not understand or even seek to comprehend the basic principles that underlay the tools and techniques responsible for the West's advantages.

When assessing the tsar, Kliuchevskii summarized the two main points of view, without discussing in detail the Slavophil criticism that Peter had broken decisively with the past and placed his homeland upon a foreign and false path or the Westerner position. However, he cited Pushkin's praise, particularly the statement that "Peter summoned Russia, and Russia answered," and Soloviev's panegyric, "Never had any people accomplished such an achievement as the Russian people did in the first quarter of the eighteenth century." He sought to view Peter in historical perspective, seeing him as neither an enlightened monarch nor a revolutionary. His reign was not a turning point nor a crossing of the Rubicon, but "more a shock than a revolution." The damages he caused were approximately equal to the advances he achieved. Russia's surface and facade changed during his years of power, but he did not touch the foundation. In many ways, his rule "resembled a spring shower that strips branches from the trees but nonetheless refreshes the air and encourages new seeds to grow."

Perhaps Peter's greatest contribution was stimulating an appetite for knowledge. Promotion of education, scientific research, and publishing helped shunt the Church from the center of life toward the periphery. Kliuchevskii barely mentioned the Church under Peter, except for melting church bells for the army and attacking some religious customs. He failed to indicate that Peter had abolished the patriarchate and replaced it with the Holy Synod. This neglect reflected his judgment that the Church quietly lost its senior position after the schism.

Peter's second most important achievement was also intangible, for his methods jolted Russia into regaining some of the self-confidence that the Time of Troubles and schism had destroyed. In addition, an accomplishment that most admirers placed first, he transformed "a poor, weak, almost unknown people" into a powerful, secure nation. He restructured society, "civilized" the country, freed its new capital from Swedish invasion, and moved Russia's western and southwestern boundaries toward "natural frontiers." Finally, he completed the first step toward the Europeanization of Russian culture and gave Russia its deserved position as a member of the European state system.

Appreciation for these achievements was balanced by judgments concerning the costs and damages. Kliuchevskii ordinarily ignored suffering and the losses in lives that barbarous rule, civil conflict, and wars entailed, but he stressed the human cost of Peter's programs. St. Petersburg, "a mass grave" and "Egyptian pyramid in the swamps of the Neva," was "a gigantic product of despotism" and a symbol of the tsar's disregard of the people's welfare. Not even victories over five Swedens would have justified the enormous financial and moral strain he placed upon the population: "In order to defend his native land from enemies, Peter caused more destruction than any enemy." An especially tragic moral loss was amalgamating the varieties of serfdom into the most debased form and extending the range of the fatal institution: this illustrated the price that autocrats made Russia pay for borrowing.[9]

Moreover, Peter's adopting European techniques was disorganized, hasty, and wasteful. He "created institutions as a thrifty mother makes clothes far too large that will fit her children only when they grow up." He introduced superfluous elements, but neglected those most necessary. Western influence at the higher levels of society and government produced "a mixture of foreign vices with ugly national virtues." Peter also ignored the national-religious unity that had sustained Russia for centuries. He not only fostered disunity but neglected the state's primary mission, regaining the Russian peoples beyond the state's boundaries, who numbered more than half the Russians when Peter became tsar.

But the major price was strengthening the autocracy, providing it a rationale and philosophical base and in a sense "justifying it," as Stalinists would later justify that dictator's rule. Under Peter and his successors, the autocracy and its crippling bureaucracy defined politics and morality and subordinated all, even the monarch and the monarchy, to the state. He strengthened the state but neither enlightened nor enriched the people and caused a visible decline of moral strength. In sum, his autocratic methods moved Russia further from the freedoms at the root of the Western achievements that Russians envied.

Peter's final disastrous act was leaving the succession unclear, allowing "free will and accident" to decide a crucial question that any thoughtful ruler would have settled in advance. The tsar deprived the nobles of the boyar council, so they lacked an instrument to fill the vacuum at his death. Instead, the guards regiments ruled, using Western military weapons and organizational systems that Peter had introduced and illustrating the irony of borrowing. In short, the dreadful years after 1725 were Peter's responsibility and legacy.

In the lectures on Western influence after Peter and in the *Course of Russian History*, completed almost two decades later, Kliuchevskii devoted only one-quarter as much space to the interlude between Peter and Catherine as to Peter's reign. He considered that period one of the most dreary and destructive in Russian history, but not devoid of progress. The army became professional. Poll and land taxes replaced the direct tax, industry and foreign trade increased, and the government opened Moscow University and built more schools. Above all, Russia concluded a sensible alliance with Poland and resumed gathering the lands and people.

The clearest opportunity in the eighteenth century to move from autocracy toward a more responsive government occurred in 1730 when a brief break occurred in the autocratic facade. Kliuchevskii devoted a full lecture, a fifth of the pages he allotted to these thirty-seven years, to the unsuccessful effort Prince Dmitrii M. Golitsyn made to limit Anna's power when Peter II's death in 1730 left the succession unclear.

One might judge that Golitsyn's placing conditions on Anna before her election as empress constituted a step toward limited monarchy. But Kliuchevskii explained that this was not Golitsyn's purpose and that he could not have succeeded even if this had been his goal. The nobility held more than half the population in serfdom, and none of them understood the concept of liberty.

Golitsyn was respected but was unpopular and isolated. The great families had few common interests. Moreover, he would have limited the autocrat's power for the sole advantage of these families, perhaps even for the Golitsyns. This would have caused discord and conflict, weakening the state when Russia, as always, needed unity. The autocracy had deep roots and had become a "historical necessity," while the nobles had no sense of corporate or national responsibility. In short, Russia lacked the foundations to move toward limited government. In Golitsyn's words, "The banquet was ready, but the guests were not worthy to partake of it."

Consequently, the years after Peter witnessed the collapse of most of his innovations, disintegration of many ties that had held Russia together, and rule by praetorian regiments. The symbol of these years was replacement of the assembly of the land by regiments. St. Petersburg became a German city, "a foreign enemy colony," commanded by "the Tatar-German Bironshchina" of Biron, Lowenfeld, and Ostermann, "the Mephistopheles from the West." The intelligent and kind-hearted Elizabeth, who succeeded Anna in 1741, at least reduced the influence of "the rascal foreigners," but she was totally dissolute and did not even know that England was an island. In a society in which more than half the population were serfs, she owned fifteen thousand dresses. During this "golden age of the aristocracy," the views of such men as Rousseau and Voltaire saturated Russia's ruling class. Immorality and luxury prevailed. The nobles freed themselves from many service obligations that Peter had imposed and made the government their instrument. Adopting all of Europe's vices and none of its virtues, they alienated themselves from their land and people. Above all, the governments between Peter and Catherine neglected the goal of reuniting the Russian lands and people and fumbled opportunities to make Russia the decisive European power.

Peter III, the worst of Elizabeth's unpleasant legacies, was a symbol of the era. A wretch more German than Russian who hated the country he ruled, he freed the nobility from their obligations while allowing them to retain their privileges, especially authority over serfs. This was the supreme irony: at a time when the European states that Russian nobles considered models were beginning to eliminate serfdom, the most Europeanized Russians moved in precisely the other direction.

Catherine exercised the same fascination as had Peter the Great. Her ideas concerning education and corrupting the nobles were favorite topics in the 1890s, and Kliuchevskii devoted the ten public lectures on Western influence to her reign. For the hundredth anniversary of Catherine's death, he wrote an essay for *Russian Thought* reviewing her qualities and period of rule. In 1897, he presented a talk on Catherine's work as a historian and promoter of historical scholarship.

The biographical detail on Catherine's character and personality reflects his conviction that the personal qualities of individuals in high position had become important in modern history. The psychological portrait emphasized upbringing, education, the "prejudices" she carried from northern Germany, and the total absence of moral principles. He considered her energetic, courageous, cheerful, intelligent, and creative, but by no means a genius. Unlike Peter the Great, she was "always on stage," more interested in appearance and reputation than in the national welfare. Her image-making Legislative Commission, correspondence with European intellectuals, subsidies to European scholars, and generous flattery led some contemporary intellectuals to declare her the most enlightened ruler in Europe.

Catherine's early lonely and unhappy days in the court had informed her of the intricacies of St. Petersburg life. However, neither these two decades nor her travel in European Russia taught her much about the country: she remained ignorant and concluded that the Russians were much like the north Germans or French. A freethinker, she could not understand a country in which the union of people and religion was fundamental. Moreover, she considered Russia backward, failing to appreciate that "while not all was good among us, it was not worse than among other peoples."

In Kliuchevskii's judgment, Catherine's principal goal was to strengthen her personal position and reputation. She also hoped to transform the Russian state and people into Europeans, using "the intellectual baggage" she carried to "the northern hothouse." The early manifesto promising to create an equitable state based on the rule of law brought these two goals together. This led to the spectacular but doomed Legislative Commission, an ethnographic exhibition and public relations exercise which Kliuchevskii discussed in great detail. One-tenth of the pages on Catherine's reign in the *Course of Russian History* described the *Instruction* (*Nakaz*) and the commission's discussion. Catherine learned much about the country's needs and the nobility's special interests from these sessions. However, while the "exotic and half-baked ideas" of Beccaria, Montesquieu, Condorcet, Rousseau, and Voltaire remained an active creed, she ultimately realized that she could not put into effect ideas so radical that the French government would not allow publication of the document. However, her proposal that Russian nobles "live Russian but think European" attracted many serf-owning "knights of freedom and equality" into totally illusory dreams.

In spite of her international reputation as a liberal, Catherine was a complete autocrat, exercising personal rule in "a Tibetan state" as vigorously as Peter had. She won the nobles' support by endorsing Peter III's decree exempting them from state service and awarding them authority in their localities. The 1785 charter recognized their corporate rights but freed them from responsibilities. In short, Catherine increased autocratic power, solidified serfdom, corrupted the nobility, poisoned the country, and destroyed the system's moral foundation. She illustrated perfectly the dilemma Russia encountered when rulers tried to introduce Western ways. The damage she caused was especially great because she borrowed to bolster her position and reputation, not to strengthen the country.

In a different way than Peter, she bungled the succession by poisoning the character of Paul and the education of Alexander I. Finally, in the process of placing Russia firmly in the European state system, she increased Western influence at the state level and committed a series of blunders that harmed Russian national interests in international politics for several generations.

A central quality of her reign was thirty-four years of almost constant war, making it "one of Russia's most bloodstained." These conflicts were responsible for her principal achievement, the return of much of "Little Russia" and Belorussia, acquisition of the north shore of the Black Sea from the Dniester River to the Kuban', and a strengthened position for Russia as a great power. The population expanded from 19 million in 1762 to 36 million in 1796. Except for Finland and Bessarabia, Russia acquired its "national frontiers" in the West.

Catherine's other main accomplishment was stimulating interest in Russian history, strengthening national consciousness, and increasing national self-esteem. Her foreign policy and imaginative propaganda instilled pride in a people who felt themselves on the fringe of the world. Kliuchevskii devoted an essay to her *Notes on Russian History* and praised her for collecting and publishing historical materials, sponsoring scholarship, and admiring Boltin.

However, her achievements did not compensate for the disasters. One of the most destructive was deepening and solidifying serfdom: the domestic history of her reign was the history of the "wretched institution." "Civilized barbarism" degraded moral and intellectual life, removed Russia from the community of advanced states, and threatened the country's survival. Kliuchevskii paid little attention to the revolts that scarred Russian history, but noted that they were more frequent and ferocious under Catherine than earlier and were directed against the state rather than the nobles.

Kliuchevskii rarely described alternative policies from which a ruler might have chosen, but he suggested that Catherine could have selected far more fruitful programs. Making conditions less onerous for the serfs would have transformed them and made the nobility into a useful class, encouraged them to adopt ways to improve their country, and raised the moral level. Above all, it would have reconciled the classes and strengthened the nation.

One of her most damaging choices involved education, on which Kliuchevskii felt especially competent to comment because of his professional activities and writing on national goals and the best ways to achieve them. On education, Catherine ignored geography, history, and tradition, just as the *Instruction* "sought answers to Russian problems in non-Russian theories based on non-Russian experiences." In addition, she accepted the unsound and dangerous view that humans are by nature good and that a wise government could shape a child into any kind of person it desired. Catherine even believed that Russia could use translated French textbooks, making the book a hindrance to enlightenment rather than a bearer of it.

She also proposed that the state should remove parents from the educational process when the child was two or three years old and rely instead on the rule of nature and the heart. "Work was the inherited responsibility of the lower sort," but the nobility's children should prepare for endless leisure by acquiring social graces, the ability to dance, and a taste for the arts. In Kliuchevskii's judgment, Russia's nobles were "the least educated nobility in Europe," demoralized, bored, and parasitical. They read and talked about human rights, but owned serfs. They had been taught to love books, but despised learning. Above all, they were isolated from the life of their homeland. Their adoption of French ideas under Catherine caused more damage than had the Time of Troubles.

Catherine fostered destructive Western influence not only through her policies on education but also those on the western borderlands and the Balkans. These increased contact with the West and vastly complicated relations with the outside world. Above all, she gave territorial advancement and stature priority over freeing West Russians from foreign rule, ignoring "an imperative demand of Russian national-religious sentiment." She compounded this error by helping to eliminate Poland as a nation-state and venturing into the complicated Balkans prematurely, soiling relations with the West for generations.

Catherine's participation in the first division of Polish territory was a blunder because it allowed Austria to gain control over Galicia, a purely Russian land. Kliuchevskii was confident that Galicia and other lands he considered Russian would one day rejoin the motherland, but Catherine delayed the process and increased the likelihood that reunification would involve conflict with Austria and Germany.

Failing to maintain an independent Poland, even one dissatisfied with its boundaries, was even more harmful, for it assigned Galicia to Austria and surrendered to alien rule millions of others he considered Russian. Even a Poland whose domestic and foreign policies annoyed Russia would have been a barrier against Austria, Prussia, and Turkey. In addition, including millions of Catholic Poles within Russia created permanent domestic tensions: "We have annexed Poland but not the Poles, acquired the country but lost the people." The indissoluble Poles would serve as a carrier of Western ideas, strain Russia's political resources, and utilize other domestic dissatisfactions to produce permanent instability, which other states would manipulate. Kliuchevskii's wry accounts of Alexander I's unsuccessful effort to woo the Poles by establishing the Kingdom of Poland, Nicholas II's crushing the rebellion of 1830–31, and Alexander II's attempt to satisfy Polish aspirations for self-rule that led to the 1863 revolt all proved that Catherine had created a permanent problem. The division of Poland may have brought Russia, Prussia, and Austria together, but it surrendered control over foreign policy to neighboring states that had not supported Russia during the Crimean War and might turn against Russia in the future. Moreover, the alliance increased the likelihood of Russia's becoming involved in European conflicts that did not engage its national interest and widened the gap between eastern and western Europe.

Control over millions of Poles also exposed Kliuchevskii's native land to criticism from Western states, who would be tempted to interfere in Russian internal affairs. In addition, Catherine's Pyrrhic activities crippled Russia's capability to liberate orthodox Slavs from Germans and Turkish Muslims. How could a Russia that ruled millions of unruly Poles lead a campaign to free other Slavs and create a harmonious Slavic community?

The final penalty rose from her foolhardy "Greek project" to place the grand duke in Constantinople as a Russian viceroy. This made the Eastern Question the core of Russia's relations with the outside world before it had gathered all Russians and established firm and defensible boundaries. Britain and France concluded from this error and her Polish policy that Russia was imperialistic in central Europe, the Balkans, and Asia as well. This myth about Russian aggression poisoned Russian-European relations. It was an especially bitter tragedy because Britain and France also sought to liberate the Balkan Christians, although their motives differed from Russia's. However, Catherine's policies persuaded them to establish a protectorate over the Ottoman Empire. An unthinking ruler ignorant of Slavic and Orthodox realities who did not comprehend Russia's long-term interests thus delayed Balkan liberation, lost enormous advantages for Russia, and led to decades of needless tension and conflict.

As indicated earlier, Kliuchevskii considered that the Belorussians and Ukrainians were Russian and possessed virtually no knowledge of peoples in the empire other than Russians. However, his description of Catherine's foreign policy and Russia's participation in Balkan affairs after 1875 lured him into some interest in the Slavic peoples in the Balkans and central Europe. The crisis then launched a slow process which increased his knowledge of the millions of Orthodox Slavs under Ottoman rule and convinced him that Russia had an opportunity, perhaps an obligation, to promote their liberation. His views over his last thirty years acquired an increasing tinge of Pan-Orthodoxy and Pan-Slavism, quite alien and even destructive to his basic position but revealing another aspect of the way in which relations with the West affected him.

The first evidence of his awareness of other Slavs appeared in a May 1876 talk on the 170th anniversary of P. J. Shafarik, Czech philologist and archeologist. This tribute may have been stimulated by the recent death of Frantisek Palacký, the Czech historian who had been an honorary member of the Society of Russian History and Antiquity and whose books had helped awaken Czech nationalism. Newspaper clippings and notes in Kliuchevskii's archives reveal that he became concerned about developments in the Balkans then, although he opposed Russia's going to war. The Congress of Berlin embittered him, because it deprived the Russians and those whom they had helped of the fruits of Russian military actions.

In his last two decades, he paid increasing attention to the Balkan peoples. His lectures in 1893–95 to Grand Duke Georgii Aleksandr praised Nicholas I's efforts to help the Greeks. An essay in January 1895 quoted Novikov's description of the first Turkish war as "a struggle against foreign enemies of Western civilization" and acquisition of Sevastopol' as "the best instrument for a Russian protectorate over the Eastern Christians."

The lectures in 1896 on Alexander II assessed defeat in the Crimean War as a blessing in disguise because it exposed weaknesses that Russia could and would repair. A talk on the 190th anniversary of Shafarik's death summarized the rise of Czech nationalism from the losses to the Jesuits and Germans in the seventeenth century through its flowering in the nineteenth. Three years later, he celebrated the one-hundredth anniversary of Palacký's birth and his devotion to Slavic freedom and unity. The pessimistic 1898 draft paper "On the Brink" bemoaned that not all Russians lived in one state, but anticipated unity of the entire Slavic world as part of a slow but almost inevitable process.

Kliuchevskii's final publications reveal further engagement. Thus, the 1909 summary volume of his university lectures contained materials on religious friction between the Poles and Russians that had not appeared in earlier editions, even that of 1908. In addition, it praised Catherine's 1774 treaty with Turkey for acquiring a Russian protectorate over Christians in the Ottoman Empire. Both that edition and the final volume of his famous set noted that the French Revolution had awakened the Balkan peoples but that Russia in the nineteenth century "had brought the Orthodox and Slavic peoples of the East to life." At the end of his career, he concluded that Russia's involvement in the Balkans had made foreign policy the state's main concern and raised the possibility that Russia might emerge as head of an Orthodox Slavic Empire.

Kliuchevskii wrote little about the nineteenth century. The chapters in the *Course of Russian History* on that period were scrappy and lacked his usual polish. However, relations with the West remained a central theme, and he concluded that the autocrats then had mismanaged the dilemma as badly as their predecessors had.

In his view, Russia's rulers in the nineteenth century recognized the riddle involved in "borrowing the scientific instruments Russia needed to retain its place in European politics without adopting the spirit and concepts of European civilization," but their programs to modernize through education or borrowing were fraudulent. They talked of reform but were concerned mainly with preserving the dynasty: they "constructed Asian edifices with European facades." They provoked or encouraged change but punished the agents of change as soon as reforms began to become effective. Alexander I considered raising the level of knowledge while preserving absolute authority: to repeat an Uvarov phrase that Kliuchevskii cited often, he wanted "a fire that would not burn." Nicholas I recognized the dilemma and the danger: this explained his muddled approach to education and serfdom. Alexander II was the supreme example. The "tsar-reformer, tsar-provocateur" abolished serfdom and reformed the judiciary and the army, but turned back from building an equitable and free society as soon as he appreciated the threat to his position and the system.

In his chapters on the reigns of Peter and Catherine, Kliuchevskii gave more attention to the role of individuals and Russia's participation in international affairs than he had on earlier periods of history. These modifications continued in his work on the years after Catherine. Thus, the pages on Paul's reign concentrated upon a psychological portrait of the tsar, especially his education, character, and relations with Catherine, and upon the conundrum posed by relations with the West. Similarly, the key to Alexander I's reign was the tsar, "a beautiful flower unable to accommodate to Russian soil" because of his personality, isolation from reality, and romantic dreams, those of "a petty tyrant of liberalism as well as of despotism." Speranskii, "the best intellect near the throne since Ordin-Nashchokin," was "a Voltaire in an Orthodox theological jacket," an eighteenth-century prisoner of the illusion that Russia was a tabula rasa on which one could put Western ideas into practice. "As skilled with abstractions as a pianist playing Liszt," he advocated principles that were alien and dangerous. He did not even recognize that emancipation should precede government by law.

Kliuchevskii placed the Decembrists, a small group of nobles who tried to overthrow the government during the confusion after Alexander I's death in 1825, in the same category as Speranskii and others led astray by Western ideas. Their revolt was a consequence of European education, "a social-moral symptom" of French ideas that prevailed during Catherine's reign, supplemented by those Napoleon's wars spread. The Decembrists were not radicals or revolutionaries but inept young patriots ignorant of their homeland. "Their fathers were Russians educated to be Frenchmen; the children by education were French but wanted to become Russians." The incident was an accident that had little effect.

In summary, Russia's relations with the West constituted an increasingly profound dilemma. Russia had been a part of Europe from its origins, and the relationship became close as time advanced. The autocrats' ideas about education and introducing Western techniques and values to strengthen the state, enhance their authority, and advance Russia's international status undermined the fragile unity that had survived the religious schism and created new strains and fractures. Similarly, in another paradox, the autocrats' success in the "natural and necessary" process of gathering the Russian land and people moved Kliuchevskii's native land toward unity, but at the same time added peoples who carried dangerous Western infections. Moreover, colonization of the western borderlands increased involvement in international affairs, led to conflict with the West over Poland and the Balkans, and increased Western influence in particular by engaging Russia in a struggle for non-Russian territories.

In order to meet Russia's new responsibilities and reduce the hazards that borrowing and closer ties with the West produced, the autocrats became increasingly repressive. Russia became a serf society, a hollow Asian edifice masquerading as a European state. Kliuchevskii accepted the need for a strong central government and sought to produce a dispassionate account of the past. Even so, his balanced analysis of the eighteenth century and brief sections on the nineteenth century constituted a depressing description of an increasingly autocratic and inefficient system of rule. His pessimism concerning his country was as distinct as Lermontov's, and the sense of gloom that pervaded his last years resembled that of Chekhov.

PART FOUR

Trying to Create a Nation

THIRTEEN

"Teacher of a Nation"

One must love that which one teaches and those whom one teaches to be a good instructor.

—V. O. Kliuchevskii

As an instructor of undergraduates, Kliuchevskii provided the basic framework and essential information concerning the full sweep of Russian history and excited among thousands of students a lifelong affection for their national past. His classroom procedures and artistry as a lecturer were important instruments, but dedication to his craft, the intellectual quality of his lectures, and his standards were principal instructional means: they taught that understanding Russian history was a civic responsibility and that all intellectual achievement required intensive effort. His determination to use knowledge of the past to help make Russia a nation was crucial to his success.

In many ways, Kliuchevskii was a self-trained scholar-teacher. Soloviev provided little guidance, except as a model of integrity and dedication, so he learned from observing his preceptors and studying carefully the art of instruction. He also reflected about Russia's educational needs. Some of his most thoughtful essays discuss the nature of education and the most effective means to develop character and intellectual power. He recognized that education played a central role in human development and the formation of a national community. For example, the course he taught at the military school devoted considerable attention to opposing philosophies concerning the nature of humanity and their effects. In his survey course he discussed education's role in early Russian history, for which it was difficult to locate information, and emphasized the role innovative rulers had assigned education. In the winter of 1889–90, his series of ten public lectures on "Western Influence in Russia after Peter" concentrated upon education. In them, he recognized that classroom teaching was only the most visible aspect of a teacher's responsibilities, and that many not formally teachers contribute immensely to education. In fact, parents were the most essential instructors.

However one defines the purposes of instruction or measures excellence, Kliuchevskii was a superb instructor. Students of all political persuasions flooded his classes in five institutions. They carried his ideas, lithographed copies of lectures, and legends about him to every corner of the land and helped to educate generations in Russian history. He became the most popular lecturer in Moscow, and a cult of Kliuchevskii as a teacher flourished in his last thirty years. For educated Russians at the turn of the century, Chaliapin, Tolstoy, and Kliuchevskii represented the highest qualities of Russian culture.

In addition, his example and exacting standards attracted into historical studies and helped train young men who as library and archive staff members helped to preserve and organize the basic sources necessary for scholarship. These and the twenty whom he prepared for professional study of history became a corps, carrying his emphasis upon research in primary sources, integrity, independence, and other professional qualities deep into the Soviet period of Russian history. The publications that he considered the obverse side of his lectures extended his teaching to groups and generations far from Moscow classrooms and auditoriums.

University and other authorities recognized his position in Russian culture as early as 1880, when his first major address was part of a ceremony honoring Pushkin, one overshadowed by Dostoevsky's famous oration on the same day. He published ten lectures or essays prepared for jubilees of writers such as Ivan Aksakov, Pushkin, Lermontov, and Granovskii as well as addresses to celebrate institutional anniversaries. The 1888 talk on the anniversary of the introduction of Christianity in Russia, often reprinted, was a compelling description of the Church's role in civilizing Russia. Other statements not only were important contributions to the contemporary discussion of Russian culture but also demonstrated the importance of celebrating anniversaries to bind past and present.

After the state closed Ger'e's program in 1888, Kliuchevskii gave an inspiring lecture at the dinner celebrating its achievements and urged renewed efforts to provide educational opportunities for women. In the 1890s alone, he completed essays honoring four men under whom he had studied, two on younger colleagues who had died, four on archivists and librarians, and carefully researched papers on great teachers or scholars of the recent or distant past. He joined civic-minded colleagues and men he had helped train in regenerating the Moscow Committee for Literacy, founded in the early thaw of Alexander II's reign. Probably his most illuminating contribution was a lecture at a fundraising meeting on February 1, 1893, comparing educational arrangements of early Russian history with those that Catherine the Great sought to establish. *Russian Thought* published "Two Educations," and a fundraising collection of

Kliuchevskii at Sergiev Posad, 1909. Source: M. V. Nechkina,
Vasilii Osipovich Kliuchevskii. Istoriia zhizni i tvorchestva (Moscow:
Nauka, 1974).

essays by humanists and scientists reprinted the seminal paper in 1894. Other
journals also reprinted it to support the committee, which became so effective
that the state placed it under the Ministry of Education in 1899.[1]

For many in the university community, as for Tolstoy and other leading Russians, alleviating the consequences of the famine in the early 1890s was closely
related to efforts to eradicate illiteracy. One of Kliuchevskii's most revealing
essays was a lecture to support that campaign in the Museum of History on
December 12, 1891, "The Good People of Ancient Russia." This appeared
first in the academy's *Theological Journal*. The Committee on Literacy and
similar organizations reprinted it in numerous editions within the following
twenty-five years, and it has appeared again in Russia since 1985.

Kliuchevskii usually declined requests from journals and newspapers for essays, but he honored appeals from organizations that provided instructional
materials for those teaching others to read. Thus, he contributed to magazines
such as *The Journal for All*, a St. Petersburg publication sponsored by Chekhov
and Gorky that had eighty thousand subscribers. With Vinogradov and others,
he organized the publication of seventeen books by the Library for Self-Edu-
cation, founded in 1898 by one of his more radical students, Vasilii N.

Storozhev, and a publisher, I. D. Sytin. Similarly, he supported Books for Practical Knowledge, founded by a conservative student, Liubavskii, to which at least four of those whom he had trained contributed volumes. In the last two years of his life, he cooperated with five young men to publish six volumes of documents on Russian history.

His publications and papers in his archives concerning the need to provide all Russians basic literacy, plus a trade or skill, together explain his views. At the core was the conviction that moral virtue, loving one's country, and supporting oneself and one's family were more important than "scientific knowledge." Moreover, not all humans are capable of mastering secondary education, and "we cannot create any kind of man we want." Therefore, education's first priority was the development of individuals who would follow Christian principles and love their country. One should then provide basic knowledge of geography and history and a trade, craft, or other skill.

In the most fundamental education, elementary, the home was central. With the support of the parish and community, it should provide moral and intellectual ideals and goals in a total living environment. Parents are the most important and usually most competent educators: they work with their own, while the school employs strangers as teachers. The father should lead, utilizing physical punishment when appropriate: a whip is "the eradicator of evil and the cultivator of virtue." A teacher at any level resembles an actor, who can perform only if he understands the play and his part. He must comprehend the circumstances in which the action occurs and the values and roles of his fellows. The parents, of course, are the most qualified "actors" because they understand the conditions, the cast, and the role each plays.

All education is a form of public service, and Kliuchevskii assigned the state the central role after parents had completed their responsibilities in the child's early years: he was critical of those who declared that Peter the Great had introduced "intellectual slavery" when he gave the state responsibility for higher education. He quoted Uvarov's famous remark that the state in education sought a fire that would not burn, but suggested that the autocracy was building foundations that would one day enable Russians to achieve intellectual independence.

Novikov and Granovskii were heroes. Novikov, some of whose books Kliuchevskii read as a youngster in Penza, served the nation by producing serious volumes (not novels!) late in the eighteenth century, when the streets of Moscow were "paved with ignorance." He emphasized that education must give priority to morality, love of one's country and its ways, and "useful sciences" and stress local circumstances. In words Kliuchevskii treasured, Novikov wrote that a teacher "must cut the cloth to fit the shoulders," not act blindly "like a butterfly flying at night." He especially lauded Novikov's campaign against Catherine the Great's "hothouse plans" for the northern Russian forests that encouraged French ideas in a society in which they were totally alien. Granovskii carried on the struggle at a later time, in different circumstances and at the university. Both appreciated that "education is beneficial only when it leads one to understand the circumstances that surround us and serve the country in which we live." Like Bacon, they respected those who provided people new information, but honored even more those who introduce the process through which one could acquire knowledge.

The time and energy that Kliuchevskii devoted to instruction at the high school, undergraduate, and graduate level testify to his commitment to teaching. From 1869 until 1906, when he retired from the academy, his responsibilities in five different institutions varied from ten to sixteen hours a week. In his last two decades, he arranged occasional informal seminars for graduate students at his home on Wednesday evenings or Sunday afternoons, and he devoted generous time to private discussions with students. In addition, he helped direct perhaps fifty young men in advanced study. Some became librarians and archivists, others ultimately obtained advanced degrees in fields other than Russian history. Still others became professional historians. He also presented a large number of public lectures, particularly between 1885 and 1900. These talks were not casual, because he devoted weeks to each, some of which attracted crowds of two thousand in the Polytechnical Museum. When he spoke in 1888 and 1892 at Trinity Monastery in Sergiev Posad in honor of the nine-hundredth anniversary of the Grand Duke Vladimir's conversion and the five-hundredth anniversary of the birth of Saint Sergei, many students, colleagues, and leading Muscovites traveled by train to attend. Twenty-five years later, Miliukov remembered the first talk in detail. Trubetskoi declared the latter talk "without a doubt the most fervent, the most deep and emotional of all those he wrote."

One of Kliuchevskii's principal goals was encouraging undergraduates to develop a lifelong practice of reading. He did not require that students read his works or those of Soloviev, but he recommended Soloviev's textbook and readings from Soloviev's *History of Russia*. His lectures also discussed source materials and historiography to encourage independent reading and thinking. Probing essay examinations required that students demonstrate an understanding of the principal issues and events as well as the ability to write clearly.

He believed that students learned from undertaking research of their own and writing reports that required knowledge and thought. Freshmen therefore had to write papers on subjects he assigned based on research in archives and libraries. All upperclassmen and graduate students in advanced courses completed a research paper each semester. The academy required each senior to write a *kandidat* essay on history or theology. Kliuchevskii directed most history essays, acted as a second commentator upon the remainder, and read many theology papers, some of which were five hundred pages long. The academy's *Journal* published the critiques of theses he graded, and his archives indicate that comments on university papers were also rigorous, noting factual errors and unclear writing with equal solicitude. Helpful in identifying questions that the students should have considered and in commenting upon conclusions, he emphasized that students avoid projecting their values onto an earlier period: the intent of objectivity constituted "the essential responsibility of a historian." *Dogmatism* was a favorite word of criticism.

The core of his courses consisted of lectures: this helps explain why lithographed copies were so popular. Students were also aware of his personal interest in them and his generosity toward those hampered by financial problems, illness, or family troubles. In their judgment, he was a demanding, busy, but kindhearted scholar-teacher of enormous renown.

Kliuchevskii's concentration upon stimulating interest in history led him to direct his talents to the primary goal, exciting Russians of all ages in increasing their knowledge and understanding of Russia's past. This definition of needs and responsibilities, his skills as a speaker, and the numbers who attended even his advanced classes precluded another important aspect of instruction: discussion of sources, methods, and interpretation with students. Moreover, he did not furnish undergraduates exercises in assessment and problem-solving. He was not systematic in passing on technical skills to graduate students, and did not monitor their research closely. However, students at all stages learned from his expositions how he acquired and assessed evidence and formed his conception of the past.

Some did not consider him a successful teacher. Pokrovskii, deputy Soviet Commissar of Enlightenment and the most prominent and influential Soviet historian from 1917 until his death in 1932, studied under Kliuchevskii as an undergraduate and for two years as a graduate student and contributed to the 1909 *Festschrift* honoring him. While recognizing that Kliuchevskii wrote with the grace of Turgenev, he considered him a failure as a teacher: he did not influence students' intellectual development or provide a distinct world view, and he was eclectic, the cardinal sin for those who emphasize the class struggle.

Trubetskoi, a member of a distinguished cultivated, religious, and "liberal" clan, represented a different class and political view from Pokrovskii's. He studied with Kliuchevskii six years earlier than Pokrovskii but shared his misgivings: "He was not a teacher but a very learned and artistic lector." The views of Michael Karpovich, who attended Kliuchevskii's class in 1908, were similar. "Karpy" served in the Embassy of the Provisional Government in Washington after the March revolution, and was a generous and popular teacher for thirty years at Harvard University. But about Kliuchevskii he wrote: "I cannot say that he taught me. He had a contagious interest and love for Russian history and gave his audience great aesthetic enjoyment—people went to hear his lectures the way they went to hear Chaliapin or to see the plays of the Moscow Art Theater—but he did not teach his students the methodology of history."[2]

The evidence is overwhelming that Kliuchevskii excelled in interesting students in history, exciting them to think about it and encouraging them to become teachers. Enthusiasm boomed among undergraduates and graduates, those who became bureaucrats, teachers in obscure parish schools, or famous poets, artists, or statesmen. Government officials and professional historians, conservatives and liberals, Orthodox priests and Communists, all felt the impact. "He democratized history: everyone heard him." From the day he offered his first university class, the auditorium was full. The administration moved the class from the Philology Auditorium, which accommodated three hundred, to the much larger Theological Auditorium, but even that did not suffice. Most students in law, medicine, and the sciences attended, even though they did not register and often could not have done so. Some attended the class prior to his so that they could hold seats. Other faculty members scheduled their courses to avoid a conflict with his: he "emptied the classrooms." Moscow high-school students memorized his lithographed lectures and looked forward to attending his classes. One student who became a teacher in Odessa wrote, "In imitation of Chateaubriand, I can say that I heard Chaliapin in Boris, Rodichev in the First State Duma, and Professor Kliuchevskii at Moscow University, and neither on the Russian stage nor on the tribune nor at the university has anyone ever affected me as much as he."[3]

Memoirs of students at the military school indicate that the lectures became the subject of long evening discussions. The officers and their wives, senior officers from the Moscow garrison, and the minister of defense when he was in Moscow audited Kliuchevskii's lectures. The minister of education enjoyed his talks: in 1901, when General P. S. Vannovskii journeyed to Moscow to consider the faculty committee report on student troubles (which he rejected), he attended a Kliuchevskii class. At the academy, students audited his course all four years. One described Kliuchevskii's two days in Sergiev Posad each week as "a holiday, the highest intellectual and artistic experience."

University colleagues, such as Kovalevskii, attended to increase their comprehension of Russian history and grasp the magic of Kliuchevskii's appeal. Platonov enjoyed listening for the same reason when in Moscow to visit his wife's family. Bernard Pares, who came to Moscow at the turn of the century to begin studying Russian history and whose views Kliuchevskii profoundly affected, marveled at the "perfect lucidity." The class was "an intellectual treat . . . a sure guide through all the complexities of Russian domestic history and all the tangles of Russian public thought." Vinogradov, reflecting in England on his years at the university, wrote that Kliuchevskii was "sensitive, endowed with the artistic genius of a kind of Rembrandt, revealing the essence of historical character and movements by a combination of intuition and keen criticism." Even the critical Trubetskoi declared, "I have never in my life met such an artist in the classroom."

The quality of Kliuchevskii's instructional program was so superior to that of his contemporaries that his renown spread swiftly and far. The lithograph of his first university lectures in 1879–80 reached the undergraduate Platonov in St. Petersburg in the summer of 1880. From that time, Platonov considered himself a student of Kliuchevskii. Dozens of letters from former students teaching in parish or *zemstvo* schools, high schools, technical schools, and other educational institutions thanked Kliuchevskii for engaging them in teaching the history of Russia. They carried on his work, using their notes, lithographs of lectures, and ultimately copies of his *Course of Russian History*. Placing a dot on each place on the map of European Russia in which a former student taught shows that they had scattered to every corner of the land.

Kliuchevskii's remarkable impact in the classroom and lecture hall derived in part from the relaxations and reforms that Alexander II had introduced and the growing thirst for science and knowledge, including history, at every level of society. He benefited too from being part of the second generation of historians, a successor to Granovskii and Soloviev, who had helped stir interest and establish standards. Moreover, his brilliance shone brightly because of the character of the competition: Soloviev and most of his colleagues thought that reading lectures constituted effective teaching, as the nicknames students gave them reveal. In addition, he stressed economic and social developments, classes and institutions, portraits of individuals, and the people, rather than the state, all of which coincided with public interest. He also included the "darker side" of Russian history without alarming the administrators, their observers, or state censors. Indeed, the candor with which he described Russia's shortcomings and failures must have stunned Russians then as it does Russian and Western readers today. But his consummate and disarming skill made irony, sarcasm, and the "oppositional tone" so difficult to identify and condemn that he "turned away the wrath" of potential critics.

Kliuchevskii recognized early that Russia was a state, not a nation, and that it lagged behind Western states in creating the traditions, loyalties, and understanding of the common past that bound a people together. As he wryly informed an advanced class of young men who planned to become teachers: "Russian history does not occupy an especially visible place in the intellectual interests of educated Russians." His determination to increase knowledge of the past in order to bring Russians together helped account for his spectacular achievements.

Related to that goal was his exalted view of the teacher and his commitment to instruction as the central purpose of life. He was always eager to teach, "to get the attention of the young," and spent a total of 108 academic years in the classroom at five different institutions. He attended every class, substituted for ailing colleagues, and arranged special sessions for students when disorders or strikes closed the university. Identifying himself frequently as a student of Soloviev and indirectly of Granovskii, he reminded those whom he trained that they were responsible for continuing the great tradition.

A constant student refrain saluted his affection for Russia and recognition that "one must love that which one teaches and those whom one teaches in order to be a successful instructor." He felt part of the *narod*, not an educated person above them or alienated from them, but a Russian among other Russians. Boltin was a favorite, in part because "more than anything else he loved the Russia of his time" and "defended the honor of national history." Students admired Kliuchevskii's candor concerning Russia's flaws and failures and applauded his making patriotism respectable. Kliuchevskii would have endorsed the statement of Braudel, whose inclusive approach to history a century later was similar and who also loved his land. "I love France as Michelet did without distinguishing between its virtues and its flaws, between what I prefer and what I prefer less easily. But this passion will not affect the pages of this work . . . for I shall try to speak of France as if it were another *pays*, another *patrie*, another nation."[4]

This abiding patriotism offended none and attracted many. Those students, such as Iakovlev, Pokrovskii, and Storozhev, who were radicals in the 1890s and became Communists, accepted without complaint Kliuchevskii's affection for his native land. Lenin (who became an admiring reader early in the 1890s), political prisoners, and workers also respected that affection.

Those who studied with Kliuchevskii recognized his integrity and immense erudition and gloried in the scholarship at the base of his teaching. Somehow he created the impression that he had interrupted his research to present a lecture. Stern against those who spoke or wrote without careful study, he insisted that one must never produce "on credit." He did not separate research and instruction, two sides of the same coin. He would have endorsed the words of an unknown Catholic scholar: "Research is to teaching as sin is to the confessional. If you have not done the first, you have nothing to say in the second."

He was an illustrious classroom instructor also because he applied the lessons he learned from careful study of the art and science of learning and teaching. His archives, letters from undergraduate days, articles on Soloviev and other instructors, and essays on education all reveal keen interest in the theory and practice of classroom instruction. Early in his career, he learned that purveying facts was not the goal: the purpose was to ensure that the student understood "the past as a shade hanging over us." The teacher must combine logic and art to instill understanding into the mind of the student, who must perceive, not just see. The teacher must "pay attention neither to the ear nor to the eye of the listener. Speak only so that those listening do not hear your words but see your subject and feel your point." "To develop a thought in a talk, one must first insert it into the mind of the listener, then produce it in clear comparison in imagination, and, finally, in soft lyrical lining place it in the heart of the listener. Even a prisoner of war will not run away, even when you free him, and will remain eternally your listening client."[5]

He understood first that students were ignorant and accepted their world on faith. They had no knowledge of the effort that millions had made to create the circumstances from which they benefited, but assumed that "blankets, food, sidewalks, cabs, even professors and beliefs" were simple, natural, and eternal gifts. The historian's first obligation was to assist them to break away from those assumptions, to comprehend and appreciate the work that others had completed to create the imperfect society in which they lived. This approach explains in part why he devoted such attention in the first weeks of his course to geography, climate, and economic factors, the "harsh circumstances" of Russia's past.

His talks were as carefully planned as a Soviet May Day parade or the entertainment between the halves of an American professional football game. After determining the character of the audience, he designed the most appropriate organization and style: a teacher must know his students, as an actor must understand his audience and the play in which he performs. The lectures he gave in the School of Painting, Sculpture, and Architecture were therefore different from those for university students, although the substance was similar. "If the professor before students is a scholar but not an artist, only students will read him; if he is an artist but not a scholar, he will be read everywhere, but not by students."[6]

Each lecture or talk stressed the basic factors or issues, provided a narrative account, and returned in the summary to the most essential points. He paid painstaking attention to detail, from the proportions of each part of the lecture to the whole to vocabulary and voice intonation. He adroitly avoided the temptation to examine more issues or cram more information into one exercise than listeners could comprehend.

The grace and lucidity with which Kliuchevskii spoke and the mastery with which he wrote contributed directly to his achievements. The sense of drama imparted into clashes of will and crises riveted audiences and readers, but he was equally skillful in creating the mood of a period. Occasional dialogue, masterly biographies, and character portraits of individuals that some students could repeat from memory years later reflected his dexterity with words, matching language and thought. Perhaps the finest expressions of his skills are the visual scenes he created and the phrases and aphorisms for which he became famous. Indeed, his mastery of physical detail resembled that of his contemporaries in the theater and opera, Stanislavsky and Chaliapin. These visual touches helped the least-informed to comprehend and remember what he spoke and wrote. Who could forget his comparing Patriarch Nikon to "a sail which is itself only in a storm, but in still weather flaps from its mast like a useless rag"? Or his comment that Alexander I was "a beautiful flower, but of a hothouse variety, which lacked perhaps time, perhaps ability, to be acclimated to the Russian soul"?[7]

Similarly, the description of the forbidding landscape one could envision from a monastery wall in the fifteenth century created an unforgettable picture of the vast, dreary areas through which the monks pressed north. The description of the way the Dnieper River and its tributaries bound the Kievan princedom together is as vivid as a photograph from a satellite. To portray the way in which ideas grew from facts and the two draw together, he recalled in childhood seeing the columns of a mansion entwined by vines that seemed to grow from the marble and give the cold stone fresh life. Similarly, the description of a pious man who gave his fortune to build a church but slept on straw helped listeners to understand the good people of old Russia. Students appreciated the fragile character of "the free urban communities in the north and the Cossack groups in the south" when he compared them to the white foam of waves "that quickly disappeared when they struck the shore."

No one recorded Kliuchevskii's pliant and flexible voice, but many commented upon his golden, husky tenor and the way he modulated the tone according to the situation. Diction and pronunciation were so distinct that everyone in a crowded auditorium could understand even whispers. He spoke slowly, using pauses to conceal the remnants of a boyhood stutter and increase attention. He combined vocabulary and inflection to illuminate differences between the chronicles of Kievan and Muscovite Russia. Moreover, the pace of his talks enabled all to complete annotations and some to transcribe his lectures. The total impact was so profound that some could repeat long passages hours after they had left the auditorium. One scholar declared the talks so vivid that he heard Kliuchevskii's voice years later whenever he read anything the historian wrote.

Finally, he was a superb mimic and actor, so skilled and artless that he never seemed so. His dress, actions, voice, and mannerisms appeared utterly genuine, as perfectly related to thought as the vine that encircles the marble: he was doing what came naturally, or at least easily.

He arrived in the auditorium just before the hour, plain, simple, short-sighted, dressed in a nondescript way and resembling an old Russian priest. With him, he brought a bag containing manuscripts, books, and papers, placed on or near the lectern but never used. The plain Russian visage seemed to announce that he was going to discuss Russian history. In Leonid Pasternak's words, he was "a man of the purest old Russian style" who "seemed inexpressibly unforgettable." One who heard Kliuchevskii at thirty-eight noted that he seemed old even then, although students always considered him a contemporary. None of his lectures was impersonal, and he made each talk a joint venture, using *we* frequently. He had the ability to make listeners believe that he knew the men described, that he had lived in Novgorod in the thirteenth century, and that he and his audience were participants or observers of events he discussed. Although he avoided eye contact with any listener, many concluded that he was speaking directly to them. His mastery of the subject was so complete that some thought he was reading, while others have recorded that he did not look at the papers before him but had memorized the text. In fact, he had devoted so much time and care that he probably had memorized each lecture. Mrs. Kliuchevskii at one of his most famous public lectures informed her neighbor that he had memorized the talk, although he appeared to be reading it.

Above all, he was an artist at the lectern. As Miliukov said, "He borrowed everything, but it was all original." He was born with great talents as a classroom lecturer, but his achievements also reflected "the infinite capacity for taking pains" that all geniuses possess. Because he did not separate research from teaching, but considered them the two sides of a coin, the published version of the university survey course brought the same qualities in his account of the past to millions of readers.

FOURTEEN

Kliuchevskii as a Nation-Builder

History, geography, religion, literature, even the common will are not
enough to define a nation. It is that which is natural or native in it which
gives its force to the world nation. A nation is a character.
—Salvador de Madariaga

Scholars usually attribute the principal role in establishing nations and states
to military forces, economic factors, political parties, and such statesmen as
Cavour and Bismarck, Nasser and Ben Gurion. But linguists, folksingers, poets, playwrights, philosophers, religious leaders, and educators contribute by
creating national languages and cultures and building the pride, self-
confidence, and sense of nationhood on which more heroic and visible warriors
and statesmen erect political structures.

In 1873, Kliuchevskii told a class that the nineteenth century was one in
which Europeans concentrated upon constructing nation-states, a process in
which Russia was errant. He then set out to remedy this tardiness by building
the national consciousness that lies at the base of every nation-state through
providing a coherent account of his people's past. Teaching at five Moscow
institutions, using every forum he could reach, and transforming his lectures
into the *Course of Russian History* were obvious and significant instruments, but
attracting able and highly motivated men into the historical profession was
another tool. The intellectual quality and commitment of fifty men, of whom
twenty became scholar-teachers, several of considerable distinction, and others
librarians and archivists, carried his approach and many of his fundamental
ideas deep into the Soviet period and beyond through the men and women
whom they excited and helped train.

This extended chain of the order that Granovskii launched shows that the
Kliuchevskii school and his works served as a bridge between the pre- and
postrevolutionary Russias. His successors in the historical craft showed the
dedication to the study of history and survival skills that he had, although their

circumstances were far more challenging and hazardous than those he faced. Their careers provided insight into the ways institutions and men remained alive even under the greatest repression. The recovery of Russia after the nightmare of more than seven decades of Communist rule rests in part upon the qualities that earlier generations kept alive.

Kliuchevskii failed to achieve his goal: almost a century after his death, Russia has not yet become a nation. Before and after the revolution, its leaders' efforts to maintain and even expand the empire rather than construct a nation formed the principal obstructions. But the definition of Russia and Russians that Kliuchevskii and others formulated is one of many contributors to his homeland's remaining "an unfinished building."

During Kliuchevskii's life, as in the years before and since, Russia possessed and in some ways was possessed by a strong state. The rulers impressed an autocratic political structure upon the populace in apparent response to the harsh circumstances, external pressures, and opportunities to expand. They were so successful that many, including historians such as Karamzin and Soloviev, considered that Russia *was* the state.

However, Kliuchevskii recognized that his homeland was not a nation, "a materially and morally integrated society" characterized by "the relative moral, mental, and cultural unity of its inhabitants, who consciously support the state and its laws." Instead, it was a state, "a geographically delimited segment of human society united by common obedience to a single sovereign." In this, it resembled other European states. Cavour's Italy, Bismarck's Germany, and the king and Parliament in Britain encountered many of the same difficulties as Russia, although shared language, history, values, traditions, and *lieder*, folklore, Dante, Goethe, and Shakespeare helped them move toward national unity. Even France, where revolution had given nation-building impetus, was not a nation until schoolteachers in the Third Republic converted deeply traditional provinces, each with its own varieties of cheeses, into a national community. In this process, instructors in a national educational system used a standard French language and depiction of French history to create the sense of nationhood, as teachers did in other countries.

Early in the *Course of Russian History,* Kliuchevskii commented that Russians should understand that the vast country included more areas and peoples than its government could administer. However, size was only one problem. Russia's shortcomings were more spiritual than material: until the people formed a national community, Russia could not achieve or maintain "its rightful international position." Kliuchevskii had little knowledge of the millions of non-Russians in the state and omitted them from his analysis. But even "his" Russians' many disunities undermined the nation's concord. They lacked a common language. Within the European part of the country that constituted Russia for him, economic disparities and the strength of the class structure divided his compatriots into economic and social classes. Many Russians had rejected the Russian Orthodox Church and were members of one of several varieties of Old Believers, small sects, or other Christian faiths. Others, especially among the elite, had no religious beliefs and in his judgment were no longer Russians. More important, few of the more than one hundred million inhabitants were knowledgeable concerning the Russian past or the history and traditions that should have bound them into a community. There were in fact several Russias.

The most visible division, one that he thought most significant and also easy to overcome, was that between the tsar and his ruling group and what he called "society." The rulers and those informed and able citizens competent to advise and support had "parted ways" in the nineteenth century, dividing the state and nation at the very pinnacle. Closing that gap and the other fissures was the first need, one he believed that he and other historians could help meet by instructing, encouraging teachers, training scholars, and publishing.

In his judgment, Russia possessed a "historical personality" and distinct national character, no better and no worse than others'. The autocracy, Church, nobility, army, and some agreement concerning external enemies brought many Russians into a temporary and fragile union. But the country lacked a common language and "memories of the past which hold a people together, bind them into a whole." Study of Russian history was less than a century old and historiography still younger. Russians did not possess common legends or comprehend how they had spread to fill almost every corner of the land. They did not appreciate that shared knowledge creates "a people that lives together and acts together, with one language and a common fate," or that history shapes a nation, "unites a people into a community." They needed a consistent view of its past, a national educational system to promote that knowledge, a unifying constitution, a system of justice and legal order, and popular national institutions.

Kliuchevskii understood little about American history, so he did not comprehend the role a successful revolution and federal system had played in creating the United States. Russia lacked the shared dreams of an ever freer and more prosperous society that brought Americans together. The arrangements, aspirations, and myths that helped transform millions of immigrants into loyal Americans were also absent. His Russia not only had no program or facilities to absorb and convert the millions its continuous expansion added, but deliberately excluded many newcomers and most non-Russians and non-Orthodox from active participation in the state. It also lacked a "national market" to contribute toward economic unity. The transportation and communications systems, media, and mass-produced nationally advertised consumer goods, news, and entertainment that bind some societies together at the end of the twentieth century were absent. Consequently, those who sought to create a common sense of the past enjoyed a special opportunity to create a community.

To help build the nation by providing a synoptic view of the nation-building process that began in the tenth century, he designed *Boyar Council*, his major courses, and the five-volume account of the past. They related each aspect of the past to the whole and emphasized the totality of the national experience. Love for his country and candor about its flaws persuaded listeners and readers, whatever their political views, that they should understand the human experience of which they were a part and become active citizens. Those hostile to the political and social system were attracted by his critical detachment, conviction that the study of history was one of a people's great creative activities, veneration for science, oppositional tone, and visible hostility toward the undeserving rich; he was in a sense a national liberal. For those who feared change, his patriotism, affection for Russian ways, unpolitical stances, and historicism were especially compelling: he was in a sense a national conservative. In short, his account of the Russian peoples' experiences, their failures as well as their achievements over centuries, helped to create the sense of national consciousness he considered vital. In his dedication to spreading knowledge and converting students and readers into participation in a nation, he resembled Michelet, Ranke, Macaulay, Frederick Jackson Turner, and other historians who undertook the same role, perhaps less consciously than he.

Kliuchevskii's achievements were so considerable in part because of the nature of Russia and the circumstances in which he worked. Throughout his lifetime, his homeland was a major European power and an active participant in the principal international events. The Crimean War, the Balkan crisis, and the Russo-Japanese War weakened its diplomatic and military record, as similar failures had revealed Italian and French shortcomings. The revolutionary change in material and intellectual aspects of life that had transformed some major European countries had barely begun to affect Russia. The gap in resources and power between Russia and other major states that the failed wars had revealed therefore grew ever larger, suggesting that the foundations of "the bear" or the "steamroller" that many Europeans feared were inadequate for Russia's status and role. The country's elite divided and hesitated over moving forward after Alexander II's reform decade, trying to freeze the political and social system just when continued modifications were most necessary to strengthen the economy and bind the society together freely. The industrial revolution, of which Kliuchevskii caught glimpses on his first railroad trip in 1861 and when striking workers paraded past his home in 1905, placed additional strains upon the political structure.

In addition, Russia lacked a national system of primary and secondary education, and its system of higher education was tiny, although the quality was high. Enrollment at every level of education was far lower in Russia in 1861 and 1911 than in the United States, although Russia's population was substantially larger. When Kliuchevskii replaced Soloviev, he was the university's only historian of Russia. In 1910, the faculty included one other professor, two associate professors, and six instructors on the Russian past; of the nine, Kliuchevskii had trained seven. The St. Petersburg faculty was smaller, and the other universities each had fewer than five. Professional historical scholarship was just beginning, but it was somewhat more advanced in Russia than in the

United States until late in the nineteenth century, even though there were fewer than two hundred historians in Russia at the time of his death. Russia also lacked a professional association, although the American one formed in 1884 had almost three thousand members thirty years later.

Thus, Kliuchevskii was a rare influence, and his impact spread easily. As soon as he began lecturing at the university and had published *Boyar Council,* those Russians engaged in intellectual activity saluted him as the country's premier historian and he became a national figure. Critical acclaim from scholars joined the popular chorus from student cohorts to create a Kliuchevskii legend that equaled that of Tolstoy and Chaliapin. Each year at one university, he attracted a substantial percentage of the total national student population. Few Moscow University graduates, whatever their field of study, failed to attend his courses before dispersing throughout the country. Many became active in the bureaucracy or professions and helped shape the country's intellectual foundation.

Finally, Kliuchevskii was part of the blooming of Russian culture in the nineteenth century, a phenomenon that created an atmosphere which assisted his development and one to which he contributed. In the first half of the nineteenth century, Pushkin, Gogol, and Lermontov created a language and standards that prepared the way for the great writers of Kliuchevskii's age. Tolstoy, Dostoevsky, and Turgenev were only the best-known of the talents who made the second half of the century one of the richest periods in the history of world literature. Tchaikovsky, Mussorgsky, Chaliapin, Chekhov, and Stanislavsky were equally prominent at the world level in music and theater, and Russian ballet at the turn of the century was recognized everywhere as supreme. In art, Repin, Levitan, and Serov were among Europe's greatest painters. D. I. Mendeleev in chemistry, N. I. Lobachevskii in mathematics, and A.D. Stoletov in physics were giants. The contributions that men such as these made to the national pride and consciousness resemble those of Shakespeare and Molière, Cervantes and Goethe, Pasteur and Edison. Vinogradov in medieval European history, Kondakov in Byzantine art, and Soloviev in early Russian history were among the other leading members of this cluster in that remarkable era. The "new history" that emerged in the last third of the nineteenth century was only one of the cultural eruptions that marked that time, and Kliuchevskii only the finest of a group of outstanding historians.

One of the most signal attractions was his civilized love of the land and people, distinct from the aggressive hostility toward non-Russians of his friend Karpov and other prominent nationalists of the era. His patriotism was so pervasive, genuine, and friendly that those whose professional training he guided as well as those who heard or read him readily adopted it.

Nationalism, distinct from patriotism, was also central. Its most fundamental but least obvious expression was limiting the account of the past to European Russia and Russians, ignoring other areas and peoples. Second, by placing Russia's origins on the eastern slopes of the Carpathians and the foundation of the state and people in Kiev, he quietly asserted that Ukrainians and Belorussians were Russians. Insistence that the "idea of the Russian land" was crucial in the early centuries made his nationalism from its beginning more territorial and cultural than ethnic. Gathering the land and people became the main thread in the quest for national unity, one he considered an indelible factor in all Russian history. This made a profound appeal to "his" Russians and was attractive even to others, as the theme of "manifest destiny" was to Americans, whatever their ethnic background or the time they had arrived in the United States.

His historicism also contributed. He believed that the historical process was organic, moved by a law of constant change and a series of economic and social forces that humans could influence in character and timing but not direct. The constant changes that economic and social forces in particular produced in the structural materials that underlay society were at the core of the historical process. The record of the past was therefore a slow, gradual flow, unmarked by violence, revolts, or war and unaffected by intellectuals or radicals of the left or right. This was an important source of confidence and faith: Russia had survived in spite of difficult circumstances, external pressures, and rulers' follies and had grown ineluctably. It helped make participation in the national community a simple process, as it eased the way in which Marxist historical "laws" conquered the minds of many educated Russians, including some he trained.

Another distinguishing concept was the prominence he awarded Russia's relations with the West, a central issue throughout his lifetime and since. He declared Russia a part of Europe from the moment the Varangians arrived to help organize what he termed the first Russian state. Alas, though, Russia stood at the eastern edge of Europe, so that costly and debilitating service as a bulwark against Asia deeply affected Russia's institutions and national character and allowed European peoples and states to bloom at Russia's expense. Moreover, the costs of "catching up" seemed as worthy an explanation of Russia's position and political system as harsh circumstances had of earlier history. He did not utilize international politics or military affairs, even the wars of Peter and Catherine, to stimulate patriotic feeling. He also impressed listeners and readers because he worked with a relatively open mind, following paths that facts unearthed. He did develop several basic themes, but he had no gods, devils, or heroes, and his theses were not fixed molds. Economic, social, and administrative institutions at society's foundations and the gradual impact they exerted upon continuity and change were more fundamental than political, military, or cultural history. Elite social classes were especially important because they and changes that affected them helped to shape society's institutions and character. *Boyar Council* in particular helped lead those he taught and many others to emphasize the economic and social factors of increasing importance in that age.

At a time when "science" was popular among scholars and students, Kliuchevskii also stressed intensive analysis of primary sources in archives, which seems elementary but was not then and often is not a century later. Although he neglected or was ignorant of parts of Russia's past, he set a standard for wide-ranging, catholic search for the "fuel of history." Just as James Harvey Robinson's "new history" in the first decade of this century expanded beyond political history into other aspects of America's past, so Kliuchevskii broke through the traditional walls, even into psychology.

The message he conveyed to students also emphasized relentless imagination, keen probing into sources, and constant inquiry concerning causes and consequences. His common sense and penetrating reasoning created insights and raised questions that helped make the study of history an art form and national service. In the words of Terence J. Emmons, he and his school examined the total society and widened the agenda of historical studies.[1] Finally, he made the study of history more than a concern of specialists, but a national service as well as an art requiring the same skills in communication that great composers, artists, and singers master.

Kliuchevskii's ability to excite young men and women about their nation's past and stimulate many to join the order that Granovskii had launched was crucial for his achievement. His view of the relationship between scholarship and teaching and his assigning important roles to collectors and preservers of source materials and to teachers at every level gave his profession a sense of pride that attracted and motivated. The example he provided of the scholar-teacher in action made the "call" even more powerful. Consequently, he inspired hundreds of students from the university, the academy, and Ger'e's program to become teachers. At a celebration honoring his thirty years of service in 1901, he learned that half of Moscow's history teachers had been his students. Letters in his archives reveal that dozens he taught were serving in *zemstvo* and parish schools in European Russia: Orshov and Elets, Kozlovsk, Kremenchug and Kursk, Pereiaslavl' and Petrozavodsk, Vorzel' and Voznesensk, Syzran' and Viaz'ma, Kiev and Vitebsk, Rostov and Tver', as well as Irkutsk and Tiflis. Many who completed their studies in the academy staffed seminaries in Olenets, Nizhnii Novgorod, and Tula and hundreds of parish schools. Others were instructors in technical and commercial programs for women and workers and adult educational programs, especially in Moscow but in provincial cities as well. Most, perhaps all, taught in several institutions, as Kliuchevskii had. Some advanced students served briefly as university instructors and then devoted their careers to editing journals. Most cherished the lithographs of his course and became purchasers and promoters of his book. All shared his enthusiasm and determination to unite Russia through teaching history. In short, they constituted a kind of missionary order carrying his vision of history as a unifying force throughout the nation.

In addition, Kliuchevskii reached thousands of eager listeners through public addresses at anniversaries of institutions and poets, historians, tsars, and saints. He spoke at dinners honoring colleagues, at meetings to collect funds for famine victims and literacy programs, and in lecture series resembling the Chautauqua programs in the United States then. A century later, these are familiar opportunities for recognized scholars who are effective speakers. Kliuchevskii spoke at a time and in a country not saturated by banquets, service club meetings, conferences, movies, and television, but in which public addresses, touring minstrels, theatrical groups, and Chaliapin concerts exercised enormous influence. Moreover, his brilliant lectures affected listeners in ways only great artists can, especially because his interpretation emphasized the full sweep of Russian history, of which everyone was a part.

In addition to those scholar-teachers who formed the so-called Kliuchevskii school, many who studied with him as undergraduate and graduate students became professors of general history, law, or literature. Three who obtained their undergraduate and graduate degrees at the academy continued to teach and carry on research there. In 1909, three of the sixteen members of the university law faculty had studied history with him, as had three others in comparative literature and classics. In addition, those teaching Russian history in Dorpat, Kazan, Kharkov, and Odessa had completed doctorates with him.

The careers of those whom Kliuchevskii inspired to join the historical profession and helped train as scholar-teachers, librarians, and archivists were rich, varied, and often dramatic. Most of them continued work in Moscow after the revolution, but some served in Kazan, Minsk, and Kiev, and even abroad. All who remained in the Soviet Union were caught up in the whirlwind that struck in the late 1920s, were arrested, and spent four or five years in prison and internal exile. Five of those who returned to Moscow rejoined the university faculty, became members of the Institute of History of the Academy of Sciences when it was established, and became members of the Academy. They and their fellows taught, helped collect and preserve materials, carried on research, and contributed to the new textbooks Stalin ordained after 1936.

Description of these scholars' careers requires another volume, but even a brief account demonstrates that they carried on the Kliuchevskii tradition and deepened and widened his influence. In particular, they helped create the Soviet historical profession by instructing the first generation and part of the second. They directed the publication of large editions of Kliuchevskii's principal books in the 1920s and 1930s and ensured their accuracy.

These scholars did not constitute a school in the sense that Kliuchevskii converted eager young men into disciples or followers. He did not establish a paternal system, implement a fixed interpretation of the past, or promote a philosophy that explained the nation's record. But, paradoxically, ignoring the political views and actions of his advanced graduate students and encouraging them to learn together provided a relaxed and informal system of guidance. This helped them form an informal, closely knit professional group that held together throughout the turmoil and strife until the last survivor died after Stalin's death. Mutual reinforcement not only helped these men survive but made their collective effort more powerful than the sum of their individual contributions.

The core of Kliuchevskii's approach rested on the dedication, high standards, and example he established and the exacting demands he quietly laid upon the apprentices. He proffered little direct guidance, but in his last two decades he arranged occasional informal seminars at his home on Wednesday evenings or Sunday afternoons, often with other senior scholars participating. These became as instructive and often as inspiring for these young men as the evenings he had spent with his mentors. As students, the men worked together on the second floor of the main university building and in nearby libraries and archives, which served almost as clubhouses for young and old interested in Russian history. Teaching and learning occurred as they walked to and from the repositories, worked at adjacent desks and tables, and enjoyed social evenings. As members of an informal association, they discussed themes, problems, discoveries, and interpretations. As time passed, they taught in high schools, Ger'e's program, and other secondary institutions, advised each other of experiences and opportunities, served as each other's examiners for advanced degrees, and collaborated in publishing readers and collections of essays and documents. The successive world of advanced students advised and directed the younger ones as they moved along. Thus, George Vernadsky, in his four years as an undergraduate, took classes with Kliuchevskii and six of the professors he had trained. The students also worked together as research assistants, instructors at the university and other Moscow institutions, and staff members in libraries and archives. Some, young and old, lived as neighbors, often in the same apartment building, before and after they were scattered in internal exile. Five lived in the same building when evacuated to Tashkent in the Second World War.

Many were related. For example, Sergei K. Bogoiavlenskii was a nephew of Miliukov, whose wife was a sister of one of Kliuchevskii's young apprentices at the Moscow Ecclesiastical Academy. The first wife of V. I. Picheta and Liubavskii's wife were sisters. The two men remained close throughout their lives, even though Picheta was a radical who became a Communist and Liubavskii was a fervent monarchist. In 1930, both were sentenced to internal exile. Liubavskii died there in 1936, but Picheta returned to serve at Moscow University and the Institute of History and to membership in the Academy, to which Liubavskii had been elected seventeen years earlier. Similarly, Bogoiavlenskii married Bogoslovskii's sister. The men remained close associates, although Bogoiavlenskii until his death in 1947 served the state in an archive the KGB controlled and became a corresponding member of the Academy, while Bogoslovskii was a deeply pious conservative who was also an Academician.

In sum, aided by the ways of the academic community then and the physical arrangements for living and working—both quite different from those with which most American historians are familiar—Kliuchevskii helped create a group of historians that survived and enabled each member to carry forward some of the principles and approaches he had emphasized.

Thus, Pokrovskii, a radical who became a Communist and the most powerful force in the Soviet historical community, helped his constitutionalist and even monarchist associates in the group to obtain apartments, positions, and appointments to educational and archival commissions. When he led a team of eleven scholars to participate in "Russian History Week" in Germany in 1928, the first travel abroad for historians, he selected Picheta and Liubavskii. Before the war, he and Kizevetter, a liberal who became one of the founders of the Kadet party, cooperated in writing a book on Russia in the nineteenth century. During the civil war, Pokrovskii twice obtained Kizevetter's release from prison. He even tolerated Kizevetter's serving as editor of the Kliuchevskii volumes published between 1918 and 1923. On the other hand, Kizevetter's resistance to the reorganization of Moscow University and Soviet policy in general so annoyed him that he rejoiced when Lenin expelled his old colleague from Russia in August 1922. He may even have recommended that step.

The most visible way in which Kliuchevskii's former apprentices contributed was in preserving and organizing materials. Thus, the Rumiantsev Library (which became the Lenin Library and then the Russian State Library) in the two decades before and after 1917 employed at least four of Kliuchevskii's advanced students on its small staff, including the deputy director, while the director of the State Historical Museum and four members of its staff in the 1920s had worked with him. The archives of the Ministry of Justice, which became part of the Russian State Archive of Ancient Acts, the principal repository for early Russian history, employed at least two Kliuchevskii alumni in senior positions through the 1940s. Still others occupied high posts in the archives of the Ministry of Foreign Affairs. In sum, men trained by Kliuchevskii dominated the most significant libraries and archives between 1890 and 1930.

During the civil war and until the whirlwind struck, those Kliuchevskii students who had been members of the Moscow University faculty continued their careers there and also taught at the Institute of History of RANION, the Association of Research Institutions of the Social Sciences, where they helped train their successors. Most also served on archive staffs, arranged instructional programs for new archivists, and helped preserve and enlarge collections, edited documents, and contributed essays to the first edition of the *Great Soviet Encyclopedia*. They also continued research and publication.

Bogoslovskii, who died in 1929, reflected their dedication when he wrote at the end of his manuscript on Peter's youth: "It is impossible to see when my book will see the light of day and if it will ever be published. Through the years I have continued my work, increasingly upheld in recent years by the example of old analysts and copyists who did not allow themselves to be stopped by the thought that their work would remain for long years just manuscripts."[2] The five volumes describing in detail Peter the Great's life, which he called "materials for a biography," were published posthumously between 1940 and 1948. The thousands of pages of notes on the history of the Bashkirs that Liubavskii compiled while in internal exile in Ufa until he died in 1936 and the thirteen hundred pages of neatly typed manuscripts that he completed reflect the same Kliuchevskii trait. These materials have not yet been published, but Russian scholars now write favorably of Liubavskii's work, and interest in the Bashkirs and other national minorities continues to rise.

Providing professional instruction and guidance to the first generation of Soviet scholars was the most important instrument for inducting that group into the great chain that Granovskii had begun. Briefly, they helped shape the Soviet historical profession in the 1920s. Some assisted in rebuilding it when Stalin allowed instruction to resume after 1934. They even participated in producing the new textbooks published under Stalin's mandate after 1936.

Lev Cherepnin, Tikhomirov, and Nechkina, all of whom became members of the Soviet Academy of Sciences and were widely recognized abroad, are among the many Soviet historians who in the 1920s participated in classes and seminars with those whom Kliuchevskii had trained. Cherepnin produced several works with Aleksei I. Iakovlev, a member of the school who also became an Academician, published essays on a number of others, and left a manuscript in his archives entitled "The Kliuchevskii School of Russian History." In a conversation in the 1970s with an eminent American scholar whose father had been a student of Kliuchevskii, he remarked discreetly that the most important lesson Soviet scholars learned from their predecessors was that "one must know how to renounce the old world and live one's way into the new one.[3]

Kliuchevskii's apprentices made their most visible contribution by ensuring scrupulous editorship of their mentor's work after the revolution—Kizevetter of the early editions published in the Soviet Union, and Iakovlev, Got'e, and Sergei V. Bakrushin of the edition published in 1937. These responsibilities are symbolic of the manner in which Kliuchevskii's influence has spread, for they brought together his teaching of undergraduates, his published research, and some of the professional historians he trained. The 1956–59 edition was edited by Tikhomirov, a "grandson" of Kliuchevskii, and by Zimin, a "great-grandson," who was a student of Cherepnin's and, like Cherepnin, completed excellent analyses of Kliuchevskii.

In the English-speaking world, Gibbon's *Decline and Fall of the Roman Empire* remains a classic more than two hundred years after its publication, but more as a masterpiece of historical literature than as a scholarly study. Macaulay, Parkinson, Morrison, Michelet, Mommsen, and Ranke remain great names as historical writers, but few read their volumes today. Even fewer masterpieces derive from lecture courses and so blend teaching and scholarship that they illustrate the ideal relationship between the two. Yet, Kliuchevskii's five-volume *Course of Russian History*, the published version of a survey course presented in several Moscow institutions from 1868 through 1910 which began to appear in 1904, has enjoyed several massive new editions, attracts millions of readers, and retains the respect of scholars in Russia and around the world.

Kliuchevskii devoted much of his last decade to transforming his survey course into the *Course of Russian History*. For thousands of his contemporaries and millions of Russians after his death, including many professional historians, these volumes provided the first and most enduring account of their native land's past. In the original and in translation, they have exercised profound influence for almost a century upon foreigners' conceptions of Russian history. Their Russia was the Russia these volumes described.

From its first appearance, the *Course of Russian History* exercised an enormous impact. Pobedonostsev so enjoyed the first two volumes that surviving to read the final three was one of his deepest wishes. Struve announced in 1909 that the set was "read by all educated Russians." Bogoslovskii agreed: the *Course of Russian History* is "the bedside book of every educated Russian." Early in the 1920s, Kizevetter and Platonov declared Kliuchevskii "the most popular and authoritative national historian." Trotsky chose to reread the *Course of Russian History* on his way to internal exile in Alma Ata. In 1932, Fedotov, who regretted Kliuchevskii's emphasis upon Muscovy and neglect of the Church's role, concluded that it was "not one of many but the single Russian history on which two generations of Russian people were educated."[4] In 1957, Tikhomirov wrote that "any young student-historian who had not read the *Course of Russian History* and mastered its fundamental positions would have been an illiterate in history." Sixteen years later, the great physicist Petr Kapitsa turned to Kliuchevskii for "Russia's real history." In 1985 Yevgeny Yevtushenko lauded the *Course*, especially compared to "the periodically retouched pages . . . interspersed with white spots of silence and concealment" of Soviet scholarship.

Enthusiasm among the public for these volumes has been as great as the admiration lavished by scholars and public figures. The first printing of 10,000 copies of the first volume sold in less than a month, and three editions of 10,000 each of the first three volumes appeared during Kliuchevskii's lifetime. The Bolsheviks in the six years after the revolution published large editions that disappeared just as rapidly. Increasingly large Soviet reprints between 1937 and 1940, 1956 and 1958, 1987 and 1990 have multiplied the impact. Subscriptions for the most recent edition of 250,000 copies were rapidly exhausted, and copies were as rare and expensive in 1992 as earlier ones in 1986. Another three-volume edition of 75,000 copies appeared in 1993 to meet the continuing demand.

The saga of the editions of Kliuchevskii's great work published over more than a century illustrates its enduring attraction and helps explain his contribution toward creating Russian national consciousness. In his lifetime, lectures played the central role in higher education. Books were scarce. Most publishers, even in Moscow, were only printers, and no textbook industry existed. Thus, Soloviev was forced to employ several printers to produce different volumes of his *History of Russia*. Kliuchevskii also turned to several, one even in Vladimir, to publish his works. After he had obtained the pages, he organized binding and arranged sales through Moscow and St. Petersburg bookstores.

Because of the shortage of printed materials, instructors ordinarily required that students master the lectures for examinations. Enterprising students such as young Kliuchevskii therefore transcribed, rewrote, and lithographed their versions of lectures for sale. In the form of lithographs, Kliuchevskii's university lectures appeared twenty-five years before he published the first volume of the *Course of Russian History*. The Ministry of Education forbade transcripts in 1887, but copies have survived for every year from 1879 through 1890, and two students or sets of students prepared independent versions in some years. In the 1990s, every major Moscow and St. Petersburg library possessed at least one set, and several owned fifteen. Many scholars' archives contain copies, and some European and American libraries possess lithographs of versions made as early as 1882–83. Teachers at Moscow high schools began to use them in 1880. Some young men came to study with Kliuchevskii because they had used transcripts in high schools as distant as Simbirsk, Kazan, Samara, and Orenburg. Platonov has confided that he read and reread a copy when he was an undergraduate in St. Petersburg in 1881 and while preparing his major works. Lenin, intellectuals in St. Petersburg, the empress, young radicals in Nizhnii Novgorod, and prisoners in Samara read them. Allegedly, Gorky memorized parts of one volume while still a young man. When Minister of Education Ivan D. Delianov requested a copy in the fall of 1893, Kliuchevskii responded that he possessed only one tattered and much-revised issue. By 1902, mint copies were so rare that one sold for a hundred rubles.

The *Course* was Kliuchevskii's main scholarly concern during his last decade, and he devoted approximately two years to each volume. However, he continued to meet his first obligation and love, teaching, and devoted more time to graduate students than before. He also completed major revisions of *Boyar Council* in 1902 and 1909, prepared several editions of the guide to his course that included materials on the period after 1905, and published eleven articles. The Russo-Japanese War in 1904–1905, the 1905 revolution and its aftermath, and the political excitement of those years consumed time and intellectual energy, and he remained an active member of his intellectual-social circle. But the *Course* constituted his major interest.

Archives for this period provide detailed information concerning his progress. He utilized thousands of notes and drafts and final copies of his published works, but relied heavily on lithographs, especially those from 1882–83 and 1883–84 and from Ger'e's program. Young men such as Iakovlev, Kizevetter, and Semevskii, who became outstanding scholars, had made transcripts, and Kliuchevskii had corrected them before they were lithographed, so they provided a sound base.

Boris served as a full-time aide, collecting materials, confirming accuracy, typing, and reading proofs. However, the major research assistant was Iakov L. Barskov, a former student who had produced a lithograph of the 1883–84 lecture. After graduation, some graduate work, and teaching history in a Moscow high school, where he introduced the lithographs and urged students to study with their author, he moved to the archives of the Ministry of Foreign Affairs.

Barskov collected copies of the various versions, organized other materials, and helped prepare the final version for publication. Many semifinal drafts are in his handwriting. Kliuchevskii acknowledged his contribution, and Barskov received a share of the royalties.

Kliuchevskii rewrote some major portions, such as the chapters on the period before Kiev, the expansion north and east from Moscow and Vladimir, and Peter the Great. On the expansion northward, he returned to materials he had collected in the 1860s on the growth of monastic landholdings and the pages amassed for his M.A. thesis on the lives of Russian saints. His diary indicates that he also read again the volumes of Soloviev and Chicherin, the latter most when he was completing the first two volumes, and Soloviev when he was reviewing pages on Peter the Great. He also turned often to Taine and Guizot.

Unfortunately, Kliuchevskii did not complete the fifth volume, which began with Catherine the Great and was to end with the abolition of serfdom. One-third was ready for the press by July 1910, and he was engaged in a draft of the remainder. However, because of constant pain and several operations during his last ten months, he wrote only intermittently and ceased completely in February 1911. With the approval of Boris, Kizevetter, and others whom Kliuchevskii had helped train, Barskov added a sixty-page summary of the history of Russia since Peter the Great published in the 1909 study guide as well as the 1894 speech on Alexander III that had caused some student discontent. He completed the final volume, which was published in 1921.

Publication of the *Course of Russian History* in effect began in 1880 with the lithographed versions of Kliuchevskii's lectures. The three-volume Witte edition of the set of lithographs appeared again in 1906 in an unauthorized version of six thousand copies published by radical students. However, the press of the Holy Synod, the largest in Moscow, in 1904 and 1906 published the first two volumes as well as a second edition of the first volume. Boris arranged with four different private printers to produce the other volumes and the successive prerevolutionary editions. In December 1917, the Soviet government nationalized Kliuchevskii's publications and authorized the first of a series of large editions, an action some intellectuals opposed because they considered nationalization a threat to their independence. In short, Kliuchevskii's students, Witte, radical students, the Holy Synod Press, his son, and the Soviet government all contributed to producing and distributing the early editions, demonstrating that Kliuchevskii from the beginning attracted many different segments of Russian society.

Reviews were full of praise. Many commented upon the volumes in their diaries and correspondence. Waiters in Moscow's best restaurants inquired of Boris about the appearance of succeeding volumes. A 1911 study revealed that workers borrowed Kliuchevskii's volumes from Moscow libraries far more than other historical works. A 1913 letter in police archives complained that copies were never available in the library or bookstores. An enterprising journalist established a periodical that sold thirty thousand copies serially in an eighteen-month period in 1912 and 1913. The competition from such unauthorized versions was such that Kliuchevskii inserted warnings in each volume demanding respect for authors' rights and declaring that only the Holy Synod editions and those he arranged privately were accurate.

Boris played a central role in publishing and selling his father's work. His parents and he were very close, corresponding affectionately when they were separated, even when Boris was a little boy. Father and son enjoyed fishing, playing chess, and long walks in the country with their dog, and Boris was a member of his parents' social and intellectual circle. He completed undergraduate degrees in history and civil law, but technological innovations fascinated him. He installed a telephone in the family home when such an instrument was a rarity, and he acquired a motorcycle. However, he found purpose in life only when he served as his father's research assistant, publisher, and business manager.

After his father's death, publishing new editions became a flourishing enterprise for Boris. The sixth edition of the first volume and the fourth edition of the second appeared in 1916, and the third edition of the third and fourth volumes in 1915. He also produced the second edition of his father's undergraduate thesis, published in 1866, *Foreigners' Tales about the Moscow State,* and three volumes of his father's essays, the first in 1912, the second in 1913, and the third in 1915, when he also brought out a second edition of the first volume. When the revolution broke out, he was preparing a fourth volume, including materials that the Academy of Sciences published in 1983. During the war years, he arranged publication of some of his father's popular essays as brochures.[5]

Lenin was a great admirer of Kliuchevskii's work and placed the Bolshevik imprimatur upon it. In the mid-eighties, he read Kliuchevskii articles in *Russian Thought,* after his sister Mariia had obtained the journal for him. He made his first reference to Kluchevskii's views in 1888, and his letters contain several comments. The Kremlin library contains a copy of the 1883–84 lithograph with his annotations in the margins. Soviet scholars demonstrated that Lenin in 1906 used materials from the lithographed lectures in polemics on the character of the landholding system in the sixteenth century. Zimin has even suggested that Lenin borrowed terminology from Kliuchevskii, particularly the phrase "Moscow tsardom" (*Moskovskoe tsarstvo*).

Only seven weeks after the Bolshevik seizure of power, at Lenin's request the executive committee of the new government on December 29, 1917, nationalized the works of Kliuchevskii, the only historian among the fifty-eight prominent writers whose publications the new state placed under its control. On March 16, 1918, the Commissariat of Enlightenment announced publication of the *Course of Russian History,* as well as its guide, the lectures he gave on estates, *Boyar Council,* the three volumes of essays, and his undergraduate thesis. This launched the first of four waves of Soviet editions that helped make Kliuchevskii a powerful force in the Russian historical scene throughout the Soviet period.

It is impossible to determine how many printings appeared in the chaotic early Soviet years, because central statistics do not exist and data in the many copies scattered around Russia and the Western world are not clear. In 1921, the Soviet Union published only one-quarter as many books as in 1917, and only 102 of the volumes printed were in history. However, the 1921 edition, which included the first printing of the fifth volume, consisted of 50,000 copies. In 1922–24 it produced other editions of the five volumes. It appears that at least 100,000 copies of each volume were published during these years, plus smaller numbers of the other works.[6]

Under the Soviet system, research and instruction in history were subject to the same sudden shifts of party policy as other aspects of Soviet life. A decade of organization and creation of a new generation of scholar-teachers after 1917 was followed by tight controls and arrests. Most of those whom Kliuchevskii had attracted and helped train survived arrest and internment from 1930 until 1935, when Stalin suddenly decreed "mastery of the historical inheritance" a goal and allowed them to resume their careers. This led to a new edition of the *Course of Russian History* in 1937, 20,000 copies in Russian and 10,000 each in Ukrainian and Belorussian. Scholars who had been students of Kliuchevskii were editors.[7]

As part of the thaw after Stalin's death, the Academy of Sciences between 1956 and 1959 produced an eight-volume edition of Kliuchevskii's writings, including the *Course of Russian History*. The edition included 75,000 copies of each volume of the *Course* and 55,000, 53,000, and 54,000 copies of some of the other works at a time when university textbook editions ranged in size from 50,000 to 60,000 volumes.[8]

The editors of this excellent set completed an intensive survey of archival material and identified primary and secondary sources on which Kliuchevskii had based information and judgments. Footnotes identified the corrections he wrote upon the various lithographed editions as well as those added when he was completing the final version. Above all, they demonstrated that the basic outline and themes and some of the language survived from lectures he had given in the early 1880s.

The size and scholarly quality of this edition, the warning issued about the hazards it created for Soviet orthodoxy, and publication of other histories to counter its impact reveal Kliuchevskii's continuing appeal as an alternative to official history as well as the ambivalence of the official view. Thus, the volume that Moscow University published in 1955 to celebrate its two-hundredth anniversary characterized him as a reactionary and mentioned favorably only his skills as a writer. Later, Nechkina, who devoted much of her scholarly career to study of Kliuchevskii, declared that exposing a new generation to such a bourgeois scholar was dangerous. She helped arrange publication of some of Pokrovskii's writings as "a necessary counterweight," but this selection appeared in 1965–66 in an edition of only 15,000 copies.

Tikhomirov, who helped persuade the Academy to publish the new edition and was the general editor, in *Questions of History* in August 1958 revealed disagreements within the party and historical profession, for he reiterated the warnings issued with the 1937 edition. Kliuchevskii was "our inheritance." His imagination in locating sources, conscientious scholarship, and compelling style deserved praise, as did his attention to ethnography, the life of the people, and social forces. However, much of his popularity was due to the works' "oppositional flavor" and the absence of other competent national histories. Moreover, Tikhomirov noted factual errors, neglect of uprisings, the Mongols, and Siberia, and portraits of individuals "extremely far from reality." Finally, the *Course* was irrelevant because contemporary scholarship had undermined or even demolished Kliuchevskii's analysis of such issues as the role trade played in Kiev.

Kliuchevskii and his work have become increasingly popular among historians and the reading public. Soviet scholars produced almost three hundred books and articles about him after 1917. The flow was constant except for the early 1930s and the period between 1947 and 1953 and a rising high level since 1988. The Academy of Sciences published an edition of 40,000 copies of his letters in 1968 and a handsome volume of Nechkina's major description of his life and work in 13,500 copies in 1973, when Soviet publishers ordinarily printed 2,000 or 3,000 copies of a scholarly biography. In 1980, the Academy reproduced 10,000 copies of the 1902 edition of the volume on saints' lives as historical sources, with twenty pages of favorable comment by a senior specialist on Novgorod, Academician V. L. Ianin. Three years later, it published 90,000 copies of a volume that included some previously unpublished essays "for the wide circle of readers interested in Russian history in the eighteenth and nineteenth centuries and the history of Russian culture."

Above all, the State Committee on Publishing between 1987 and 1990 produced a new edition in 250,000 copies (the original announcement was of 150,000) because bookstores were selling copies of the previous set for a thousand rubles: the original price had been twenty-eight. This ten-volume set and a three-volume set in 1993 in 75,000 copies reflected the revival of popular interest in history and rebellion against the dull compilations and distortions the official account of the past had inflicted upon the reading public, as well as dissatisfaction with living conditions, restraints, and national and religious discontents. It was also a response to a national campaign led by Academician Dmitrii S. Likhachev, a humanistic scholar respected throughout the world for his work in early Russian history, art, and folklore who had spent four and a half years in labor camps. A founder of the All-Russian Society for the Preservation of History and Culture, he provided the campaign to reprint the

Course of Russian History the same dignity, prestige, and protection that Academician Andrei Sakharov supplied the movement for a democratic society, in which Likhachev was also active.

Editor Ianin's comments in the new edition were far more laudatory than those of earlier editors, and he acknowledged that Kliuchevskii had created a school of scholarship, which earlier Soviet scholars had vigorously denied. The new edition contained some essays that earlier Soviet editors had ignored, but excluded *Boyar Council* and other works and the articles on religion, Church, and church leaders. However, in 1990 Ianin edited a handsome volume entitled *Historical Portraits: Leaders of Historical Thought* by "one of the leaders of Russian and world culture." Among the essays not published since before 1917 were two of Kliuchevskii's most deeply religious and popular works, "The Good People of Ancient Russia" and "The Significance of Saint Sergei for the Russian People and State." Their reappearance in an edition of 2 million copies and in journals in 1992 and 1993 reveals that the political and academic communities recognize religious and national aspects of Kliuchevskii's work previously ignored.

The influence of the *Course of Russian History* and Kliuchevskii's teaching has extended far beyond Russia's borders and contributed to the world's growing recognition of nineteenth-century Russian culture. The origins of European and American interest in Russia began in the last third of the nineteenth century with Russia's increasing role in international politics. At the same time, translations of Turgenev, Dostoevsky, Tolstoy, and other great writers became fashionable and then popular. The enthusiastic reception given literature helped to introduce Russian music abroad, and ballet and theater followed. By 1914, Russian culture had become an important part of the intellectual life of educated Europeans and Americans.

Kliuchevskii was an important figure in this flowering. The translations into languages other than Russian and the academic achievements of those English and American pioneers in Russian studies whom he attracted and helped train were part of the wave of Russian culture that swept over Europe and the United States. Early translations into Finnish, Czech, French, Japanese, German, and English, and later Italian, Danish, Hungarian, Hebrew, and Turkish, served as the fundamental guides for professional historians and the informed reading public at the formative stage, when study of Russian history was beginning.

The early translation into English and the career of Bernard Pares, who spent 1898–99 in Moscow attending Kliuchevskii's classes, provide a practical illustration as well as a symbol of the way his teaching and research together spread knowledge and understanding of Russia's past, in this case throughout the English-speaking world. This translation was especially important because the first volume appeared in 1910, three others before 1914, and the fifth in 1926, making it the first full scholarly history of Russia in English. Kliuchevskii had planned that his son and Kizevetter translate the volumes, but Dent and Sons in London offered an attractive contract under which C. J. Hogarth, a friend of Vinogradov at Oxford, would serve as the translator. Hogarth ultimately became an excellent translator, but he was then much less able than those who had presented Russia's great novelists to the English public. His renditions are incomplete and inaccurate and possess none of the grace and irony of the original. Even so, his translation spread throughout the English-speaking world. A second edition appeared in 1960.[9]

The first scholarly history of Russia published in English was that in 1926 by Pares, the founder of Russian studies in England, a frequent instructor in American universities, and a popular lecturer there after 1924. Seven editions of this volume appeared before an American textbook was published. However, Pares's volume was not a rival, for he was briefly a student of Kliuchevskii and he and his book were surrogates for Kliuchevskii. He devoted more attention to military affairs, intellectuals, and individuals than his Moscow mentor, but he adopted Kliuchevskii's framework, concept of the flow of Russian history, and positions on events and individuals. Pares invited Kliuchevskii to England in 1902 to lecture at the opening of the first British university program in Russian studies, an honor that Kliuchevskii declined, and he made two men whom Kliuchevskii had trained members of the editorial board of his new journal, the first in England devoted to Russia. Thus, he placed a Kliuchevskii stamp upon the English and American approach to Russian history in the crucial formative period. In the words of Karpovich, who studied under Kliuchevskii, scholars outside Russia "have remained to a large extent within the Kliuchevskii tradition," a heritage that Vernadsky and he sustained when they began their American academic careers at Yale and Harvard, respectively.

Truly "a teacher affects eternity: he can never tell when his influence stops."

FIFTEEN

Last Days

After 1905, Kliuchevskii concentrated upon completing his masterpiece, but he continued teaching, converted sections of his volumes to essays in popular journals, and produced new editions of the textbook for his classes. In his last year, he continued writing and revising the last volume and drafted an article to celebrate the fiftieth anniversary of the abolition of serfdom. This final venture was especially appropriate because his opportunity for an academic career rested upon Alexander II's reforms and he considered celebrating anniversaries an important way to strengthen the bond between past and present.

Those years brought a major disappointment, the end of service in the academy in circumstances that offended and saddened him. An enormous amount of information is available concerning the rupture, but the causes remain somewhat unclear, as they often do in such incidents in the academic world. The strains of war and revolution contributed. Dismay over slowness in completing the *Course of Russian History* may also have been a factor: devoting two days each week to the academy was hampering him. On the other hand, he did not refer to this, maintained his schedule at the university, and taught one afternoon a week at the School of Painting, Sculpture, and Architecture until October 1910.

The difficulties began in January 1905, when the rector, Bishop Evdokim, heard rumors that students were planning a demonstration against the war after a Kliuchevskii lecture. Kliuchevskii frostily rejected Evdokim's suggestion that he cancel the class to cripple the demonstration, probably because teaching was a sacred obligation, but also because the rector's writing to him, rather than discussing it, was an affront. Later that year, he was one of twenty-two faculty members who signed a petition that the Holy Synod grant the academy autonomy, which enraged the rector. Kliuchevskii in a private conversation with the rector suggested that a student threat to strike was a youthful prank. When Evdokim cited this remark in a talk to the student body, Kliuchevskii was outraged.

Last Days

Kliuchevskii at his dacha, July 1909. Photograph by S. I. Smirnov. Source: M. V. Nechkina, *Vasilii Osipovich Kliuchevskii. Istoriia zhizni i tvorchestva* (Moscow: Nauka, 1974).

Whatever the causes of his discontent, on August 29, 1905, he requested that he be allowed to retire. A faculty meeting a week later voted to accept the resignation but sent a delegation requesting that he reconsider. Sergiev Posad and Moscow newspapers then published a letter from five colleagues alleging that the rector had invited several unqualified teachers to the meeting who had voted to accept Kliuchevskii's withdrawal. While the rector proceeded with the administrative work involved, the students petitioned and threatened to strike. Ultimately, on January 2, 1906, Kliuchevskii resigned formally by letter, saying that his honor had been engaged and that resignation in the confused circumstances constituted a last service to his beloved institution. He rejected a visiting professorship and an honorary title and refused to suggest scholars to succeed him. Correspondence concerning the return of books borrowed from the library was cold, and he was convinced that Evdokim sought to humiliate him. Sergei I. Smirnov, an outstanding scholar-teacher whose graduate work he had directed, resigned from the faculty in disgust and became an instructor at the university.

On the other hand, Kliuchevskii's years of gradual withdrawal from the university were pleasant. In 1906 he resigned from university and Academy of Sciences prize committees and other such functions. Two years later, he yielded his seminars to former students, concentrated upon an undergraduate course, and devoted increased time to encouraging scholars he had helped train. In a way, evenings with these younger men replaced the warm relationships that he had enjoyed at the academy. His old friend from student days, Kirpichnikov, and Liubavskii, senior administrators at the university, were considerate, encouraging him to reduce his teaching responsibilities and present his courses at particularly convenient hours. They arranged research leave for the academic year 1909–10 and organized a celebration on December 5, 1909, the thirtieth anniversary of his first lecture as successor to Soloviev. Hundreds of letters from all parts of the country poured into the university and his home, and the university published a *Festschrift* more than eight hundred pages long. This included a bibliography of his publications and essays by more than forty scholars, fifteen of whom had obtained advanced degrees under his direction. On that day, the *Russian Journal* saluted him as "a Russian national monument."

He insisted on teaching, but on September 15, 1910, he requested leave for a semester when he learned that he faced an operation for cancer. In April 1911, the university made him an honorary member of the faculty, a distinction he had previously declined. He remained actively interested in the selection of his successor, debating between supporting Kizevetter or Bogoslovskii. He ultimately endorsed Kizevetter, but the faculty chose Bogoslovskii, who had succeeded him at the academy.

During these years, Kliuchevskii enjoyed teaching at the School of Painting, Sculpture, and Architecture, where he felt "an artist among artists." He gave his last lecture there on October 19, 1910, just before he underwent the first of a series of operations. During his months in the hospital, he worked on lectures for the school, corrected student papers, drafted an article, and continued writing the fifth volume of the *Course of Russian History*. He insisted on dying at home, and passed away on May 12, 1911.

The funeral was one of the largest in the city's history. Administrators and colleagues from the institutions at which he had taught, Platonov and other scholars from St. Petersburg, and hundreds of archivists, librarians, students, artists, priests, teachers, army officers, and Muscovites of all ages who had heard him lecture or had read his books crowded the streets. Two bishops and fifteen priests, all former students, celebrated the services in the university church. Thousands watched the cortege as it traveled two miles from Zhitnaia Street to the university and three miles to the Donskoi Monastery cemetery. Newspapers and journals published long obituaries, letters, and memoirs. Telegrams from Witte and other officials, hundreds of other Russians, all the universities, and many libraries, schools, learned societies, and liberal and conservative political groups showered upon Boris. However, the mayor of Moscow and the superintendent of the educational district were the only elected or appointed government officials who attended the services, illustrating the leaders' blindness to the contribution the scholar-teacher had made toward bringing society and state together and creating a nation.

ABBREVIATIONS

VOK   Vasilii O. Kliuchevskii

PUBLICATIONS BY KLIUCHEVSKII

Boiarskaia duma   *Boiarskaia duma drevnei Rusi.* 3rd ed. Moscow, 1902.

Istoricheskie portrety   *Istoricheskie portrety. Deiateli istoricheskie mysli.* Moscow, 1990.

Kurs   *Sochineniia, Kurs russkoi istorii.* Moscow, 1956–58.

Kurs, Sochineniia   *Kurs, Sochineniia v deviati tomakh.* Moscow, 1986–89.

Neopublikovannye   *Neopublikovannye proizvedeniia.* Moscow, 1983.

Ocherki i rechi   *Ocherki i rechi. Vtoroi sbornik statei V. Kliuchevskogo.* Moscow, 1913.

Opyty i issledovaniia   *Opyty i issledovaniia. Pervyi sbornik statei V. Kliuchevskogo.* 2nd ed. Moscow, 1915.

Otzyvy i otvety   *Otzyvy i otvety. Tretii sbornik statei V. Kliuchevskogo.* Moscow, 1914.

Pis'ma   *Pis'ma. Dnevniki. Aforizmy i mysli ob istorii.* Moscow, 1968.

Pis'ma k Gvozdevu   *Pis'ma V. O. Kliuchevskogo k P. I. Gvozdevu, 1861–1870.* Moscow, 1924.

JOURNALS

BV   *Bogoslovskii vestnik.*

Chteniia   *Chteniia v Imperatorskom obshchestve istorii i drevnostei rossiiskikh pri Moskovskom universitete.*

IV   *Istoricheskii vestnik.*

PO   *Pravoslavnoe obozrenie.*

RM   *Russkaia mysl'.*

RV   *Russkii vestnik.*

SIE   *Sovetskaia istoricheskaia entsiklopediia.*

VI   *Voprosy istorii.*

NOTES

1. "UNDER THE BELLS" OF PENZA

1. Father I. A. Artobolevskii, "K biografii V. O. Kliuchevskogo. Kliuchevskii do universiteta," *Golos minuvshago*, No. 5 (1911), 159; Elizaveta O. Virginskaia, "Vospominaniia o V. O. Kliuchevskom, 1856–1861," *Chteniia*, CCXLVIV, Book I, Part III (1914), 414–16.

2. A. V. Tiustin, "Penza," *SIE*, X (1967), 961–62; *Entsiklopedicheskii slovar'*, LXXVI (1903), 494–95; Isabella T. Kreindler, "The Mordvinians: A Doomed Soviet Nationality," *Cahiers du monde russe et soviétique*, XXVI, No. 1 (1985), 43–62.

3. Leonid Pasternak, who became acquainted with Kliuchevskii during the last thirteen years of the historian's life and painted his portrait in 1909, remarked that Kliuchevskii's sister Elizaveta told him that the family was not Russian in origin. A Mordovian scholar of Mordovian history claimed that Kliuchevskii was one of the few Mordovians who received a higher education and professional opportunities in the nineteenth century. However, no other evidence supports this. Leonid Pasternak, *Zapisi raznykh let* (Moscow, 1975), 156; Ivan A. Iashkin, *Mordovskaia sotsialisticheskaia natsiiadetishche Oktiabria* (Saransk, 1978), 46–48.

4. A. G. Rashin, *Naselenie Rossii za sto let* (Moscow, 1956), 295; Regina G. Eimontova, "Prosveshchenie v Rossii pervoi poloviny XIX veka," *VI*, No. 1 (1986), 92–93.

5. Sergei A. Belokurov, comp., "Vasilii Osipovich Kliuchevskii. Materialy dlia ego biografii," *Chteniia*, CCXLVIII, Book I, Part III (1914), 17.

6. State Archive of the Penza Oblast, Penza Seminary Archive, f. 21, o. 1, d. 2; Belokurov, "Kliuchevskii," 17–95.

7. Gregory L. Freeze, *The Russian Levites: Parish Clergy in the Nineteenth Century* (Cambridge, Mass., 1977), 96.

8. Father Aleksii Rozhdestvenskii, "Vospominaniia o V. O. Kliuchevskom," *Chteniia*, CCXVLII, Book I, Part III (1914), 429, 432; Belokurov, "Kliuchevskii," xvi.

9. V. O. Kliuchevskii (hereafter VOK), *Pis'ma. Dnevniki. Aforizmy i mysli ob istorii* (Moscow, 1968), 13–17.

10. Belokurov, "Kliuchevskii," 312–13; Rozhdestvenskii, "Vospominaniia, 423–30.

2. "I HAVE STARTED ON THE ROAD TO SCIENCE"

1. P. Mizhuev, "Rossiia. Prosveshchenie. Uchebnoe delo," *Entsiklopedicheskii slovar'*, XXVII A (1899), 382–409; Regina D. Eimontova, "Universitetskaia reforma 1863 g.," *Istoricheskie zapiski*, No. 70 (1961), 163–70.

2. Akademiia Nauk SSSR, Institut istorii, *Istoriia Moskvy v shestikh tomakh* (Moscow, 1953–59), V, 15–16; *Moskovskii putevoditel'-spravochnik, 1897* (Moscow, 1897), 2; Robert E. Johnson, *Peasant and Proletarian: The Working Class of Moscow in the Late Nineteenth Century* (New Brunswick, N.J., 1979), 31–32.

3. S. Moldavan et al., eds., *Moskva, Illiustrirovannaia istoriia v dvukh tomakh* (Mos-

cow, 1984–86), I, 278–85; Akademiia Nauk, *Istoriia Moskvy,* I, 18; III, 511, 544–47, 558–62.

4. Aleksandr I. Kirpichnikov, "Pervyi den' v universitete. Otryvok iz vospominanii," *IV,* LCVIII, No. 6 (1897), 748.

5. Galina I. Shchetinina, *Universitety v Rossii i ustav 1884 goda* (Moscow, 1976), 182–83.

6. Moscow University, *Otchet o sostoianii i deistviiakh ʒa 1880* (Moscow, 1881), 56, 103; . . . ʒa *1901* (Moscow, 1902), 18–19; . . . ʒa *1907* (Moscow, 1908), 83–85; . . . ʒa *1910* (Moscow, 1911), 95, 106.

7. VOK, *Pis'ma,* 47–53; VOK, *Pis'ma k Gvoʒdevu,* 56–57, 63–66.

3. "THE GUIDING STARS"

1. L. Hamilton Rhinelander, "Exiled Russian Scholars in Prague," *Canadian Slavonic Papers,* XVI (1974), 331.

2. Nikolai L. Gudzii, *Iʒuchenie russkoi literatury v Moskovskom universitete (dooktiabr'skii period)* (Moscow, 1958), 54.

3. Elliot Benowitz, *B. N. Chicherin: Rationalism and Liberalism in Nineteenth-Century Russia,* University of Wisconsin Ph.D. thesis (1966), 82–86; Andrzej Walicki, *Legal Philosophies of Russian Liberalism* (Oxford, 1987), 105–64, especially 115.

4. Nicholas V. Riasanovsky, *The Image of Peter the Great in Russian History and Thought* (New York, 1985), 154.

5. Russian State Historical Archive, Ministry of Education archive, f. 733, o. 141, d. 92; o. 147, d. 409; Russian State Library, Moscow, Manuscript Division, Sergei M. Soloviev archive, f. 285, o. 46, d. 69; Vladimir I. Ger'e archive, f. 70, o. 34, d. 86.

6. VOK, "Pamiati S. M. Solov'eva," *Nauchnoe slovo,* No. 8 (1904), 117–32.

7. VOK, "Nabrosok rechi, posviashchennoi 150-letiiu Moskovskogo universiteta," *Neopublikovannye,* 196–97; VOK, "Pamiati T. N. Granovskogo, umer 4-go oktiabria 1855g.," *RV,* XLIII, No. 263 (October 8, 1905), 3.

4. "YEARS OF PREPARATION AND CHANGE"

1. Gennadii F. Karpov, *V ʒashchitu Bogdana Khmel'nitskogo* (Moscow, 1890), 48, 104.

2. Russian State Library, Moscow, Manuscript Division, A. A. Kizevetter archive, f. 566, o. 47, d. 9, VOK, "Istoriia Rossii," Part 2 (1873–1874), *Lektsii V. O. Kliuchevskogo;* Kizevetter, "Pervyi kurs V. O. Kliuchevskogo, 1873–1874," Russkii nauchnyi institut, Belgrade, *Zapiski,* III (1931), 279–306, especially 281, 284, 304–305; A. A. Zimin, "Formirovanie istoricheskikh vzgliadov V. O. Kliuchevskogo v 60-e gody XIX v.," *Istoricheskie ʒapiski,* No. 69 (1961), 194.

3. Vladimir I. Kedrin, *Aleksandrovskoe voennoe uchilishche,* 1863–1901 (Moscow, 1901).

4. Militsa V. Nechkina, *Vasilii Osipovich Kliuchevskii. Istoriia ʒhiʒni i tvorchestva* (Moscow, 1974), 137, 176.

5. Ibid., 146–49, 170–71, emphasized that writing this volume was a dangerous and courageous act. The editor of the edition of Kliuchevskii's works published between 1987 and 1990 asserted that the Holy Synod prevented a second edition (Vladimir L. Ianin, *Nedelia* [October 20–26, 1986]). I have found no evidence for this statement.

6. VOK, "Velikiia Minei Chetii," *Moskva*, No. 90 (June 20, 1868).

7. Aleksandr V. Gorskii, *Dnevnik A. V. Gorskogo, s primechaniiami prof. S. Smirnova* (Moscow, 1885); Moskovskaia dukhovnaia akademiia, *Spiski studentov, okonchivshikh polnyi kurs za pervoe stoletie eia sushchestvovaniia, 1814–1914 gg.* (Sergiev Posad, 1915), 51–147; Nikolai A. Zaozerskii, "V. O. Kliuchevskii i ego retsenziia dissertatsii na uchenye stepeni professorov i studentov Moskovskoi dukhovnoi akademii," in Matvei V. Liubavskii, ed., *Vasilii Osipovich Kliuchevskii. Biograficheskii ocherk, rechi, proiznesennye v torzhestvennom zasedanii 12 noiabria 1911 goda, i materialy dlia ego biografii* (Moscow, 1914), 72–122. Published as volume CCXLVIII of *Chteniia* of the Society of Russian History and Antiquity.

8. Iurii V. Got'e, "Primechaniia," in VOK, *Kurs russkoi istorii* (Moscow, 1937), III, 401, 403; Got'e, who found Sergiev Posad an occasional haven from Moscow during the revolution and civil war, put "the monastery's magnificent library, one in perfect order," under the protection of the Rumiantsev Museum, to which it was later moved. Got'e, *Time of Troubles: The Diary of Iurii Vladimirovich Got'e. Moscow. July 8, 1917– July 23, 1922*, translated, edited, and introduced by Terence J. Emmons (Princeton, N.J., 1988), 313, 319, 378.

5. THE BREAKTHROUGH: THE *BOYAR COUNCIL*

1. Robert O. Crummey, "Kliuchevskii's Portrait of the Boyars," *Canadian-American Slavic Studies*, XX, No. 3–4 (1986), 341.

2. Zimin, "Formirovanie istoricheskikh vzgliadov Kliuchevskogo," 178–96.

3. VOK, *Boiarskaia duma drevnei Rusi*, 3rd ed. (Moscow, 1902), 3.

4. Ibid., 202.

5. VOK, "Boiarskaia duma," *Russkaia mysl'*, I, No. 3 (1880), 50.

6. VOK, *Boiarskaia duma*, 168, footnote.

7. Ibid., 29.

8. Ibid., 285–93, 302–309, 315.

9. In the first edition of *Boiarskaia duma*, Kliuchevskii considered the economic crisis the main explanation for the boyars' indifference to power. In the third edition, it was one of the main reasons.

6. A PROFESSOR'S LIFE

1. Sergei F. Platonov, "Pamiati V. O. Kliuchevskogo," in *V. O. Kliuchevskii. Kharakteristiki i vospominaniia* (Moscow, 1912), 98.

2. Prince B. A. Shchetinin, "M. M. Kovalevskii i Moskovskii universitet 80-kh godov. Stranichka iz vospominanii," *IV*, CXLIV, No. 5 (1916), 484; Shchetinina, *Universitety*, 157–58; Pavel N. Miliukov, "Universitety v Rossii," *Entsiklopedicheskii slovar'*, XXXIV A (1902), 793–802; Robert J. Burch, *Social Unrest in Imperial Russia: The Student Movement at Moscow University, 1897–1905*, University of Washington Ph.D. thesis (1972), 42–56.

3. Russian Academy of Sciences, Institute of Russian History, Moscow, VOK archive, f. 4, o. 1, d. 6, "Nabroski o russkoi istorii i uchenykh"; VOK, *Kurs russkoi istorii* (Moscow, 1904), I, 40–42; VOK, "Istoriia soslovii v Rossii," *Sochineniia*, VI (Moscow, 1959), 299–306, 475.

4. Russian Academy of Sciences, Institute of Russian History, Moscow, VOK

archive, f. 4, o. 1, d. 28; VOK, "Prilozhenie k razdelu 'Istoriografiia,' " *Sochineniia v deviati tomakh* (Moscow, 1989), VII, 428–30.

5. In 1912, the society library contained 1,500 manuscripts and 14,000 books and periodicals.

7. THE OUTSIDE WORLD INTERVENES

1. VOK, *Pis'ma*, 343, 347, 388.

2. Russian State Library, Moscow, Manuscript Division, VOK archive, f. 131, o. 30, d. 4; State Archive of the Russian Federation, Moscow Police Department archive, f. 102, d. 1888 g.

3. Evidence on this incident is abundant, but determining the exact chronology, numbers expelled and arrested, and shifting views is difficult. The most complete source is the detailed diary kept by Bogolepov, "Stranitsa iz zhizni Moskovskogo universiteta," *Russkii arkhiv*, LI, Book I (1913), 8–68. The seventy-page report of the faculty committee to review the incident has also survived. Ministry of Education and police reports constitute more than a thousand pages: State Archive of the Russian Federation, Moscow University archive, f. 63, o. 7, d. 357.2; Russian State Historical Archive, Moscow Police Department archive, f. 30, o. 1895, d. 7. Kliuchevskii's papers in the archive of the Institute of History in Moscow contain his work on the faculty committee report, the superintendent's comments on it, a diary he kept during the disorders, student circulars and leaflets, reports of student meetings at other universities, summaries of police reports that a friend in the university administration must have given him, official memoranda, other papers, and letters on this period. Some colleagues and students have published letters and memoirs, and the secondary literature on the student movement is vast.

4. Russian Academy of Sciences, Moscow, Archive, Aleksei I. Iakovlev archive, f. 640, o. 1, d. 40; Russian State Library, Moscow, Manuscript Division, VOK archive, f. 131, o. 30, d. 15, 22; o. 34, d. 76; Russian Academy of Sciences, Moscow, Institute of Russian History, Archive, VOK archive, f. 4, o. 1, d. 65.

5. Russian National Library, St. Petersburg, Manuscript Division, Dmitrii F. Kobeko archive, f. 9, opis'; Russian State Library, Moscow, Manuscript Division, VOK archive, f. 131, o. 32, d. 13; Russian Academy of Sciences, Institute of Russian History, Moscow archive, VOK archive, f. 4, o. 3, d. 1. 4, cloth v. 3 53, 146.

6. Russian State Library, Moscow, Manuscript Division, Vladimir I. Ger'e archive, f. 70, o. 70, d. 9, "Zapiski o prichinakh studencheskikh volnenii"; VOK archive, f. 131, o. 20, d. 27, "Materialy po studencheskomu dvizheniiu v 1890–1900s," Russian Academy of Sciences, Institute of Russian History, Archive, VOK archive, f. 4, o. 2, d. 7, 8, 47.

7. Ibid., f. 4, o. 3, d. 1, 4; f. 4, o. 4, d. 14; State Archive of the Russian Federation, Moscow University Archive, f. 63, o. 7, d. 357.2; Russian State Library, Moscow, Manuscript Division, VOK archive, f. 131, o. 22, d. 17; o. 34, d. 64.

8. VOK, *Pis'ma*, 298–300, 342.

9. Ibid., 203–205, 303, 310, 382–84, 476.

8. THE SCHOLAR

1. George Fedotov, *The Russian Religious Mind* (Cambridge, Mass., 1966), especially II, 180, and "Rossiia Kliuchevskogo," *Sovremennye zapiski*, I (1932), 340–62, con-

tribute a particularly cogent critique of Kliuchevskii's neglect of the cultural and spiritual aspects of early Russian history.

2. Russian Academy of Sciences, Institute of Russian History, Moscow, Archive, VOK archive, f. 4, o. 41, d. 92, VOK, "Metodologiia russkoi istorii," 66.

3. VOK, *Pis'ma*, 343.

4. Fernand Braudel, *L'Identité de France*, I: *L'Espace et l'histoire* (Paris, 1986), 11–12.

5. VOK, "Boiarskaia duma," *Russkaia mysl'*, I, Part II (1880), 48–52; Braudel, *On History*, translated by Sarah Matthews (Chicago, 1980), 10–11.

6. Boris I. Syromiatnikov, "V. O. Kliuchevskii i B. N. Chicherin," in *V. O. Kliuchevskii. Kharakteristiki i vospominaniia* (Moscow, 1912) 61.

7. VOK, *Pis'ma*, 335.

8. He published many of his reviews of theses. The annual *Zhurnaly* of the Ecclesiastical Academy from 1887 through 1907 contained his comments on student papers.

9. Following Kliuchevskii's death, Iushkov published an edition in 1913, Kliuchevskii's son Boris published one in 1914, and the new Soviet government published one in 1918. Three other editions have appeared since 1918.

10. Edward Gibbon, *The History of the Decline and Fall of the Roman Empire*, Introduction by J. B. Bury (London, 1909), I, vii.

9. THE ORIGINS OF RUSSIA AND THE RUSSIANS

1. Quoted in Raisa Kireeva, *Izuchenie otechestvennoi istoriografii v dorevoliutsionnoi Rossii v seredine XIX v. do 1917 g.* (Moscow, 1983), 190.

2. Russian Academy of Sciences, Institute of Russian History, Moscow, Archive, VOK archive, f. 4, d. 27, "Metodologiia i terminologiia (Programma i kurs lektsii, chitannyi v Moskovskom universitete v 1884–1885 gg.)," 67–68; VOK, *Pis'ma*, 223.

3. VOK, *Kurs*, I (Moscow, 1956), 281–82, 382–84; II (1957), 213, 398–99.

4. Specialists still disagree concerning the time and place of the Slavs' first appearance in history, an issue on which archeological research may provide additional information. But in the 1970s and 1980s, Western and Russian scholarship demonstrated quite conclusively that the Varangian influence was dominant in Kiev not only in the political and economic realm but also in law and the arts. Most scholars agree that the word *Rus'* derives from an old Finnish word.

5. VOK, *Kurs*, I (Moscow, 1956), 94–95, 284–86, 291.

6. Ibid., 31–32.

7. Russian Academy of Sciences, Institute of Russian History, Moscow, Archive, VOK archive, f. 4, o. 40, d. 26; Russian State Library, Moscow, Manuscript Division, VOK archive, f. 131, o. 40, d. 13, "Zapiski po vseobshchei istorii. Lektsii, chitannye v Aleksandrovskom voennom uchilishche v 1871–1872 i 1872–1873 uchebnykh godakh," 52.

8. Ibid., 238, 375.

9. Russian State Library, Moscow, Manuscript Division, VOK archive, f. 131, o. 1, d. 12; VOK, "F. M. Dostoevskii," *Neopublikovannye*, 320–21; Vadim A. Aleksandrov and A. A. Zimin, "Kommentarii," VOK, *Kurs*, V (Moscow, 1958), 432.

10. VOK, "Prilozhenie k kursu 'Metodologiia russkoi istorii,' " *Sochineniia v deviati tomakh*, VI (Moscow, 1989), 398–400; "Chestvovanie," *IV*, LXXXVII (1902), 751–52.

11. VOK, "Dobrye liudi drevnei Rusi," *Ocherki i rechi. Vtoroi sbornik statei* (Moscow, 1913), 157.

12. VOK, *Kurs*, V (Moscow, 1958), 313–14.

10. THE FLOW OF RUSSIAN HISTORY

1. Russian Academy of Sciences, Institute of Russian History, Moscow, Archive, VOK archive, f. 4, d. 27, "Metodologiia i terminologiia," 66; Hayden White, *Metahistory: The Historical Imagination in Nineteenth-Century Europe* (Baltimore, 1973), ix–xx, 192, 428.

2. Mikhail M. Bogoslovskii, "Professor Vasilii Osipovich Kliuchevskii (16 ianvaria 1841–12 maia 1911 g.)," in Moskovskaia dukhovnaia akademiia, *Pamiati pochivshikh nastavnikov* (Sergiev Posad, 1914), 347–50.

3. Braudel, *On History*, 4.

4. Russian Academy of Sciences, Institute of Russian History, Moscow, Archive, VOK archive, f. 4, o. 1, d. 93, "Konspekt 3-kh klassov vvodnykh lektsii po russkoi istorii, Uchilishche Vaianiia i . . . "; d. 94, "Lektsii (4 vechera) o krasote i pom. v drevnei Rusi."

5. Quoted by Aleksandrov and Zimin, "Kommentarii," in VOK, *Kurs*, II (Moscow, 1957), 418.

6. Richard Hellie, *Enserfment and Military Change in Muscovy* (Chicago, 1971), 3–4, 276–77.

7. VOK, "Imperatritsa Ekaterina II, 1796–1896," *Ocherki i rechi*, 336.

8. VOK, "Otmena krepostnogo prava," *Sochineniia v deviati tomakh*, V (Moscow, 1958), 468.

11. THE CHURCH AND THE RELIGIOUS SCHISM

1. VOK, "Drevniaia i novaia Rossiia," *Neopublikovannye*, 358–59.

2. VOK, *Kurs*, III (Moscow, 1958), 91.

3. These papers assume that those outside the Church, none of whom he mentions, would allow their children to receive primary education in an Orthodox school and accept the parish as an administrative unit. He was so completely Russian and Orthodox and lived in such a restricted circle that he did not comprehend those of other faiths. None of his published works, correspondence, or archival material or the information others provide about him contains a reference to Islam or other faiths, even some of ancient provenance such as the Armenian church in the Caucasus, or the non-Russians devoted to these beliefs. He did not mention the Lutherans, other smaller Protestant groups, or the sects that distinguished Russian religious life.

4. VOK, "Otzyv V. Pospelova. Tserkovno-gosudarstvennye otnosheniia russkoi ierarkhii v xiv–xvi vekakh," *Chteniia*, CCXLVIII, Book I, Part II (1914), 94.

5. Fedotov, *The Russian Religious Mind*, II, 186.

6. Russian Academy of Sciences, Institute of Russian History, Moscow, Archive, VOK archive, f. 4, o. 11, d. 26, "Uchastie monastyria v kolonizatsii Severovostochnoi Rossii."

7. VOK, "Sodeistvie tserkvi uspekham russkogo grazhdanskogo prava i poriadka," *Ocherki i rechi*, 114–16; VOK, *Kurs russkoi istorii*, III (Moscow, 1908), 328.

8. VOK, *Kurs*, III (Moscow, 1957), 297.

12. THE AUTOCRACY AND THE AUTOCRATS' POLICIES

1. VOK, "Noveishaia istoriia Zapadnoi Evropy v sviazi s istoriei Rossii," *Neopublikovannye*, 231.
2. VOK, *Kurs*, IV (Moscow, 1958), 214.
3. VOK, "Noveishaia istoriia Zapadnoi Evropy," 231.
4. VOK, *Pis'ma*, 302.
5. VOK, *Kurs*, III (Moscow, 1958), 325–27.
6. VOK, "Drevniaia i novaia Rossiia," *Neopublikovannye*, 358–59.
7. VOK, "Sostav predstavitel'stva na zemskikh soborakh drevnei Rusi. Posviashchastsia B. N. Chicherinu," *Opyty i issledovaniia*, 422, 547; VOK, *Kurs*, VIII (Moscow, 1958), 21.
8. Ibid., IV (Moscow, 1937), 214.
9. Ibid., 145.

13. "TEACHER OF A NATION"

1. An American specialist has termed this essay "the pioneering work in the history of childhood and the family in Russia." Max Okenfuss, "Two Educations," *History of Education Quarterly*, XVII (1977), 417.
2. Philip E. Mosely, "Professor Michael Karpovich," in Hugh McLean, Martin Malia, and George Fischer, eds., *Russian Thought and Politics* (Cambridge, Mass., 1957), 4.
3. Russian Academy of Sciences, Institute of Russian History, Moscow, Archive, VOK archive, f. 4, o. 1, d. 61, 119.
4. Braudel, *L'Identité de la France*, 9.
5. VOK, *Pis'ma*, 356.
6. Ibid., 24.
7. VOK, *Kurs*, I (Moscow, 1956), 17; III (Moscow, 1957), 386.

14. KLIUCHEVSKII AS A NATION-BUILDER

1. Terence J. Emmons, "Kliuchevskii i ego ucheniki," *VI*, No. 10 (1990), 45–61. I am indebted to this essay for many insights.
2. Quoted by Franco Venturi, *Historiens du xx-e siècle* (Geneva, 1966), 185.
3. Nicholas V. Riasanovsky, review of *Otechestvennye istoriki XVIII–XX vv., Sbornik statei, vystuplenii, vospominanii*, by L. V. Cherepnin (Moscow: Nauka, 1984), *Slavic Review*, XLV (1986), 110.
4. Georges Fedotov, "Rossiia Kliuchevskogo," *Sovremennye zapiski* (Paris), I (1932), 340.
5. Boris resided in the family home until the early 1930s, working as an automobile mechanic and a translator of books about automobiles from English and German. In 1918 he signed agreements with the Commission for Preserving Monuments of Art and History and the Commissariat for Enlightenment recognizing state ownership of his father's library, which the Russian National Library later acquired. His parents' friends and their children remained close to him until his arrest in 1933 and internal exile to Alma Alta. Two friends in the late 1930s helped persuade Soviet authorities to allow his return to Moscow, where he died in 1944.

6. Pokrovskii was indignant that the Soviet government had published the "archaic" fifth volume, and some of Kliuchevskii's warmest admirers were distressed. All succeeding Soviet editions have included it, as have the foreign translations.

7. Soviet historians dutifully declared Kliuchevskii one of the most able historical inheritors, and one whom they should study while creating Marxist-Leninist historical science.

8. Other publishing ventures at that time place the significance of this edition in perspective. Between 1959 and 1966, a much less prestigious publisher than the Academy of Sciences produced the first Soviet edition of Soloviev's *History of Russia* in fifteen unannotated volumes, the first two in printings of 8,000 copies and the final thirteen varying from 45,000 to 50,000 copies. The Academy of Sciences between 1957 and 1962 published a collection of the works of Academician Evgenii V. Tarle in twelve volumes in printings that varied between 27,000 and 30,000 copies.

9. Several fine English translations of the Kliuchevskii volumes on the seventeenth century and Peter the Great have been published, in some cases in several editions. English and American journals have produced translations of some of Kliuchevskii's most important essays. In addition, the American Council of Learned Societies published the five volumes in Kliuchevskii's matchless Russian in 1948, when Russian studies began to expand in the United States.

BIBLIOGRAPHICAL ESSAY

This study, the first major one of Kliuchevskii in a language other than Russian, profits from earlier analyses. However, it relies mainly upon examination of Kliuchevskii's publications and those of his teachers, colleagues, and students; the record of his academic career; and his immense archives. The works of the men with whom he studied and whom he taught and other friends and associates and their archival collections were also useful, as were the archives of Moscow University, the Ministry of Education, and the Moscow Police Department.

Kliuchevskii, his colleagues, and his friends were acutely conscious of the central role well-organized libraries and archives play in a nation's culture and of the value of historical records. Because of this awareness, they preserved their professional and personal papers and arranged for their deposit in archives in Moscow and St. Petersburg. Successive generations of librarians and archivists, some of whom they helped inspire and train, organized these materials and prepared guides and inventories. Consequently, archival sources concerning the Kliuchevskii generation are as rich and well-organized as those of that generation in any European country or the United States. They enable the scholar to trace the creation of Kliuchevskii's courses and of his major works from their inception in the masses of notes from archival documents through numerous drafts and revisions, even of page proof, to final publication.

The bulk of Kliuchevskii's archives consists of his research notes, copies of hundreds of documents, outlines of lectures and essays, drafts of publications, lithographed courses, corrected proof sheets, and manuscripts, some of which have been published in the past two decades. He preserved the various lithographed texts of courses he presented in the Third Aleksandrovskoe Military School and the Women's Higher Courses of Professor Ger'e in the 1870s and 1880s. These served as the foundation for the class he presented for thirty years at Moscow University, of which twenty-one versions from the period between 1879 and 1890 survive, some with his marginal annotations. Archives of some students and colleagues also contain copies of these lithographed lectures, as do a number of major libraries in Moscow, St. Petersburg, and several European and American cities.

Kliuchevskii retained many other valuable materials. These include almost a thousand letters he received, those from Penza when he was an undergraduate as well as missives from schoolboys in the countryside who sought copies of his books, former students, and colleagues. He did all writing by hand, so that only letters that associates or officials retained have survived, but even these are numerous because many Russians recognized early that he was a figure of historical importance.

Comments upon student reports and theses, papers concerning appointments and promotions, clippings from newspapers on the Balkan crisis in the 1870s, family photographs, committee reports, and his schedules from the five institutions at which he taught also enrich the observer's understanding. The archives contain quantities of personal information, such as passes to the university, libraries, diaries, account books, and comments on student unrest, the 1904–1906 turmoil, and Church and political affairs.

Finally, draft aphorisms, poems, and short stories are illuminating. In sum, his papers allow one admission to his private life as well as to the "laboratory" from which his work emerged.

Kliuchevskii was a dedicated and immensely successful teacher at a variety of institutions: a high school, a seminary, a special program for women, Russia's outstanding institution for artists, and Moscow University. The classroom and auditorium were only the most visible sites of his instructional work, because he considered public lectures at anniversaries or memorials equally significant educational forums. All the materials on his years of teaching and lecturing are therefore significant.

I have examined carefully the data concerning his years at the Third Aleksandrovskoe Military School and at the Moscow Ecclesiastical Academy, and essays and books he published in the 1870s, before he became famous. Although these materials add considerable insight into his life and work, Russian scholars have neglected them. The evidence from his years of teaching in the Women's Higher Courses of Professor Ger'e also provides important insights into his views. The lithographs of his lectures in the military school and the Ger'e program, some available both in draft and in final form only in archives and others in published form, were immensely valuable. For example, the lithographed lectures he gave on the origins and consequences of the French Revolution at the military school not only illuminated his intellectual development between 1868 and 1883 but revealed much concerning his knowledge and views concerning Russia's relations with the West.

Unfortunately, we lack access to Kliuchevskii's collection of books and journals, in which he wrote comments in the margins. Sometime in the 1920s, his library was transferred to what is now the Russian State Library, which scattered it throughout its vast repositories.

The Manuscript Division of the Russian State Library contains the largest and most valuable collection of Kliuchevskii's papers, 15,000 pages described in an inventory 154 pages long. The materials in the Archives of the Institute of Russian History of the Russian Academy of Sciences in Moscow are almost as valuable. The other most important resources rest in the archives of the Russian Academy of Sciences in Moscow and the library and archives of the St. Petersburg branch of the Institute of Russian History.

The Academy of Sciences archives and the Manuscript Division of the Russian State Library, formerly the Lenin Library, together contain the papers of about forty of Kliuchevskii's colleagues, associates, and students, but the State Historical Museum, the Russian State Historical Archive, the State Russian Archive of Literature and Art, and the State Archive of the Russian Federation (formerly the Central State Archive of the October Revolution) contain others. The last one possesses the papers of the Ministry of Education and some of those of the Moscow Police Department, while the Central State Archive of the City of Moscow contains the remainder from the police department. The archives of Moscow University are divided between the State Archive of the Russian Federation and the Central State Archive of the City of Moscow. The archives of the Penza Seminary were fruitful, but those of the Moscow Ecclesiastical Academy were not. I was not able to locate the papers of the Third Aleksandrovskoe Military School, which may not have been preserved.

No lithographs of Kliuchevskii's lectures at the Ecclesiastical Academy have survived, but his archives, those of his colleagues, and those of the academy together con-

Bibliographical Essay

tain significant information. The academy's annual reports, official documents, and journal, the jubilee volume published in 1914 in honor of its presence in Trinity Monastery, and the record of the 1896 and 1901 celebrations honoring his service supplement student letters and memoirs of students and colleagues. Kliuchevskii's comments on almost 150 undergraduate theses and M.A. exams are also helpful.

Kliuchevskii's high place in Russian culture was evident so early that the institutions with which he was connected, his associates, and students at every level began early to preserve records of their relations with him. The memoir literature concerning his life is extraordinarily plentiful. University colleagues such as Buslaev and Nikolai Davydov left important accounts. Above all, students at every institution at which he studied and taught published recollections of him, sometimes in several different formats. Those whom he taught as undergraduates and then as advanced students at Moscow University and who became significant scholars were especially helpful: few scholars have had as many distinguished students write such detailed and perceptive accounts of a teacher and colleague. The essays by Bogoslovskii, Got'e, Kizevetter, Miliukov, and Liubavskii were especially rich in information and insight. In addition, Liubavskii and Belokurov helped collect and publish important collections of documentary materials on his life and the reminiscences of other students and associates. Another, Nikolai A. Zaozerskii, collected and published the comments Kliuchevskii made on papers by undergraduates and advanced students in the Moscow Ecclesiastical Academy, an unusual but important source.

Especially rewarding were Kliuchevskii's colleagues' papers, especially those of Ger'e, Tikhonravov, and Korelin, on Kliuchevskii as a member of the university community and as a friend. Those of his students were even more rich, especially on Kliuchevskii as a seminar instructor and a guide. Almost all those he helped collected and retained significant materials, but those of Belokurov, Bogoslovskii, Got'e, Kizevetter, and Liubavskii were particularly valuable. Iakovlev, who as a freshman in 1896 attracted his mentor's attention and who continued advanced study with him, left massive amounts of information concerning his teaching, newspaper clippings concerning his death and funeral, and information on Kliuchevskii that had appeared in the Soviet Union before Iakovlev's death in 1951. Iakovlev interested scholars of succeeding generations in his mentor's work, so that their memoirs and scholarly studies also contain valuable information.

Kliuchevskii has stimulated dozens of studies. Except for the two most repressive periods of Stalinist rule, interest in his work has remained consistently high in Russia, never more so than in the years since 1985. This bibliography includes only the most significant of the hundreds of reviews of his work and analyses of his career, but even so it shows that many Russians, Europeans, Americans, and Japanese have examined his publications from a variety of angles. A number of able Soviet scholars produced analyses: those by Cherepnin, Kireeva, Nechkina, and Zimin were especially perceptive. The first forty-six pages of Nechkina's *Vasilii Osipovich Kliuchevskii: istoriia zhizni i tvorchestva* (Moscow, 1974) surveys much of the literature in Russian concerning Kliuchevskii and the major issues with which he dealt. In addition, see the studies by Robert F. Byrnes, "Nechkina's *Kliuchevskii*, Review Article," *Russian Review*, XXXVII (1978), 68–81; Byrnes, "Soviet Historical Views of Kliuchevskii," *Canadian-American Slavic Studies*, XX, No. 3–4 (1986), 437–454; and Riasanovsky, "Kliuchevsky in Recent Soviet Historiography," ibid., 455–466, for assessments of later studies.

Bibliographical Essay

The secondary literature on late imperial Russia and on the institutions and issues important for Kliuchevskii is vast and rich. The bibliography includes all the primary sources but only those secondary studies of most value: for example, it excludes many of the materials and studies useful for the pages on the Penza seminary and the publication of Kliuchevskii's works after 1918.

BIBLIOGRAPHY

PRIMARY SOURCES

A. Books by Kliuchevskii

Aforizmy. Istoricheskie portrety i etiudy. Dnevniki. Moscow, 1993.

Boiarskaia duma drevnei Rusi. Opyt pravitel'stvennogo uchrezhdeniia v sviazi s istoriei obshchestva. Moscow, 1881. Other editions were produced in 1882, 1902, 1909, 1914, and 1919, all in Moscow except for the last one, in Petrograd. A reprint of the fourth edition was published in The Hague in 1965. The original version appeared in a series of articles in *Russkaia mysl'* in 1880–81.

Drevnerusskie zhitiia sviatykh kak istoricheskii istochnik. Moscow, 1871. This was reprinted in Moscow in 1980. Other reprints were produced in The Hague in 1968, in Farnsborough, England, in 1969, and in the German Democratic Republic in 1971.

Istoricheskie portrety. Deiateli istoricheskoi mysli. Moscow, 1990. Ed. Valentin L. Ianin.

Istoriia soslovii v Rossii. Moscow, 1913. A lithographed version appeared in 1887. A second edition of the 1913 volume appeared in 1914 and a third in 1919. It was also published in the sixth volume of the two *Sochineniia*, in 1958 and 1989. A reprint of the 1919 edition was published in Hattiesburg, Mississippi, in 1969.

Kratkoe posobie po russkoi istorii: Chastnoe izdanie tol'ko dlia slushatelei avtora. Moscow, 1899. Eight other editions were published in 1900, 1903, 1905, 1906, 1908, 1909, 1917, and 1992. Kliuchevskii's principal archival collections and Russian, Finnish, and American libraries have copies of this volume's lithographed predecessor, *Posobie dlia prigotovleniia k polukursovomu ispytaniiu po russkoi istorii, sostavleno po kursu russkoi istorii, chitannomu v 1890/91 g. professorom V. O. Kliuchevskim.* Moscow, 1890–91. Later versions appeared in 1895, 1897, and 1900.

Kurs russkoi istorii. 1st ed., vols. 1–4, Moscow, 1904–10; vol. 5, Petrograd, 1922. First Soviet edition, Petrograd, 1918–22; Moscow edition, 1937; Kiev edition, 1938–40, in Ukrainian; Minsk edition, 1938–40, in Belorussian. Moscow edition, 1956–58, first five volumes of *Sochineniia* in eight volumes; Moscow edition, 1986–88, first five volumes of *Sochineniia v deviati tomakh.* The most recent edition, entitled *Russkaia istoriia. Polnyi kurs lektsii v trekh knigakh,* was published in Moscow in 1993. Three unauthorized editions also exist: *Lektsii po russkoi istorii professora Moskovskogo universiteta V. O. Kliuchevskogo* (St. Petersburg, 1902); *Russkaia istoriia* (St. Petersburg, 1907); *Kurs russkoi istorii* (Moscow, 1912–13), in the journal *Narodnoe blago.*

    A. A. Zimin in *Kurs russkoi istorii* (Moscow, 1958), vol. V, 470–72, provides a list of twenty-two lithographed editions of the university lecture course produced between 1879–80 and 1907 that have survived. Many are among Kliuchevskii's papers, but others are in various Moscow and St. Petersburg libraries, especially the Moscow University library. I have found others in the archives of scholars such as Kizevetter and Karpov. In addition, lithographs from the lecture courses on Russian history that Kliuchevskii offered in the 1870s in the Women's Higher Courses of Professor Ger'e are in the Manuscript Division of the Russian State Library. In chronological order, those in this group I found most useful:

Programma chtenii na Lubianskikh kursakh v 1870 g. Ekaterina S. Nekrasova archive, f. 196.

Kurs lektsii 70-kh gg. Kliuchevskii archive, f. 131.

Lektsii V. O. Kliuchevskogo po russkoi istorii, I. Kurs chitannyi na Vysshikh zhenskikh kursakh po ikh otkrytii V. I. Ger'e v 1872 g. Kurs zapisannyi Evdokiei Ivanovnoi Ger'e. Moscow, 1872. Vladimir I. Ger'e archive, f. 70.

Translations, in whole or in part, of *Kurs russkoi istorii:*

Russké dejíny. Prel. Stanislav Minarik, Dil 1–5. Prague, 1927–29.

A History of Russia, by V. O. Kliuchevsky. Translated by C. J. Hogarth. London, 1911–26. 5 vols. Reprinted in 1960.

Peter the Great. Translated by Liliana Archibald. New York, 1958.

The Rise of the Romanovs. Translated by Liliana Archibald, assisted by Mark Scholl. London, 1970.

A Course in Russian History: The Seventeenth Century. Translated by Natalie Duddington. Introduced by Alfred J. Rieber. Chicago, 1968.

Pierre le Grand et son oeuvre. Traduit du russe par H. de Witte. Paris, 1930. Reprinted in 1953.

Histoire de Russie. Traduit du russe et annoté par C. Andronikof. Préface de Pierre Pascal. Vol. I. Paris, 1956.

Venäjän historian pääpürteet. Suomekski tormitataneet T. Kaila ja Jvos I. Mikola. Vol. I. Porvoosa, Finland, 1910.

Geschichte Russlands. Herausgegeben Prof. Dr. Friedrich Braun und Reinhold von Walter. Vols. 1–4. Leipzig and Berlin, 1925–26.

Peter der Grosse und andere Porträts aus der Russischen Geschichte. Ubers. Reinhold von Walter. Leipzig, 1940. Reprinted in 1953.

Russische Geschichte von Peter dem Grossen bis Nikolaus I. Ubers. Waldemar Jolles. Zurich, 1945. 2 vols.

Kurs russkoi istorii. (In Hebrew) Translated by Michael Confino. Tel Aviv, 1968. 3 vols.

Neopublikovannye proizvedeniia. Moscow, 1983.

Ocherki i rechi. Vtoroi sbornik statei. Moscow, 1913. Reprinted in 1918.

Opyty i issledovaniia. Pervyi sbornik statei. Moscow, 1912. 2nd ed., 1915. Reprinted in 1918.

Otzyvy i otvety. Tretii sbornik statei. Moscow, 1914. Reprinted in 1918.

Skazaniia inostrantsev o Moskovskom gosudarstve. Moscow, 1866. The Society for Disseminating Useful Books published a second printing in 1866, and a third edition appeared in Petrograd in 1918.

Sochineniia. Moscow, 1956–59. 8 vols. Academician Mikhail N. Tikhomirov was the general editor of this set, but Zimin and V. A. Aleksandrov completed the thorough editing.

Sochineniia v deviati tomakh. Moscow, 1987–90. 9 vols. Ed. Academician Valentin L. Ianin.

Vseobshchaia istoriia. From 1868 through 1883, Kliuchevskii taught a course on the origins, course, and consequences of the French Revolution, sometimes entitled "A History of European Man," "Europe since the Seventeenth Century," "General History," "Notes on General History," "Recent History," and "The French Revolution." Nineteen lithographed copies of this course have survived in various Russian libraries and archives, especially the Russian National Library in St. Petersburg. Nechkina published one set, that for 1871–72 and 1872–73, in *Novaia i noveishaia istoriia*, No. 5 (1969), 116–21, and No. 6 (1969), 92–102. The original is in the manuscript division of the Russian National Library. In addition, *Neopublikovannye* in 1983, 198–291, published this course as Kliuchevskii presented it to Grand Duke Georgii Aleksandr in 1894–95.

I used most the lithographs for the 1874 and 1875 courses, *Zapiski po vseobshchei istorii* and *Zapiski istorii*, respectively, and those for the years from 1880 through 1883, which he entitled *Noveishaia istoriia*, all in the Russian National Library. I also utilized the course for 1879–80, which he entitled *Evropa nakanune frantsuzskoi revoliutsii*, in the Bogoslovskii archive, f. 442, in the State Historical Museum in Moscow.

B. Other Works by Kliuchevskii

1. HISTORICAL RESEARCH

"Boiarskaia duma drevnei Rusi. Opyt istorii pravitel'stvennogo uchrezhdeniia v sviazi s istoriei obshchestva." *RM*, I, No. 1, Part II (1880), 40–76; I, No. 3, Part II (1880), 45–74; I, No. 4, Part II (1881), 31–37; I, No. 10, Part II (1881), 64–95; I, No. 11, Part II (1881), 126–54; II, No. 3 (1881), 245–72; No. 8 (1881), 184–230; No. 10 (1881), 148–92; II, No. 11 (1881), 80–113.

"Ch'ia zemlia pod gorodskimi riadami na Krasnoi ploshchadi." *RV*, No. 125 (1887).

"Etnograficheskie sledstviia russkoi kolonizatsii verkhnego povolzh'ia. Vliianie prirody verkhnego Povolzh'ia na narodnoe khoziaistvo Velikorossii i na plemennoi kharakter velikorossa." *Istoricheskie portrety*, 40–62.

"Krepostnoi vopros nakanune zakonodatel'nogo ego vozbuzhdeniia." *Kriticheskoe obozrenie*, No. 3 (1879), 1–14. Reprinted in *Otzyvy i otvety*, 297–320; *Sochineniia*, VII, 106–125; *Sochineniia v deviati tomakh*, VIII, 31–49.

"Nabroski po variazhskomu voprosu." *Neopublikovannye*, 113–23. Reprinted in *Sochineniia v deviati tomakh*, VII, 136–148.

"O khlebnoi mere v drevnei Rusi." *Drevnosti*, X (1885), 68–69.

"O peredelakh u krest'ian na severe." Ibid., Book I (1890), 192.

"Otmena krepostnogo prava." *Sochineniia v deviati tomakh*, V, 371–394.

"Podushnaia podat' i otmena kholopstva v Rossii." *RM*, VI, No. 5 (1886), 106–127; No. 7, 1–19; No. 9, 72–87; No. 10, 1–20. Reprinted in *Opyty i issledovaniia*, 311–416; *Sochineniia*, VII, 318–402; *Sochineniia v deviati tomakh*, IX, 194–270.

"Predislovie." *Sbornik Moskovskogo Glavnago Arkhiva Ministerstva Inostrannykh Del*, VII (1900), v–ix.

"Proiskhozhdenie krepostnogo prava v Rossii." *RM*, VI, No. 8 (1885), 1–36; No. 10, 1–46. Reprinted in *Opyty i issledovaniia*, 212–310; *Sochineniia*, VII, 237–317; *Sochineniia v deviati tomakh*, VIII, 120–193.

"Pskovskaia Pravda." *Sochineniia*, VI, 105–128; *Sochineniia v deviati tomakh*, VII, 100–121. Also published as a booklet.

"Russkaia Pravda." *Sochineniia*, VI, 88–104; *Sochineniia v deviati tomakh*, VII, 100–121.

Bibliography

"Russkii rubl' XVI–XVIII v. v ego otnoshenii k nyneshnemu." *Chteniia*, CXXVIII, Book I (1884), 1–72. Reprinted in *Opyty i issledovaniia*, 123–211; *Sochineniia*, VII, 170–236; *Sochineniia v deviati tomakh*, VIII, 59–220.

"Skazaniia inostrantsev o Moskovskom gosudarstve." Predislovie R. Skrynnikova. *Nashe nasledie*, No. 1 (1988), 95–102.

"Smena. Boiarstvo i dvorianstvo." *RM*, XX, No. 1 (1899), 200–221.

"Sostav predstavitel'stva na zemskikh soborakh drevnei Rusi, posviashchaetsia B. N. Chicherinu." *RM*, XI, No. 1 (1890), 141–178; XII, No. 1 (1891), 132–147; XIII, No. 1 (1892), 140–172. Reprinted in *Opyty i issledovaniia*, 417–551; *Sochineniia*, VIII, 5–112; *Sochineniia v deviati tomakh*, VIII, 277–374. Reprinted also as a booklet.

"Zaiavlenie v zasedanii Imperatorskogo moskovskogo arkheologicheskogo obshchestva 21 aprelia 1900 g. o sostavlenii kart." *Drevnosti*, XIX, Book II (1902), 40.

"Zamechanie o grivne kune." Ibid., X, No. 3 (1986), 86.

"Zamechaniia o Sudebnike Tsaria Fedora." *Sudebnik Tsaria Fedora Ivanovicha 1589. Po spisku sobraniia F. F. Mazurina*. Moscow, 1900, xxv–xxxviii.

2. LECTURE COURSES

"Drevniaia i novaia Rossiia." *Neopublikovannye*, 353–361.

"Istochniki russkoi istorii." *Sochineniia v deviati tomakh*, VII, 5–83.

"Istoriia soslovii v Rossii." *Sochineniia*, VI, 276–466; *Sochineniia v deviati tomakh*, VI, 224–391. Also published as a book in 1913, 1914, and 1918.

"Konspekt lektsii kursa istoriografii o Palitsyne, Khvorostinine. 10 oktiabria 1891g." Zimin and Kireeva, eds. "Iz rukopisnogo naslediia V. O. Kliuchevskogo. Novye materialy k kursu po russkoi istoriografii." *Istoriia i istoriki. Istoriograficheskii ezhegodnik, 1972* (Moscow, 1973), 323–325. Reprinted in *Sochineniia v deviati tomakh*, VIII, 166–167.

"Kurs lektsii po istochnikovedeniiu." *Sochineniia*, VI, 5–87; *Sochineniia v deviati tomakh*, VII, 5–83.

"Lektsii po russkoi istoriografii." *Sochineniia*, VIII, 396–452; *Sochineniia v deviati tomakh*, VII, 185–233.

"Metodologiia russkoi istorii. 1884–1885 ak. god." *Sochineniia v deviati tomakh*, VI, 5–93.

"Noveishaia istoriia Zapadnoi Evropy v sviazi s istoriei Rossii." *Neopublikovannye*, 198–291.

"Prikliuchenie k kursu 'Istoriia soslovii v Rossii.' " *Sochineniia v deviati tomakh*, VI, 413–431.

"Prikliuchenie k kursu 'Metodologiia russkoi istorii.' " Ibid., 392–401.

"Prikliuchenie k kursu 'Noveishaia istoriia Zapadnoi Evropy v sviazi s istoriei Rossii.' " *Neopublikovannye*, 366–370.

"Prikliuchenie k kursu 'Terminologiia russkoi istorii.' " *Sochineniia v deviati tomakh*, VI, 401–413.

"Prikliuchenie k kursu 'Zapadnoe vliianie v Rossii posle Petra.' " *Neopublikovannye*, 349–359.

"Prikliuchenie k razdelu, 'Istochnikovedenie. Spetsial'noe izuchenie otdelov 1891, sent. 12. Istochniki.' (*Kurs* 1894 g.)." *Sochineniia v deviati tomakh*, VII, 401–407.

"Prilozhenie k kursu 'Metodologiia russkoi istorii.' " Ibid., VI, 392–401.

"Prilozhenie k razdelu, 'Istoriograficheskie etiudy.' " *Neopublikovannye*, 364–366.

"Prilozhenie k razdelu 'Istoriografiia.' " *Sochineniia v deviati tomakh*, VII, 408–430.

"Russkaia istoriografiia, 1861–1893 gg." *Neopublikovannye*, 180–186; *Sochineniia v deviati tomakh*, VII, 381–388; *Istoricheskie portrety*, 551–558.

3. HISTORIOGRAPHY

"K. N. Bestuzhev-Riumin." *Neopublikovannye*, 153–168. Reprinted in *Sochineniia v deviati tomakh*, VII, 352–370.

"I. N. Boltin (+6-go oktiabria 1792 g.)." *RM*, XIII, No. 11 (1892), 107–130. Reprinted in *Ocherki i rechi*, 163–198; *Kurs* (Moscow, 1937), V, 456–488; *Sochineniia*, VIII, 133–163; *Sochineniia v deviati tomakh*, VI, 234–261; *Istoricheskie portrety*, 447–475.

"Dvadtsatipiatiletie istorii Rossii S. M. Solov'eva." *Drevniaia i novaia Rossiia*, I (1877), 107–113.

"D. I. Ilovaiskii i I. E. Zabelin." *Neopublikovannye*, 117. Reprinted in *Sochineniia v deviati tomakh*, VII, 379.

"N. M. Karamzin." Ibid., 133–137; *Sochineniia v deviati tomakh*, VII, 274–279; *Istoricheskie portrety*, 488–490.

"N. I. Kostomarov." Ibid., 177–178. Reprinted in *Sochineniia v deviati tomakh*, VII, 379–380.

"O trudakh imperatritsy Ekateriny II po russkoi istorii." *Chteniia*, CLXXXIV, Book II (1897), 137.

"Obzor istoriografii o tsarstvovanii Ivana Groznogo. Istoriografiia Smutnogo Vremeni." Zimin and Kireeva, "Iz rukopisnogo naslediia V. O. Kliuchevskogo. Novye materialy k kursu po russkoi istoriografii." *Istoriia i istoriki. Istoriograficheskii ezhegodnik, 1972* (Moscow, 1973), 311–322. Reprinted in *Sochineniia v deviati tomakh*, VII, 149–165.

"Pamiati I. N. Boltina," *RM*, XIII, No. 11 (1892), 107–130. Reprinted in *Sochineniia*, VIII, 164–176; *Sochineniia v deviati tomakh*, VII, 262–273; *Istoricheskie portrety*, 476–487.

"Pamiati T. N. Granovskogo, umer 4-go oktiabria 1855 g." *RV*, XLIII, No. 263 (October 8, 1905). Reprinted in *Sochineniia*, VIII, 390–395; *Sochineniia v deviati tomakh*, VII, 298–302; *Istoricheskie portrety*, 491–495.

"M. P. Pogodin." *Neopublikovannye*, 138–152. Reprinted in *Sochineniia v deviati tomakh*, VII, 280–297.

"V. N. Tatishchev." Ibid., 124–129. Reprinted in *Sochineniia v deviati tomakh*, VII, 178–184.

"Terminologiia russkoi istorii." *Sochineniia*, VI, 129–175; *Sochineniia v deviati tomakh*, VI, 94–224.

"I. Timofeev, Kniaz' Khvorostinin i A. Palitsyn." Zimin and Kireeva, "Iz rukopisnogo naslediia V. O. Kliuchevskogo," *Istoriia i istoriki. Istoriograficheskii ezhegodnik, 1972* (Moscow, 1973), 326–336. Reprinted in *Sochineniia v deviati tomakh*, VII, 166–177.

"I. E. Zabelin." *Neopublikovannye*, 170–177. Reprinted in *Sochineniia v deviati tomakh*, VII, 371–378.

4. ON RELIGION AND THE CHURCH

"Alliluiia i otets Pafnutii." *Sovremennye izvestiia*, No. 75 (March 17, 1872). Reprinted in *Otzyvy i otvety*, 209–215.

Bibliography

"Dobrye liudi drevnei Rusi." *BV*, IV, No. 1 (1892), 77–96. Reprinted in *Ocherki i rechi*, 140–162, in *Istoricheskie portrety*, 77–94, and in *Iasnaia Poliana*, No. 4 (1991), 187–199. Reprinted many times in large editions as a booklet.

"Grecheskaia tserkov' v Londone v pervoi polovine XVIII v." *PO*, III, No. 1 (1871), 43–62.

"Khoziaistvennaia deiatel'nost' Solovetskogo monastyria v Belomorskom krae." *Moskovskie universitetskie izvestiia*, No. 7 (1866–67), 541–574. Reprinted in *Opyty i issledovaniia*, 1–36; *Sochineniia*, VII, 5–32; *Sochineniia v deviati tomakh*, VIII, 5–35.

"Novootkrytyi pamiatnik po istorii raskola." *BV*, VIII, No. 7 (1896), 490–499.

"O prosvetitel'noi roli Sv. Stefana Permskogo." *Chteniia*, CLXXXV, Book II (1898), 14.

"Obraztsovye pisateli russkikh zhitii v XV veke." *PO*, II, No. 8 (1870), 178–210; No. 9, 328–353; No. 10, 479–503.

"Pis'mo frantsuzhenki." *Neopublikovannye*, 326–333.

"Predislovie, Inok German, *Zhitie prepodobnogo Filippa Iranskogo*." Obshchestvo liubitelei drevnei pis'mennosti, *Pamiatniki drevnei pis'mennosti*, XLVI (1879), x–xliv. Reprinted as a booklet.

"Predislovie, *Skazaniia o chudesakh Vladimirskoi ikony Boshiei materi*." Ibid., XXX (1879), 114–117. Reprinted as a booklet.

"Pskovskie spory." *PO*, IV, No. 9 (1872), 382–307; No. 10, 466–491; No. 12, 711–741. Reprinted in *Opyty i issledovaniia*, 37–122; *Sochineniia v deviati tomakh*, VIII, 33–105.

"Russkaia tserkovno-istoricheskaia literatura." *PO*, III, No. 9 (1871), 328–340; No. 11, 709–728.

"Sodeistvie tserkvi uspekham russkogo grazhdanskogo prava i poriadka." *Tvoreniia sviatykh ottsov*, IV (1888), 382–412. Reprinted in *Ocherki i rechi*, 90–116, in *Moskva*, No. 6 (1992), 152–161, and as a booklet.

"Tserkov' po otnosheniiu k umstvennomu razvitiiu drevnei Rusi. Rets. na sochinenie A. Shchapova, *Sotsial'no-pedagogicheskie usloviia umstvennogo razvitiia russkogo naroda*. *PO*, II, No. 2 (1870), 307–337. Reprinted in *Otzyvy i otvety*, 133–169.

"Velikiia Minei Chetii." *Moskva*, No. 90 (June 20, 1868). Reprinted in *Otzyvy i otvety*, 1–19.

"Verovanie i myshlenie." *Neopublikovannye*, 308–309.

"Znachenie prepodobnogo Sergiia dlia russkogo naroda i gosudarstva." *Troitskii tsvetok*, No. 9 (1892), 1–32. Reprinted in *BV*, IV, No. 11 (1892), 190–204; *Ocherki i rechi*, 199–215; *Istoricheskie portrety*, 63–76; A. P. Rogovich, *Prepodobnyi Sergei Radonezhskii* (Berlin, 1922), 29–47; *Russkii arkhiv*, No. 1 (1990), 75–85; *Khudozhnik*, No. 7 (1992), 7–13. Also published on many occasions and in several countries as a booklet, sometimes entitled *Blagodatnyi vospitatel' russkogo narodnogo dukha*. Translated, "St. Sergius: The Importance of His Life and Work," *Russian Review* (England), II, No. 3 (1913), 45–59.

5. ON RUSSIAN CULTURAL LEADERS

"I. S. Aksakov." *Neopublikovannye*, 317–318.

"A. P. Chekhov." Ibid., 323–324.

"F. M. Dostoevskii." Ibid., 320–323.

"Evgenii Onegin i ego predki." *RM*, VIII, No. 2 (1887), 291–306. Reprinted in *Ocherki i rechi*, 67–89; *Kurs* (Moscow, 1937), V, 315–335; *Sochineniia*, VII, 403–422; *Isto-*

richeskie portrety, 408–426; *Rossiia i Pushkin. Sbornik statei, 1837–1937* (Kharbin, 1937), 125–139. Translated by Marshall S. Shatz, "Eugene Onegin and His Ancestors," *Canadian-American Slavic Studies,* XVI (1982), 227–246.
"Nedorosl' Fonvizina. Opyt istoricheskogo ob"iasneniia uchebnoi p'esy." *Iskusstvo i nauka,* No. 1 (1896), 5–26. Reprinted in *Ocherki i rechi,* 283–311; *Kurs* (Moscow, 1937), V, 489–514; *Sochineniia,* VIII, 263–287; *Sochineniia v deviati tomakh,* IX, 55–77; *Istoricheskie portrety,* 341–363.
"N. V. Gogol'." *Neopublikovannye,* 312–315.
"I. A. Goncharov." Ibid., 319–320.
"Grust'. (Pamiati M. Iu. Lermontova, umer 15 iiulia 1841 g.)." *RM,* XII, No. 7 (1891), 1–18. Reprinted in *Ocherki i rechi,* 117–139; *Sochineniia,* VIII, 113–132; *Istoricheskie portrety,* 427–444.
"K Kislovodsku. (Podrazhanie Pushkinu)." *Neopublikovannye,* 333–336.
"M. Iu. Lermontov." Ibid., 311–312.
"Ob intelligentsii." Ibid., 298–308.
"Pamiati A. S. Pushkina." *Sochineniia,* VIII, 306–313; *Sochineniia v deviati tomakh,* IX, 101–108; *Istoricheskie portrety,* 400–407.
"Rech', proiznesennaia v torzhestvennom sobranii Moskovskogo universiteta 6-go iiunia 1880 g. v den' otkrytiia pamiatnika Pushkinu." *RM,* I, No. 6 (1880), 20–27. Reprinted in *Venok na pamiatnik Pushkinu* (St. Petersburg, 1880), 271–278; *Ocherki i rechi,* 57–66; *Sochineniia,* VII, 145–152; *Sochineniia v deviati tomakh,* IX, 77–84; *Istoricheskie portrety,* 392–399.
"Vospominaniia o N. I. Novikove i ego vremeni." *RM,* XVI, No. 1 (1895), 38–60. Reprinted in *Ocherki i rechi,* 248–282; *Kurs* (Moscow, 1937), V, 424–455; *Sochineniia,* VIII, 223–252; *Sochineniia v deviati tomakh,* IX, 28–55; *Istoricheskie portrety,* 364–391.

6. ON RELATIONS WITH THE WEST

"Zapadnoe vliianie v Rossii posle Petra." *Neopublikovannye,* 11–112. Also published as a booklet. Translated by Marshall Shatz, "Western Influence in Russia after Peter the Great," *Canadian-American Slavic Studies,* XX, No. 3–4 (1986), 467–484; XXIV, No. 4 (1990), 431–454.
"Zapadnoe vliianie v Rossii XVII v. Istoriko-psikhologicheskii ocherk." *Voprosy filosofii i psikhologii,* No. 36 (1897), 137–155; No. 38, 535–558; No. 39, 760–800. Reprinted in *Ocherki i rechi,* 386–470. Also published as a booklet.

7. THESIS DEFENSES

"Disput M. M. Bogoslovskogo." *IV,* XCI (1903), 382–383.
"Disput V. E. Iakushkina." *Istoricheskoe obozrenie,* I (1890), 300–301.
"Disput A. A. Kizevettera." *RV,* No. 349 (December 20, 1903); No. 350 (December 21, 1903).
"Disput M. K. Liubavskogo." Ibid., No. 146 (May 29, 1901).
"Disput N. A. Rozhkova." Ibid., No. 139 (May 20, 1900).
"Doktorskii disput g. Subbotina v Moskovskoi dukhovnoi akademii." *PO,* VI, No. 5 (1874), 327–337. Reprinted in *Otzyvy i otvety,* 260–278.
"Mnenie dotsenta Vasiliia Kliuchevskogo po povodu *otzyva sostavlennogo komissiei isto-*

richeskogo otdeleniia Akademii o dissertatsii prof. Kazanskogo." *Chteniia,* CCXLVIII, Book I, Part II (1914), 80–82.

"Mnenie o sochinenii ekstraordinarnogo professora Golubinskogo *Istoriia russkoi tserkvi*" (Tom I-yi polovina I-ia). Ibid., 82–84.

"Otzyv Nikolaia Kedrova, *Dukhovnyi reglament v sviazi s preobrazovatel'noiu deiatel'nost'iu Petra Velikogo.*" Ibid., 108–109.

"Otzyv o dissertatsii N. N. Firsova, *Russkie torgovo-promyshlennye kompanii v I-uiu polovinu XVIII stoletiia.*" *RV,* No. 143 (May 16, 1897).

"Otzyv ob issledovanii P. N. Miliukova, *Gosudarstvennoe khoziaistvo Rossii v pervuiu chetvert' XVIII v. i reforma Petra Velikogo.*" *Sochineniia,* VIII, 177–183.

"Otzyv o sochinenii M. I. Gorchakova, *O zemel'nykh vladeniiakh Vserossiiskikh mitropolitov, patriarkhov i Sv. Sinoda.*" *Izvestiia Akademii nauk,* XXI, No. 1 (1872), 130–134. Reprinted in *Otzyvy i otvety,* 170–208.

"Otzyv o sochinenii professora Moskovskoi dukhovnoi akademii N. F. Kaptereva, *Snoshenie Ierusalimskogo patriarkha Dosifeia s russkim pravitel'stvom, 1669–1707,* Moscow, 1891." *Zhurnaly soveta Moskovskoi dukhovnoi akademii za 1891 g.* (1892), 362–367.

"Otzyv o sochinenii N. A. Rozhkova, *Sel'skoe khoziaistvo Moskovskoi Rusi v XVI veke.*" *Otchet o sorok chetvertom prisuzhdenii nagrad gr. Uvarova* (St. Petersburg, 1904), 19–37. Reprinted in *Otzyvy i otvety,* 455–481; *Sochineniia,* VIII, 368–389.

"Otzyv ob issledovanii V. I. Semevskogo, *Krest'ianskii vopros v Rossii v XVII i pervoi polovine XIX v.*" *Sochineniia,* VII, 423–428; *Sochineniia v deviati tomakh,* VIII, 271–276.

"Otzyv ob otchete professorskogo stipendiata S. I. Smirnova ob ego zaniatiiakh v techenie 1895–1896 uchebnogo goda." *Zhurnaly Soveta Moskovskoi dukhovnoi akademii za 1896 g.* (1898), 380.

8. REVIEWS

"Th. von Bernhardi, *Geschichte Russlands und der europäischen Politik in den Jahren 1814–1831.*" *Historische Zeitschrift,* XXXVI (1876), 648–670. Reprinted in *Otzyvy i otvety,* Supplement, 1–25.

"Kriticheskoe obozrenie. *Istoriia Moskovskoi dukhovnoi akademii do eia preobrazovaniia, 1814–1870 gg.* S. Smirnova, M. 1879 g." *PO,* XI, No. 4 (1879), 802–825. Reprinted in *Otzyvy i otvety,* 321–347.

"Novyi trud po tserkovnomu pravu. Rets. na sochinenie N. Suvorova, *O tserkovnykh nakazaniiakh. Opyt issledovaniia po tserkovnomu pravu.*" *PO,* IX, No. 5 (1877), 173–182. Reprinted in *Otzyvy i otvety,* 285–296.

"Novye issledovaniia po istorii drevnerusskikh monastyrei." *PO,* II, No. 10 and 12 (1869). Reprinted in *Otzyvy i otvety,* 20–84.

"Ob"iasnenie po povodu odnoi retsenzii. Otvet Vladimirskomu—Budanova." *RM,* II, No. 2 (1881). Reprinted in *Otzyvy i otvety,* 377–387.

"*Ocherk istorii russkogo naroda do XVII stoletiia. Obshchinnyi byt drevnei Rusi.* D. D. Sontsova, Moscow, 1875." *Uchebnovospitatel'naia biblioteka,* I, Part II (1876), 92–100. Reprinted in *Otzyvy i otvety,* 279–284.

"Otvet D. I. Ilovaiskomu." *Sochineniia,* VII, 163–169.

"Otzyv Nikolaia Kedrova, *Dukhovnyi reglament v sviazi s preobrazovatel'noiu deiatel'nost'iu Petra Velikogo.*" *Chteniia,* CCXLVIII, Book I, Part II (1914), 108–109.

"Otzyv o knige S. Smirnova, *Istoriia Moskovskoi dukhovnoi akademii do eia preobra-*

ʒovaniia, 1814–1870 g., M, 1879 g." *PO*, XII, No. 4 (1879). Reprinted in *Otʒyvy i otvety*, 321–347.

"Otzyv ob issledovanii S. F. Platonova, *Drevnerusskie skaʒaniia i povesti o Smutnom vremeni XVII veka kak istoricheskii istochnik*, St. P., 1888." *Otchet o 31-m prisuʒhdenii nagrad gr. Uvarova* (St. Petersburg, 1890), 55–66. Reprinted in *Otʒyvy i otvety*, 388–405; *Sochineniia*, VII, 439–453; *Sochineniia v deviati tomakh*, VII, 122–135.

"Po povodu stat'i D. Golokhvostova, 'Istoricheskoe znachenie slova 'kormlenii.' " *Russkii arkhiv*, No. 5 (1889), 135–145. Reprinted in *Sochineniia*, VII, 429–438.

"Popravki k odnoi antikritike (V. S. Ikonnikovu)." *PO*, II, No. 4 (1870), 124–141. Reprinted in *Otʒyvy i otvety*, 84–105.

"Pravo i fakt v istorii krest'ianskogo voprosa. Pis'mo k redaktoru." *Rus'*, No. 28 (May 23, 1881), 14–17. Reprinted in *Otʒyvy i otvety*, 365–376; *Sochineniia*, VII, 153–162; *Sochineniia v deviati tomakh*, VIII, 51–58.

"G. Rambo, istorik Rossii." *Kriticheskoe oboʒrenie*, No. 80 (1879), 1–10. Reprinted in *Otʒyvy i otvety*, 348–364.

"Razbor issledovanii N. D. Chechulina, *Goroda Moskovskogo gosudarstva v XVII veke.*" *Otchet o tridtsat' tret'em prisuʒhdenii nagrad gr. Uvarova* (St. Petersburg, 1892), 276–315. Reprinted in *Otʒyvy i otvety*, 406–454; *Sochineniia*, VIII, 184–222. Also published as a booklet.

"Razbor sochineniia M. I. Gorchakova, *O ʒemel'nykh vladeniiakh vserossiiskikh mitropolitov, patriarkhov i Sv. Sinoda, 998–1738 gg.*, *Otchet o 15-m prisuʒhdenii nagrad gr. Uvarova*, St. Petersburg." *PO*, III (1871), 209–211. Reprinted in *Otʒyvy i otvety*, 216–259. Also published as a booklet.

"Vozrazheniia I. A. Linnichenko na ego doklad, 'Desiatinnaia organizatsiia naroda v drevnei Rusi.' " *Drevnosti*, XVII (1900), 70–72.

9. LETTERS AND REMINISCENCES

"Avtobiografiia." *Neopublikovannye*, 342–348.

"Dnevnik zasedanii III Arkheologicheskogo s"ezda v Kieve, 1874g." *Pis'ma*, 249–257.

"Iz proshlogo." *Biulleteni literatury i ʒhiʒni*, XXI (1913), 934–940.

"G. F. Karpov." *Chteniia*, CLX, Book I, Protokoly (1892), 41–45.

"M. S. Korelin. 3 ianvaria 1899." *Voprosy filosofii i psikhologii*, No. 1–2 (1899), viii–xix.

"O F. I. Buslaeve kak o prepodavatele i issledovatele." *Chteniia*, CLXXXV, Book II, Protokoly (1898), 51–53. Reprinted in *Sochineniia*, VIII, 288–294; *Sochineniia v deviati tomakh*, VII, 345–357; *Istoricheskie portrety*, 544–550; Iurii N. Emel'ianov, ed., *Moskovskii universitet v vospominaniiakh sovremennikov, 1755–1917* (Moscow, 1989), 223–229.

"Aleksei Nikolaevich Olenin (1893 g.)." *Neopublikovannye*, 130–132.

"Pamiati G. V. Iollosa." *RV*, XLIV, No. 61 (March 16, 1907).

"Pamiati S. M. Solov'eva, umer 4 oktiabria 1879 g." *Nauchnoe slovo*, No. 8 (1904), 117–132. Reprinted in *Ocherki i rechi*, 36–56; *Sochineniia*, VIII, 351–367; *Sochineniia v deviati tomakh*, VII, 329–344.

"Aleksei Stepanovich Pavlov." *Chteniia*, CLXXXIX, Book II (1898), Smes', 16.

Pis'ma. Dnevniki. Aforiʒmy i mysli ob istorii. Moscow, 1968.

"Pis'ma, otnosiashchiesia k epokhe proiskhozhdeniia universitetskogo kursa, 1861–1863 gg." *Golos minuvshago*, No. 5 (1913), 226–233.

"Predislovie." *Sochineniia S. V. Usova* (Moscow, 1892), v–vii.

"Rech' pamiati A. S. Usova." *Drevnosti*, XI, No. 3 (1887), xii–xvii. Reprinted also as a booklet.

"Rech', proiznesennaia posle pokhoron A. N. Zertsalova." *Neopublikovannye*, 137–138.

"Rukopisnaia biblioteka V. M. Undol'skogo." *PO*, II, No. 5 (1870), 872–894. Reprinted in *Otzyvy i otvety*, 106–132.

"Russkii istorik-iurist nedavnego proshlogo." *Neopublikovannye*, 168–170.

"S. M. Solov'ev." *Kriticheskoe obozrenie*, No. 20 (1879), 37–40.

"S. M. Solov'ev (umer 4 oktiabria 1879)." *Rechi i otcheti, chitannye v torzhestvennom sobranii Imp. Moskovskogo universiteta 12 ianvaria 1880 g.* (Moscow, 1880), 51–73. Reprinted in *Ocherki i rechi*, 1–23; *Sochineniia*, VII, 126–144; *Sochineniia v deviati tomakh*, VII, 303–319; *Istoricheskie portrety*, 496–514. Also published as a booklet.

"S. M. Solov'ev kak prepodavatel'." *Izdaniia istoricheskogo obshchestva pri Imperatorskom Moskovskom universitete*, I (1896), 184–194. Reprinted in *Vospominaniia o studencheskoi zhizni* (Moscow, 1899), 3–26; *Ocherki i rechi*, 24–35; *Sochineniia*, VIII, 253–262; *Sochineniia v deviati tomakh*, VII, 321–328; Emel'ianov, *Moskovskii universitet v vospominaniiakh sovremennikov*, 351–359; *Vysshee obrazovanie v Rossii*, No. 6 (1992), 116–123.

"Vospominaniia P. S. Kazanskogo ob A. V. Gorskom." *BV*, X, No. 11 (1900), 544–560.

"Vospominaniia o D. V. Maslovskom." *Chteniia*, CLXXIII, Book II, Smes' (1895), 26–27.

"Vospominaniia o N. S. Tikhonravove." *Vestnik Evropy* (March 1897), 218–224. Reprinted in *Sochinenie N. S. Tikhonravova* (Moscow, 1898), I, lxxxiii–lxxxix.

10. ANNIVERSARIES

"Iubilei Obshchestva istorii i drevnostei rossiiskikh." *Neopublikovannye*, 187–196; reprinted in *Sochineniia v deviati tomakh*, VII, 389–400; *Istoricheskie portrety*, 559–570.

"Nabrosok rechi, posviashchennoi 150-letiiu Moskovskogo universiteta." *Neopublikovannye*, 196–197.

"Rech' pri otkrytii zasedaniia v pamiat' P. I. Shafarika." *Chteniia*, CLXXIX, Book IV, Smes' (1896), 25–27.

"Rech' pri zakrytii (vysshikh zhenskikh kursov)." *Neopublikovannye*, 178–180.

11. ON ARTISTIC THEMES

"Dva vospitaniia." *RM*, XIV, No. 3 (1893), 88–99. Reprinted in *V pol'zu voskresnykh shkol* (Moscow, 1894), 36–64, in *Ocherki i rechi*, 216–247, and in *Prepodavanie istorii v shkole*, No. 1 (1991), 24–43. Translated by Max J. Okenfuss, "Two Educations," *History of Education Quarterly*, XVII, No. 4 (1977), 419–447.

"Iskusstvo i moral'." *Neopublikovannye*, 309–310.

"Kharakteristiki obshchestvennykh tipov." Ibid., 292–295.

"Nabrosok rechi, posviashchennoi 150-letiiu Moskovskogo universiteta." *Neopublikovannye*, 196–197.

"Neokonchennaia skazka pro Vanichku Dokhlogo i Pet'ku Golovana." Ibid., 336–337.

"Nerastorzhima sviaz' vremeni." *Zhurnalist*, No. 2 (1988), 104–105.

"O vzgliade khudozhnika na obstanovku i ubor izobrazhaemogo im litsa." *Sochineniia*, VIII, 295–305; *Istoricheskie portrety*, 29–39.

"Prikliuchenie s avantiuristkoi." *Neopublikovannye*, 337–339.

Bibliography

"Razroznennye aforizmy, 1889–1899 gg." *Sochineniia v deviati tomakh*, IX, 406–446.
"Stikhotvoreniia i proza." *Neopublikovannye*, 324–326.
"Vechernie chteniia v Abastumane." *Neopublikovannye*, 296–298.
"Zabytym byt' ne mozhem. Sebe i liudiam." *Nedelia* (September 23–29, 1962). Reprinted in Gosudarstvennaia publichnaia istoricheskaia biblioteka, *Izvestiia* (Moscow, 1963), 135–141.
"Zadachi nauchnoi populiarizatsii." *Nauchnoe slovo*, No. 1 (1903), 1–12.
"Zakholustnye melodii." *Neopublikovannye*, 339–342.

12. PORTRAITS

"Drevniaia i novaia Rossiia." *Neopublikovannye*, 355–364.
"Imperatritsa Ekaterina II." *Istoricheskie portrety*, 255–281.
"Imperatritsa Ekaterina II, 1796–1896." *RM*, XVII, No. 11 (1896), 130–177. Reprinted in *Ocherki i rechi*, 312–385; *Kurs* (Moscow, 1937), V, 357–423; *Sochineniia*, V, 309–371; *Sochineniia v deviati tomakh*, V, 282–339; *Istoricheskie portrety*, 282–340.
"Kharakteristika tsaria Ivana Groznogo." *Istoricheskie portrety*, 95–106. Published many times as a booklet.
"Kn. V. V. Golitsyn—Podgotovka i programmy reformy." *Istoricheskie portrety*, 139–150.
"Moskva i eia kniaz'ia udel'nogo veka." *Zhurnal dlia vsekh*, No. 1 (1905), 34–38.
"Novaia Rossiia i prolog eia istorii." *RM*, XXVIII, No. 1 (1907), 1–18.
"A. L. Ordin-Nashchokin, Moskovskii gosudarstvennyi chelovek XVII veka." *Nauchnoe slovo*, No. 3 (1904), 121–138. Reprinted in *Istoricheskie portrety*, 121–138.
"Pamiati v Boze pochivshego Gosudaria Imperatora Aleksandra III." *Chteniia*, CLXXI, Book IV (1894), 1–7.
"Perevorot 25 iiunia 1761 g." *Istoricheskie portrety*, 245–254.
"Petr Velikii, ego naruzhnost', privychki, obraz zhizni i mysli, kharakter." Ibid., 174–192.
"Petr Velikii sredi svoikh sotrudnikov." *Zhurnal dlia vsekh*, No. 1 (1901), 54–72; No. 3, 321–334; No. 4, 446–454. Reprinted in *Ocherki i rechi*, 471–514; *Sochineniia*, VIII, 314–350; *Sochineniia v deviati tomakh*, VIII, 375–408; *Istoricheskie portrety*, 193–227; and several times as a booklet.
"Russkoe gosudarstvo okolo poloviny XVIII v . . . Imperatritsa Elizaveta—Imperator Petr II." *Istoricheskie portrety*, 228–244.
"Russkoe obshchestvo v minutu smerti Petra Velikogo." *RM*, XXX, No. 1 (1909), 1–24. Reprinted also as a pamphlet.
"Tsar' Aleksei Mikhailovich—F. M. Rtishchev." *Istoricheskie portrety*, 107–120.
"Zhizn' Petra Velikogo do nachala severnoi voiny." Ibid., 151–174.
"Znachenie Petra I. (Komment. Iu. Vorob'eva)." *Znanie—sila*, No. 1 (1989), 66–71.

C. Memoirs

1. ON PENZA

Anon. "V. O. Kliuchevskii. Rodilsia 16 ianv. 1841 + 12 maia 1911." *BV*, No. 5 (1911), 5–24.

————. "V. O. Kliuchevskii v dukhovnoi akademii. Po lichnym vospominaniiam." *Russkoe slovo* (May 13, 1911).

Artobolevskii, Father I. A. "K biografii V. O. Kliuchevskogo. Kliuchevskii do universiteta." *Golos minuvshago*, No. 5 (1911), 158–173.

Burlutskii, I. "Protoierei Andrei Lukich Ovsov." *Penʒenskie eparkhial'nye vedomosti*, No. 3 (1870), 76–86; No. 4, 103–117.

Gromoglasov, Il'ia M. "Vospominaniia o Kliuchevskom." *Russkoe slovo* (May 13, 14 [26, 27], 1911).

Malovskii, Protoierei Vasilii. "Vospominaniia o V. O. Kliuchevskom, 1856–1861." *Chteniia*, CCXLVIII, Book I, Part III (1914), 419–422.

Rozhdestvenskii, Father Aleksei. "Vospominaniia o V. O. Kliuchevskom." Ibid., 422–434.

Satserdotov, M. I. "Iz proshlogo Penzenskoi eparkhii." *IV*, LXXXVI (1901), 654–667.

Sektorov, Father Petr. "Vospominaniia o vysokopreosviashchennom Varlaame, byvshem arkhiepiskope Penzenskom, s 1855 g. po 1862." *Penʒenskie eparkhial'nye vedomosti*, No. 20 (1881), 11–20.

Selivanov, Aleksei F. "V. O. Kliuchevskii." *Penʒenskie gubernskie vedomosti* (November 27, 1900).

————. "Vasilii Osipovich Kliuchevskii." *Pamiatnaia kniʒhka Penʒenskoi gubernii na 1889* (Penza, 1888), 423–424.

Stolypin, D. A. "Sviashchennik Aleksandr Afanas'evich Stolypin. Nekrolog." *Penʒenskie eparkhial'nye vedomosti*, No. 24 (1894), 1107–1112.

Troitskii, Aleksandr I. *Istoricheskaia ʒapiska o Penʒenskoi dukhovnoi seminarii ʒa istekshii poslednii period ee sushchestvovaniia.* Penza, 1901.

Virginskaia, Elizaveta O. "Vospominaniia o V. O. Kliuchevskom, 1856–1861." *Chteniia*, CCXLVIII, Book I, Part III (1914), 419–429.

Voznesenskii, S. "Pamiati Vasiliia Osipovicha Kliuchevskogo." *Russkoe slovo*, No. 9 (1911), 126–138.

2. ON THE MOSCOW ECCLESIASTICAL ACADEMY

Belov, Aleksei M. "V. O. Kliuchevskii kak lektor. Iz vospominanii ego slushatelia." *IV*, CXXIV, No. 6 (1911), 986–990.

Beskii, N. "V. O. Kliuchevskii v dukhovnoi akademii." *Russkoe slovo* (May 13 [26], 1911).

Bogorodskii, Nikolai N. "Vasilii Osipovich Kliuchevskii. Vospominaniia slushatelia." *Polotsko-Vitebskaia starina*, Book I (1911), 1–12.

Fedorov, Ivan. "Pamiati professora-istorika." *Smolenskii vestnik* (May 15, 1911).

Golubtsova, Mariia A. "Vospominaniia o V. O. Kliuchevskom." *U Troitsy v Akademii, 1814–1914. Iubileinyi sbornik istoricheskikh materialov* (Moscow, 1914), 670–682. Reprinted in *Moskovskii ʒhurnal*, No. 11 (1991), 3–7.

————. *Zapiski, dnevnik, vospominaniia, pis'ma.* Moscow, 1929.

Gorskii, Father A. V. *Dnevnik A. V. Gorskogo.* Moscow, 1885.

————. "Iz arkhiva A. V. Gorskogo. I. Epizod iz istorii opisaniia slavianskikh rukopisei Moskovskoi Sinodal'noi Biblioteki." *BV*, X, No. 11 (1900), 475–515.

Iakhontov, Stepan D. "Pamiati V. O. Kliuchevskogo." *Trudy Riaʒanskoi uchenoi arkhivnoi komissii*, XXV (1911), 75–79.

Kabanov, Andrei K., and N. M. Likin. *Pamiati professora V. O. Kliuchevskogo +12 maia 1911 g. Sbornik statei.* Nizhnii Novgorod, 1911.

Kolosov, Nikolai A. "Professor V. O. Kliuchevskii. Kratkii nekrolog i lichnye vospominaniia." *Dushepoleznoe chtenie,* No. 2, 7–8 (1911), 304–316.

Moskovskaia dukhovnaia akademiia. *Otchet o sostoianii Moskovskoi dukhovnoi akademii v kontse 1869–1870 g. i v techenie 1870–1871 uchebnogo goda.* Moscow, 1972.

Nuretov, Mitrofan D. "Iz vospominanii studenta Moskovskoi dukhovnoi akademii XXXII kursa (1873–1877 g.)." *BV,* III, No. 10–11 (1914), 646–676; III, No. 10–12 (1915), 700–784; III, No. 10–12 (1916), 582–612.

Rezun D. Ia. "V. O. Kliuchevskii kak prepodavatel'." *Prepodavanie istorii v shkole,* No. 4 (1972), 15–28.

Rudakov, Vasilii E. "Pamiati V. O. Kliuchevskogo." *IV,* CXXIV, No. 6 (1911), 975–985.

———. "Moskovskaia dukhovnaia akademiia v 1881." Undated report in Russian State Library, Moscow.

Sokolov, Vasilii A. "Gody studenchestva, 1870–1874." *BV,* I, No. 2 (1916), 246–275; No. 3/4, 385–420; II, No. 5 (1916), 3–36.

Student semidesiatykh godov. "Kratkie vospominaniia o Moskovskoi akademii v periode 1876–1880 gg." *U Troitsy v Akademii,* 172–201.

Tikhonravov, V. "Na lektsii V. O. Kliuchevskogo." *Kievskaia pochta* (May 16, 1911).

3. ON MOSCOW UNIVERSITY

Anon. *Vasilii Osipovich Kliuchevskii. Ocherk i kharakteristiki lichnosti i mirovozzreniia pochivshego istorika.* Moscow, 1912.

Arsen'ev, N. S. "Moi vospominaniia o Moskovskom universitete, 1906–1910 gg." *Zapiski russkoi akademicheskoi gruppy v SShA,* I (1967), 7–22.

Bobrinskoi, Count P. A.; B. N. Beliaev; A. P. Matveev; and S. K. Sochivko, eds. *Sbornik vospominanii. Pamiati russkogo studenchestva kontsa XIX, nachala XX vekov.* Paris, 1934.

Bogoiavlenskii, Sergei K. "Vospominaniia S. K. Bogoiavlenskogo o V. O. Kliuchevskom." *Arkheologicheskii ezhegodnik za 1980 god* (Moscow, 1981), 308–314.

Bogoslovskii, Mikhail M. "Iz vospominanii o V. O. Kliuchevskom." *Chteniia,* CCXLVIII, Book I (1914), 123–130.

———. "Pamiati V. O. Kliuchevskogo. Iz zhizni V. O. Kliuchevskogo." *Russkoe slovo* (May 14, 1911).

———. "Vospominaniia o Kliuchevskom." Ibid. (May 11, 14, 1911).

Borozdin, Il'ia N. "V. O. Kliuchevskii. K tridtsatiletiiu ego nauchno-prepodavatel'skoi deiatel'nosti." *Russkaia starina,* CXLII (1910), 154–158.

———. "V. O. Kliuchevskii. Nekrolog." *Drevnosti,* No. 3 (1913), 315–318.

———. "Pamiati Vasiliia Osipovicha Kliuchevskogo. Bolezn' i konchina." *Russkoe slovo* (May 13, 1911).

———. "Pamiati V. O. Kliuchevskogo." *Sovremennyi mir,* No. 5 (1911), 309–312.

Briusov, Valerii Ia. *Dnevniki, 1891–1910.* Moscow, 1927.

Buslaev, Fedor I. *Moi vospominaniia.* Moscow, 1897. Originally in *Vestnik Evropy,* No. 10 (1890); No. 2 (1892).

Bystrenin, Vladimir P. "Ukhodiashchee." *Golos minuvshago,* No. 1 (1922), 31–50; No. 2, 91–107; No. 1 (1923), 175–200.

Chicherin, Boris N. *Vospominaniia.* Moscow, 1929–1934. 4 vols.

Davydov, Nikolai V. "Iz lichnykh vospominanii o V. A. Gol'tseve." Viktor Gol'tsev, *Pamiati Viktora Aleksandrovicha Gol'tseva* (Moscow, 1910), 128–134.

———. *Iz proshlogo.* Moscow, 1913.

Efimovskii, E. L. "Lektsii V. O. Kliuchevskogo v zhizni Moskovskogo studenchestva." Obshchestvo slavianskoi kul'tury. *Izvestiia,* I, Book I (1912), 9–12.

El'iashevich, V. B. "Iz vospominanii starogo moskovskogo studenta, 1892–1896 gg." Bobrinskoi, *Sbornik vospominanii,* 106–114.

Filin, M. D. "Dnevnikovye zapisi A. N. Savina o V. O. Kliuchevskom." *Arkheograficheskii ezhegodnik za 1978 god* (Moscow, 1879), 327–332.

Firsov, Nikolai N. "Pamiati V. O. Kliuchevskogo." Firsov, *Istoricheskie kharakteristiki i eskizy, 1890–1920 gg.* (Kazan, 1922), II, 243–244.

Fisher, H. A. L. *Paul Vinogradoff: A Memoir.* Oxford, 1927.

Golitsyn, Prince V. M. "Moskovskii universitet v 60-kh godakh." *Golos minuvshago,* No. 11–12 (1917), 173–240.

Got'e, Iurii V. "V. O. Kliuchevskii kak rukovoditel' nachinaiushchikh uchenykh. Iz lichnykh vospominanii." *V. O. Kliuchevskii. Kharakteristiki i vospominaniia* (Moscow, 1912), 177–182.

———. *Time of Troubles: The Diary of Iurii Vladimirovich Got'e. Moscow, July 8, 1917– July 23, 1922.* Translated, edited, and introduced by Terence J. Emmons. Princeton, N.J., 1988. Published as "Moi zametki," *Voprosy istorii,* No. 6 (1991), 150–175; No. 7–8 (1991), 164–190; No. 11 (1991), 150–177; No. 12 (1991), 137–164; No. 1 (1992), 119–138; No. 2/3 (1992), 143–161; No. 4/5 (1992), 107–118; No. 11/12 (1992), 124–159.

———. "Universitet." *Vestnik Moskovskogo universiteta.* Seriia B. *Istoriia,* No. 4 (1982), 113–127.

Kareev, Nikolai I. "Pamiati dvukh istorikov, V. I. Ger'e i I. V. Luchitskii." *Annaly,* No. 1 (1922), 157–174.

Kirpichnikov, Aleksandr I. "Pervyi den' v universitete. Otryvok iz vospominanii." *IV,* LCVIII, No. 6 (1897), 746–760. Reprinted in *Vospominaniia o studencheskoi zhizni,* 133–164.

Kizevetter, Aleksandr A. "Iz vospominanii vos'midesiatnika. 1. Moskva. 2. Studenchestvo. 3. Professora." *Golos minuvshago na chuzhoi storone,* No. 1 (1926), 119–132; No. 2, 139–153; No. 3, 123–152.

———. *Na rubezhe dvukh stoletii. Vospominaniia, 1881–1914.* Prague, 1929.

———. "Pamiati V. O. Kliuchevskogo." *RM,* XXXII, No. 6 (1911), 135–140.

———. "Pamiati V. O. Kliuchevskogo. Bolezn' i smert' Kliuchevskogo. Kratkie biograficheskie svedeniia o V. O. Kliuchevskom." *RV,* No. 11 (May 13, 1911).

V. O. Kliuchevskii. Kharakteristiki i vospominaniia. Moscow, 1912.

Klochkov, Mikhail V. "Iz traurnykh vospominanii. V. O. Kliuchevskii, 1839–1911." *Sovremennik,* No. 5 (1911), 344–353.

Kolubovskii, Ia. "Iz literaturnykh vospominanii." *IV,* CXLVI, No. 4 (1914), 134–149.

Kondakov, Nikodim P. *Vospominaniia i dumy.* Prague, 1927.

Kotliarevskii, Nestor A. "V. O. Kliuchevskii. Nekrolog." *Otchet o deiatel'nosti otdeleniia russkogo iazyka i slovesnosti imp. Akad. nauk za 1911 g.* (St. Petersburg, 1911), 30–34.

Kovalevskii, E. P., comp. "Otryvki iz vospominanii prof. Maksima Kovalevskogo." Vasilii B. El'iashevich, A. A. Kizevetter, and M. M. Novikov, eds., *Moskovskii universitet. 1755–1930. Iubileinyi sbornik* (Paris, 1930), 275–293.

Kovalevskii, Maksim M. "Moskovskii universitet v kontse 70-kh i nachale 80-kh godov proshlogo veka." *Vestnik Evropy*, No. 5 (1910), 187–189. Reprinted in Petr A. Zaionchkovskii and A. N. Sokolov, eds., *Moskovskii universitet v vospominaniiakh sovremennikov* (Moscow, 1956), 287–294.

Lappo-Danilevskii, Aleksandr S. "V. O. Kliuchevskii. Nekrolog." *Izvestiia Imperatorskoi akademii nauk*, Seriia 6, V, No. 6 (1911), 921–924.

———. "Pamiati V. O. Kliuchevskogo." *Vestnik Evropy*, No. 8 (1911), 335–353.

Mel'gunov, Sergei P. *Vospominaniia i dnevniki.* Paris, 1964. 2 vols.

Miliukov, Pavel N. "Moi universitetskie gody." El'iashevich, Kizevetter, and Novikov, eds., *Moskovskii universitet*, 262–274.

———. *Vospominaniia, 1859–1917.* Ed. M. M. Karpovicha and B. I. El'kina. New York, 1955. 2 vols.

Pares, Sir Bernard. *A Wandering Student.* Syracuse, 1948.

Pasternak, Leonid. *Zapisi raznykh let.* Moscow, 1975.

Picheta, Vladimir I. "Vospominaniia o Moskovskom universitete, 1897–1901." *Slaviane v epokhu feodalizma. K 100-letiiu akademika V. I. Pichety* (Moscow, 1978), 52–65.

Putintsev, Nikolai. "Pamiati istorika Vasiliia Osipovicha Kliuchevskogo." *Voennyi mir*, No. 2 (1912), 57–65.

"Rechi, proiznesennye v chrezvychainom zasedanii Obshchestva 12 noiabria 1911 g., posviashchennye pamiati Kliuchevskogo." *Chteniia*, CCXLVIII, Book I, Part II (1914), 37–130.

Shchetinin, Prince Boris A. "Iz vospominanii o V. O. Kliuchevskom." *IV*, CXXV, No. 7 (1911), 223–226.

Shchetinin, Prince Vasilii B. *V Moskovskom universitete. Iz nedavnogo proshlogo.* Moscow, 1906.

Trubetskaia, Princess Ol'ga. *Kniaz' S. N. Trubetskoi. Vospominaniia sestry.* New York, 1953.

Trubetskoi, Prince Serge N. *Vospominaniia.* Sofia, 1921.

Umov, Nikolai A. "Ot 'nauchnogo slova.' " *Kliuchevskii. Kharakteristiki i vospominaniia*, 1–4.

Vasilenko, Sergei N. *Stranitsy vospominanii.* Moscow, 1948. Reprinted in Zaionchkovskii and Sokolov, *Moskovskii universitet v vospominaniiakh sovremennikov*, 336–340.

Vipper, Robert Iu. "Pamiati velikogo uchenogo. Pis'mo k redaktsii." *RV* (May 17, 1911).

Vysotskii, Nikolai G. "Iz dalekogo proshlogo. Vospominaniia o studencheskikh godakh v Moskovskom universitete." *Vestnik vospitaniia*, No. 7 (1910), 130–170.

Zaionchkovskii, Petr A., and A. N. Sokolov, eds. *Moskovskii universitet v vospominaniiakh sovremennikov.* Moscow, 1956.

4. ON THE THIRD ALEKSANDROVSKOE MILITARY SCHOOL

Baiov, Aleksei K. *Znachenie V. O. Kliuchevskogo dlia russkoi voenno-istoricheskoi nauki.* St. Petersburg, 1911.

Kedrin, Vladimir I. *Aleksandrovskoe voennoe uchilishche, 1863–1901.* Moscow, 1901.

Petrov, Viktor A. "Vospominaniia o zaniatiiakh V. O. Kliuchevskogo v Aleksandrovskom voennom uchilishche." Ibid., 435–450.

Putintsev, Nikolai. "Pamiat' istorika Vasiliia Osipovicha Kliuchevskogo." *Voennyi mir*, No. 2 (1912), 57–65.

5. WOMEN'S HIGHER COURSES

Bobrova, L. A. "Vysshie zhenskie kursy professora Ger'e v Moskve, 1872–1888." *Trudy Moskovskogo gosudarstvennogo istoriko-arkhivnogo instituta*, XVI (1961), 253–265.

Grishina, Z. V. "Vysshee obrazovanie zhenshchin v dorevoliutsionnoi Rossii i Moskovskom universitete." *Vestnik Moskovskogo universiteta*, Seriia 8, *Istoriia*, No. 1 (1984), 52–63.

Shchepkina, Ekaterina N. "Pervye gody Vysshykh zhenskikh kursov." *Russkoe proshloe*, No. 5 (1923), 134–145.

Valk, S. N., et al. *Sankt-Peterburgskie vysshie (Bestuzhevskie) kursy, 1878–1918. Sbornik statei*. Leningrad, 1965.

Vinogradskaia, Ol'ga A. *Pamiati Ol'gi Afinogenovny Vinogradskoi. Biografiia i vospominaniia*. Moscow, 1916.

6. OTHER MEMOIRS

Belokurov, Sergei A. "K prebyvaniiu V. O. Kliuchevskogo v Abbas-Tiumane v 1893–1895 gg." *U Troitsy v Akademii 1814–1914. Iubileinyi sbornik istoricheskikh materialov* (Moscow, 1914), 683–691.

Gol'tsev, Viktor A. *Pamiati Viktora Aleksandrovicha Gol'tseva*. Ed. A. A. Kizevetter. Moscow, 1910.

Koni, Anatolii F. "Vasilii Osipovich Kliuchevskii." *Na zhiznennom puti* (St. Petersburg, 1912), II, 170–172.

———. "Vospominaniia o V. O. Kliuchevskom." *Kliuchevskii. Kharakteristiki i vospominaniia*, 145–163.

Kryzhanovskii, Sergei E. *Vospominaniia. Iz bumag poslednego gosudarstvennogo sekretaria Rossiiskoi imperii*. Berlin, n.d.

Maklakov, Vasilii A. *The First State Duma: Contemporary Reminiscences*. Translated by Mary Belkin. Bloomington, Ind., 1964.

———. *Iz vospominanii*. New York, 1954.

———. "Otryvki iz vospominanii." El'iashevich, Kizevetter, and Novikov, *Moskovskii universitet*, 294–318.

———. *Vlast' i obshchestvennost' na zakate staroi Rossii. Vospominaniia sovremennika*. Paris, 1936.

———. "Vinogradov." *Slavonic Review*, XIII, No. 39 (1935), 633–640.

Pasternak, Alexander. *A Vanished Present: The Memoirs of Alexander Pasternak*. Ed. and trans. Ana Pasternak Slater. New York, 1984.

Pasternak, Boris. *Essai d'autobiographie*. Paris, 1958.

Platonov, Sergei F. "Pamiati V. O. Kliuchevskogo." *Kliuchevskii. Kharakteristiki i vospominaniia*, 94–99.

Shaliapin, Fedor. *Stranitsy iz moei zhizni. Avtobiografiia*. Leningrad, 1926.

Shipov, Dmitrii N. *Vospominaniia i dumy o perezhitom*. Moscow, 1918.

D. SELECTED JOURNALS

Bogoslovskii vestnik, 1892–1917. Published by the Moscow Ecclesiastical Academy.
Chteniia, 1865–1918. Published by the Society of Russian History and Antiquity.
Drevnosti, 1880–1917. Published by the Imperial Moscow Archeological Society.
Istoricheskii vestnik, 1880–1917.

Zhurnal dlia vsekh, 1896–1906.
Zhurnal Soveta Moskovskoi dukhovnoi akademii, 1880–1917.

SECONDARY SOURCES

A. Russian Works on Kliuchevskii Published before 1917

1. PRINCIPAL AUTHORS

Bogoslovskii, Mikhail M. "Kliuchevskii—pedagog." Bogoslovskii, *Istoriografiia, memuaristika, epistoliariia. Nauchnoe nasledie* (Moscow, 1987), 36–63.
————. "V. O. Kljucevsky. Gest. 12/25 Mai 1911." *Zeitschrift für osteuropäische Geschichte*, III (1913), 309–318.
————. "V. O. Kliuchevskii kak uchenyi." *Kliuchevskii. Kharakteristiki i vospominaniia*, 26–44. Reprinted in Bogoslovskii, *Istoriografiia*, 22–36.
————. "Professor Vasilii Osipovich Kliuchevskii (16 ianvaria 1841–12 maia 1911 g.)." Moskovskaia dukhovnaia akademiia, *Pamiati pochivshikh nastavnikov* (Sergiev Posad, 1914), 325–356.
Kizevetter, Aleksandr A. "Detskie i shkol'nye gody V. O. Kliuchevskogo." Kizevetter, *Istoricheskie otkliki* (Moscow, 1915), 361–370.
————. "V. O. Kliuchevskii." *RV*, No. 279 (December 5, 1905).
————. "V. O. Kliuchevskii kak prepodavatel'." *RM*, No. 12 (1911), 1–14. Reprinted in Kizevetter, *Istoricheskie otkliki*, 371–390, and *Kliuchevskii. Kharakteristiki i vospominaniia*, 164–176.
————. "Kliuchevskii i 'sotsializatsiia klassikov.'" *Svoboda Rossii* (May 25 [12], 1918).
————. "V. O. Kliuchevskii kak uchenyi istorik Rossii." *RV* (May 14, 15, 1911).
————. "Prof. V. O. Kliuchevskii. *Kurs russkoi istorii*. C III. M., 1908 g." *RM*, XXIX, No. 3 (1908), 47–49.
————. "V. Kliuchevskii. *Kurs russkoi istorii*. C IV. M., 1910 g." Ibid., XXXI, No. 2 (1910), 31–33.
————. *V. O. Kliuchevskii. Zodchii russkoi kul'tury*. Prague, 1926.
————. "Klyuchevsky and His *Course of Russian History*." *Slavonic Review*, I (1922), 504–522.
————. "Pervyi kurs V. O. Kliuchevskogo, 1873–1874." Russkii nauchnyi institut, Belgrade, *Zapiski*, III (1931), 279–306.
————. "Prilozheniia." Kliuchevskii, *Opyty i izsledovaniia. Pervyi sbornik statei* (Moscow, 1912), i–xxiv.
Liubavskii, Matvei K. *Vasilii Osipovich Kliuchevskii*. Moscow, 1912.
————, ed. *Vasilii Osipovich Kliuchevskii. Biograficheskii ocherk, rechi, proiznesennye v torzhestvennom zasedanii 12 noiabria 1911 goda, i materialy dlia ego biografii*. Moscow, 1914.
————. "Vasilii Osipovich Kliuchevskii (+ 12 maia 1911). Biograficheskii ocherk." *Chteniia*, CCXLVIII, Part I (1914), 1–34.
————. "Solov'ev i Kliuchevskii." *Kliuchevskii. Kharakteristiki i vospominaniia*, 45–58. Reprinted in *Chteniia*, CCXLVIII, Part II (1914), 41–52.
Miliukov, Pavel N. "V. O. Kliuchevskii." *Rech'* (May 17, 24, 25, 1911).
————. "V. O. Kliuchevskii." *Kliuchevskii. Kharakteristiki i vospominaniia*, 183–217.
————. "V. O. Kliuchevskii i ego uchenyi trudy. Doklad." *Izvestiia Obshchestva slavianskoi kul'tury*, I, Book I (1912), 30–59.

————. "V. O. Kliuchevskii kak lichnost'." *Poslednie novosti*, Paris (January 24, 26, 1932).

————. "Klyuchevsky." *Encyclopedia of the Social Sciences* (New York, 1930–35), VIII, 577–578.

2. OTHER WORKS

Aikhenval'd, Iulii I. "Kliuchevskii, myslitel' i khudozhnik." *Kliuchevskii. Kharakteristiki i vospominaniia*, 117–144.

Aleksandrov, Mikhail S. *Gosudarstvo, biurokratiia i absoliutizm v istorii Rossii*. St. Petersburg, 1910.

Baiov, Aleksei K. "Znachenie V. O. Kliuchevskogo dlia russkoi voenno-istoricheskoi nauki." *Izvestiia Imperatorskoi nikolaevskoi voennoi akademii*, No. 21 (1911), 901–915.

Barskov, Iakov L., ed. *Sbornik statei, posviashchennykh Vasiliiu Osipovichu Kliuchevskomu ego uchenikami, druz'iami i pochitateliami ko dniu tridtsatiletiia ego professorskoi deiatel'-nosti v Moskovskom universitete (5 dekabria 1879–5 dekabria 1909 goda)*. Moscow, 1909.

Barsov, Elpidifor V. "Doktorskii disput E. E. Golubinskogo v Moskovskoi dukhovnoi akademii." *Chteniia*, CCXVI, Book III (1913), 29–39.

————. "V. O. Kliuchevskii—kak predsedatel' Obshchestva." *Chteniia*, CCXLVIII, Book I (1914), 37–40.

————. "Mnenie V. O. Kliuchevskogo o Maksime Gor'kom. Zapisano 25 sent. 1907 g." *U Troitsy v Akademii*, 692–693.

Belokurov, Sergei A. "K prebyvaniiu V. O. Kliuchevskogo v Abbas-Tiumane v 1893–1895 gg." *U Troitsy v Akademii*, 683–691.

————. "Kliuchevskii." *Bogoslovskaia entsiklopediia*, XI (1910), 275–290.

————, comp. "Vasilii Osipovich Kliuchevskii. Materialy dlia ego biografii." *Chteniia*, CCXLVIII, Book I, Part III (1914), 476 pp.

Filin, N. D. "Dnevnikovye zapisi A. N. Savina o V. O. Kliuchevskom." *Arkheograficheskii ezhegodnik za 1966 god*. (Moscow, 1968), 327–332.

Golubtsov, Sergei A. "V. O. Kliuchevskii v studencheskie gody." VOK, *Pis'ma k Gvozdevu*, 7–37.

Khvostov, Veniamin M. *Istoricheskoe mirovozzrenie V. O. Kliuchevskogo*. Moscow, 1910. Reprinted in Khvostov, *Nravstvennaia lichnost' i obshchestvo. Ocherki po etike i sotsiologii* (Moscow, 1911), 184–230.

Klochkov, Mikhail V. "V. O. Kliuchevskii o Gosudarstvennoi dume." *IV*, CXXXII (1913), 243–249.

————. *Ocherki pravitel'stvennoi deiatel'nosti vremeni Pavla I*. Petrograd, 1916.

Koialovich, Mikhail O. *Istoriia russkogo samosoznaniia po istoricheskim pamiatnikam i nauchnym sochineniiam*. St. Petersburg, 1901. 3rd ed.

Korolev, Aleksandr V. *V. O. Kliuchevskii*. Khar'kov, 1911.

Korsakov, D. A. "Po povodu dvukh monografii V. O. Kliuchevskogo." *IV*, CXXVI (1911), 236–251.

Kotliarevskii, Sergei A. "Chto daet 'Boiarskaia duma' V. O. Kliuchevskogo dlia gosudarstvovedeniia." *Sbornik statei, posviashchennykh Vasiliiu Osipovichu Kliuchevskomu* (Moscow, 1909), 244–253.

————. "V. O. Kliuchevskii kak istorik uchrezhdeniia." *Voprosy prava*, VIII, No. 4 (1911), 1–14.

Kovalevskii, Maksim. "Vasilii Osipovich Kliuchevskii." *Vestnik Evropy*, No. 6 (1911), 406–411.

Lappo-Danilevskii, Aleksandr S. "Istoricheskie vzgliady V. O. Kliuchevskogo." *Kliuchevskii. Kharakteristiki i vospominaniia*, 100–116.

Lashnikov, Ivan V. "Ocherki russkoi istoriografii." *Universitetskie izvestiia*, (Kiev), Part II, No. 6 (1872), 8–10.

Lednitskii, A. R. "V. O. Kliuchevskii kak istorik slavianin." *Izvestiia Obshchestva slavianskoi kul'tury*, I, Book I (1912), 1–8.

Levitskii, Anatolii I. "Boiarskaia duma." *Zhurnal Ministerstva narodnogo prosveshcheniia*, CCXXXV (1884), 86–132; CCXXXVI (1884), 27–63.

L'vov, L. "Kliuchevskii o Rossii." *Svoboda Rossii*, No. 34 (May 25 [12], 1918).

Mikhailovskii, Nikolai K. "Literatura i zhizn'." *RM*, XIII, No. 6 (1892), 182–183.

Miroslavskii, V. *Professor Moskovskoi dukhovnoi akademii V. O. Kliuchevskii*. Iaroslavl', 1912.

Nikolaev, V. "Professor V. O. Kliuchevskii, *Dobrye liudi drevnei Rusi*, Sergiev Posad, 1892." *Bibliograficheskie zapiski*, I, No. 2 (1892), 147–148.

Petukhov, Evgenii V. *Russkaia literatura. Drevnii period*. Iur'ev, 1912.

Picheta, Vladimir I. "Istoricheskie vzgliady i metodologicheskie printsipy V. O. Kliuchevskogo." *Izvestiia Obshchestva slavianskoi kul'tury*, I, Book I (1912), 13–29.

Platonov, Sergei F. *V. O. Kliuchevskii, 1841–1911*. St. Petersburg, 1911.

———. "V. O. Kliuchevskii, 1841–1911. Nekrolog." *Zhurnal ministerstva narodnogo prosveshcheniia*, New Series, XXXVL, No. 11 (1911), 30–36.

———. "Vasilii Osipovich Kliuchevskii." Platonov, *Stat'i po russkoi istorii, 1883–1912*, 2nd ed. (St. Petersburg, 1912), 495–503.

———. "Pamiati V. O. Kliuchevskogo." *Kliuchevskii. Kharakteristiki i vospominaniia*, 94–99.

Rozanov, Vasilii V. "V. O. Kliuchevskii o drevnei Rusi." *Russkii vestnik*, No. 7 (1892), 213–227.

Samarin, Dmitrii. "Teoriia o nedostatochnosti krest'ianskikh nadelov po ucheniiu professora Iu E. Iansona." *Rus'*, No. 1 (November 15, 1881), 10–14; No. 2 (November 22, 1881), 9–13.

Shpakov, Aleksei Ia. *V. O. Kliuchevskii. K 75-letiiu so dnia rozhdeniia*. Odessa, 1916.

Smirnov, Pavel P. "V. O. Kliuchevskii." *Voenno-istoricheskii vestnik*, Book I (1912), 79–86; Book II, 65–77.

Smirnov, Sergei I. "Issledovanie V. O. Kliuchevskogo *Drevnerusskie zhitiia sviatykh kak istoricheskii istochnik*." *Chteniia*, CCXLVIII, Book I (1914), 53–71.

———. "V. O. Kliuchevskii i ego ponimanie natsional'nogo vospitaniia." Vladimir Volzhanin, V. F. Dinze, and S. D. Smirnov, eds., *O natsional'noi shkole. Sbornik statei* (Petrograd, 1916), 67–80.

Sobolevskii, A. I. "Russkaia literatura XVII veka v osveshchenii V. O. Kliuchevskogo." *Russkii filologicheskii vestnik*, LX, No. 4 (1908), 365–368.

Syromiatnikov, Boris I. "V. O. Kliuchevskii i B. N. Chicherin." *Kliuchevskii. Kharakteristiki i vospominaniia*, 59–93.

———. "V. O. Kliuchevskii i russkaia istoricheskaia nauka." *Voprosy prava*, Book VII, No. 4 (1911), 15–41.

Vladimirskii-Budanov, Mikhail F. "Novoe issledovanie o Boiarskoi Dume." V. P. Bezobrazov, ed., *Sbornik gosudarstvennykh znanii*, VIII (1880), 104–124.

Zaozerskii, Nikolai A. "Dvadtsatipiatiletie professorskoi sluzhby V. O. Kliuchevskogo v Moskovskoi dukhovnoi akademii." *BV*, No. 12 (1896), 475–489.

———. "V. O. Kliuchevskii v ego retsenziiakh dissertatsii na uchenye stepeni professorov i studentov Moskovskoi dukhovnoi akademii." *Chteniia*, CCXLVIII, Book I (1914), 72–122.

B. Russian Studies of Kliuchevskii Published after 1917

1. PRINCIPAL AUTHORS

Aleksandrov, Vadim A. "Kliuchevskii, Vasilii Osipovich." *SIE*, VII (1965), 433–435.

———. "Vasilii Osipovich Kliuchevskii, 1841–1911." VOK, *Istoricheskie portrety*, 5–26.

———. "Vasilii Osipovich Kliuchevskii, 1841–1911. K 150-letiiu so dnia rozhdeniia." *Istoriia SSSR*, No. 5 (1991), 57–69.

———. "Kommentarii." *Sochineniia v deviati tomakh*, I, 370–412; II, 398–408; III, 365–372; IV, 359–368; V, 395–472; VI, 469–510; VIII, 419–438.

———. "Posleslovie." Ibid., I, 367–368; II, 374–393; III, 343–362; IV, 332–351; V, 361–381; VIII, 408–418.

———, and A. A. Zimin. "Kommentarii." VOK, *Kurs, Sochineniia*, I, 370–412; II, 398–408; III, 365–372; IV, 359–368; V, 395–472; VI, 469–510.

———, and V. G. Zimina. "Kommentarii." VOK, *Kurs. Sochineniia v deviati tomakh*, IV, 352–387; VIII, 419–438.

Kireeva, Raisa A. "Dekabristskaia tema v dorevoliutsionnoi istoriograficheskoi literature." *Istoriia i istoriki. Istoriografiia istorii SSSR, 1976* (Moscow, 1979), 116–131.

———. "Istochniki istoriograficheskikh rabot V. O. Kliuchevskogo." *Arkheograficheskii ezhegodnik za 1962* (Moscow, 1963), 323–330.

———, ed. "Istoricheskie miniatiury. V. O. Kliuchevskii." *Nedelia*, No. 24 (July 9–15, 1963), 11.

———. "Istoriograficheskii kurs V. O. Kliuchevskogo." *Istoriia SSSR*, No. 2 (1964), 91–100.

———. *V. O. Kliuchevskii kak istorik russkoi istoricheskoi nauki.* Moscow, 1966.

———. "V. O. Kliuchevskii kak istorik istoriograficheskoi nauki. Russkaia istoriografiia pervoi poloviny XIX v." *Istoriia i istoriki. Istoriografiia istorii SSSR. 1965* (Moscow, 1966), 397–428.

———. "Kommentarii." VOK, *Sochineniia v deviati tomakh*, IX, 463–507.

———. "Posleslovie." Ibid., VI, 432–451; VII, 431–447; IX, 447–462.

———. "Primechaniia." Kliuchevskii, *Pis'ma*, 417–484.

———. "Problema periodizatsii russkoi istoriografii v trudakh burzhuaznykh istorikov serediny XIX–nachala XX v." *Istoriia i istoriki. Istoriograficheskii ezhegodnik. 1971* (Moscow, 1973), 109–137.

———, ed. "Slovo—zoloto. Aforizmy V. O. Kliuchevskogo." *Nedelia*, No. 39 (September 23–29, 1962), 24.

———. "Vospominaniia i dnevnikovye zapisi deiatelei kul'tury o V. O. Kliuchevskom." *Arkheograficheskii ezhegodnik za 1980 god* (Moscow, 1981), 314–319.

———, and A. A. Zimin. "Arkheograficheskoe posleslovie." VOK, *Neopublikovannye*, 371–375.

Nechkina, Militsa V. "Istoriia izucheniia V. O. Kliuchevskogo." *Istoricheskie zapiski*, LXXXIV (1966), 216–254.

———. "Iunye gody V. O. Kliuchevskogo." *VI*, No. 9 (1969), 67–90.

———. "K kharakteristike V. O. Kliuchevskogo kak sotsiologa (v sviazi s izdaniem V

Bibliography

toma *Kursa russkoi istorii* V. O. Kliuchevskogo)." *Vestnik prosveshcheniia* (Kazan), No. 1–2 (1923), 28–39.

———. "V. O. Kliuchevskii." Mikhail N. Pokrovskii, ed., *Russkaia istoricheskaia literatura v klassovom osveshchenii* (Moscow, 1927–30), II, 217–352.

———. "Kliuchevskii, Vasilii Osipovich." *Malaia sovetskaia entsiklopediia*, III (1931), 813–815.

———. *Vasilii Osipovich Kliuchevskii: Istoriia zhizni i tvorchestva*. Moscow, 1974.

———. "V. O. Kliuchevskii o frantsuzskoi revoliutsii 1789 goda." *Novaia i noveishaia istoriia*, No. 5 (1969), 109–115.

———. "V. O. Kliuchevskii—student." *VI*, No. 5 (1971), 61–79.

———. "Magisterskaia dissertatsiia V. O. Kliuchevskogo." *Istoricheskie zapiski*, XL (1972), 244–302.

———. "O neopublikovannykh materialakh V. O. Kliuchevskogo." *Istoricheskii zhurnal*, No. 5 (1942), 171–172.

———. "Pervaia nauchnaia rabota V. O. Kliuchevskogo." *VI*, No. 6 (1972), 47–59.

———. "Predislovie." VOK, *Neopublikovannye*, 3–10.

———. "Vzgliad V. O. Kliuchevskogo na rol' 'idei' v istoricheskom protsesse. (Iz rabot o predshestvennikakh ekonomicheskogo materializma v russkoi istoriografii)." *Krasnaia nov'*, No. 5 (1923), 174–203.

Rubinshtein, Nikolai L. "K vykhodu v svet *Kursa russkoi istorii* V. O. Kliuchevskogo." *Kniga i proletarskaia revoliutsiia*, No. 9 (1937), 88–91.

———. "Vasilii O. Kliuchevskii." *Istoricheskii zhurnal*, No. 6 (1941), 34–42.

———. "V. O. Kliuchevskii, 1841–1911 gg." Kliuchevskii, *Kurs* (Moscow, 1937), I, iii–xviii.

———. "Kliuchevskii i ego *Kurs russkoi istorii*." *Pravda* (August 15, 1937).

Zimin, Aleksandr A. "Arkhiv V. O. Kliuchevskogo." Gosudarstvennaia ordena Lenina Biblioteka SSSR imeni V. I. Lenina, *Zapiski otdela rukopisei*, XII (1951), 76–86.

———. "Formirovanie istoricheskikh vzgliadov V. O. Kliuchevskogo v 60-e gody XIX v." *Istoricheskie zapiski*, No. 69 (1961), 178–196.

———. "Iz rukopisnogo naslediia V. O. Kliuchevskogo. Novye materialy k kursu po russkoi istoriografii." *Istoriia i istoriki. Istoriograficheskii ezhegodnik. 1972* (Moscow, 1973), 307–336.

———. "K izdaniiu *Sochinenii* V. O. Kliuchevskogo." *Istoriia SSSR*, No. 2 (1957), 266–267.

———. "Kliuchevskii, V. O. God 1812-i." *Nedelia*, No. 41 (October 7–13, 1962), 13.

———. "Kniazheskaia znat' i formirovanie sostava boiarskoi dumy vo vtoroi polovine XIV–pervoi treti XVI v." *Istoricheskie zapiski*, No. 103 (1979), 195–241.

———. "Trudnye voprosy metodiki istochnikovedeniia drevnei Rusi." *Istochnikovedenie. Teoreticheskie i metodologicheskie problemy* (Moscow, 1969), 427–449.

2. OTHER WORKS

Abramov, V. K. "Vasilii Osipovich Kliuchevskii. K 150-letiiu so dnia rozhdeniia." *Vestnik Mordovskogo universiteta*, No. 1 (1991), 56–60.

Arkhipov, Konstantin A. "V. O. Kliuchevskii kak gosudarstvoved." *Sovetskoe pravo*, No. 2 (1927), 28–51.

Astakhov, Viktor I. "V. O. Kliuchevskii—vydaiushchiisia predstavitel' burzhuaznoi istoriografii poreformennogo perioda." Astakhov, *Kurs lektsii po russkoi istoriografii (do kontsa XIX v.)* (Khar'kov, 1965), 170–202.

Avtokratova, M. I., and V. N. Samoshenko. "Rabota dorevoliutsionnykh istorikov v chital'nykh zalakh arkhivov, voshedshikh v sostav TsGADA." *Sovetskie arkhivy*, No. 4 (1988), 51–58.

Bochkarev, Valentin N. "Vasilii Osipovich Kliuchevskii. K 120-letiiu so dnia rozhdeniia i 50-letiiu so dnia smerti." *Trudy nauchno-issledovatel'skogo instituta literatury, istorii i ekonomiki pri Sovete ministrov Mordovskoi ASSR* (Saransk), XXI, Seriia 1 (1961), 158–171.

Bogoiavlenskii, Sergei K. "Primechaniia k V tomu." VOK, *Kurs* (Moscow, 1937), V, 536–648.

Bushuev, K. "V. O. Kliuchevskii. K vykhodu iz pechati *Kursa russkoi istorii*." *Uchitel'skaia gazeta* (July 23, 1938), 2.

Cherepnin, Lev V. "V. O. Kliuchevskii." Akademiia nauk, Institut istorii, *Ocherki istorii istoricheskoi nauki*, II, 146–170.

———. "V. O. Kliuchevskii kak istochnikoved." *Arkheograficheskii ezhegodnik za 1980 god* (Moscow, 1981), 332–340.

———. "V. O. Kliuchevskii o russkikh pisateliakh." *Trudy Moskovskogo istoriko-arkhivnogo instituta*, No. 3 (1963), 99–100.

Chumachenko, Evgeniia G. *V. O. Kliuchevskii—istochnikoved.* Moscow, 1970.

———. "Neokonchennaia stat'ia V. O. Kliuchevskogo o Gogole. Iz neopublikovannykh materialov." Gosudarstvennaia ordena Lenina Biblioteka SSSR imeni V. I. Lenina, *Zapiski otdela rukopisei*, XXIV (1961), 409–414.

———. "O priemakh issledovaniia V. O. Kliuchevskim istochnikov drevnerusskikh zhitii sviatykh." *Trudy Moskovskogo istoriko-arkhivnogo instituta*, XXIV (1966), 191–202.

———. "Obzor neopublikovannykh rukopisei V. O. Kliuchevskogo o russkoi literature XIX–nachala XX vv." Ibid., XVI (1961), 301–315.

———. Priemy raboty V. O. Kliuchevskogo nad skazaniiami inostrantsev o Rossii XV–XVI vv." Ibid., XXIV (1965), 202–223. Reprinted in *Arkheograficheskii ezhegodnik za 1966* (Moscow, 1968), 105–115.

Dodonov, Ivan. "Zur Geschichtsauffassung Kljucevskija." *Jahrbuch für Geschichte der UdSSR der volksdemokratischen Länder Europas*, III (1959), 318–330. Translated from Russian by Erich Donnert.

Dvorzhanskii, A. I. "Iubilei 150 let so dnia rozhdeniia V. O. Kliuchevskogo." *Penzenskii vremennik liubitelei stariny*, No. 1 (1991), 1–4.

Filin, N. "Blestiashchii ispolnitel' lektsii. O pedagogicheskom masterstve V. O. Kliuchevskogo." *Uchitel'skaia gazeta*, No. 3 (January 15–22, 1991).

Golubtsov, Sergei A. "V. O. Kliuchevskii v studencheskie gody." VOK, *Pis'ma k Gvozdevu*, 9–37.

———. "Teoreticheskie vzgliady V. O. Kliuchevskogo." *Russkii istoricheskii zhurnal*, VIII (1922), 178–202.

Golyga, Arsenii V. *Iskusstvo istorii.* Moscow, 1980.

Got'e, Iurii V. "Primechaniia." VOK, *Kurs* (Moscow, 1937), II, 426–435; III, 395–405.

Iakovlev, Aleksei I. "V. O. Kliuchevskii, 1841–1911." *Zapiski nauchno-issledovatel'skogo instituta pri Sovete ministrov Mordovskoi ASSR, Istoriia i arkheologiia*, VI (1946), 94–131.

———. "Primechaniia." VOK, *Kurs russkoi istorii* (Moscow, 1937), I, 385–390.

Illeritskii, V. E. "Istoriografiia." Akademiia nauk, Institut istorii, *Ocherki istorii istoricheskoi nauki*, II, 548–574.

Bibliography

————. "V. O. Kliuchevskii—vydaiushchiisia burzhuaznyi istorik poreformennogo perioda." Illeritskii and I. A. Kudriavtsev, eds., *Istoriografiia istorii SSSR s drevneishikh vremen do velikoi oktiabr'skoi sotsialisticheskoi revoliutsii* (Moscow, 1961), 305–316.

————, and I. A. Kudriavtsev. "V. O. Kliuchevskii—vydaiushchiisia burzhuaznyi istorik poreformennogo perioda." Illeritskii and I. A. Kudriavtsev, eds., *Istoriografiia istorii SSSR* (Moscow, 1971), 270–281. 2nd ed.

Karagodin, Anatolii I. *Filosofiia istorii V. O. Kliuchevskogo.* Saratov, 1976.

————. *Metodologicheskie printsipy istoricheskikh issledovanii V. O. Kliuchevskogo.* Saratov, 1982.

Kazak, A. P. "Ob evoliutsii teoreticheskikh osnov kontseptsii istoricheskogo znaniia V. O. Kliuchevskogo." *Filosofskie nauki,* No. 10 (1984), 140–144.

Kedrov, Konstantin. "Nash sovremennik Vasilii Kliuchevskii." *Izvestiia* (January 9, 1988).

Korobov, Sergei A. "Novoe o detstve V. O. Kliuchevskogo." *VI,* No. 1 (1992), 187–188.

————. "Novoe o Kliuchevskom." *Penzenskii vremennik liubitelei stariny,* No. 2 (1991), 14–15.

Korol'kov, I. "K voprosu o proiskhozhdenii krepostnogo prava i klassovoi bor'by v Rossii v osveshchenii V. O. Kliuchevskogo." *Uchenye zapiski Chitinskogo pedagogicheskogo instituta,* No. 7 (1961), 3–30.

Krasnobaev, B. I. "V. O. Kliuchevskii o russkoi kul'ture XVII–XIX vekov." *Istoriia SSSR,* No. 5 (1981), 131–149.

————. "V. O. Kljucevski über die Kulturbeziehungen zwischen Russland und Europa im 17. und 18. Jahrhundert." Wolfgang Kessler, Henryk Rietz, and Gert Robel, eds., *Kulturbeziehungen in Mittel- und Osteuropa im 18. und 19. Jahrhundert* (Berlin, 1982), 291–298.

Lapitskii, M. I. "Dialogi. Glazami Kliuchevskogo: Nashe proshloe, nastoiashchee, budushchee." *Politicheskie issledovaniia,* No. 4 (1991), 116–125.

Laptev, Vladimir V. "V. O. Kliuchevskii v sovetskoi istoriografii." Leningrad, *Gosudarstvennyi pedagogicheskii institut imeni A. I. Gertsena. Uchenye zapiski,* CCXCVIII (1971), 221–237.

Leont'ev, M. F., comp. "Izrecheniia i aforizmy V. O. Kliuchevskogo." *VI,* No. 7 (1965), 208–214.

Lur'e, Ia. S. "Ivan Groznyi i ego vremia." *Istoriia SSSR,* No. 5 (1990), 174–177.

Markov, N. O. "V. O. Kliuchevskii o vzaimootnoshenii prirody i obshchestva. Rol' geograficheskoi sredy v obshchestvenno-istoricheskom protsesse." *Trudy nauchno-issledovatel'skogo instituta iazykov, literatury, istorii i ekonomiki pri Sovete ministrov Mordovskoi ASSR,* XLVII (1974), 101–143.

————. "Problema svoeobraziia russkogo istoricheskogo protsessa v sotsiologicheskoi kontseptsii V. O. Kliuchevskogo." Ibid., 89–100.

Nardin, V. V. "Voprosy istorii srednevekovoi Rossii v trudakh V. O. Kliuchevskogo i M. N. Pokrovskogo." *Voprosy metodologii i istorii istoricheskoi nauki* (Moscow, 1977), 95–133.

Parkhomenko, Vladimir A. "Drevniaia istoriia Rossii (Kievskaia Rus') v osveshchenii Kliuchevskogo i Presniakova." *Vestnik drevnei istorii,* No. 3 (1938), 189–203.

Piontkovskii, Sergei A. "Velikoderzhavnye tendentsii v istoriografii Rossii." *Istorik-Marksist,* XVII (1930), 21–26.

————. "Velikorusskaia burzhuaznaia istoriografiia poslednego desiatiletiia. Preniia po dokladu. Vystupleniia t. t. Shestakova, Mameta i Tatarova." Ibid., XVIII–XIX (1930), 157–176.

Pokrovskii, Mikhail N. "*Kurs russkoi istorii* prof. V. Kliuchevskogo." Pokrovskii, *Izbrannye proizvedeniia* (Moscow, 1967), IV, 266–271.

————. "O *Kurse russkoi istorii* V. O. Kliuchevskogo, T. V." *Pechat' i revoliutsiia*, No. 3 (1923), 101–104. Reprinted in *Izbrannye proizvedeniia*, IV (Moscow, 1967), 272–276, and in other collections.

Presniakov, Aleksandr E. "V. O. Kliuchevskii, 1911–1921." *Russkii istoricheskii zhurnal*, No. 8 (1922), 203–224.

Rabinovich, M. D. "Evoliutsiia kursa vseobshchei istorii V. O. Kliuchevskogo. (Po materialam lektsionnogo kursa 1879–1880 g.)." *Novaia i noveishaia istoriia*, No. 6 (1969), 103–108.

————. "V. O. Kliuchevskii ob arkhivakh." *Sovetskie arkhivy*, No. 6 (1969), 58–63.

Rezun, D. Ia. "K voprosu ob izobrazhenii V. O. Kliuchevskim sotsial'noi bor'by v drevnei Rusi." *Voprosy istorii Sibiri dosovetskogo perioda* (*Bakhrushinskie chteniia, 1969*) (Novosibirsk, 1973), 29–44.

Rybakov, Boris A. *Kievskaia Rus' i russkie kniazhestva XII–XIII vv.* Moscow, 1982.

Shirinkina, Tat'iana G. "Nekotorye problemy dukhovnoi zhizni russkogo obshchestva v trudakh V. O. Kliuchevskogo." *Problemy dukhovnoi zhizni sotsialisticheskogo obshchevsta* (Omsk, 1984), 155–163.

Shmidt, Sigurd O. "V. I. Lenin—chitatel' V. O. Kliuchevskogo." G. M. Amashina, ed., *Problemy istorii obshchestvennogo dvizheniia i istoriografii* (Moscow, 1971), 354–364.

Shteingauz, Iziaslav X. "V. O. Kliuchevskii o gosudarstve i revoliutsii." *Ocherki istorii Sibiri, Sbornik statei* (Irkutsk, 1973), IV, 126–135.

————. *Sotsiologicheskie vzgliady V. O. Kliuchevskogo.* Irkutsk, 1974.

Simonov, I. S. "V. O. Kliuchevskii. K desiatiletnei godovshchine po smerti 1911 12 (25) V–1921." *Pedagogicheskaia mysl'*, No. 5–8 (1921), 115–120.

Stanislavskaia, A. M. "V. O. Kliuchevskii." Akademiia nauk, Institut istorii, *Ocherki istorii istoricheskoi nauki v SSSR*, III (1960), 146–170.

Tikhomirov, Mikhail N. "K vykhodu pervykh trekh tomov *Sobraniia sochinenii* V. O. Kliuchevskogo." *VI*, No. 8 (1958), 154–159.

————. "Predislovie." VOK, *Kurs*, I, 5–12.

————. "Pskovskie povesti o krest'ianskoi voine v Rossii nachala XVII v." *Iz istorii sotsial'no-politicheskikh idei. Sbornik statei k 75-letiiu V. P. Volgina* (Moscow, 1953), 181–188.

————. "Soslovno-predstavitel'nye uchrezhdeniia (zemskie sobory) v Rossii XVI v." *VI*, No. 5 (1958), 2–22.

Tkhorzhevskii, Sergei I. "V. O. Kliuchevskii kak sotsiolog i politicheskii myslitel'." *Dela i dni*, II (1921), 152–179.

Tsamutali, Aleksei N. "Liberal'noe napravlenie. V. O. Kliuchevskii. A. S. Lappo-Danilevskii." *Bor'ba napravlenii v russkoi istoriografii v period imperializma. Istoriograficheskie ocherki* (Leningrad, 1986), 134–155.

Unpelev, A. G., and G. A. Unpelev. *Istoriograficheskie ocherki k problemam metodologii istoricheskoi nauki.* Vladivostok, 1983.

Vladimirov, A. "Vzgliady V. O. Kliuchevskogo na sushchnost' i faktory istoricheskogo protsessa." *Prosveshchenie i kul'tura*, No. 3–4 (1922), 6–19.

Vvedenskii, Andrei A. *Lekstii po dokumental'nomu istochnikovedeniiu istorii SSSR.* Kiev, 1963.

————. "Pytannia diplomatyky v pratsiakh V. O. Kliuchevskogo." *Ukrain'skii istoricheski zhurnal*, No. 1 (1959), 106–115.

———. "Voprosy diplomatiki v trudakh V. O. Kliuchevskogo." Vvedenskii, *Lektsii po dokumental'nomu istochnikovedeniiu SSSR*, 59–75.

C. WORKS ON KLIUCHEVSKII PUBLISHED ABROAD

Amfiteatrov, Aleksandr V. "V. O. Kliuchevskii kak khudozhnik slova." *Literaturnyi al'manakh Grani* (Berlin), I (1922), 175–197.

Byrnes, Robert F. "Between Two Fires: Kliuchevskii on Religion and the Russian Orthodox Church." *Modern Greek Studies*, VI (1990), 157–185.

———. "Kliuchevskii's View of the Flow of Russian History." *Review of Politics*, LV (1993), 565–591.

———. "Undergraduate Teaching: The V. O. Kliuchevskii Example." *The History Teacher*, XXVII (1994), 177–194.

———. "The Young Kliuchevskii: 'Under the Bells' of Penza." *Slavonic and East European Review*, LXVII (1989), 564–580.

Confino, Michael. "History as an Art Form: V. O. Klyuchevsky and His *Course of Russian History*. Introduction to the Hebrew translation of V. O. Klyuchevsky's *History of Russia*." VOK, *History of Russia* (in Hebrew) (1968), I, 5–25.

Cracraft, James. "Kliuchevskii on Peter the Great." *Canadian-American Slavic Studies*, XX, No. 3–4 (1986), 367–381.

Crummey, Robert O. "Kliuchevskii's Portrait of the Boyars." Ibid., 341–356.

Dilkes, Thomas P. Jr. *Values in the Historiography of Vasilii Osipovich Kliuchevskii*. University of Iowa Ph.D. thesis, 1964.

Emmons, Terence J. "Kliuchevskii i ego ucheniki." *VI*, No. 10 (1990), 45–61.

Fedotov, Georges. "Rossiia Kliuchevskogo." *Sovremennye zapiski* (Paris), I (1932), 340–362.

Fosburg, Nina. "Review of Vasilii Osipovich Kliuchevskii, *Pis'ma. Dnevniki. Aforizmy i mysli ob istorii*, Moscow, 1968." *Kritika*, No. 3 (1970), 145–158.

Freeze, Gregory L. "Russian Orthodoxy in Pre-revolutionary Historiography: The Case of V. O. Kliuchevskii." *Canadian-American Slavic Studies*, XX, No. 3–4 (1986), 287–297.

Hotta, Hideo. "Formation of the Historian Kliuchevsky: Seminary and University Years" (in Japanese). *Shikan* (Tokyo), No. 140 (1978).

Kaiser, Daniel H. "Medieval Russian Legal Sources in the Historical Writings of V. O. Kliuchevskii." Ibid., 287–297.

Karpovich, Michael. "Klyuchevsky and Recent Trends in Russian Historiography." *Slavonic and East European Review*, XXI (1943), 31–39.

Khota, Kh. "Formirovanie V. O. Kliuchevskogo kak istorika. Gody ucheby v dukhovnoi seminarii i universitete" (in Japanese). *Shikan* (Tokyo), No. 78 (1969), 1–80.

Kleimola, Ann M. "Kliuchevskii and the Boyars: The Master and His Model." *Canadian-American Slavic Studies*, XX, No. 3–4 (1986), 331–340.

Klimenko, N. K. "V. O. Kliuchevskii." *Vozrozhdenie* (Paris), No. 118 (1961), 64–78.

Knorring, N. "V. O. Kliuchevskii v ego pervye moskovskie gody." *Golos minuvshago na chuzhoi storone*, XV, No. 2 (1926), 315–321.

Kotliarevskii, Nestor A. "V. O. Kliuchevskii." Kotliarevskii, *Kholmy rodiny* (Berlin, 1923), 88–97.

Langer, Lawrence N. "In the Path of History: The Place of Novgorod and Pskov in

Kliuchevskii's *History of Russia*." *Canadian-American Slavic Studies*, XX, No. 3–4 (1986), 243–257.

Leitsch, Walter. "Kliuchevskii's Study on the Reports of Foreign Travelers about Muscovy: A Belated Review." Ibid., 299–308.

Maklakov, Basil. "Klyuchevsky." *Slavonic Review*, XIII (1935), 320–329.

Mazour, Anatole G. "V. O. Kliuchevsky: The Making of an Historian." *Russian Review*, XXXI, No. 4 (1972), 345–359; XXXIII, No. 1 (1973), 1–27.

———. "V. O. Kliuchevsky: The Scholar and Teacher." *Russian Review*, XXXII, No. 1 (January 1973), 15–27.

Osipov, N. "V. O. Kliuchevskii o pol'skom voprose." *Mosty. Literaturno-khudozhestvennyi i obshchestvenno-politicheskii al'manakh* (Munich), VI (1961), 300–310.

Parry, Albert. "Vasilii Osipovich Kliuchevsky." Bernadotte E. Schmitt, ed., *Some Historians of Modern Europe* (Chicago, 1942), 196–216.

Raba, Joel. "Russian Medieval Cities: Kliuchevskii's Vision and Archeological Reality." *Canadian-American Slavic Studies*, XX, No. 3–4 (1986), 259–272.

Raeff, Marc. "Kliuchevskii: Historian of the Eighteenth Century." Ibid., 383–398.

———. "*Neopublikovannye proizvedeniia*. By V. O. Kliuchevskii. Moscow, 1983." *Slavic Review*, XLIII, No. 2 (1984), 291–292.

Riasanovsky, Nicholas V. "Kliuchevskii in Recent Soviet Historiography." *Canadian-American Slavic Studies*, XX, No. 3–4 (1986), 455–466.

Sanders, Thomas. *The Past in the Service of the Fathers: Russian Historians and Russian Society*. Stanford University, Ph.D. thesis, 1989.

Serman, Il'ia. "Kliuchevskii i russkaia literatura." *Canadian-American Slavic Studies*, XX, No. 3–4 (1986), 417–436.

Stokes, A.D. "The System of Succession to the Thrones of Russia, 1054–1113." Robert Auty, L. R. Lewitter, and A. P. Vlasto, eds., *Gorski Vijenac: A Garland of Essays Offered to Professor E. M. Hill* (Cambridge, UK, 1970), 268–275.

Torke, Hans. "Kliuchevskii's *Istoriia Soslovii*." *Canadian-American Slavic Studies*, XX, No. 3–4 (1986), 309–329.

Vernadsky, George. "V. O. Kliuchevskii." Vernadsky, *Russian Historiography: A History* (Belmont, Mass., 1978), 128–139.

Vodoff, V. "Remarques critiques sur le cours de terminologie d'histoire russe de V. O. Klucevskij." *Canadian-American Slavic Studies*, XX, No. 3–4 (1986), 273–285.

Wittfogel, Karl A. "Russia and the East: A Comparison and Contrast." *Slavic Review*, XXII, No. 4 (1963), 627–643.

Topical Sources

A. Religion and the Church

Elliot, Alison Godard. *Road to Paradise: Reading the Lives of the Early Saints*. Hanover, N.H., 1988.

Fedotov, George P. "The Problem of Old Russian Culture." *Slavic Review*, XXI (1962), 1–15.

———. *The Russian Religious Mind*. Cambridge, Mass., 1966. 2 vols.

Florovskii, George V. *Puti russkogo bogosloviia*. Paris, 1937.

Bibliography

Freeze, Gregory L. *The Parish Clergy in Nineteenth Century Russia: Crisis, Reform, Counter-Reform.* Princeton, 1983.

————. *The Russian Levites: Parish Clergy in the Nineteenth Century.* Cambridge, 1977.

————. "Tserkov', religiia i politicheskaia kul'tura na zakate staroi Rossii." *Istoriia SSSR,* No. 2 (1991), 107–119.

Pomialovskii, Nikolai G. *Ocherki bursy.* Moscow, 1936. Translated by Alfred Kuhn, *Seminary Sketches* (Ithaca, N.Y., 1973).

B. Learning and Education

Aleksandrovskoe voennoe uchilishche za XXXV let. 1863–1898. Moscow, 1900.

Alston, Patrick L. "The Dynamics of Educational Expansion in Russia." In Konrad J. Jarausch, ed., *The Transformation of Higher Learning, 1860–1930* (Chicago, 1983), 89–107.

Education and the State in Czarist Russia. Stanford, 1969.

Balmuth, Daniel. *Censorship in Russia, 1865–1905.* Washington, D.C., 1979.

Besançon, Alain. *Éducation et société en Russie dans le second tiers du XIXe siècle.* The Hague, 1974.

Bohachevsky-Chomiak, Martha. *Sergei N. Trubetskoi: An Intellectual among the Intelligentsia in Prerevolutionary Russia.* Belmont, Mass., 1976.

Bohachevsky-Chomiak, Martha, and Bernice Glatzer Rozenthal, eds. *A Revolution of the Spirit: Crisis of Value in Russia, 1890–1918.* Translated by Marian Schwartz. Newtonville, Mass., 1982.

Brooks, Jeffrey. *When Russia Learned to Read: Literacy and Popular Literature, 1861–1917.* Princeton, 1985.

Choldin, Marianna T. *A Fence around the Empire: Russian Censorship of Western Ideas under the Tsars.* Durham, N.C., 1985.

Dmitrieva, Nina A. *Moskovskoe uchilishche zhivopisi, vaianiia i zodchestva.* Moscow, 1950.

Eimontova, Regina G. "Professora starye i novye na rubezhe 50–60-kh godov XIX v." In *Problemy istorii russkogo obshchestvennogo dvizheniia i istoricheskoi nauki* (Moscow, 1981), 128–138.

————. "Prosveshchenie v Rossii pervoi poloviny XIX veka." *VI,* No. 1 (1986), 92–93.

————. *Russkie universitety na grani dvukh epokh. Ot Rossii krepostnoi k Rossii kapitalisticheskoi.* Moscow, 1985.

————. "Universitetskaia reforma 1863 g." *Istoricheskie zapiski,* No. 70 (1961), 163–196.

————. "Universitetskii vopros i russkaia obshchestvennost' v 50–60-kh godakh XIX v." *Istoriia SSSR,* No. 6 (1971), 144–157.

Kassow, Samuel D. *Students, Professors, and the State in Tsarist Russia.* Berkeley, 1989.

Kedrov, Nikolai I. *Moskovskaia dukhovnaia akademiia 1814–1899. Kratkii istoricheskii ocherk. S prilozheniem spiskov nachal'nikov, nastavnikov i vospitannikov.* Moscow, 1889.

Krichevskii, G. G. "Uchenye stepeni v universitetakh dorevoliutsionnoi Rossii." *Istoriia SSSR,* No. 2 (1982), 141–153.

Leikina-Svirskaia, Vera R. *Intelligentsiia v Rossii vo vtoroi polovine XIX veka.* Moscow, 1971.

McClelland, James C. *Autocrats and Academics: Education, Culture, and Society in Tsarist Russia.* Chicago, 1979.

Mathes, William L. *The Struggle for University Autonomy in the Russian Empire during the First Decade of the Reign of Alexander II.* Columbia University Ph.D. thesis, 1966.

Shchetinina, Galina I. *Universitety v Rossii i ustav 1884 goda.* Moscow, 1976.

Shkurinov, Pavel S. *Pozitivizm v Rossii XIX v.* Moscow, 1980.

Tkachenko, P. S. *Uchashchaiasia molodezh' v revoliutsionnom dvizhenii 60–70kh gg. XIX v.* Moscow, 1978.

U Troitsy v Akademii, 1814–1914 gg.: iubileinyi sbornik istoricheskikh materialov. Izdanie byvshikh vospitannikov Moskovskoi dukhovnoi akademii. Moscow, 1914.

Vucinich, Alexander S. *Science in Russian Culture: A History to 1860.* Stanford, 1963.

————. *Science in Russian Culture, 1861–1917.* Stanford, 1970.

————. *Social Thought in Tsarist Russia: The Quest for a General Science of Society, 1861–1917.* Chicago, 1976.

C. Moscow and Moscow University

Akademiia nauk, Institut istorii. *Istoriia Moskvy v shesti tomakh.* Moscow, 1953–1959. 6 vols.

Bogolepov, N. P. "Stranitsa iz zhizni Moskovskogo universiteta. Iz zapisok professora N. P. Bogolepova." *Russkii arkhiv,* LI, Book I (1913), 8–68.

Bogoslovskii, Mikhail M. "Moskva v 1870–1890-kh godakh." Bogoslovskii, *Istoriografiia, memuaristika, epistoliariia. Nauchnoe nasledie* (Moscow, 1987), 107–137.

Burch, Robert J. *Social Unrest in Imperial Russia: The Student Movement at Moscow University, 1887–1905.* University of Washington Ph.D. thesis, 1972.

Buslaev, Fedor I. *Moi dosugi: sobrannye iz periodicheskikh izdanii melkiia sochineniia Fedora Buslaeva.* Moscow, 1886. 2 vols.

Demidov, I. A., and V. V. Ishutin. "Obshchestvo istorii i drevnostei rossiiskikh pri Moskovskom universitete." *Istoriia i istoriki. Bibliograficheskii ezhegodnik, 1975* (Moscow, 1978), 250–280.

Dmitriev, S. S. "Istoricheskaia nauka v Moskovskom universitete v 60–90-kh godakh XIX veka." *Vestnik Moskovskogo universiteta,* No. 7 (1954), 95–115.

Emel'ianov, Iurii N., ed. *Moskovskii universitet v vospominaniiakh sovremennikov, 1755–1917.* Moscow, 1989.

Engelstein, Laura. *Moscow, 1905: Working-Class Organizations and Political Conflict.* Stanford, 1982.

Eshevskii, Stepan V. "Moskovskii universitet v 1861 godu. Iz zapisok S. V. Eshevskogo." *Russkaia starina,* XCIV, No. 6 (1898), 577–603.

Ivantsov, M. "M. S. Korelin kak professor i rukovoditel' studencheskikh zaniatii." *RM,* No. 10, Part II (1898), 137–148.

Johnson, Robert E. *Peasant and Proletarian: The Working Class of Moscow in the Late Nineteenth Century.* New Brunswick, N.J., 1979.

Karataev, Nikolai K. *Ekonomicheskie nauki v Moskovskom universitete, 1755–1955.* Moscow, 1956.

Kheraskov, Ivan. "Iz istorii studencheskogo dvizheniia v Moskovskom universitete. Vospominaniia uchastnika, 1897–1903." In Vasilii B. El'iashevich, A. A. Kizevetter, and M. M. Novikov, eds., *Moskovskii universitet, 1755–1930, iubileinyi sbornik* (Paris, 1930), 431–449.

Latysheva, O. I. *Moskovskii universitet v revoliutsionnoi bor'be v period pervoi russkoi revoliutsii 1905–1907 gg.* Moscow State University thesis, 1956.

Mel'gunov, Sergei P. "Moskovskii universitet v 1894 g. Po povodu vospominanii prof. Bogolepova." *Golos minuvshago*, No. 5 (1913), 182–218.

———. *Studencheskie organizatsii 80–90kh gg. v Moskovskom universitete. Po arkhivnym dannym.* Moscow, 1908.

Moldavan, S., et al.; eds. *Moskva. Illiustrirovannaia istoriia v dvukh tomakh.* Moscow, 1984–86. 2 vols.

Moscow University. *Doklad Komissii, izbrannoi Sovetom Imperatorskogo moskovskogo universiteta 28-go fevralia 1901 goda dlia vyiasneniia prichin studencheskikh volnenii i mer k uporiadocheniiu universitetskoi zhizni.* Moscow, 1901. Reprinted in Stuttgart in 1904 and in London in 1906.

———. *K voprosu ob ustroistve studencheskikh obshchezhitii pri Imperatorskom moskovskom universitete.* Moscow, 1898.

———. *Otchet o sostoianii i deistviiakh 1-go Moskovskogo universiteta.* Moscow, 1847–1927.

Orlov, V. I. *Studencheskoe dvizhenie Moskovskogo universiteta v XIX stoletii.* Moscow, 1934.

Shchetinin, Prince B. A. "M. M. Kovalevskii i Moskovskii universitet 80-kh godov. Stranichka iz vospominanii." *IV,* CXLIX, No. 5 (1916), 483–490.

Shchipanov, Ia., ed. *Moskovskii universitet i razvitie filosofskoi i obshchestvenno-politicheskoi mysli v Rossii.* Moscow, 1957.

Sliuzberg, G. B. "Dorevoliutsionnoe russkoe studenchestvo." *Sbornik vospominanii. Pamiati russkogo studenchestva kontsa XIX–nachala XX vekov* (Paris, 1934), 82–95.

Syromiatnikov, A. "Moskovskii universitet v oktiabr'skie dni 1905 g." *Krasnyi arkhiv,* LXXIV (1936), 195–204.

Tikhonravov, Nikolai S. *Sochineniia.* Moscow, 1898. 4 vols.

Tkachenko, Petr S. *Moskovskoe studenchestvo v obshchestvenno-politicheskoi zhizni Rossii vtoroi poloviny XIX veka.* Moscow, 1958.

Tsetlin, Lev S. *Iz istorii nauchnoi mysli v Rossii. Nauka i uchenye v Moskovskom universitete vo vtoroi polovine XIX veka.* Moscow, 1958.

D. Women's Higher Courses

Andreeva, I. N. "V. I. Ger'e—organizator vysshikh zhenskikh kursov v Moskve." *Sovetskaia pedagogika*, No. 9 (1987), 107–112.

Bobrova, L. A. "Vysshie zhenskie kursy professora Ger'e' v Moskve, 1872–1888." *Trudy Moskovskogo gosudarstvennogo istoriko-arkhivnogo instituta,* XVI (1961), 253–265.

Dudgeon, Ruth. *Women and Higher Education in Russia, 1855–1905.* George Washington University Ph.D. thesis, 1975.

Filippova, L. D. "Iz istorii zhenskogo obrazovaniia v Rossii." *VI,* XXXVIII, No. 2 (1963), 209–218.

Grishina, Z. V. "Vysshee obrazovanie zhenshchin v dorevoliutsionnoi Rossii i Moskovskii universitet." *Vestnik Moskovskogo universiteta,* Seriia 8, *Istoriia*, No. 1 (1984), 52–63.

Johanson, Christine. *Women's Struggle for Higher Education in Russia, 1855–1900.* Kingston and Montreal, 1987.
Likhacheva, Elena M. *Materialy dlia istorii zhenskogo obrazovaniia v Rossii, 1086–1856.* St. Petersburg, 1899–1901. 2 vols.
Moskovskie vysshie zhenskie kursy. *Otchet Vysshikh zhenskikh kursov.* Moscow, 1875–1905.
Nekrasova, Ekaterina S. *Iz proshlogo zhenskikh kursov.* Moscow, 1886.

E. 1905

Chuloshnikov, A. "Predislovie k istorii manifesta 6 avgusta 1905 g." *Krasnyi arkhiv,* XIV, No. 1 (1926), 462–470.
Emmons, Terence. "The Beseda Circle, 1899–1905." *Slavic Review,* XXXII, No. 3 (1973), 461–496.
———. *The Formation of Political Parties and the First National Elections in Russia.* Cambridge, 1983.
Galai, Shmuel. *The Liberation Movement in Russia, 1900–1905.* Cambridge, 1973.
Healy, Ann E. *The Russian Autocracy in Crisis, 1905–1907.* Hamden, Conn., 1976.
Moskovskaia dukhovnaia akademiia. "Otchet o sostoianii Moskovskoi dukhovnoi akademii v 1905–1906 uchebnom godu." *BV,* XV, No. 3 (1906), 1–54.
Pares, Bernard. "The Peterhof Conference (on the Draft Project of the Imperial Duma), August 1–5, 1905." *Russian Review* (England) (November 1913), 87–120.
Protokoly zasedanii soveshchaniia pod lichnym Ego Imperatorskogo Velichestva predstavitel'stvom dlia obsuzhdeniia prednachertanii, ukazannykh v vysochaishem reskripte 18 fevralia 1905 goda. 19, 21, 23, 25, i 26 iiulia 1905 goda. St. Petersburg, 1905.
Snow, George. "The Peterhof Conference and the Bulygin Duma." *Russian History/Histoire Russe,* II, Part II (1975), 149–162.
Tagantsev, Nikolai S. *Perezhitoe. Uchrezhdenie gosudarstvennoi dumy v 1905–1906 gg.* Petrograd, 1919.

F. Basic Historical Studies

Amburger, Eric. *Geschichte der Behördenorganisation Russlands vom Peter dem Grossen bis 1917.* Leiden, 1966.
Anderson, Benedict. *Imagined Communities: Reflections on the Origins and Spread of Nationalism.* London, 1983.
Anisimov, Evgenii V. *Podatnaia reforma Petra I. Vvedenie podushnoi podati v Rossii, 1719–1728.* Leningrad, 1982.
Backus, Oswald P. *Motives of West Russian Nobles in Deserting Lithuania for Moscow, 1377–1514.* Lawrence, Kans., 1987.
Basarab, John. *Pereiaslav 1654: A Historiographical Study.* Edmonton, Alberta, 1982.
Becker, Seymour. *Nobility and Privilege in Late Imperial Russia.* De Kalb, Ill., 1988.
Benowitz, Elliot. *B. N. Chicherin: Rationalism and Liberalism in Nineteenth-Century Russia.* University of Wisconsin Ph.D. thesis, 1966.
Birnbaum, Henrik, and Michael S. Flyer, eds. *Medieval Russian Culture.* Berkeley, 1984.

Blum, Jerome. *Land and Peasant in Russia from the Ninth to the Nineteenth Century.* Princeton, 1961.

Bradley, Joseph. *Muzhik and Muscovite: Urbanization in Late Imperial Russia.* Berkeley, 1985.

Cherepnin, Lev V. *Zemskie sobory russkogo gosudarstva v XVI–XVII vv.* Moscow, 1978.

Confino, Michael. *Domaines et seigneurs en Russie vers la fin du XVIII siècle. Etude de structures agraires et de mentalités économiques.* Paris, 1963.

————. *Systèmes agraires et progrès agricole. L'Assolement triennal en Russie aux XVIII et XIX siècles. Etude d'économie et de sociologie rurales.* Paris, 1969.

Crummey, Robert O. *Aristocrats and Servitors: The Boyar Elite in Russia, 1613–1689.* Princeton, 1983.

————. *The Formation of Muscovy, 1304–1613.* London, New York, 1987.

————. "Ivan the Terrible." In Samuel H. Baron and Nancy W. Heer, eds., *Windows on the Russian Past* (Columbus, Ohio, 1977), 57–74.

Fennel, John L. *The Emergence of Moscow, 1304–1359.* Berkeley, 1968.

Freeze, Gregory L. "The *Soslovie* (Estate) Paradigm and Russian Social History." *American Historical Review,* XCI (1986), 11–36.

Frieden, Nancy M. *Russian Physicians in an Age of Reform and Revolution, 1856–1905.* Princeton, 1981.

Hanson, Gary A. *Afanasii Prokof'evich Shchapov, 1830–1876: Russian Historian and Social Thinker.* University of Wisconsin Ph.D. thesis, 1971.

Hellie, Richard. *Enserfment and Military Change in Muscovy.* Chicago, 1971.

Ianin, Valentin L. *Novgorodskie posadniki.* Moscow, 1962.

Ilovaiskii, Dmitrii I. *Dopolnitel'naia polemika po voprosam variago-russkomu i bolgaro-gunnskomu.* Moscow, 1886.

————. "Poborniki normanizma i turanizma." *Russkaia starina,* XXXVI (1882), 585–620.

Karpov, Gennadii F. *V zashchitu Bogdana Khmel'nitskogo.* Moscow, 1890.

Keep, John L. H. "The Decline of the Zemsky Sobor." *Slavonic and East European Review,* XXXVI (1957), 100–122.

Kleimola, Ann M. "Patterns of Duma Recruitment, 1505–1550." Daniel C. Waugh, ed., *Essays in Honor of A. A. Zimin* (Columbus, Ohio, 1985), 232–257.

Kollmann, Nancy S. *Kinship and Politics: The Making of the Muscovite Political System, 1345–1547.* Stanford, 1987.

Likhachev, Nikolai P. *Razriadnye d'iaki XVI veka. Opyt istoricheskogo issledovaniia.* St. Petersburg, 1888.

Okenfuss, Max J. *The Discovery of Childhood in Russia: The Evidence of the Slavic Primer.* Newtonville, Mass., 1980.

Owens, Thomas C. *Capitalism and Politics in Russia: A Social History of the Moscow Merchants, 1885–1905.* New York, 1981.

Pasczkiewicz, Henryk. *The Origin of Russia.* London, 1954.

————. *The Making of the Russian Nation.* London, 1963.

Pavlov-Silvanskii, N. P. *Feodalizm v udel'noi Rossii.* St. Petersburg, 1907.

Raeff, Marc. *Understanding Imperial Russia: State and Society in the Old Regime.* New York, 1984.

Riasanovsky, Nicholas V. *The Image of Peter the Great in Russian History and Thought.* New York, 1985.

Rieber, Alfred J. *Merchants and Entrepreneurs in Imperial Russia.* Chapel Hill, N.C., 1982.

Shmidt, Sigurd O. *Rossiiskoe gosudarstvo v seredine XVI stoletiia: tsarskii arkhiv i litsevye letopisi vremeni Ivana Groznogo.* Moscow, 1984.

Smirnov, Ivan I. *Ocherki politicheskoi istorii russkogo gosudarstva 30–50-kh godov XVI veka.* Leningrad, 1958.

Torke, Hans J. *Die staatsbedingte Gesellschaft im Moskauer Reich. Zar und Zemlja in der altrussischen Herrschaftsverfassung, 1613–1689.* Leiden, 1974.

Velychenko, Stephen. "The Origins of the Official Soviet Interpretation of Eastern Slavonic History: A Case Study of Policy Formulation." *Forschungen zur osteeuropäischen Geschichte,* XLVI (1992), 221–253.

Vladimirskii-Budanov, Mikhail. *Obzor istorii russkogo prava.* Kiev, 1915.

Zagoskin, Nikolai P. *Istoriia prava moskovskogo gosudarstva.* Kazan, 1877–79. 2 vols.

G. Historiography

Adelung, Friedrich. *Kritiko-literaturnoe obozrenie puteshestvennikov po Rossii do 1700 goda i ikh sochinenii.* St. Petersburg, 1846.

Akademiia nauk SSSR, Institut istorii. *Ocherki istorii istoricheskoi nauki v SSSR.* Moscow, 1955–85. 5 vols.

Braudel, Fernand. *L'Identité de la France.* I: *L'Espace et l'histoire.* Paris, 1986.

———. *On History.* Translated by Sarah Matthews. Chicago, 1980.

Byrnes, Robert F. "Soviet Historical Views of Kliuchevskii." *Canadian-American Slavic Studies,* XX, No. 3–4 (1986), 437–454.

———. "Nechkina's *Kliuchevskii.* Review Article." *Russian Review,* XXXVII (1978), 68–81.

Cherepnin, Lev V. *Otechestvennye istoriki XVIII–XX vv. Sbornik statei, vystuplenii, vospominanii.* Moscow, 1984.

Dalin, Viktor M. *Liudi i idei. Iz istorii revoliutsionnogo i sotsialisticheskogo dvizheniia vo Frantsii.* Moscow, 1970.

Grekov, Boris. *Kievskaia Rus'.* Moscow, 1953.

———. *Krest'iane na Rusi s drevneishikh vremen do XVIII veka.* 2nd ed. Moscow, 1954. 2 vols.

Grothusen, Klaus-Detlev. *Die historische Rechtsschule Russlands. Ein Beitrag zur russischen Geistesgeschichte in der zweiten Hälfte des 19. Jahrhunderts.* Giessen, 1962.

Hecker, Hans. *Russische Universalgeschichtsscheibung von den "Vierziger Jahren" der 19. Jahrhunderts bis zur sowjetischen "Weltgeschichte" 1855–1965.* Munich-Vienna, 1983.

Karpov, Gennadii F. *Kostomarov kak istorik Malorossii.* Moscow, 1871.

Kireeva, Raisa A. *Izuchenie otechestvennoi istoriografii v dorevoliutsionnoi Rossii v seredine XIX v. do 1917 g.* Moscow, 1983.

Likhachev, Dmitri S. "Literaturnyi etiket drevnei Rusi (k probleme izucheniia)." *Trudy otdela drevnerusskoi literatury Instituta russkoi literatury,* XVII (1961), 5–16.

Mogol'nitskii, B. G. "P. G. Vinogradov kak istorik istoricheskoi nauki." *Istoriia i istoriki. Istoriograficheskii ezhegodnik, 1973* (Moscow, 1975), 214–231.

Pokrovskii, Mikhail N. *Istoricheskaia nauka i bor'ba klassov.* Moscow, 1933. 2 vols.

Radzialowski, Thaddeus C. *The Life and Work of N. P. Pavlov-Silvanskii, 1869–1908.* University of Michigan Ph.D. thesis, 1979.

Raskin, A. G. *Naselenie Rossii za sto let.* Moscow, 1956.

Reddel, Carl W. *Sergei Mikhailovich Solov'ev: The Early Years, 1820–1848.* Indiana University Ph.D. thesis, 1973.

Riha, Thomas. *A Russian European: Paul Miliukov in Russian Politics.* Notre Dame, 1969.

Roosevelt, Priscilla. *Apostle of Russian Liberalism: Timofei Granovski.* Newtonville, Mass., 1986.

Rubinshtein, Nikolai L. *Russkaia istoriografiia.* Moscow, 1941.

Safronov, Boris B. *Istoricheskoe mirovozzrenie R. Iu. Vippera i ego vremia.* Moscow, 1976.

Schelting, Alexander von. *Russland und Europa in russischen Geschichtsdenken.* Bern, 1948.

———. *Russland und der Westen im russischen Geschichtsdenken der zweiten Hälfte der 19. Jahrhunderts.* Berlin, 1989.

Thurston, Gary J. "Alexis de Tocqueville in Russia." *Journal of the History of Ideas,* XXXVII (1976), 289–306.

Tsamutali, Aleksei N. *Bor'ba napravlenii v russkoi istoriografii v periode imperializma.* Leningrad, 1986.

Venturi, Franco. *Historiens du xx-e siècle.* Geneva, 1966.

Vernadsky, George. *Russian Historiography: A History.* Belmont, Mass., 1978.

INDEX

Robert F. Byrnes is Distinguished Professor of History, Emeritus, at Indiana University, Bloomington. He has written numerous books on American, French, East European, and Russian history and Russian–American cultural relations.